Politics and Culture in Eighteenth-Century Russia

Politics and Culture in Eighteenth-Century Russia

Collected Essays by
Isabel de Madariaga

LONGMAN
London and New York

Addison Wesley Longman Limited
Edinburgh Gate,
Harlow, Essex CM20 2JE, United Kingdom
and Associated Companies throughout the world

Published in the United States of America by Addison Wesley Longman Inc., New York

First published 1998

ISBN 0582 322553 PPR
ISBN 0582 322561 CSD

Visit Addison Wesley Longman on the world wide web at http://www.awl-he.com

British Library Cataloguing in Publication Data

A catalogue record for this book is available from the British Library

Library of Congress Cataloging-in-Publication Data

A catalogue record for this book is available from the Library of Congress

Set by 35 in 10/12 pt Bembo
Produced by Addison Wesley Longman Singapore (Pte) Ltd.,
Printed in Singapore

Contents

Acknowledgements

The publishers would like to thank the following for permission to reproduce copyright material:

'Tsar into emperor: the title of Peter the Great' was originally published in *Royal and Republican Sovereignty in Early Modern Europe. Essays in Honour of Ragnhild Hatton*, ed. R. Oresko, G.C. Gibbs and H.M. Scott (Cambridge: Cambridge University Press, 1997), pp. 351–81. Used by permission.

'Autocracy and sovereignty' was originally published in *Canadian-American Slavic Studies*, 16, Nos 3–4. Fall–Winter 1982, pp. 369–87. Used by permission of Charles J. Schlacks Jr.

'Portrait of an eighteenth-century Russian statesman: Prince Dmitry Mikhaylovich Golitsyn' was originally published in *Slavonic and East European Review*, 62, No. 1, 1984, pp. 36–60. Used by permission of the editors.

'The eighteenth-century origin of Russian civil rights' will also be published in *Katharina II., Russland und Europa. Beiträge zur Internationalen Forschung*, ed. Claus Scharf (Mainz: Veröffentlichungen des Instituts für Europäische Geschichte, 1998).

'Penal policy in the age of Catherine II' was originally published in *La Leopoldina*, 11, 1990 (Milan, Giuffrè), pp. 497–535. Used by permission of Professor Luigi Berlinguer.

'Catherine II and the serfs: a reconsideration of some problems' was originally published in *Slavonic and East European Review*, 52, No. 1, 1974, pp. 34–62. Used by permission of the editors.

'Freemasonry in eighteenth-century Russia' was originally published in *Il Vieusseux*, December 1994, pp. 80–102. Used by permission of Professor P. Bagnoli of the Gabinetto Vieusseux.

'Catherine II and the foundation of the Russian educational system' was originally published as 'The foundation of the Russian educational system by Catherine II' in *Slavonic and East European Review*, 57, No. 3, 1979, pp. 369–95. Used by permission of the editors.

'Catherine II and enlightened absolutism' was originally published as 'Catherine the Great' in *Enlightened Absolutism: Reform and Reformers in Later Eighteenth-Century Europe*, ed. H.M. Scott (London and Michigan: Macmillan and University of Michigan Press, 1990), pp. 289–312. Used by permission.

'Catherine II and the *philosophes*' was originally published in *Russia and the West in the Eighteenth Century. Proceedings of the Second International Conference of the Study Group on Eighteenth-Century Russia, 17–22 July 1981*, pp. 30–52. Used by permission of Professor A.G. Cross.

'Catherine II and Montesquieu between Prince M.M. Shcherbatov and Denis Diderot' was originally published in *Studi storici sull settecento europeo in onore di Franco Venturi*, II (Naples, 1985), pp. 611–50. Used by permission of casa edittrice Jovene.

'Catherine II and the literary and cultural life of Russia' was originally published as 'Catherine II et la littérature' in *Histoire de la littérature russe*, I, ed. I. Serman *et al.* (Paris: Maison Arthème Fayard, 1992). Used by permission.

Introduction

The essays presented here have been written over some twenty-five years and therefore represent an evolution in my conception of Russian history. (I would not, for instance, today use the word 'bureaucrat' to describe Russian officials in the eighteenth century.) But they are not reproduced here in chronological order of publication. Indeed, the first essay was the last but one to be published and only appeared in January 1997. Some are carefully thought out scholarly papers, such as the essay on 'Catherine II and the Serfs' (1974), which was a by-product of the research for my book, *Russia in the Age of Catherine the Great*, (1981). Other essays are more in the nature of a lecture given at a seminar and subsequently worked up into a full-scale paper, such as for instance 'Russia and the Enlightenment', which was originally given as a talk to students in St Andrews, but has been subsequently developed.

The order in which the essays have been presented here is the result of an attempt to group them according to the inner logic of their subject matter. The first four deal with the nature of the Russian government and its relation to society. The second group is composed of essays concerned with the way in which the government dealt with social and administrative problems, and the third deals with the relationship between Catherine II, Russian society, and the *philosophes* and their world of ideas.

The subject of 'Tsar into emperor' first struck me some years ago while meditating on the reasons why Peter I chose to abandon the perfectly good title of 'tsar', which he and his advisers knew quite well meant 'emperor', in favour of the foreign sounding title of 'imperator'. Where did he get the very idea of changing his title from? And why did it take the form he gave it? Usually dealt with in general or particular histories as a sudden change which historians need not bother to explain, it seemed to me that it must have roots in the past of Russian relations with European and non-European powers. The subject took me right back to Russian medieval history. My conclusion, which I hope is clear from the article included here, is that Peter was anxious to take up a position in the European states system, to which Russia had only marginally belonged until then, by sharing in the heritage of the Roman

Empire. But to make his point more effectively, he claimed descent from the Roman Empire and dated the ancestry of the Russian ruling house to Augustus, emperor of an undivided Roman Empire. It is easy to lose sight of Russian insistence on descent from the Roman Empire because of the constant use of the words Byzantium/Byzantine to describe their heritage, words which colour our perception and lead us to envisage Russia in terms of the Orthodox Hellenistic East to the exclusion of Roman Rome.[1]

The second article reproduced here, 'Autocracy and sovereignty', was my first effort to develop a theme which has come to exercise me a great deal (and which I did indeed take up again in the article on 'Tsar into emperor'). It is the theme of the impossibility of finding exact equivalents of words and concepts in different languages. Historians of Russia have long been aware of the difficulty in translating, say, seventeenth-century Russian court ranks into an acceptable English or French terminology (German is for many reasons easier).[2] Take, for example, the difficulty of translating *okolnichi* or *stol'nik* into English ('someone who is near to the ruler', or 'table attendant', both long and clumsy formulas). There can never be a satisfactory translation of *boyar*, which has too many meanings. The translation of abstract concepts or of the names of institutions is even more perilous. How can one translate the eighteenth-century sense of *pravitel'stvo* (tribunal) or the very subtle meaning of *prisustvennoye mesto* (the place where the presence is). This led me to examine the meaning of the Russian word *samoderzhaviye*, and how other European languages have been slowly but irrevocably sliding into translating it by 'autocracy', which because it is a calque of the equivalent and original Greek word, sounds more accurate even though it may not be so. I had been hoping that my effort to prove that at any rate until the eighteenth century *samoderzhaviye* should be translated as 'sovereignty' might provoke some debate. Alas it did not and has not.[3] And so we still slither around in a slippery terminological morass where *gosudar'* is translated both as 'sovereign' and as 'lord', and we are no nearer reaching agreement on definitions in a dictionary of the major political concepts of Russian public life.[4] But beyond this very precise question of definitions there is a further very elusive element to the meaning of words, deriving from personal relations and habits, traditional forms of courtesy, religious traditions and observations, the way political institutions worked. How far does the universal use of name and patronymic in Russia colour the social relationships across class and caste, and underline the fraternity of Christian man to a degree

1. I owe to the kindness of Professor Averil Cameron the information that the Roman Empire of the East did not begin to be described as Byzantium until the end of the sixteenth century.
2. See glossary in D. Griffiths and G. Munro, trs. and eds, *Catherine II's Charters of 1785 to the Nobility and the Towns*, Charles Schlacks Jr, Salt Lake City, Utah, 1991.
3. In a furious argument between Voltaire and the Russian historian G.F. Müller, when Voltaire was putting together his history of Peter the Great, Müller declared that Voltaire was wrong to translate the word 'autocrator' as 'conservateur' since 'il signifie souverain'. See E. Shmurlo, *Vol'ter i ego kniga o Petre velikom*, Prague, 1929, pp. 311–12.
4. R. Pipes, in the introduction to his edition of Karamzin's *Memoir on Ancient and Modern Russia*, Harvard University Press, 1959, already pointed out that the term *samoderzhaviye* performed the function of 'sovereignty' in Russian political literature.

incomprehensible to Saxon villeins and Norman barons? Latin has been the mother tongue or the *lingua franca* of all non-Orthodox Christian Europe, and has provided a common vocabulary for political and liturgical use. But Russia is neither Latin nor Greek in culture, it is Old Church Slavonic. And concepts simply do not quite correspond and translations leave one dissatisfied because they increase rather than reduce the cultural distance. The word *gosudarstvo*, for instance, is now ubiquitously translated as 'state'. But state in what sense? Has it always meant, even when we speak of the Kievan 'state', a unit of government monopolizing all coercive and administrative power in a specific territory? Does it mean state at all, or is it closer to the German *Herrschaft*, the concept of rulership before a state even existed, rulership within an area with ill-defined borders, a concept which applies more to the nature of the ruler's power than to that which is ruled over?

The 'Portrait of a Russian eighteenth-century statesman' is in a sense an unfinished sketch because its subject is difficult to seize. The uniquely fascinating moment, lasting a mere few weeks, during which some in the Russian political elite attempted to impose legal limits on the unlimited power of the tsar, or in this case the tsaritsa, offers many avenues for future research. There is more to be sought and to be found and to be published. (G.A. Protasov's doctoral thesis was not available to foreign readers. Is it available now? Does it cast any new light on the subject?) This is a question which needs to be approached by scholars like those Stalin once called archive rats, who will burrow and beaver away, seeking to establish the course of events hour by hour and day by day, to clarify individual actions, to establish the subsequent incidence of rewards and punishments, and to assess eighteenth- and nineteenth-century verdicts on a page of Russian history which has aroused very conflicting judgements among historians, according to their own political culture, whether Russian Marxist, American democratic, or European aristocratic-constitutionalist. There is also always the hope that some day it will be possible to flesh out the characters of the major and minor protagonists in this episode, to turn them from puppets into human beings.

The final essay in this section on 'The eighteenth-century origin of Russian civil rights' is an as yet unpublished revised version of a paper, first produced in 1986 and brought up to date for a conference held in Zerbst, the ancestral home of Catherine II, in 1996, on the occasion of the 200th anniversary of the death of Germany's greatest daughter. Zerbst was in East Germany, and the ravages of both war and reconstruction are both clear to see. But this charming small town still conveys very well the atmosphere of the small German eighteenth-century principalities.

When did Russians begin to have civil rights, and when did they begin to think they had any, or ought to have them? And was it possible to enjoy civil rights in a regime as absolute as that of the tsars? Even in the occasional spurts of revolt against the despotic nature of Russian absolutism, few Russians thought of defining what they wanted in terms of 'civil rights'. The abstract language of the law did not come readily to Russians until the study of law abroad became frequent in the eighteenth century. Catherine herself was scathing about the existence of the rights of the nobility in Russia in her marginal comments on Strube de Pyrmont's *Lettres russiennes.*[5] And Karamzin, in his criticism, addressed to Alexander I, of Speransky's draft of a civil code for Russia, based on the Code Napoleon, exclaimed: 'Is it advisable, for instance to open the Russian code with a chapter on civil rights, which properly speaking Russia neither had nor has?'[6] If Russia had no civil rights of the kind enshrined in the Declaration of the Rights of Man, there was before the eighteenth century a well-established conviction of the existence of a right to property, based on customary law. The state should not be entitled to confiscate property, and certainly not without compensation and due legal process. This right, together with established norms for the division of property within family and kin or lineage, moved into the forefront of the minds of property owners in the eighteenth century, when property ownership became more precarious under the increasing pressure of the Petrine state. The historiography of law does not really march hand in hand with social and political history in Russia, otherwise the significance for Russian civil rights of the property rights of women, or of the right of the people to own *kholopi*, or slaves, would not be dismissed so airily.[7] It is too easily assumed that the only rights worth having are rights against the state, whereas rights against one's fellowmen are frequently even more important.

It is particularly in the sphere of civil rights that the new Russian historiography has made extraordinary progress of a kind which should be drawn to the attention of foreign historians if textbooks are not to continue misleading students and the general public. I refer specifically to the work of O.A. Omelchenko, who in recent years has uncovered far more evidence of the direction of Catherine's political thought, along lines already opened up by Marc Raeff. Catherine was fascinated by the British form of government, and her attempts to borrow and adapt from the Bill of Rights, and from other British constitutional documents, her struggle to find a political solution to the problem of representation in Russian central government institutions can now be followed in the drafts of her papers which have survived.

'Penal policy in the age of Catherine II' was also originally a paper, prepared in 1986 for a conference to commemorate the 200th anniversary of the criminal code of Leopold of Tuscany, held in Siena. The invitation to contribute a paper on Russia to this essentially Italian occasion was irresistible, given the subject and the venue, and indeed I have never attended a conference in which pleasure and work were so equally divided, indeed at which it was such a pleasure to work. Moreover, it gave me an opportunity to study a subject

5. F.H. Strube de Piermont, *Lettres russiennes*, ed. Corrado Rosso, Pisa, 1978, Catherine's comments on pp. 218–20.
6. Karamzin, *Memoir*, p. 185.
7. For women's property rights see the unpublished Ph.D. thesis by Michelle L. Marrese, 'A Woman's Kingdom: Women and the Control of Property in Russia, 1700–1861', North Western University, Illinois; and for litigation over ownership of slaves, see R. Hellie, *Slavery in Russia, 1450–1725*, University of Chicago Press, 1982.

which I had hitherto somewhat neglected. But I found it difficult to embark on an interpretation of Russian penal policy in general, and Catherine's in particular, because so little had been written in English on the bare facts of Russian eighteenth-century penal policy. There was not, in English, any account of the policy to interpret. So I turned to a study of what Catherine's policy actually was, what she inherited and what she did with her inheritance. I have not attempted in this paper to tackle the application to Russia of the theories of Michel Foucault as expounded in his *Surveiller et punir*, with which I admit I have little sympathy. Obviously the approach to crime and punishment has changed considerably over time for social reasons, but to dismiss humanitarianism as a fig leaf, meant to cover up with hypocritical concern a basic determination to maintain existing power relations and the dominance of a ruling class, seems to me shortsighted, unscientific and unproved. The phasing out of the death penalty in a country short of labour may have been rational enough even though so many convicts died on the way to Siberia where they worked off their punishment. But only the argument for humanitarianism will explain the elimination or reduction of physical pain not only as part of the death penalty where it was still inflicted but as part of punishment, and the almost complete elimination of torture as part of the legal process.[8] Humanitarianism was a movement which swept over Europe and the fact that individuals continued to show extreme cruelty where they could freely do so and that the twentieth century has seen more refinements of cruelty in torture, execution and punishment than ever before is no reason to doubt the genuineness of eighteenth-century sensibilities on the subject. The ideologues of the French Revolution did not use torture as did those of the twentieth century, and the guillotine was introduced as a humane way of executing traitors. It only shows that there is no such thing as linear progress in the evolution of human society.

A full history of penal policy, in theory and in practice, in eighteenth-century Russia, based on court records and judicial practice, remains to be written. It cannot be treated simply as a continuation of the seventeenth-century legal situation (though much of the seventeenth-century practice survived) because of the vast number of new laws introduced by Peter I, with new concepts of crime and new penalties. The massive borrowings from Sweden, for instance in the Military Code of 1716, introduced a European dimension which had been lacking before. Moreover, there has been no systematic study of court verdicts in criminal (or civil) cases, of appeals procedure and of the implementation of sentences. Until this is undertaken, which now seems more possible in the new historiographical climate in Russia, much will remain uncertain about the Russian penal system, and much of the

8. In eighteenth-century England torture had been phased out, and in any case it had previously been illegal under the common law. It had been applied under the prerogative, particularly in the sixteenth century, but it could not be applied to nobles, though it could to the gentry. Under Peter I it had been applied to all classes, but under Catherine nobles do not seem ever to have been tortured.

speculation on the role of the state in the maintenance of the ruling class will continue to be built on air.

Strange as it may seem, V.I. Semevsky's classical work, *Krest'yane v tsarstvovaniye Yekateriny II* (1903), remains the starting point for any study of the peasantry in the reign of Catherine II. Some of Semevsky's interpretations have been challenged, notably by R. Bartlett. But Semevsky's basic picture, strongly tinged by deep political, populist disapproval, remains the standard, for instance in the work of J. Blum[9] and many other Western historians who do not think it necessary to question anything he wrote or re-examine any of his conclusions. Thus the article 'Catherine II and the serfs: a reconsideration of some problems' was, more than any of the others reproduced here, the product of my dissatisfaction with the existing state of scholarship on serfdom under Catherine II when I was writing my book *Russia in the Age of Catherine the Great.* I attempted to tackle only three major issues, in the context of the generally accepted view at the time that Catherine, in the first ten years of her reign, acted with the deliberate intention of strengthening the power of the nobles over their serfs in order to win the support of the former for her usurpation of the throne. The three issues were: the power granted to nobles to exile serfs to Siberia (granted in fact by Elizabeth in 1760); the alleged prohibition of serfs to complain of ill-treatment by their masters; and the alleged transformation of large numbers of state peasants into serfs by means of the grants of settled land given by the Empress to nobles in order to win their support. Semevsky's papers have been preserved in what was at the time the archive of the Moscow section of the Academy of Sciences of the USSR. They include copies of petitions from serfs complaining of ill-treatment and a full chronological list of all those who received grants of land under Catherine. Since I published this article in 1974, to my knowledge this archive has not been examined by any Western or Russian historian in order to test or confirm the assumptions which are still echoed from textbook to textbook.

Similarly, no further investigation has been made of the policy behind the granting of large numbers of relatively small estates to Russian nobles in lands confiscated from Poland at the first and subsequent partitions, though Princess Dashkova confirms in her memoirs that this policy was intended to increase the presence of Russian landowners in the elective local government institutions introduced by the Statute of 1775.[10]

'Freemasonry in eighteenth-century Russian society' was written as part of a symposium on European freemasonry to be published by the Gabinetto Vieusseux in Florence. Here again, as with the subject of penal policy, I did not think that I could approach the subject of the masonic impact on Russian society without providing a good deal more information to the Italian reader on what the Russian masonic movement was like. I therefore attempted to provide a general overview of its development, particularly in that period in

9. J. Blum, *Lord and Peasant in Russia from the Ninth to the Nineteenth Century*, Princeton, 1961.
10. Princess E.R. Dashkova, *Memoirs*, ed. K. Fitzlyon, London, 1958, p. 196.

the eighteenth century when it reached its maximum influence, before the lodges were closed down by Catherine II in the 1790s, and before the movement re-emerged in different form under Alexander I, transformed by the French Revolution and the Napoleonic empire into other kinds of secret societies, culminating in the Decembrist movement. There is no doubt in my mind that freemasonry in Russia developed as it did because of a deep dissatisfaction with the kind of spiritual nourishment offered on the one hand by the Orthodox Church and on the other hand by the rationalism of the *philosophes* of the Enlightenment. One has only to look at the kind of works translated into Russian, mainly from German, but sometimes from Latin: Jacob Böhme, Meister Eckhart, J. Arndt, the *Chemische Hochzeit* of Christian Rosencreutz, the *Paracelsi Handbibel*, Haugwitz's *Hirtenbrief*, to realize the longing for some kind of spiritual poetry. Some of this longing is expressed in the literary works of major (and minor) poets who were masons, like for instance M.N. Kheraskov, who wrote one of the hymns in use among them, 'Kol slaven'. It is also reflected in the original masonic writings of the masons themselves, about which much less is known since they remain unpublished, but which have now been subjected to an initial exploration by Stephen L. Baehr in the *Modern Encyclopedia of Russian and Soviet Literature* and by Rafaella Faggionato in the *Rivista Storica Italiana*.[11]

The downfall of N.I. Novikov in 1792 and the closing of the lodges in 1794 were not only the consequences of Catherine's increasing fear of the spread of revolutionary ideas from France through Poland. They were also in part the result of internal stresses, even feuds, within the masonic movement itself which have not been sufficiently explored. The various types of freemasonry were rivals for the control of Russian freemasonry. The competition between the Swedish Templars and the Yelagin/Reichel lodges was solved by Catherine when she sent the head of the Templars, Prince G.P. Gagarin, to honourable exile in Moscow. But he promptly engaged in a struggle with the Rosicrucians for control of the Moscow masons. It was Gagarin who, in 1786, denounced Novikov to Prince A.A. Prozorovsky, who was not at the time governor general of Moscow, for allegedly running schools and a hospital in Moscow, which in fact did not exist, though subsequent historians have believed that they did on his denunciation alone. When the crisis occurred in Moscow in 1792, Prozorovsky, by then governor general and commander in chief, was already prejudiced and forewarned.[12]

The article on 'Catherine II and the foundation of the Russian educational system' has been included here because though it is in the nature of a first version of a chapter of my *Russia in the Age of Catherine the Great*, the present version treats the subject in a more leisurely way and provides more background

11. Stephen L. Baehr, vol. VIII, pp. 28–36; Rafaella Faggionato, 'La fine di un "Utopia" – contributo alla storia della massoneria nella Russia di Caterina II', *Rivista Storica Italiana*, cv, I, 1993, pp. 36–179. Much additional material on Russian freemasonry has now also been published by A.G. Cross.
12. G. Vernadsky, *Russkoye masonstvo*, Petrograd, 1917, p. 210.

detail. Since its first publication in 1979, there have been a number of interesting studies both in Russia and in the West which have contributed to fill out the picture. Max Okenfuss's criticism of Catherine's pedagogical methods were noted briefly in the corresponding chapter of my book. As he puts it, 'In the search for an alternative to the role of memorization of classical texts in grammar schools, Catherine selected not the Lockean or Rousseauian "natural" education but a very Germanic regimen of discipline, repetition and order'. But fashions in pedagogy change. Nowhere in Catherine's day were the methods of *Emile* practised, and though progressive schools may have adopted some of them in recent years, educationalists in Britain are turning their back on 'natural' and child-centred education. It seems inappropriate to criticize Catherine for adopting a pedagogical method known in her time to work.

More relevant perhaps is G. Marker's study of the implementation of the law of 1786 setting up the national school system. He stresses the extent to which the normative element in the teaching programme was adapted by teachers on the spot in order to cope with lack of funds, local official indifference, shortage of qualified teachers and so forth. His conclusion is that the failure of the government to exercise the strict control prescribed in order to produce uniformity in the event led to the resounding success of the schools.[13] Their relative success is also confirmed by some figures for literacy provided by Boris Mironov. For male town-dwellers aged between ten and nineteen, they were 19.3 per cent in 1757, 27.3 per cent in 1777, rising to 31.35 per cent in 1787 (one year after the promulgation of the act setting up the national schools), 34.3 per cent in 1797 and 38.8 per cent in 1807. The figures for women were correspondingly lower, rising from 5.2 per cent in 1757 to 18.7 per cent in 1807; and the figures for peasants were lowest of all, 3.2 per cent males in 1757 rising to 9.6 per cent in 1807.[14] These figures refer only to a small cohort of the population, but they suggest that we have often been too hasty in assuming the total illiteracy of the Russian town population.

One of the well-worn subjects of debate for many years past was the extent to which Catherine II could truly be described as an enlightened despot, or as I prefer it, an enlightened absolutist ruler. There are two aspects to this question: first, was Catherine a reformer at all, or was she merely a hypocrite, mouthing the noble sentiments of the *philosophes*, and calmly pursuing her oppressive policies? And were the policies she did pursue 'enlightened', and if so in what sense? I have long held that Catherine was a reformer by temperament, and a

13. G. Marker, 'Who Rules the Word? Public School Education and the Fate of Universality in Russia, 1782–1803', *Russian History*, 20, Nos 1–4, 1993, pp. 15–34. See also my paper, 'The Educational Reforms of Peter I and Catherine II: The Darlington Report in Retrospect' in *Thomas Darlington's Report on Education in Russia*, papers from the 75th anniversary conference, December 1984, and Janet Hartley, 'The Boards of Social Welfare and the Financing of Catherine II's State Schools', *Slavonic and East European Review*, 67, No. 2, April 1989, pp. 211–27.

14. B.N. Mironov, *Istoriya v tsifrakh*, Leningrad, 1991, pp. 80–4, quoted in G. Smagina, 'Die Schulreform Katharinas II: Idee und Realisierung', paper presented at the international conference on the 200th anniversary of the death of Catherine II, organized by the Institute of European History of Mainz and the city of Zerbst, 26–31 August 1996, p. 31.

woman who meant to rule, not merely reign. I also think that the whole tenor of her life, from adolescence to maturity, shows her to have been an intellectual, if of a pragmatic rather than a theoretical kind. It is clear, at any rate to me, that many of her reforms are based on ideas current at the time, which cannot necessarily be traced to the influence of any individual *philosophe*, except perhaps for Montesquieu, and that she hoped by following rational policies and making good laws to improve the condition of her people. The essay 'Catherine the Great' represents a summary of the view that Catherine belongs squarely in the tradition of the 'enlightened' monarchs of the second half of the eighteenth century. But what do we mean by 'enlightened'? This is a question which has often arisen in academic dispute with American colleagues in particular, who tend to confuse 'Enlightenment' with what is today described as 'liberal' in the United States, that is to say pliable and accommodating, rather than rigid and disciplinarian policies. This 'liberal' interpretation seems to me to fail to understand the extent to which the 'Enlightenment' could be authoritarian. One has only to read Rousseau's *Contrat Social* to appreciate this.

The next two papers reproduced here deal with Catherine's relations with Voltaire, Diderot, Montesquieu and Rousseau, either directly, or in the second case through the intermediary of a Russian *philosophe*, Prince M.M. Shcherbatov. The two papers belong together. It will be observed that I am far more critical of the attitude of the *philosophes* (all French, except Rousseau who was French-influenced) to Russia than the majority of historians both in Soviet Russia and in the West who have tended almost invariably to blame Catherine for failing to implement the ideas of any or all of the four named above. It simply does not occur to these historians that the *philosophes* could actually be wrong about Russia! (I would exclude Montesquieu, whose generalizations are few, more subtle and less didactic.) This patronizing attitude towards Russia starts with Voltaire, who could not be bothered to use the correct names for Russian towns (though I like Veronise, a cross between Verona and Venice, for Voronezh) and felt forced to draw a veil over his real opinion of the execution of Aleksey Petrovich by Peter I. Rousseau believed that Russia, having taken the wrong turning under Peter I, would soon be overrun by the Tartars – it has not been to this day. Diderot, the only *philosophe* to visit Russia, was totally ignorant of actual conditions outside St Petersburg, and concerned only with putting forward his own plans and projects without much sense of Russian reality. He did not have the courage to voice his criticism of Russia openly, but on his return to France he published them in Raynal's *Histoire des Etablissements et du Commerce des Deux Indes*, in Raynal's name, where they did indeed arouse Catherine's indignation when she read them – not knowing of course that they were his. This patronizing attitude of contemporary French *philosophes* as well as later French historians (see for instance Lortholary's classic work, *Le Mirage russe en France au XVIIIe siècle*) is typical of their view of inferior cultures – one need only compare it with Desdevizes du Desert's work on enlightened Spain. Moreover, one must not forget that the *philosophes* were fighting out their battles with each other in their comments on Catherine II and her *Great Instruction*. Voltaire, it is true, was always a faithful admirer, and to my knowledge was not her pensioner in the way Diderot was. But he was very critical of Montesquieu and detested Rousseau.

The paper on 'Russia and the Enlightenment' was delivered to a history society in St Andrews, and is really an introductory survey not so much of the intellectual content of the cultural impact of the Enlightenment in Russia as of the extent of its impact over time. This paper, though originally delivered in 1986, has been recast and has drawn on recent scholarship more than the others in this collection because it existed only in manuscript, and needed therefore to be re-written in any case. It is a subject which requires a whole book, since the influence of the Enlightenment is really only one strand in the cultural life of Russia in the eighteenth century, and there is no doubt that concentration on this particular aspect distorts the general picture. We are left with an account of a rather thin intellectual trend by which the impact of the West on Russia is measured, whereas much of Russian life rolled on with its own traditional entertainments, rites, sorrows and rejoicings, songs and ballads, proverbs, religious and pagan ceremonies and reading matter. Moreover, were Peter I's celebrations of victory in the streets of Moscow or St Petersburg's canals not closer to Renaissance spectacle? It is this concentration on Western influences on Russia which may well have led to the hardening into accepted fact of the notion of the existence of a deep cultural divide between the nobility and the peasantry, serving to render more acute the incipient Russian class conflict and to alienate the nobles from the people.[15] I have found this assumption unproven, since it seems to me that the cultural gulf between the noble and the peasant is no greater in Russia than in France or Spain. Peasants lived in their own world everywhere, and in many ways in Russia they were closer to their masters than in many other European cultures.

Finally I include a brief piece on the literary activity of Catherine herself. Here again, in the space available to me it was scarcely possible to do justice to the large variety of her intellectual interests and her efforts at composition in various fields and genres. Her *Instruction* and her letters to Voltaire and Grimm are well known, because they were written in French. Her plays were written in Russian, doubtless corrected for her by one or other of her secretaries. As a genuine Russian patriot, Catherine took very seriously her writings on Russian history. She read widely in Russian and foreign published histories of Russia and collected manuscripts, either borrowing them from her noble friends or obtaining copies from monasteries, and she is known to have possessed a copy of the 'Slovo o polku Igoreve',[16] the great Russian medieval ballad, in her library of over 140 manuscripts. Catherine could not read Old Church Slavonic easily and apart from the copy of the original 'Slovo' made for her she was provided with a translation into Russian made from the original Old

15. G. Hosking, *Russia, People and Empire*, London, 1997, pp. 156–7.
16. See the article by the late G.N. Moiseyeva, '"Slovo o polku Igoreve" i Yekaterina' in *Vosemnadsatyy vek*, sbornik 18, Nauka, 1993, pp. 3–30.

Church Slavonic, which belonged to the bibliophile A.I. Musin Pushkin, which was destroyed in the fire of Moscow in 1812. The publication of the 'Slovo' in 1800 was based on the copy in Catherine's archives which thus seems to be the only surviving example of the original text, if not the original manuscript. Catherine also prepared genealogical tables of the princes of Rus' to 1140, and she was in close contact with the leading Russian amateurs of history in the 1790s, such as I.I. Boltin, I.P. Elagin and of course A.I. Musin Pushkin. Later historians have sneered at her efforts, but in her own time, when the history of the early middle ages in Russia was in its infancy, her work was respected.[17] When one studies the timetable of the Empress's day, the number of official engagements, ukazy, reports, despatches etc. to be read and studied, one realizes why she got up at six in the morning to write her plays and her laws.

17. Moiseyeva, *op. cit.*, p. 30.

PART ONE

Russian Government and Society

CHAPTER ONE

Tsar into emperor: the title of Peter the Great

I

> C'est par ces riens d'étiquette que se marque la considération d'un pays, que s'affirme sa puissance, que s'établit sa grandeur . . .
>
> Jean Baptiste Colbert, Marquis de Torcy*

On 30 August 1721, the long Great Northern War came to an end and peace was signed between Russia and Sweden at Nystadt. The peace consolidated the gains made by Russia, notably the acquisition of the Baltic provinces of Livonia and Estonia, part of Finland and the estuary of the Neva on which St Petersburg had been founded in 1703. Russia had now replaced Sweden as the principal naval power in the Baltic Sea.

A thanksgiving service was to take place in the new capital on 22 October 1721, and two days before, on the 20th, the Senate and the Synod, in joint session, decided to beg the tsar, in the name of the whole Russian people, to accept the titles of Father of the Fatherland (*otets otechestva*), All Russian Emperor (*imperator vserossiyskiy*) and Peter the Great, in gratitude for the graces and great services he had rendered to his country in both peace and war. In fulfilment of this decision, Prince A.D. Menshikov, the most corrupt and well loved of Peter's 'fledglings', was charged by the Senate to submit to Peter a written request, 'in the name of all the orders in the All-Russian state' (*vserossiyskogo gosudarstva chinov*), that he should condescend to accept this title, and allow the Senate to submit the proposal to him in the course of a solemn church ceremony. Peter, in reply to Menshikov's proposal, said that he would first like to consult with a few members of the Senate. Whereupon a number of senators, and the archbishops of Pskov and Novgorod, who were the vice-presidents of the Synod, waited upon Peter and humbly presented their petition again. 'With his usual praiseworthy modesty and moderation' Peter at

* *Journal inédit de Jean-Baptiste Colbert, marquis de Torcy, Ministre et Secrétaire d'état, 1685*, ed. F. Masson (Paris, 1884), p. xiv. This chapter was completed before the publication of R. Wortman, *Scenarios of Power: Myth and Ceremony in Russian Monarchy*, vol. I (Princeton, 1995). I was therefore unable to make use of his insights.

first refused to agree, giving many substantial reasons. But he finally gave way and, as we know, on 22 October 1721, at the solemn service of thanksgiving for the peace with Sweden, in the Holy Trinity Church in St Petersburg, the archbishop of Pskov, Feofan Prokopovich, proclaimed in his sermon the services to his people which entitled Peter to be called by these new titles. After the sermon, all the senators approached Peter, and the chancellor, Count Golovkin, made a fulsome speech praising Peter for having 'brought his faithful subjects from the darkness of ignorance to the theatre of glory of the whole world, from not-being to being', and for 'introducing them into the society of political peoples'.[1]

The difficulties experienced by Peter I in obtaining recognition of his new title by the other European powers have been quite extensively studied. But the change from the traditional Slavonic title of 'tsar' to the Latin title of 'imperator' raises a number of interesting questions which do not seem to have attracted so much scholarly attention in English. First of all, what did the titles 'tsar' and 'emperor' mean in traditional Russian usage? Secondly, what grounds, if any, did Peter have for wishing to change from the traditional Russian title of tsar to that of emperor? What kind of emperor was he thinking of, and what consequences would the change have for the status of Russia in international relations?[2]

In considering the meaning of titles, one must bear in mind that before the late seventeenth century there was a certain lack of precision about their use among European powers. The supremacy traditionally granted to the Holy Roman Emperor was being undermined already in the sixteenth century by the concept of 'Rex imperator in regno suo' which had a respectable medieval ancestry. The growing discrepancy between the actual power of the emperor and his claims to supremacy, blatantly revealed by the religious wars of the sixteenth and seventeenth centuries, further weakened the imperial position. Europe, moreover, since the discoveries, was no longer a 'Christian Commonwealth', and the peace settlements of 1648 opened the way to a restructuring of international relations on the basis of the equality of sovereign states.[3] Russia had now to insert herself at her proper rank into this new network of states.

The title 'imperator' goes back to republican Rome, where it meant only a military commander, and was a title of honour bestowed on victorious generals by the acclamation of their soldiers, and subsequently endorsed by the

1. *Polnoye sobraniye zakonov Rossiyskoy imperii*, 45 vols. (St Petersburg, 1830), pt. I, vol. V, No. 3840, 22 October 1721; see also *Istoriya Pravitel'stvuyushchego Senata*, vol. I, pp. 92ff. All dates are given in the old style unless indicated by N.S. I am grateful to Dr W.F. Ryan, Academic Librarian of the Warburg Institute, for much guidance through the bibliographical rapids, and also to Dr O.A. Omel'chenko of the Vsesoyuznyy Yuridicheskiy Zaochnyy Institut, Moscow, who has very kindly looked up and copied sources for me in the Russian State Archives in Moscow, and with whom I have corresponded on the subject.
2. See the lengthy bibliography in R. Wittram, *Peter I., Czar und Kaiser*, 2 vols. (Göttingen, 1964), vol. II, p. 607, note 34.
3. See H. Duchhardt, 'Imperium und Regna im Zeitalter Ludwigs XIV', *Historische Zeitschrift*, 232 (1981), pp. 555–81.

Senate.[4] After the reign of Augustus, the imperator united military, administrative, and judicial power, and religious power as Supreme Pontiff. Under Diocletian he was surrounded with the trappings of a god: petitioners had to prostrate themselves before an emperor withdrawn in his apartments, wearing rich robes and a crown. Though he was in all respects a king, even an oriental king, the sole source of power and enjoying sole power, yet he did not use the name 'king' in Rome because of the historical Roman aversion to kings as dangerous to liberty.[5] With the transfer of the capital to Byzantium and Constantine's conversion to Christianity, the role of the emperor, as head of the church and ruler by divine right, was greatly enhanced. The emperor continued to be 'elected' (or appointed by a reigning emperor) and 'acclaimed' but became also the manifestation of a power created by God. The wreath was replaced by the diadem.

At the beginning, Byzantine titles in Greek were faithful translations of the original Latin. Thus 'imperator' was translated 'autokrator'. Little by little Latin was edged out and replaced by Greek, and Greek writers often used 'basileus', which was the common title for the ruler of the eastern dependencies of the Byzantine Empire, as for instance Egypt, though the usage took some time to penetrate the chanceries. 'Basileus' was originally the Greek for the Latin 'rex', but as it came to be applied to the emperor, so it ceased to be applied to the emperor's vassals.[6] In the seventh century for the first time the title basileus was used alone as the formal title of the imperator, swallowing up autokrator, Caesar, and Augustus, 'So that at length the name of emperor and king grew to be as one although the Romans . . . so much at first distinguished them'.[7] As Bréhier puts it, 'oriental usage was stronger than Roman constitutionalism'. Later 'autokrator' revived but was applied only to the senior emperor, to the basileus who actually ruled when there was more than one, in order to reinforce his authority. Never did the Byzantines, as lords of the world, use 'basileus' to translate the Latin 'rex', and they refused to allow the title of basileus to the Carolingian and German emperors, except only to Charlemagne.[8] The Byzantine view was not accepted everywhere in the barbarian West, however: when Basil the Macedonian reproached the Holy Roman Emperor Ludwig II with presuming to use the title 'basileus', the latter replied that he was as good an

4. There is a vast literature on Rome and Byzantium. I have limited myself to some general works, such as J.P.T. Bury, *The Constitution of the Later Roman Empire*, The Creighton Lecture, 1909 (Cambridge, 1910), *passim* (I owe this reference to the kindness of the late Professor S.E. Finer); J. Bryce, *The Holy Roman Empire* (8th edn, London, 1897); N.H. Baynes and H.St.L.B. Moss, *Byzantium* (Oxford, 1948 edn); L. Bréhier, *Les institutions de l'Empire Byzantin* (Paris, 1970 edn); G. Walter (ed.), *Le mémorial des siècles*, Le Xe siècle, les évènements, *La naissance du Saint empire*, by R. Folz, Introduction at pp. 12–13. See also J. Selden, *Titles of Honor* (3rd edn, London, 1672), who says, p. 11, that in olden times a king was superior to an emperor, which denoted only a general or leader of an army.

5. Selden, *Titles of Honor*, p. 12.

6. L. Bréhier, 'L'origine des titres impériaux à Byzance', *Byzantinische Zeitschrift*, 15 (1906), pp. 161–78, at p. 170.

7. Selden, *Titles of Honor*, p. 14.

8. Bréhier, 'L'origine', p. 175.

emperor as Basil, and that anyhow basileus was only the Greek for rex, and need not mean emperor at all.[9] Indeed, in its time basileus was the favourite title used by the Saxon kings of England.[10]

It was this 'basileus autokrator' who presided over the conversion of Kievan Russia to Christianity, and who became known in early Slavonic chronicles as tsar, with his capital at Tsargrad. The word 'tsar' derives philologically from 'caesar', a derivation which was often lost sight of in the centuries to come. The title of tsar was not confined in Old Church Slavonic to the ruler of the empire in Constantinople; it was also used of kings, for instance the kings of the Old Testament, like David, or of the New Testament, like Herod, king of Judea, and indeed the kingdom of heaven was the '*tsarstvo bozhie*'. After the Mongol conquest it was also used of the rulers of the Golden Horde, and in general seems to have been used indiscriminately of Orthodox or eastern pagan or Muslim rulers, but not of the Catholic western emperors. In medieval Russian documents, the title 'kesar' was applied exclusively to the pagan Roman emperors. The alternative, 'tsesar', was used of the Christian Holy Roman emperors.[11] Thus in the early middle ages 'tsar' was used in Church Slavonic both of the emperor in Byzantium and of kings in the Bible,[12] just as 'basileus' was used by emperors in Constantinople and by kings in England.

The title used by the rulers of the Kievan principalities was knyaz', which could be both a general designation of all members of a ruling clan and could also refer specifically to one knyaz', who was the senior ruler in that clan at the time in a given city, and who later came to be known as 'velikii knyaz''. The title knyaz' has usually been translated as prince, while 'velikii knyaz'' appears as grand duke or grand prince. Neither prince nor duke is really strictly correct, since knyaz' derives from the Germanic **Kuningaz* which later developed into König, king.[13]

The whole question of the titles used by and to the rulers of the principalities of Kievan Russia is extremely complex, and there is no room, nor am I competent, to enter upon it here in any detail. It appears that in the pre-Mongol period they were addressed by Byzantine officials as *αρχοντες Ρωσιας*. Later, in the thirteenth and fourteenth centuries, they were addressed as *ρεξ* or

9. Bryce, *Holy Roman Empire*, pp. 191–2.
10. *Ibid.*, pp. 143–4; see also K.-H. Ruffman, 'England und der russische Zaren-und Kaisertitel', *Jahrbücher für Geschichte Osteuropas*, n.s., 3/3 (1955), pp. 217–24, at p. 222 n. 24. But 'imperator' or 'basileus' was not used in England after Saxon times (Selden, *Titles of Honor*, p. 17).
11. See W. Vodoff, 'L'idée impériale et la vision de Rome à Tver', XIV–XVe siècles', in his *Princes et principautés russes, Xe–XIIe siècles* (Northampton, 1989), No. XI, pp. 479–93, at p. 483 n. 39. On the derivation of tsar see M. Szeftel, 'The title of the Muscovite monarch up to the end of the seventeenth century', *Canadian American Slavic Studies*, 13/1–2 (1979), pp. 59–81, with extensive criticism of sources; and see also my article 'Autocracy and Sovereignty', *ibid.*, 16/3–4 (1982), pp. 369–95.
12. A. Lakier, 'Istoriya titula gosudarey Rossii', *Zhurnal Ministerstva narodnogo prosveshcheniya*, 56 (1847), pp. 81–156, at p. 85. This is a useful survey but it is marred by the fact that the author follows the historian Karamzin in rejecting the derivation of tsar from caesar and deriving it from oriental sources such as Nebuchadnezzar.
13. See M. Andrusiak, 'Kings of Kiev and Galicia', *Slavonic and East European Review*, 33 (1953), pp. 342–9.

μεγας ρεξ, as in *μεγας ρεξ του Τιφερου* (king or grand king of Tver'). It is possible that the Byzantine chancellery simply accepted the titles the Russian rulers gave themselves, adopting the Latin version. *Ρεξ* was in common use in Constantinople for the kings of France, Italy, Germany, etc., though it should be borne in mind that Greek writers had early learnt to use 'rex' for barbarian kings such as Odoacer.[14] Yet Michael of Tver', after receiving the *yarlyk* (edict) of the Mongol Khan in 1304 as grand prince of Vladimir and Moscow, sent an embassy to the Emperor Andronicos II in which he described himself as '*βασιλευς των Ρως*'. The Byzantine patriarchs also called the Russian princes '*ρεγες*'. The title of tsar appears very rarely in medieval Russia, but the use of 'kaiser', in German, in Russian relations with the Catholic Livonian Order appears as early as 1417.[15] Thus the distinction between basileus and rex, while very clear to the Byzantine chanceries, was not necessarily so clear to kings and princes elsewhere.

Similarly, in the Latin West, the Russian princes were usually addressed as 'rex' in early medieval times. Yaroslav the Wise was often called 'rex' in foreign chronicles. The right to make kings was one of the prerogatives of the Holy Roman Emperor, and also at times of the popes.[16] When Izyaslav was expelled from the throne of Kiev in 1073, he was granted the title of king by the Emperor Henry IV. When he received no help from the emperor he turned to the pope, Gregory VII, offering to place Russia under the Holy See if the pope helped him to recover his throne. Pope Gregory VII used the titles rex and regina to Prince Izyaslav and his wife. In the thirteenth century Honorius III addressed a missive to 'universis regibus Russiae', that is to say to all the princes of Russia. Later when the princes of Galicia sought in the West for help against the Tartar invasions of the early thirteenth century, the papacy offered Danilo the title of king. In 1253 he received the regalia and was crowned, but he proved unable to impose union with Rome on his subjects. However, he was known as 'rex Russiae', and even sometimes by the title 'korol'' (<Karl, i.e. Carolus Magnus), the Russian for 'king'.[17]

It seems that before the Mongol conquest – when Russia played an active part in the diplomacy of eastern Europe, and Russian princesses married into a number of royal houses, including those of the Empire – and particularly before the schism of 1054, the title of 'rex' was normally used in the Latin West not only for the senior ruler but for many of the minor rulers in Russia. But the usage gradually died out once the Russian principalities were overrun and became vassals of the Mongol khans.[18]

14. Bréhier, 'L'origine', p. 170.
15. W. Vodoff, 'La titulature princière en Russie du XI au début du XVI siècles', I; 'La titulature des princes russes du Xe au début du XII siècles', II; and 'La place du Grand Prince de Tver' dans les structures politiques russes de la fin du XIV et du XVe siècles', XII, in *Princes et principautés*, p. 33 n. 5. See also A.V. Soloviev, '"Reges" et "regnum Russiae" au Moyen Age', *Byzantion*, 36 (1966), pp. 144–73, at pp. 169ff: 'de grote konyng von Moskove, de rusche Kayser'.
16. *Bryce, Holy Roman Empire*, p. 250.
17. Andrusiak, 'Kings', pp. 348–9.
18. Soloviev, '"Reges" et "regnum"', pp. 152–64.

First the schism of 1054 and then the Mongol conquest set up barriers between East and West which lasted almost until the end of the fifteenth century. But several circumstances came together then to link Russia more closely with the West. It is difficult for the historian today to grasp quite how world-shattering was the fall of Constantinople in 1453 to the Christian community, coming on top of the final breach between the eastern and the western churches after the Council of Florence of 1439. In the West the Church survived but in the East there now remained only one independent Orthodox realm, as the Turks advanced throughout southern Europe. In Russia the disaster had a very special impact. In the first place Russian relations with the West had become much more frequent in the fifteenth century, as discussions began between Russia, the empire and the papacy on common action against the advancing Ottomans. Secondly, the unification of almost all the Russian principalities (except for those incorporated in Poland–Lithuania) under the authority of the grand duke of Moscow, and the formal emancipation of Russia from the Mongol yoke (dating officially from 1480), fostered a sense of the imperial role of the Muscovite grand duke as the independent ruler of All Russia. Finally, the marriage of Ivan III to the niece of the last emperor of Byzantium in 1472 led Ivan III to contemplate the possibility of inheriting some part at least of the Byzantine political and religious legacy. Thus, from 1473 he began to use intermittently, though not in his relations with western powers,[19] the more imposing Old Church Slavonic title of 'tsar' (in the sense of basileus, emperor), since there was no longer a tsar in Tsargrad.

However, in 1488 the Holy Roman Emperor offered to grant the title of 'king' to the ruler of Russia in the course of negotiations to procure an alliance between the emperor and the Grand Duke Ivan III, directed against Poland–Lithuania. The imperial envoy, Nicholas Poppel, implied that Ivan III had already asked the pope for the title, but that it was not for the pope to grant it. He offered to intercede with the Emperor Frederick III provided strict secrecy was kept. Ivan flatly refused to be condescended to, declaring that he and his ancestors had been lords in their own lands from time immemorial, and that

19. Pierangelo Catalano, 'Fin de l'Empire romain? Un problème juridico-religieux', in *Da Roma alla Terza Roma, documenti e studi: Roma – Constantinopoli – Mosca*, Edizione scientifiche italiane (Naples, 1983), pp. 543–58, at p. 549. See also Selden, *Titles of Honor*, p. 19: 'The Dukes of Muscovy . . . have had of late times this title of Emperoour or Czar which *Basilius* [Vasili III] first took to himself. Yet this title he used not to all princes. In his letters to the Emperoour, the Pope, the King of Swethland and Danemark, the governors of Prussia and Livonia and to the Great Turk he used it, but not to the Polonian . . . although . . . John Basiliowich, in his Letters to the king of *Poland* called himself Czar which is *Emperour* or *King*, but he was never saluted from the Polack by other name than Great Duke . . .'. Ivan III was called emperor in a treaty with Denmark dated 1493 ('domino Johanne totius Rutzie imperator . . .'. See N. Andreyev, 'Filofey and his epistle to Ivan Vasil'yevich', *Slavonic and East European Review*, 38 (1959), pp. 3–31, at p. 14 n. 61). And in a treaty between Vasily III and Albert of Prussia the former is called 'Imperator ac dominator totius Russiae' (see *Pamyatniki diplomaticheskikh snosheniy*, 10 vols. (1851–71) (hereafter *PDS*), vol. I, p. 1442, note). But V.I. Savva, *Moskovskiya tsari i Vizantiiskiye vasilevy* (Khar'kov, 1901), p. 276 n. 11, argues that 'imperator' may have been the translation into Latin of 'obladatel'' or 'povelitel'', commander, an argument which Szeftel in turn rejects ('Title of the Muscovite Monarch', p. 74), and so do I.

their lands had been granted by God and he needed no help from the emperor. This incidentally is not the outrageously arrogant reaction it has sometimes been taken to be, but the natural reaction of a ruler who had never been a vassal of the Holy Roman Emperor (nor indeed of the empire of the East, nor of the papacy), and who claimed to inherit the role of the basileis.[20] Already in 1492 (the year in which the world was supposed to come to an end), Zosimus, metropolitan of Moscow, had spoken of Ivan III as 'the new emperor Constantine of the new Constantinople – Moscow'.[21]

In 1499 Ivan III had his grandson Dmitri (who never reigned) crowned as grand duke, using the so-called cap of Grand Duke Vladimir Monomakh for the first time. This item of the future regalia of the tsars has a chequered history, again designed to strengthen the Russian claim to be the heirs of the empire of the East. It was reputed to be a gift from the Byzantine Emperor Constantine IX Monomakh to the Grand Duke Vladimir Monomakh, who had allegedly also been crowned with it. At about the same time, Ivan III adopted the crowned two-headed eagle as the arms of Russia.[22] Yet Ivan III acted cautiously, for it did not prove easy to get other European states to accept the new title of tsar, let alone the implication that it equalled that of emperor, either in form or in content. Had the title of the princes of Russia continued to be translated as rex (king) in the West, instead of declining to the usual 'magnus dux' after the Mongol conquest, the assimilation of Russia into the ranking order of European states would have been that much easier. But any change in the title of grand duke as normally used in the West would involve a substantial leap from a mere duke to a basileus, and would now have to cross the Russian language barrier. Moreover, the general assumption in the West was that only the Holy Roman Emperor could grant a royal title in the Christian community of nations, and he would not grant it to a schismatic ruler.

The fall of Constantinople had a particularly deep significance for Russia as the potential heir to the religious leadership of the Orthodox faithful. This was expressed in the concept of Moscow, the third Rome, a central element in the movement of ideas and sensibilities associated with the *translatio imperii* or the transfer of the Roman Empire of the East to the one remaining Orthodox power. The theory is usually associated with the epistles of a monk Filofey, who wrote to Vasily III around 1523 pointing out that all Christian kingdoms had now come together in Holy Russia, for 'two Romes have fallen, but the third still stands, and there will be no fourth'. Moscow must now take up the

20. S.M. Solov'yev, *Istoriya Rossii s drevneyshikh vremen* (Moscow, 1960), vol. III, p. 135.
21. D. Strémoukhoff, 'Moscow the Third Rome: Sources of the doctrine', *Speculum*, 28 (1953), pp. 108–25, at p. 112.
22. See M. Cherniavsky, 'Khan or basileus: An aspect of Russian mediaeval political thought', *Journal of the History of Ideas*, 20 (1959), pp. 459–76. Cherniavsky regards Dmitri's coronation as 'a copy of the Byzantine coronation for a caesar only, a junior co-emperor', Ivan III was performing the role of the 'augustus' or senior emperor. See p. 463, and notes 12 and 13. On the two-headed eagle see G. Alef, 'The adoption of the Muscovite two-headed eagle: A discordant view', *Speculum*, 41 (1966), pp. 1–21; Alef, however, argues that the adoption by Russia of the two-headed eagle on seals and on the Muscovite coat of arms was the result more of the renewed contacts between Muscovy and the Habsburgs than of the *translatio imperii* from Byzantium to Russia.

mission of defending the true faith, and accept the burden of empire. Similar claims had already been expressed earlier in veiled ecclesiastical language, but one of the more striking examples of the claim to imperial descent was put forward in the *Tale of the Princes of Vladimir*, dating from between 1499 and 1525, in which the Rurikides of the House of Moscow are alleged to descend from Prus, the brother of Augustus Caesar.[23] It is difficult to judge how seriously the Russian tsars believed in their Roman descent, but it served to underline their claim to a hereditary imperial status, going back beyond Byzantium to Rome itself, and was therefore useful for propaganda purposes. (It should be remembered that the formal name of the Byzantine Empire was Empire of the Romans.)[24]

In the event, the title of tsar tended to be used by foreign powers more often in verbal communications than in written ones. However, there was one major departure, when, on 4 August 1514, Maximilian, then king of the Romans, sent a letter to Vasily III, again seeking his alliance against Poland–Lithuania. The surviving text is in German and Maximilian, whether by accident or on purpose, speaks of the brotherly friendship between himself and the 'Grossen Herrn Vasili von Gotes Gnaden Kayser unnd Herscher aller Rewssen und Grosfurste zu Wolodimer . . . [*sic*]'.[25] (This letter was to have important consequences, for which see below, p. 33.) But Baron Herberstein, the imperial ambassador, still addressed Vasily III in 1516 as 'rex et dominus totius Russiae', so that Maximilian's letter seems to have been a flash in the pan.[26]

Ivan the Terrible took the claim to the imperial title of the ruler of Russia a stage further. He was the first Russian grand duke to be crowned tsar, in 1547 (*before* the conquest of Kazan' and Astrakhan'), in a ceremony which deliberately drew upon Byzantine precedents, and in which Ivan was anointed and took communion at the altar.[27] The Orthodox Christian theory of imperial government as expounded by Agapetus to Justinian was developed by the Metropolitan Makarius (a notable exponent of the theory of Moscow as the third Rome) in an eloquent address which had remarkably little influence on the actual conduct of the new tsar.[28] Logically enough, Ivan IV turned to the

23. The standard work is H. Schaeder, *Moskau das dritte Rom* (Darmstadt, 1929, reissued, 1957). There is a considerable literature on this subject which is usefully summarised in R. Crummey, *The Formation of Muscovy, 1304–1613* (London, 1987), pp. 136–7. Recent scholarship suggests that Filofey was the author of only one letter addressed to a high official in Pskov in 1523, and not to the tsar. See also Catalano, 'Fin de l'Empire romain?', and V. Pašuto, 'Mosca – Terza Roma', in *Da Roma alla Terza Roma*, pp. 459–74, where the various versions of the *Tale of the Princes of Vladimir* are analysed.

24. The claim might seem to belong rather to the world of Renaissance pretensions: the kings of Spain were descended from Hercules, Queen Elizabeth was descended from the Trojan Brutus, while the kings of France laid claim to descent from 'Francus', the son of Hector. See in general F. Yates, *Astraea – The Imperial Theme in the Sixteenth Century* (London, 1985 edn), pp. 115, 130–5.

25. *PDS*, vol. I, p. 1438, for the original German text. See also Soloviev, '"Reges" et "regnum"', pp. 171–3.

26. S. von Herberstein, *La Moscovie du XVIe siècle*, ed. Robert Delort (Paris, 1965).

27. David B. Miller, 'The coronation of Ivan IV', *Jahrbücher für Geschichte Osteuropas*, n.s., 15 (1967), pp. 559–74.

28. *Ibid.*, and see I. Shevchenko, 'A neglected Byzantine source of Muscovite political ideology', repr. in *Harvard Slavic Studies*, 5 (1954), pp. 141–79.

patriarch of Constantinople, the ecclesiastical superior of the Russian Orthodox Church, for confirmation of his right to the title of tsar. In the synodal letter of 1561, drafted by the patriarch and signed by most of the Greek hierarchy, the patriarch stressed that only the patriarchs of Rome and Constantinople could grant the title of emperor. Since Ivan IV was of 'imperial descent' he was authorised to be and to call himself legitimate basileus. In a second personal missive, the patriarch addressed Ivan as 'basileus of the orthodox christians of the universe', thus recognising the role of Russia as heir to Byzantium.[29] Moreover, Ivan IV was now in a position to straddle the Christian and the Muslim worlds. His title of tsar eventually reproduced not only the title of the emperor in Byzantium but also the Russian form of the title of the rulers of the Golden Horde and of the successor realms of Kazan' and Astrakhan' to which he could now lay claim.[30]

Ivan IV, like his father Vasily III and his grandfather Ivan III, did not use the title of tsar in all communications with the western world, and it was not generally acknowledged. He attempted to impose it on the Livonians on the grounds that Livonia formed part of his patrimony. In the words of the contemporary chronicler, Balthasar Russow, 'dath der Russische Keys. May. als ein Her und Erffförst der Lande tho Lyfflandt'. Russow uses the word 'Kayser' several times and also 'Majesty'.[31] The king of Poland, Sigismund, refused outright to use it, alleging that the 'royal' title needed the consent of the emperor and the pope.

The Poles in fact put up the stiffest resistance to the use of the title of tsar. They argued for instance that no Christian ruler was called tsar, which was a title only in use among *basurmany* or Muslims; or that the title belonged only to the Holy Roman Emperor, and therefore its use by Moscow could not be accepted without talks with other kings.[32] In 1581 the dialogue between King Stephen Bathory of Poland and Ivan IV sank to new depths when Ivan, as a means of putting pressure on Stephen, forwarded to him the genealogy of his descent from Caesar Augustus's brother Prus, stressing that he, Ivan, was the heir of his ancestors by the grace of God, and was not a ruler elected by a noisy assembly like the king of Poland. To which Stephen replied that Ivan should not tell tall stories about his descent from Augustus's non-existent brother.[33]

The Poles had attempted to bargain with Ivan over his title: peace for recognition. In turn, the papacy hoped to win acknowledgement of Roman supremacy in exchange for recognition of the tsar's title. In 1550, a letter from

29. Catalano, 'Fin de l'Empire romain', p. 551.
30. When Ivan IV failed to convince other powers of the validity of his claim to the title of tsar as equivalent of basileus he frequently fell back on his right to the title as ruler by conquest of the successor states of Kazan' and Astrakhan'.
31. Edward C. Thaden, 'Ivan IV in Baltic German historiography', in his *Interpreting History: Collective Essays on Russia's Relations with Europe* (New York, 1990), pp. 237–56, at pp. 242–3. Thaden quotes examples from the sixteenth-century *Chronica der Provintz Lyyflandt* by Balthasar Russow (1584). Russow considers that 'czar' is Tartar for 'king': pp. 78–90.
32. Savva, *Moskovskiye tsari*, pp. 286ff.
33. Proof of the existence of Prus for Ivan was the fact that Prussia was named after him. *Ibid.*, p. 312.

the pope was drafted for delivery to Ivan in which he was addressed as 'Universorum Ruthenorum imperator', but the papal mission to Russia never took place owing to Polish obstruction.[34] An attempt was also made in 1576 to secure Ivan's support for the election of Maximilian II to the Polish throne. Ivan was promised the help of the pope and other rulers in order that 'the whole Greek empire of the East' should belong to him ('vse tsesarstvo na vskhod solntsa'). He agreed to negotiate but did not take up the offer of the title of 'emperor of the East'.[35] In 1581 the Jesuit Antonio Possevino, who was the personal emissary of Pope Gregory XIII to Ivan IV, negotiated the Truce of Iam Zapol'skiy between the tsar and Stephen Bathory, which put a temporary end to the disastrous Livonian War. Possevino put into words the problem which faced the western powers in relations with Russia in his report to Gregory XIII:

> To promote the greater glory of God, we should realize that in addition to the dispatch of capable and discerning men, it will prove important . . . to attempt a definition of the place of the Prince of Muscovy among the Christian rulers. Negotiations can be carried on with the present Prince, or with his more gentle son [Fyodor Ivanovich], or perhaps even with his future Catholic successor . . .[36]

In the course of the negotiations Ivan insisted on the use of tsar, at any rate of tsar of Kazan' and Astrakhan'. He was even prepared to give up fortified towns in order to achieve this aim. Possevino expounded the western theory of

> the single emperor of the Christians, a title requiring confirmation by the Apostolic See . . . If the Grand Prince of Muscovy desired to have a valid title, and to enjoy a legitimate dignity, he should first negotiate with the Pope, like the rest of the Christian rulers, who were well aware that the acquisition of Kazan' and Astrakhan' was not sufficient to warrant the addition of a new title such as 'the other Caesar', which means Emperor or King. If the Prince tried to call himself Caesar, everyone would know that this title meant 'only Tsar', not Caesar, and that it was an oddity borrowed from the Tartars in an effort to approximate the title held by other Kings.

Thus the papacy at this time regarded 'tsar' as a barbarism, and rejected the derivation from Caesar. But on another occasion Possevino attempted to persuade Ivan IV that if he agreed to church unity, 'you will have every reason to expect that your titles and distinctions will enjoy greater prestige than they have heretofore, and you will soon be called Emperor of the East, if you

34. *Ibid.*, p. 370. P. Pierling, *La Russie et le Saint Siège*, 5 vols. (Paris, 1901–12), vol. I, pp. 341 and 348ff. It was Polish policy to prevent an understanding between Rome and Russia, and physical obstacles were placed in the way of the journeys of envoys. The pope, for instance, had invited Ivan to send representatives to the Council of Trent, but his messenger was not allowed to proceed through Poland. Savva, *Moskovskiye tsari*, p. 326.
35. *Ibid.*, pp. 285–6.
36. See *The Moscovia of Antonio Possevino, S.J.*, trans. and ed. Hugh F. Graham (Pittsburgh, 1977), p. 128.

advance the cause of the Orthodox Catholics there . . .'. Ivan refused the offer of the empire of the East, on the grounds that 'it was for the Lord of his own volition to assign realms to whomever he chooses'.[37]

The creation of the patriarchate in 1589, in the reign of Fyodor Ivanovich, was Boris Godunov's main contribution to the evolution of the doctrine of 'Moscow the Third Rome'. In the charter which established it, Moscow is described as the imperial city, in the language which used to be used of Constantinople, and the tsar as the sole Christian emperor (tsar) on earth, in the third Rome.[38]

In the Time of Troubles renewed efforts were made for Polish recognition of the title of tsar under Boris Godunov. The Russians pointed out that the Spanish, French, Danish and English kings and even the popes had used 'tsar'. But the Poles replied that none of these countries had been at war with Russia. They – the Poles – had. Let recognition come after perpetual peace. Most paradoxical was the claim of the false Dmitri, during the Time of Troubles, whose seizure of the Russian throne was sponsored by Poland behind the scenes, to the title of 'Imperator et Magnus Dux' in Latin, and to the title of 'tsesar', i.e. tsar in the form which was used to the Holy Roman Emperor. When King Sigismund of Poland utterly rejected his claim, Dmitri answered that 'tsar' was a title given by God. Rulers of Russia could not be counted merely as lords and princes, and had as much right to the title of tsar as the Assyrians and the Medes and even the Romans, who had no greater claims. 'We have *kings* under us, and who serve us', he declared.[39] The Russian claim to the title of emperor was by no means a secret among foreigners serving in Russia. Captain Margeret, a French mercenary in Russia in 1606, refers in his memoirs to Maximilian's letter calling Vasily III emperor, and to the Russian assertion that the title of tsar ranked above that of 'Tsisar' and 'korol' ', used of the Holy Roman Emperor and other kings.[40]

II

There can be no doubt that a corpus of doctrine had been accumulating at the Russian court, enabling the Tsars Ivan III, Vasily III and more particularly Ivan IV to pursue systematically the claim to the imperial title and parity with the Holy Roman Emperor as emperor of the East whenever they felt that the moment was opportune.[41] But the extinction of the Ryurikid dynasty and its replacement by the Romanovs, who did not descend directly from a Ryurikid ancestor,[42] weakened the position of the Russian ruler. What is more, the tsar

37. *Ibid.*, p. 68.
38. Catalano, 'Fin de l'Empire romain?', p. 553.
39. Pierling, *La Russie*, vol. IV, p. 64.
40. Jacques Margeret, *Un mousquetaire à Moscou*, ed. A. Bennigsen (Paris, 1983), pp. 47–8. Cf. G. Fletcher, *Of the Russe Commonwealth*, facsimile edn by R. Pipes (Cambridge, Mass., 1966), pp. 19–20.
41. Pašuto, 'Mosca', p. 464.
42. Mikhail Romanov was the grandson of the brother of Ivan IV's first wife. There were many princes with a far better *hereditary* claim to the throne than the Romanovs.

was now an elected ruler, which, in accordance with the tenets of the time, and indeed of Ivan IV himself, gave him a lower status than that of hereditary rulers. He required a twofold recognition, as legitimate ruler, and as tsar. Other powers could now put forward conditions for the recognition of the new tsar, and manoeuvre between the claims of Mikhail and Wladyslaw of Poland, who had been offered the throne in 1610.[43] Eventually, as most of the European powers and most of the princes of the Holy Roman Empire recognised Mikhail Romanov, the emperor accepted a *de facto* recognition, using 'zarische Hoheit' verbally to the Russian envoy, that is to say accepting the title of tsar but not of Majesty.[44]

It has been observed by recent historians that the reign of Aleksey Mikhailovich saw a wholesale 'byzantinisation' of Russia, which manifested itself not only in the cultural sphere but also in foreign policy.[45] The 'sacralisation' of the Russian monarchy, implying increasing stress on divine right to the point of identifying tsar and God, has also been lately analysed by two Russian specialists in the field of semiotics, V.M. Zhivov and B.A. Uspensky. The trend developed in the context of the idea of 'Moscow the Third Rome', which became a political concept as well as a religious one, bringing with it the rejection of cultural isolation and a renewal of the Byzantine cultural heritage. Both Alexis and his son Fyodor consciously adopted the political symbols of the Byzantine basileus. The former sent to Byzantium for an orb and a diadem on the Byzantine model, and commissioned a throne ornamented with the Latin inscription 'Potentissimus et invictissimus Moscovitiarum Imperatori Alexio', while at his coronation Tsar Fyodor communed at the altar like a basileus.[46]

The Holy Roman Emperor showed a revived interest in Russia in the middle of the seventeenth century as a result of the imperial need to set up a coalition against the Porte, and because of the problem of the Russian candidature to the Polish throne in the 1650s. An imperial embassy was sent in 1660–61, led by Augustin Freiherr von Mayerberg, to improve relations between the two powers. The negotiations were held up when the imperial envoys observed that Leopold I was not addressed by the Russians as 'kaiserliche Majestät' but as 'kaiserliche Grossmächtigkeit' (*vel'mozhnost'*). When reproached, the Russians replied that as long as the tsar was not addressed as 'Majesty' (*velichestvo*) they could not use any other form to the emperor but 'Grossmächtigkeit'. In order

43. W. Leitsch, *Moskau und die Politik des Kaiserhofes im XVII Jahrhundert*, I: *1604–1654*, Wiener Archiv für Geschichte des Slaventums und Osteuropas, vol. IV (Graz and Cologne, 1960), pp. 158 and 192. In 1615 the Venetian resident in Vienna reported that: 'L'ambasciatore di Moscovia non fu nell' audienza trattato da cesare con quelli termini che e solito farse con loro perchè non tiene il presente gran duca per legitimo principe et per non disgustar il re di Polonia col mostrar tenerlo per tale' (p. 203).
44. *Ibid.*, pp. 237ff. See also *PDS*, vol. VII, pp. 57ff, Feb. 1687.
45. See P. Longworth, *Alexis Tsar of all the Russias* (London, 1984), *passim* and pp. 214 and 230.
46. 'Tsar' i Bog: semioticheskiye aspekty sakralizatsii monarkha v Rossii', in their *Yazyki kul'tury i problemy perevedimosti* (Moscow, 1987), pp. 47–154. (I am grateful to Maria Karine Schaub for having drawn my attention to this work and provided me with a copy.) See also J. Billington, *The Icon and the Axe* (New York, 1966), p. 148.

to keep negotiations ticking over, efforts were made to find a compromise title such as 'Potentissimus'. Mayerberg eventually agreed to the use of Majestät to the tsar, subject to approval by the emperor. But Leopold refused outright after 1661 to call the tsar 'Majesty' in official documents.[47]

While there remained a possibility in the mid-seventeenth century that the Russian tsar might be elected to the throne of Poland, the papacy could still entertain hopes of a union of churches, and therefore prove more flexible regarding the Russian title. But the Peace of Andrusovo in 1667 between Poland and Russia put paid to these hopes. A further attempt at a rapprochement between Russia, the papacy and the empire took place in the 1670s, this time as part of a widespread Russian diplomatic initiative in the hope of achieving a coalition against the advancing Ottoman Empire. The Russian envoy to Rome was the Catholic Scot, Paul Menzies, who arrived in 1672, with strict instructions not to accept any document which did not include the title 'tsar'. Menzies's mission has been studied in great detail, as well as the endless memoranda by various papal officials, discussing 'ce que voulait bien dire ce mot étrange de Tsar, d'allure prétentieuse et de dérivation inexplicable'.[48] A papal councillor, Abbate Scarlatti, in a long memorandum, wrote that some people argued that 'questa parola [tsar] significa imperatore et è barbara ne puolo usarsi da Papi nelle lettere latine'. But, he countered, popes do use barbarous titles in Latin, such as 'Landgravio, Burgravio . . . Contestabile'. The princes of Muscovy were entitled to be called 'king'; but the Emperor Maximilian had had no right to have used the title of kayser (to Vasily III), since though he could make kings, only the pope could make another emperor.[49] Menzies's mission ended in failure, both with regard to forming a coalition against the Turks, and with regard to the tsar's title, in spite of Tsar Aleksey Mikhailovich's assurances to the pope that Russia had been ruled over for generations by descendants of Caesar Augustus, the ruler of the universe, and of his relative Ryurik. Not until 1685 did the papacy condescend to use 'tsar' in addressing the rulers of Russia.[50]

The Russian diplomatic initiative of the 1670s misfired, and a few years later Vienna in turn took up the defence of south-east Europe against the advancing Turks. The Holy League between Poland, the emperor and the papacy, later joined by Venice, was established in 1683. The attempt to win Russia to join in the anti-Turkish crusade was held up by the need to consolidate the temporary Peace of Andrusovo of 1667 between Poland and Russia, and this was finally achieved, on terms very unfavourable to Poland, in the 'perpetual peace' of 1686. Meanwhile the emperor sent an envoy, a Jesuit priest, Father Carlo Maurizio Vota, to Moscow in 1684, with orders to attempt

47. Klaus Meyer, '"Kayserliche Grossmächtigkeit". Titularfrage bei den Verhandlungen zwischen Kaiser und Zar, 1661/2', *Zeitschrift für Ostforschung, Länder und Völker im Ostlichen Mitteleuropa*, 12 (1983), pp. 1–12.

48. Pierling, *La Russie*, vol. IV, p. 64.

49. N.V. Charykov, *Posol'stvo v Rim i sluzhba v Moskve Pavla Meneziia, 1637–1694* (St Petersburg, 1906), pp. 204 and 206–8.

50. *Ibid.*, p. 48; Szeftel, 'Title of the Muscovite Monarch', p. 72.

to secure freedom of worship for Catholics in Russia.[51] In discussions with Prince V.V. Golitsyn, the favourite of the Regent Sophia, it was suggested that if the emperor made concessions on etiquette, Russia would show greater flexibility on religion. But the emperor continued to refuse equality of treatment, and addressed letters to the two young tsars, Ivan and Peter, 'ad serenitates vestras', not 'your Majesties', though he did use the title tsar.[52] The question surfaced again during the embassy of Boris Sheremet'yev to Vienna in 1687. Sheremet'yev was instructed not to use 'Majesty' to the emperor if the latter called the Russian tsars merely serene highnesses (*presvetleyshiye*). This time Leopold argued that the decision did not depend on him but on the electors of the Holy Roman Empire.[53]

Throughout the seventeenth century the kings of France also used different forms of address to the rulers of Russia, and this uncertainty gave rise in the eighteenth century, when Peter the Great's new title was being considered, to the drafting of long memoranda in the office of the French secretaries of state. According to one French eighteenth-century expert on earlier Franco-Russian relations, Vasily III took the title of tsar because it ranked higher than grand duke, and subsequently Ivan IV added the titles of tsar of Kazan' and Astrakhan'.

> Les savants des autres Etats de l'Europe recherchèrent quelle pouvait être la signification de ce titre. Quelques uns estimèrent qu'il dérivoit du mot hebreux zarah que l'on trouve dans le premier livre de Moyse chapitre 37 verset 25, et dans le 51e chapitre de Jérémie verset 8 et qui signifie en allemand *consacré avec onction* et ils jugèrent que le Grand Duc Basile vouloit s'honorer de ce titre parce qu'il etoit couronné et sacré comme les autres têtes couronnées.[54]

In the reign of Louis XIII there are several examples of letters dating from the 1630s calling Tsar Mikhail Fyodorovich 'Empereur des Russies', and as

51. A. Tamborra, 'La teoria politico-religiosa di "Mosca Terza Roma" nei secoli XVII–XIX: sopravivenza e linee di svolgimento', in *Da Roma alla Terza Roma*, pp. 517–39, at p. 521; some of the memoranda prepared in the Vatican have been published in *Historiae Russiae Monumenta*, ed. A.I. Turgenev, vol. II, including *Ritratto della Moscovia* by C.M. Vota, prepared on Venetian sources before he actually went there.
52. *PDS*, vol. VI, p. 1684; see also F. Tumansky, *Sobraniye raznykh zapisok i sochineniiy sluzhashchikh k dostavleniyu polnogo svedeniya o zhizni i deyaniyakh gospodina imperatora Petra Velikogo*, 10 vols. (St Petersburg, 1787), vol. IV, p. 142.
53. E. Lukinich, 'Der Kaisertitel Peters des Grossen und der Wiener Hof', *Jahrbuch für Kultur und Geschichte der Slaven*, 5 (1929), pp. 369ff. See also *PDS*, vol. VII, pp. 57ff, Feb. 1687 and Archives du Ministère des Affaires Etrangères, Paris (hereafter AAE), Correspondance Politique, Russie, vol. 2, 1686–1704, 'Relation de tout ce qui s'est passé dans l'ambassade des Moscovites faite à Vienne auprès de l'Empereur au commencement de l'année 1687'. Matters became even more complicated when the Russian ambassador, Boris Sheremet'yev, objected to the tsars Ivan and Peter being addressed as majesties in the plural instead of in the singular: 'allégeant qu'il en étoit d'Eux comme de la très Sainte Trinité que quand ils seraient trois Czars ils ne feraient qu'une Majesté'.
54. AAE, Mémoires et Documents (hereafter MD) Russie, vol. 3, fos. 253–74, 'Dissertation sur les titres donnés au Czar de la Grande Russie dans les traités et autres actes', by N. Le Dran, dated 1728. Olearius seems to have been the originator of this particular etymology. See *The Travels of Olearius in Seventeenth-Century Russia*, trans. and ed. S.H. Baron (Stanford, Calif., 1967), p. 174.

late as 1654, Louis XIV wrote to Tsar Aleksey as 'Empereur de Russie et de Moscovie'.[55] However, in the course of the seventeenth century Louis XIV decided that tsar was not the same as emperor.[56] Moreover, though in the opinion of the papal court tsar ranked below the title of king, Russia now seemed to be claiming parity with the Holy Roman Emperor:

> il paroit que ceux qui ont depuis regné en Moscovie ont prétendu que l'expression de Czar signifiat plus que Roy; qu'elle doit être regardée comme equivalente à celle de *Caesar* ou *Empereur* et qu'ils devoient être traité à l'égal de l'Empereur des Romains. Ils ont même pris pour leur armes un aigle jaune à deux testes qui est l'enseigne propre à l'Empire Romain.[57]

Quite apart from the Russian insistence on the use of tsar at least, there arose also the thorny question of the use of the appellation 'Majesty'. Louis XIV, far more punctilious than his predecessor, refused to use to P. Potemkin, Russian envoy to France in 1668, the formula 'Majesté czarée', and indeed 'on observa à son égard le cérémonial établi pour les *ambassad^{rs} des Princes Orientaux* . . .'.[58] In order to cut short all pretensions, the French now insisted on calling the tsar 'Sa Majesté le Czar', and not 'Sa Majesté Czarée', as the Russians wished, since the latter formula might more easily evolve into 'Sa Majesté Impériale'.[59] Towards the end of the 1680s, particularly after the revocation of the Edict of Nantes, relations between France and Russia cooled off and the subject was dropped.[60] Louis XIV's reluctance to allow the title of tsar to the ruler of Russia may well have been influenced by his own attitude at the time to the imperial claims to precedence, which were again under attack from many sides from the mid-seventeenth century onwards. The concept of the medieval empire was giving way to the idea of a territorial unit, and Louis XIV's internal and external propaganda was directed at asserting the pre-eminence of the sovereign kingdom of France over the elective empire of Germany. (He allowed himself, for instance, to be portrayed on inscriptions as 'imperator francorum'.[61])

A word should be added here about the attitude of England. Most of the Protestant powers in the seventeenth century, which felt no allegiance to the Holy Roman Empire, found no difficulty in addressing the ruler of Muscovy

55. AAE, MD Russie, vol. 3, fos. 253–74.
56. *Ibid.*, fos. 107ff, mémoire par Mr Le Dran, 2 April 1718 (N.S.), 'Observations sur le cérémonial des lettres écrites aux Roys de France par les Czars de la Grande Russie'.
57. AAE, MD Russie, vol. 3, by N. Le Dran, 1728.
58. AAE, MD Russie, vol. 3, 'Sur le Cérémonial observé en France à l'égard des ministres envoyez par les Czars de la Grande Russie', by N. Le Dran, Sept. 1716 (N.S.).
59. AAE, MD Russie, vol. 3, fos. 107ff, Mémoire par Mr Le Dran, 2 April 1718 (N.S.).
60. F. Groenebaum, *Frankreich in Ost und Nordeuropa. Die französisch-russische Beziehungen von 1648–1689* (Wiesbaden, 1986), p. 207, Lettre de Louis XIV aux tsars de Moscovie, Versailles, 20 Dec. 1685 (N.S.). See also Tumansky, *Sobraniye raznykh zapisok, passim*, for texts of various official letters. Tumansky is only really reliable when he gives a text in the original language. His translations into Russian tend to ignore the subtleties of diplomatic speech.
61. See Duchhardt, 'Imperium', p. 578; see also P. Burke, *The Fabrication of Louis XIV* (New Haven and London, 1992), pp. 179–80.

as 'emperor'. However, in the case of England it is quite clear that the emperor of Muscovy was regarded as on a par with Prester John and the emperor of China. Travel writers such as Giles Fletcher in the sixteenth century or Samuel Collins in the seventeenth use emperor as a matter of course.[62] In an address book prepared for Charles II it is stated that the 'Emp^r of Russia's titles' were 'Magnus dominus, Imperator et Magnus Dux'.[63]

III

Peter I shook off the tutelage of his sister Sophia in 1689 but not until 1694 can he be said to have picked up the reins of government. In the present state of our knowledge it is difficult to tell what ideas he harboured at that time about the status of Russia in Europe. In 1697 he embarked on the great embassy to foreign parts, led by his crony Admiral Lefort, in which he himself appeared only in the rank of a bombardier. Here, however, since the tsar travelled incognito, matters of etiquette could mainly be forgotten.

Peter's attitude to the title of tsar, to titles in general and to the title of emperor in particular, is at this time reflected in his not entirely playful adoption of the appellation 'Knyaz' Kesar' or 'Min Her Kenih' for Prince F. Yu. Romodanovsky, the head of the Preobrazhensky Prikaz, and of the government, during Peter's absence abroad. In his letters to Romodanovsky, the latter is frequently addressed as 'Your Majesty'. After the death of Romodanovsky in 1708, his son Ivan Fyodorovich was also appointed head of the Preobrazhensky Prikaz and was addressed by Peter as 'Your Majesty'. Similarly, the head of his band of revellers, the Synod of Drunken Fools, was entitled the Knyaz' Papa or Prince Pope, and Peter until his death scrupulously appointed a prince pope whenever a vacancy occurred.[64] But though he was evidently not a believer in the personal importance of titles, as ruler of Russia, Peter was fully aware of the need to establish his country more securely in the European states system.

From the Russian point of view, it was essential to secure recognition of the equality of tsar and emperor from the Holy Roman Emperor whose example would be followed almost automatically by the other European rulers. But it was also possible for Russian foreign policy to manoeuvre between the emperor, the papacy (alone entitled to create Christian emperors as distinct from kings which the emperor could create) and the king of France, and to bring pressure to bear on the first by, for instance, supporting the rising of Ferenz

62. See Fletcher, *Of the Russe Commonwealth*, and S. Collins, *The Present State of Russia* (London, 1671), *passim*.
63. MS Gunther, Museum of the History of Science, 60, Oxford, MS address book of Charles II, 1660–80. I am grateful to Dr W.F. Ryan for communicating this document to me. However, Duchhardt, 'Imperium', pp. 569ff, stresses that Charles II, when acting as mediator at the negotiations of the Peace of Nijmegen, together with Louis XIV used the opportunity to dispute the emperor's claims to precedence.
64. N.V. Voznesensky, *Zakonodatel'nyye akty Petra*, ANSSR (Moscow and Leningrad, 1945), Nos 230, 232, pp. 181–2.

Rákoczi in Leopold's rear, in Hungary. The pope meanwhile had rejected both Majesty and tsar, though when Prince Boris Kurakin was sent to Rome in 1707 to persuade the pope not to recognise Stanislas Leszczynski as king of Poland after the peace of Altranstadt, the pope did agree to the use of 'potentissimus czar' but not 'maesta'. Kurakin refused to accept the brief.[65]

The great victory of Poltava and the new status it gave to Russia persuaded Peter to take up again the question of recognition of the rank of Majesty and the title of emperor with the court of Vienna. Peter pointed out that even the Porte addressed the tsar as 'Majesty'.[66] Vienna replied that in no circumstances would it accept the use of Majesty, and the imperial ambassador to St Petersburg warned his court that this might lead to cutting all communications between the two courts.

The British envoy to Russia, Charles Whitworth, also sensed changes in the air. In the seventeenth century England had not hesitated to use the title 'emperor' to the tsars, because Russia was considered on a par with the empires of the East which did not form part of the Christian commonwealth of nations. But precisely when Russia was endeavouring to enter the magic circle of the European states, England, under William III and later Queen Anne, attempted to evade using the title of emperor. The reasoning is obvious: Russia was an empire as long as it was beyond the pale; but once it had to be considered within the European system of precedence, then the title and its implications could no longer be accepted. Aware of Peter's plans, Whitworth wrote to Secretary of State Boyle on 20/31 October 1709, asking for fresh instructions on the ceremonial to be observed at his audience with Peter, since his earlier ones were 'suited to the constitutions and temper of all eastern nations, but would be very disadvantagious [*sic*] to Her Majesty in the present juncture'. Peter had 'altered the ancient maxims of his government to the methods of other European courts', and as Whitworth was the first ambassador to be received under this new system, he was afraid of setting an unauthorised precedent.[67] While Whitworth did use 'Imperial Majesty' when speaking of and to the tsar, he always avoided addressing him as 'emperor'.

Whether on his own initiative or on that of the tsar, the next Russian envoy to Vienna, Baron Urbich, reopened the question in somewhat dramatic form in 1711. According to Whitworth, Urbich had turned up in Moscow after the battle of Poltava, 'and finding that court apt for any impressions or vain projects on their vast success, he preached to them their right to the Eastern empire of the Greeks and the happy opportunity of reviving that title'. But

65. A. Tamborra, 'Russia e la Santa Sede all'epoca di Pietro il Grande', *Archivio Storico Italiano*, 119 (1961), pp. 200–40, at pp. 216–19. Not until 1717 did the pope agree to use 'Majesty'.
66. Lukinich, 'Der Kaisertitel', p. 1. Report of the imperial ambassador, Count Wilczek, 28 June 1710. On Sultan Suleiman's recognition of the imperial title and 'majesty' as early as the reign of Vasily III, see Ruffman, 'England'.
67. *Sbornik imperatorskogo Russkogo istoricheskogo obshchestva*, 148 vols. (St Petersburg, 1867–1916) (henceforth *SIRIO*), vol. 50, pp. 261–2. Whitworth did not get very much guidance. Boyle replied that 'HM does not fear that the use of ancient ceremonial can be prejudicial to her' provided all ambassadors received the same treatment: *ibid.*, p. 286, 13 Dec. 1709.

when Urbich raised the question in Vienna, he received the usual rebuff from the emperor, then Joseph I. But the emperor died soon after, in April 1711, and Peter determined to press his claim again. When the dowager empress, acting as regent in the absence of the future Charles VI, sent him a letter notifying him of the death of the emperor, she used the title 'Serenity' instead of 'Majesty'. 'The Czar . . . to revenge himself' retorted in kind, addressing the empress merely as 'Serenity', since he was outraged that during an interregnum, when there was no emperor, a mere regent should insult him, and he would not take from a regent what he had submitted to from a reigning emperor.[68]

The Viennese court in turn reacted angrily. It refused to accept Peter's letter from Urbich and it was eventually returned to his house on the following day, on the grounds that the Russian chancery could not have deliberately intended to offend the empress and must have made a mistake. Urbich was a choleric man, and he and his brother both attempted to force the letter back on to the imperial messenger, in what became an unseemly brawl. But at the time it was Peter who allowed the matter to drop, in view of the impending war between Russia and the Porte in 1711, which required him to mend all his diplomatic fences. Indeed for a while he seemed on the surface to have abandoned his efforts to force recognition from the major European powers, and at a meeting in Yaroslavl' with Augustus of Saxony-Poland, he even remarked jokingly that he would rather be an admiral in the fleet of one of the great powers than '"Kaiser" in Asiatic countries'.[69]

Nevertheless, the tsar had several opportunities to lay the groundwork for recognition of his imperial title at this time. In the negotiations with the German Estates of Livonia and Estonia, at the time of their annexation after Russia's victorious campaign in 1710, he secured their acceptance both of the appellation 'Majesty' and of the title of Kaiser or emperor.[70]

Meanwhile, with the accession of George I, who was also elector of Hanover, England was proving much more stiff-necked about using even 'imperial

68. Public Record Office (hereafter PRO), SP 91/6, fols. 144ff. Whitworth to St John, 1–12 Oct. 1711, from Carlsbad, where Whitworth was attending on Peter who was taking the waters. See also Lukinich, 'Der Kaisertitel', p. 373. The note was addressed to 'Serenissimo et potentissimo Domino Tzaro et magno duci Petro Alexievicio'. However Reinhold Wittram suggests that Whitworth himself may have been responsible, for Baron Shafirov, the vice-president of the College of Foreign Affairs, drew the attention of other foreign envoys to the fact that Whitworth in February 1710 had used the formula 'Imperial Majesty' (see Wittram, *Peter I.*, vol. II, pp. 250ff). For the implications of Whitworth's formulation see Ruffmann, 'England', p. 219 n. 9.
69. Wittram, *Peter I.*, vol. I, pp. 252–3.
70. *Ibid.*, vol. II, pp. 354ff, lists a number of occasions on which Peter was called 'Czaar und Imperator von aller Reussen' in Livonia and Estonia, and also in the marriage contract of his niece Anna Ivanovna with the duke of Curland (ch. 7, n. 5). See also S.M. Solov'yev, *Istoriya*, vol. IX, p. 92. It was in 1713 that Peter ordered his envoys abroad to insist on the use of 'Russia' and not 'Muscovy' in communications addressed to them. A.D. Menshikov to Prince V.D. Dolgoruky in Copenhagen, *Ibid.*, p. 333, 1713. For the use of the imperial crown on banners from 1710, and the constant reference to the Emperor Constantine the Great, see G.B. Vilinbakhov, 'Otrazheniye idey absolyutizma v russkoy gosudarstvennoy geral'dike petrovskogo vremeni', *Study Group on Eighteenth-Century Russia Newsletter*, 15 (1987), pp. 31–40.

Majesty', particularly in the latter part of the Great Northern War when Britain and Russia were at loggerheads. In 1717, in the course of negotiations at The Hague between Whitworth and Chancellor Golovkin and Vice-Chancellor Shafirov, the Russians attempted to force acceptance of the title of emperor, because it could be found in an 'old English gilt credential'. This was rejected by Whitworth on the grounds that both appellation and gold were out of date, and to be found only in letters 'sent to Turkey, Marocco, China and other nations shut out of the pale of Christianity and the common course of correspondence, and that if they would be treated as the other Princes of Europe they must be contented with the style used to the king of France'. The two Russians, however, insisted on 'having the word "emperor" . . . used in any fashion whatsoever'.[71] In that same year, 1717, a semi-official account of the reasons why Peter had declared war on Sweden, drafted by Shafirov and revised in detail by Peter himself, was published anonymously in St Petersburg. In the German text his title appears as 'Petrus der erste, Czaar und Kayzer aller Reussen'.[72]

But the campaign really began seriously in 1718, when on 10 May a Russian translation and the alleged German original of the letter from Maximilian I to the Grand Duke Vasily III, written in 1514, was published in St Petersburg.[73] It may well have been a sudden decision, for though the existence of such a letter was known the actual text had been dug up by Shafirov's brother in the archives in Moscow. Consisting of five printed pages, the leaflet was shown, before it was published, to the foreign envoys of the empire and Hanover, and a copy was handed to the imperial envoy with a note to the effect that the text was not only interesting because of its ancient date but also because it demonstrated imperial acceptance of the Russian title of Caesar of all Russia as far back as 1514, a point which the tsar himself underlined, declaring that the latter gave him 'gutes recht' to the title. At the time, however, Peter did not insist on taking immediate steps to enforce his claim, which might alienate the court of Vienna to which his son Aleksey had just fled in February 1718.

Vienna, however, took immediate steps to dispute the authenticity of the document. No German original could be traced in the imperial archives, and the expert bibliographers of the early eighteenth century all concurred that the letter was an undoubted forgery, the product of the pen of a semi-literate Russian chancery clerk or of some German lost in the wilds of Siberia. Even Peter recognised that he had never come across such dreadful style or language.

71. Ruffman, 'England', p. 223; *SIRIO*, 66, pp. 398–9.

72. The German title was 'Raisonnement, was für rechtmässige Uhrsachen Se. Czarische Majestät Petrus der Erste, Czaar und Käyser [*sic*] aller Reussen gehabt . . .'. See also Wittram, *Peter I.*, vol. II, p. 469. The rumour that Peter intended 'als ein von Europa declarirter Kayser zu sterben' was current in Hanover in the summer of 1718.

73. A.V. Florovsky, 'Stranitsa istorii russko-avstriyskikh diplomaticheskikh otnosheniy XVIII veka', in V. Pashuto (ed.), *Feodal'naya Rossiya vo vsemirnom istoricheskom protsesse* (Moscow, 1972), pp. 389–97, at pp. 390–1. In the nineteenth century documents were discovered in the imperial archives which confirmed the authenticity of the text. See also *SIRIO*, 34, p. 338. Report from French consul La Vie of 9 May 1718.

Vienna continued for some years to reject Maximilian's letter as genuine and a war of pamphlets broke out.[74]

Peter's plans are further confirmed by the patent in Latin, dated 18 February 1721, conferring the title of count on James Bruce, one of the Russian plenipotentiaries at the peace negotiations on Åland Island with the Swedes, which was signed by Peter 'propria manu sua imperatoriae Majestatis'.[75] After the Peace of Nystadt Peter felt confident enough to proclaim his new title as a unilateral act of sovereignty, without waiting to negotiate its recognition by other powers. As we know, he chose the occasion of the thanksgiving for peace at the end of the long Northern War. He considered Russia now to be powerful enough for her alliance to be sought, an alliance which need only be granted if his conditions were met. But, as if underlining the need to place Russia firmly in the order of precedence of European states, and since the Russian 'tsar' was not accepted as equivalent to emperor, he adopted the Latin form of the imperial title, namely imperator, for use in Russia and in Russian, and abroad, not the Greek basileus.

Needless to say, such a breach with existing practice was met with hostility by the other powers. The court of Vienna regarded such a unilateral assumption of a title as unheard of. It was a question to be referred to all the powers of Europe, or at least to all the electors of the Holy Roman Empire. The Holy Roman Emperor of course viewed the assumption of an imperial title from a totally different point of view from that of the other crowned heads of Europe. He still clung to the medieval tradition of the Christian commonwealth, at a time when the theory of the equality of sovereign states in international law was gaining ground. In his view there could be only one Christian emperor. He feared the multiplication of such claims, in which case the one body of Christendom, of which he was the sole head, would have two or more heads, and he would lose his supremacy.

IV

The question now arises: what precisely did Peter I have in mind when he unilaterally proclaimed himself emperor of all the Russias? To begin with it is important to clear our minds of the present-day definition of an empire. An empire in modern usage is a territorially extensive polity in which one state rules over a number of other states or subordinate settlements. This was not enough to make an empire in Christian Europe. The ruler of far the largest realm known to modern European history, Philip II of Spain, had to content himself with the title of king of his various realms, and in 1721, Philip V still ruled over lands almost as extensive as those of Russia. Thus, when Peter I engineered the ceremony by which he was offered the title of emperor, he

74. Florovsky, 'Stranitsa'. See also Laura Ronchi de Michelis, 'L'Europa di fronte ad un nuovo imperatore', in *Da Roma a Terza Roma*, pp. 511–16 for other examples.
75. E.A. Saveleva, *Biblioteka Ya. V. Bryusa. Katalog* (Leningrad, 1989), p. 12, No. 13.

was not thinking simply that the size of his domains justified a change of title. Nowhere in the submissions made to him by his humble servants to adopt the title of emperor is the *size* of the Russian lands mentioned, only the completeness of his victory over Sweden.[76]

The change clearly formed part of the prestige policy associated with Peter's westernisation of Russia, and of his effort to enter the magic circle of European states at a high level. Russia was no longer the grand duchy of Muscovy, and the title 'tsar' was meaningless in the context of the Latin West, having no place in the table of precedence of European rulers. But, until Peter's revolutionary gesture, there had been only one western Christian empire and there was no precedent, in what was still regarded as a universal Christian community of nations, for claiming an imperial title, or setting up an empire in rivalry to the existing one. Even if a new concept of 'empire' was beginning to develop, as the supreme expression of a 'national' monarchy, no ruler had as yet claimed the title.[77]

Thus, if Peter was to lay claim to the title of emperor, it was bound to be by resurrecting the empire of the East. This is what he did. The claim to imperial rank dates back at least to the fifteenth century, according to Ihor Shevchenko, 'characterized by the first deliberate Russian (not exclusively Muscovite) attempts to transform Russian princes into the counterparts of the Byzantine emperors, and later to claim the Byzantine heritage for themselves and their lands', when the grand duke of Vladimir and Moscow also added to his title 'ruler of all-Russia', that is, when he asserted his authority over most of the other Russian princes or cities.[78] It was expressed in the word tsar, the early Russian name for the basileus, because at that time Russia tended to underline her separation from the West more than to promote westernisation by the use of foreign titles. There was no need for a tsar to call himself an imperator. Nor was his claim to the title of tsar based on rule over the successor states of the Golden Horde, since they had not as yet been conquered.

Unlike later Russian philologists, or the eighteenth-century specialists of the French chancery of foreign affairs, the Russian tsars never lost sight of the etymology of the word, and knew quite well that it derived from tsesar, the Russian pronunciation of caesar. It was rather in the West that with few exceptions the makers of foreign policy lost sight of the original rank of the rulers of Russia, *reges*, and once having downgraded them to grand dukes refused to except them as equals again, even as kings. Had they not forgotten what was

76. Voznesensky, *Zakonodatel'nyye akty*, No. 212, pp. 155–6.
77. G. Stökl, 'Imperium und Imperiale Ideologie: Erfahrungen am Beispiel des vorpetrinischen Russland', in his *Der Russische Staat im Mittelalter und früher Neuzeit* (Wiesbaden, 1981), pp. 170–1, seems to me to pay insufficient attention to the religious element in Russian thought in his search for an 'ideology' of empire. More to the point is Duchhardt's perception that a new concept of empire was coming into being with the collapse of the old Christian vision, and that at this time it took the form of a 'national monarchy': 'Imperium und regna', pp. 578ff. It is worth noting that only emperors who believed that their rights were inherited from Rome or Constantinople called themselves 'Caesar'.
78. Shevchenko, 'Neglected source', pp. 141–79.

once so well known, the connection between tsar, caesar and basileus would not have been so difficult to establish.

It is clear from the history of the Russian claims to imperial status that they descend from the theocratic Byzantine world. The Russians knew perfectly well that an empire had to be associated with a religion, and the theory of the *translatio imperii* underlay their policy throughout the fifteenth, sixteenth and seventeenth centuries. From the moment of the fall of Constantinople in 1453, long before the epistles of Filofey and the theory of Moscow the Third Rome, the idea that the ruler of Russia would become the successor not specifically of the Byzantine Empire, as a territorial entity, since Russia did not rule over any ex-Byzantine lands, but of the Orthodox Christian Empire, which had existed until then as a counterpoise to the Holy Roman Empire of the Latin Catholics, forms the counterpoint to the relations of Russia with western powers. The epistle of Filofey to Grand Duke Vasily III sums up the situation: 'all the empires of the Orthodox Christian faith have gathered into your single empire . . . you are the only tsar for Christians in the whole world . . .'.[79]

This trend became even clearer in the seventeenth century as Russia began to flex her muscles in military conflict with the West, and pushed her advance into the old lands of Kievan Russia. The pressure for recognition as the Orthodox emperor increased, particularly in the reign of Aleksey Mikhailovich. Within Russia Tsar Aleksey took on more and more of the ritual functions of Byzantine emperors, and finally reduced the Russian patriarchate to its proper role as junior partner of the secular power rather than its superior. Byzantine symbols of power appeared in imperial portraits, the orb or golden apple, the sceptre and diadem. The language of panegyrics and odes stressed the divine nature of rulers as 'icons' or images of God, or as 'anointed' Christs.[80]

In the Russian intellectual climate of the age – where colonial empires had never been heard of – the only possibility was to establish Peter's new title on the basis of the old empire of the East. Both in the draft and in the final submission to him, his servants stated that they were 'following the example of the ancients [*s prikladu drevnikh*] and particularly of the Roman and Greek peoples' in proposing that he should accept the titles offered.[81]

But Peter had a secular turn of mind, and lived in a period and among statesmen and administrators who were also influenced by the secular spirit of the age. He easily played down the religious element in the creation of the Russian Empire. He had no opinion of the Byzantine Empire, and but little of

79. M. Cherniavsky, *Tsar and People* (New York, 1969 edn), p. 38.

80. Zhivov and Uspensky, 'Tsar' i Bog', pp. 79ff.

81. Russian State Archive of Ancient Documents of the USSR (hereafter RGADA), fo. 2, d. II, 1.6, 6 ob., another probably earlier draft, of the submission to Peter (no date) makes the connection evident. When begging Peter to accept the titles of Pater Patriae, Peter the Great, and All Russian Emperor, it continues 'a title which your imperial Majesty's praiseworthy antecessor [*antetsesorom*] was already given some centuries ago by the glorious Roman Emperor Maximilian . . .' (I am grateful to Dr O.A. Omel'chenko for procuring this and other documents from the Central State Archives in Moscow.)

the Orthodox religion.[82] But one should not be misled by his remark to Augustus of Saxony Poland quoted above (p. 32). When Peter said he would rather be an admiral of the fleet of one of the great powers than 'kaiser' in an Asiatic country, he was not referring to the Byzantine Empire but to two of his other 'empires', namely the *tsarstvo* of Kazan' and the *tsarstvo* of Astrakhan'. But he was very well aware of the political importance of Russia's position as the only independent Orthodox realm and a powerful one at that. Following on the policy of his father, of championing the rights of the Orthodox, he had issued appeals to the Orthodox Christian peoples under Turkish rule to rise against their oppressor on the outbreak of the war with the Porte in 1711. He had no intention of recreating the political features of the non-existent Byzantine polity, preferring to establish his own form of political absolutism. But he did not underestimate the magnetic influence which an Orthodox empire could exercise on the Orthodox populations within the Ottoman Empire and within the Habsburg lands.

The Byzantine model is present again in the coronation of Peter's wife Catherine in 1724 as empress of Russia. Before the ceremony Peter issued a manifesto stressing that 'it is known to everyone that in all Christian realms it is the unfailing custom for potentates to crown their wives, and not only now but of old this was frequently the custom of the Orthodox Greek emperors [*imperatory*, not *basileis*]', and therefore, in view of Catherine's great services to the nation, and her devotion to him, he proposed that her coronation should take place the following year.[83]

But if Peter was indeed asserting the right of the ruler of Russia to be regarded as the heir of the Orthodox empire of Byzantium, he dressed up his claim in western clothes, and gave it a classical Roman ancestry. The title he chose was Roman and in Latin. In a ceremony modelled on the Roman one, the title was offered to him by his Senate, which was in fact modelled on a Swedish rather than a classical institution. For the occasion the Russian Senate took on the attributions of the Roman Senate. Moreover it drew attention to the model by referring to the practice of the 'Roman Senate of offering such

82. In the notes for the speech written by Peter and delivered on 22 October 1721 he says: 'We must thank God with all our hearts, but hoping for peace, we must not weaken in the art of war, so that it should not happen to us as to the Greeks, as to the Greek monarchy'. (Voznesensky, *Zakonodatel'nyye akty*, No. 213, for Peter's draft, and No. 214 for the full account, pp. 156–61.)
83. *Ibid.*, p. 179, No. 229, 15 Nov. 1723, in Peter's handwriting. In the fair copy, after the words 'Greek emperors', the manifesto continues: 'and notably the Emperor [*imperator*] Vasilisk crowned his wife Zenobia, Emperor Justinian crowned his wife Liupitsiya, Emperor Heraclius crowned his wife Martina, Emperor Leo the Wise crowned his wife Maria with the imperial crown, and others did it too, about which it is not considered necessary to say more'. There is much controversy over whether Peter intended this coronation to legitimise Catherine as his heir (he had no living sons) on the Byzantine principle that empresses could act as regents or appoint emperors. See K.G. Holum, *Theodosian Empresses, Women and Imperial Dominion in Late Antiquity* (Los Angeles and London, 1982) on the powers of early Byzantine empresses. The example of the role of Irina, the widow of Tsar Fyodor Ivanovich, to whom he left his throne, may be relevant here. Dr Lindsey Hughes confirms that none of the wives of tsars, whether Ryurikides or Romanovs, was ever crowned, but the Polish Marina, the wife of the False Dmitri, was crowned.

titles publicly to their emperors in sign of gratitude for their great deeds, and inscribing such titles as Pater Patriae, emperor and Great on statues . . .'.[84] Even more strikingly Roman (but of course also Byzantine) is the conferring of the titles by acclamation. After Chancellor Golovkin's speech, the Senate proclaimed three times 'Long live Peter the Great, Pater Patriae, emperor of all Russia', a cry taken up by all the people present and followed by salvoes from guns, blasts on trumpets and the rolling of drums and kettledrums.

As Zhivov and Uspensky have pointed out, byzantinisation cohabited easily with westernisation, indeed it increased throughout the eighteenth century in the context of the sacralisation of the ruler, which of course was of Byzantine imperial origin. Peter himself and his heirs as anointed emperors were on the one hand identified with Christ, a practice which continued though it became somewhat awkward in the case of the empresses (even Catherine II was hailed as 'Christ' in an ecclesiastical ode of 1786).[85] On the other hand, the westernising Roman trend is reflected in the influence of classical Latin literature on panegyric poetry, visual and verbal propaganda, and the identification particularly of the empresses with Astraea or Minerva.[86] In the coronation of the first Russian ruler to be *crowned* imperator, namely Peter II (1727–30), the hereditary descent from Augustus was again emphasised.[87]

As regards the common people of Russia, the change from tsar to emperor was accepted with difficulty. For the peasants, and particularly the Old Believers, held that the title 'emperor' was bestowed by the pope and hence satanic in origin, and that the symbol of the two-headed eagle was the mark of the devil, because only the devil has two heads. Moreover, 'imperator' added up in old Russian numerals to 666, the number of the great beast of the Apocalypse.[88]

The ordinary, westernised, Russian noble came to believe firmly that the title 'emperor' was superior to that of 'tsar'. Very revealing is the dialogue between Peter the Great and Alexander the Great in the other world, written by a historian and great admirer of Peter I, P. Krekshin, in the middle of the eighteenth century. Invited to enter Peter's room, Alexander greeted him as Tsar Peter Alekseyevich; the emperor rose from his chair, said 'greetings Tsar Alexander' and sat down without offering any courtesy to Alexander. Outraged, Alexander strode out of the house, and complained to Franz Lefort that he was the great Greek Tsar Alexander, and that Peter showed him no honour in speech, and did not offer him an armchair. He had done no more than greet

84. Voznesensky, *Zakonodatel'nyye akty*, p. 156, No. 213. This full account of the ceremony has been added to and corrected carefully by Peter himself.

85. Zhivov and Uspensky, 'Tsar' i Bog', pp. 79–81.

86. S. Baehr, *The Paradise Myth in Eighteenth Century Russia – Utopian Patterns in Early Secular Russian Literature and Culture* (Stanford, Calif., 1992), pp. 38–40.

87. Yu. M. Lotman and B.S. Uspensky, 'Echoes of the notion "Moscow as the Third Rome" in Peter the Great's ideology', in Lotman and Uspensky, *The Semiotics of Russian Culture*, ed. Ann Shukman (Ann Arbor, 1984), pp. 53–67, at pp. 53–4.

88. Billington, *The Icon and the Axe*, p. 199; see also W.F. Ryan, 'The Great Beast in Russia: Aleister Crowley's theatrical tour and his beastly writings on Russia', in A. MacMillin (ed.), *Symbolism and After: Essays on Russian Poetry in Honour of Georgette Donchin* (London, 1992), pp. 137–60.

Peter as Tsar Peter Alekseyevich. This explains everything, replied Lefort: 'He is emperor, not tsar; as your father Philip was raised from prince to tsar, so Peter the Great was raised from tsar to emperor.' When Alexander greeted Peter correctly, the latter rose, hailed him as great Tsar Alexander, and offered him a chair.[89]

In his public lectures on Peter the Great, S.M. Solov'yev argued that Peter had long contemplated becoming eastern emperor, not a Roman eastern emperor, but a Russian eastern emperor. 'He had nothing to do with Rome, and he rejected this antiquated notion, useless to Russia and to her history. He was working only for Russia and with Russia, with her and for her he obtained the title of emperor and he did not separate his native land from his own glory.'[90] Solov'yev was an ardent Russian nationalist, and his views are echoed by other historians, such as Savva, who reject completely the idea of any influence of the Byzantine Empire on Peter. This may partly be the result of the neglect of the cultural influence of the Orthodox Church in the secularised Petrine state in nineteenth-century historiography. On the other hand more modern Russian and western writers, such as Shevchenko, Stremoukhoff, Zhivov and Uspensky, and Baehr, do trace the features of Byzantium behind the mask of the Roman Peter the Great.[91]

89. P.N. Krekshin, *Kratkoye opisaniye slavnykh i dostopamyatnykh del imp. Petra Velikogo . . . prestavlennoye razgovory v tsarstsve mertvykh . . . B.P. Sheremet'yeva, F.A. Golovina, i samogo imperatora s . . . tsarem Ioannom Vasil'ievichem, s Shveskim korolem Karlom XII i grecheskim tsarem Aleksandrom* (St Petersburg, 1788) (written before 1763), pp. 96ff.

90. S.M. Solov'yev, *Publichnyye chteniya o Petre Velikom* (Moscow, 1984 edn), p. 124.

91. See *Istoricheskoye pokazaniye o rossiysko-imperatorskom titule s ob''yasneniyem*, by N.N. Bantysh Kamensky, dated 3 Mar. 1803, based on a questionnaire sent by Taubert to M.N. Bantysh Kamensky in 1766, RGADA, fo. 166, d. II, III, 1–305, and fond 166, op. I, d. I, 1–11, 11–115. Reference kindly supplied by Dr Omel'chenko. In the course of the eighteenth century Russia gradually persuaded the European courts to accept what was really a striking departure in international relations and to acknowledge the new Russian title. This proved relatively easy with the minor Protestant powers and was facilitated by Peter's assertion that he did not intend his new title to justify any claim to alter the existing order of precedence among European courts. Frederick William I of Prussia recognised the title as king in Prussia, though not as elector of Brandenburg; the United Provinces also recognised the imperial title in 1722, many German principalities and city states in 1722–25. France proved less accommodating: as late as 1717 the French government had so low an opinion of Russia that the regent insisted on being given precedence over Russia in all copies of the treaty of 1717 between France, Russia and Prussia, as he was given by all the other 'Puissances Orientales', and incidentally by Prussia too: see AAE, MD III, Mémoire cited in n. 52. What Vienna had always dreaded finally happened under Catherine II. In 1781 the empress insisted on the alternative (the practice by which the contracting parties each signed first on one of the copies of the treaty) in the signature of the Austro-Russian alliance of 1781, and Joseph II was compelled to give way, in secret only, and agree that the treaty should take the form of an exchange of letters: see my article 'The secret Austro-Russian Treaty of 1781', *Slavonic and East European Review* 38 (1959–60), pp. 114–45.

CHAPTER TWO

Autocracy and sovereignty⋆

I

Students of Russian history have often been struck by the difficulty inherent in translating the terminology of Russian social and political life into Western languages with any degree of precision. The difficulty stems in part from the substance, from the nature of Russian social and political institutions. In part it stems from the form, namely from semantic problems.

To take the matter of substance first: in the Kievan period there were many similarities between Russian and Western, above all Germanic, political institutions, similarities which survived even the growing divergence between the Greek East and the Latin West. But the Mongol Conquest drove Russia and Europe further apart. Either as a result of borrowings from Byzantium, or from the Mongols, or in reaction against them, the Russians developed a number of political and social institutions that had no counterparts in the Western world. To name but a few, there are no exact parallels, hence no exact translations, for such concepts as *krugovaia poruka*†; *mestnichestvo*; or indeed for that vital term *boiar*, which has a number of different meanings: it came to signify both a personal, non-hereditary rank to which the tsar appoints, and a descriptive term applicable to ancient, untitled families or clans from among whom the tsar was expected – but not bound – to select those he appointed to the personal rank of *boiar*. In the same way, the various non-hereditary Muscovite ranks of military servitors such as *okol'nichi, stol'niki, striapchie, moskovskie dvoriane*, or *zhil'tsy*, in no way corresponded in political or social significance with the hereditary dukes, counts, and barons of the West and the non-hereditary knights. No one has ever satisfactorily explained, or translated, the term *oprichnina*, let alone *tiaglo*.

The semantic difficulty derived from the gulf between Old Church Slavic with its roots in Byzantine terminology, and Latin. The use of Latin as the

⋆ An early version of this article was read to a meeting of the Study Group on Eighteenth-Century Russia on 11 January 1980. I am greatly indebted to the comments of my colleagues and above all to Dr W.F. Ryan for his invaluable assistance in dealing with the Greek texts.
† I have since learnt of the English equivalent, frankpledge.

written language of administration in much of Western Europe gave a basic unity to the political terminology in use in the West, down to the Latinized forms of Greek words, e.g., *monarchia, aristocratia*, etc.[1]

Of course the use of a common descriptive Latin word sometimes obscured vital differences between institutions – *parliamentum* is an example. But this was nothing to the semantic gulf which opened up between the political language of the West and that of Russia. The case of the title *tsar'* illustrates the point.

Marc Szeftel has provided an exhaustive account of the development of the title of *tsar'*,[2] and he states that though the derivation from *Caesar* was accepted,[3] the title tended to be applied to independent monarchs who did not have in Russian a specific traditional appellation, such as 'king' or 'prince' (*korol', kniaz'*). Hence it was applied in Russian to the kingdoms of Siberia, Kazan' and Astrakhan', whether in Russian or Tartar hands, and indeed to all Eastern potentates, before it was formally claimed as part of the title of the ruler of Muscovy. This claim was first put forward in international relations by Ivan III, and in Muscovite political thought it stood for the assertion of Muscovite independence and equality of status with the Holy Roman Emperor.[4] The rulers of Muscovy sought primarily the acceptance of the title of *tsar'*, without claiming descent from the Byzantine emperors, but basing their demand on the possession of the khanates of Siberia, Astrakhan' and Kazan'. It thus became possible for other powers to forget that *tsar'* had once been recognized as *Empereur* (in English correspondence), as *imperator*, or even as *kayzer und Herrscher aller Reussen* by the Emperor Maximilian in 1514. By the

1. An example of the way Latin was used in the West is surely the imaginative leap whereby the Latin *rex* was used for Germanic *konung*. Rex was originally a functional title, associated with *regere*, 'to steer, direct or rule', borne by those who carried out the function; *konung* was a personal title describing all the members of a leading kin group. The form *kniaz'* was borrowed very early by the Russians with the meaning of 'noble', suggests M. Hellmann, 'Slawisches, insbesondere Ostslawischen Herrschertum des Mittelalters', in *Das Königtum. Seine geistigen und rechtlichen Grundlagen* (Mainau Vorträge, Institut für geschichtliche Landesforschung des Bodensee Gebietes, vol. 3) (Lindau; Thorbecke, 1958), pp. 266–77. In Saxon England 'king' was a title used by all members of a ruling family, while the overlord was the Bretwalda. But while Germanic *koning*, 'king' eventually was identified with Latin *rex*, in Slavic it seems not to have acquired the association with ruling implied in *rex* but to have maintained its connection with the personal leadership of a kin group. It was eventually the Germanic *Karl* through *Korol'* which became identified with the *rex* as ruler.

2. The whole question of the evolution of royal and imperial titles is extremely complex. For the most up-to-date treatment in the case of Russia, see M. Szeftel, 'The Title of the Muscovite Monarch', *Canadian-American Slavic Studies*, 13, Nos 1–2 (Spring–Summer 1979) [Essays in Honor of Nikolay Andreyev], 59–81 and literature noted therein; see also M. Cherniavsky, 'Khan or Basileus: An Aspect of Russian Medieval Thought', *Journal of History of Ideas*, 20, No. 4 (Oct.–Dec. 1959), 459–76, and literature noted therein; G. Stökl, 'Die Begriffe Reich, Herrschaft und Staat bei den Orthodoxen Slaven', *Saeculum*, 5 (1954), 115ff.; R. Binner, 'Zur Datierung des Samoderžec in der russischen Herrschertitulatur', 20 (1969), 57–68; and J. Raba, 'The Authority of the Muscovite Ruler at the Dawn of the Modern Era', *Jahrbücher für Geschichte Osteuropas*, 24 (1976), 321ff.

3. D.I. Prozorovskii, 'O znachenii tsarskogo titula do priniatiia russkimi gosudariami titula imperatora', *Izvestiia Imperatorskago Arkheologicheskago obshchestva*, 10 vols. (St Petersburg: Tip. Imp. Akademii nauk, 1859–84), VIII, pts. 3 and 5, pp. 192ff. and 450ff., at p. 197f.

4. Szeftel, 'The Title', pp. 70–1.

end of the seventeenth century a spokesman of Rome could argue that the title of *tsar'* 'was not equivalent to that of emperor and could best be translated as king'.[5]

By the eighteenth century, according to Prozorovskii, many historians and philologists had even rejected the derivation of *tsar'* from *Caesar*, or had simply lost sight of it. The historian Boltin quoted, somewhat sceptically, the view of eighteenth-century scholars that *tsar'* was Assyrian in origin and was a suffix *Sar* added to the name of rulers such as Navokhodana*sar* or Balta*sar*. The Russians had allegedly taken over this suffix and applied it to Greek emperors.[6] In his ecclesiastical dictionary of 1794, Archpriest P. Alekseev described *tsar'* as a title given to minor rulers, or as derived from a Hebrew word meaning to counsel.[7] This explains much of the difficulty encountered by Peter I when he adopted the title of *Imperator*. The etymological origin of the word *tsar'* had been glossed over and the title had been devalued, while *imperator* was recognized as superior to *tsar'* and indeed as laying claim to equality with the Holy Roman Emperor.[8]

In the case of *tsar'* the difficulty arose because while *tsar'* was acceptable as a title used of Eastern potentates such as 'Morocco, Tunisia, China, etc., the adoption by Russia of its equivalent, *emperor*, in the eighteenth century might have consequences on the order of precedence among Western monarchies which had not been anticipated in the sixteenth century, when "emperor" was often used as the correct translation for *tsar*"'.[9] However, the semantic perplexities arising from the difficulty of finding exact equivalents for Muscovite institutions became much greater, and acquired more importance, in the eighteenth century. Moreover the eighteenth century added a new dimension to the problem.

The vast amount of foreign political literature translated into Russian necessitated the adaptation of old words or the invention of new ones to express new political concepts. Similarly the integration of Russia into the general European state system led to the translation into foreign tongues of official Russian documents such as texts of treaties, diplomatic dispatches, government instructions, laws, etc. Greater contact with the West led to the publication of an increasing number of works in Western languages describing Russia and Russian institutions, and their authors were faced with the problem of devising a new terminology. The situation was further complicated by the massive importation under Peter I of words of French, Dutch, German, or Latin origin to describe the new institutions he set up to which Muscovite terminology

5. *Ibid.*, pp. 71–2. But see pp. 22–3 above for my disagreement with Szeftel.

6. Prozorovskii, 'O znachenii', pp. 197ff.; Karamzin apparently shared this view of the Assyrian derivation of *tsar'* (*ibid.*, p. 459).

7. P. Alekseev, *Tserkovnyi slovar' ili istolkovanie rechenii slavianskikh, drevnikh takozh troiazychnykh bez perevoda prilozhennykh v sviashchernom pisanii i drugikh tserkovnykh knigakh*, 3 vols. (Moscow: Pechatano pri Imp. Moskovskom universitete, 1794).

8. Szeftel, 'The Title', p. 76, and literature cited therein. See also my article, 'The Secret Austro-Russian Treaty of 1781', *Slavonic and East European Review*, 38, No. 90 (1959), 114–45 on the later Russian claim to parity with the Holy Roman Emperor.

9. Szeftel, 'The Title', p. 66, and n. 22.

was unsuited (*kollegiia, reglament, registrator*), including words, e.g. *Senat*, which were used in a specifically Russian sense, and not in the usual Western context (classical Rome).

Modern historians of the eighteenth century, writing in English, have still failed to agree on a common translation for such terms as *prikaz, pravlenie*, the very subtle *prisutstvennoe mesto*, and *uchrezhdenie*. Each author provides his own translation and supplies a glossary. The same need had already been felt in the eighteenth century, which saw the compilation of a large number of lexicons, dictionaries and glossaries designed to tackle the difficult task of mediating the Russian social and political system.

II

Since it was in the eighteenth century that the first systematic effort to interpret Russian terminology was made, it is proposed to examine here whether eighteenth-century dictionaries and lexicons can cast some light on how two specific concepts were understood by eighteenth-century Russians. The two concepts are: *samoderzhets* and *gosudar'*. These words are usually translated in modern historical works as 'autocrat' and 'sovereign'. It is suggested here for the consideration of the many experts in the field, that these two concepts were originally understood in a different sense. *Samoderzhets* (*samoderzhavie*) meant 'sovereign' (sovereignty); and *gosudar'* meant 'lord', *seigneur, Herr*.

Samoderzhavie

What precisely did *samoderzhavie, samoderzhets* mean in eighteenth-century Russian political language? What did it mean to Russians? What did it mean to an eighteenth-century English, French, or German reader? Was it translated as 'autocrat' or 'autocracy', and did the word 'autocracy' carry the same overtones, convey the same meaning, to the educated reader as it does today? Did the concept of 'sovereignty' exist and how was it understood?

There are two sides to the concept of *samoderzhavie*: it applies first to relations between one crowned head and another or one state and another; and, second, it applies to the relationship between a ruler and his subjects.

Samoderzhets in the literal translation from the Byzantine Greek αὐτοκράτορ means no more than a sovereign monarch holding his power directly from God and not by delegation from any other ruler. In this sense, namely the assertion of independence from any overlord, the title *samoderzhets* was first used by Ivan III to symbolize the final overthrow of the Tartar yoke. Ivan III thus laid claim to political independence, to sovereignty in international relations. It was Ivan IV who laid claim to sovereignty in *internal* relations when he argued that 'Russian tsars derived their *samoderzhavie* from God and ruled their kingdoms themselves, not with the help of boiars and magnates'.[10] But

10. V.O. Kliuchevskii, *Sochineniia*, 8 vols. (Moscow: Gos. izd-vo polit. lit-ry, 1956–59), II, pt. 2: *Kurs russkoi istorii*, 167ff.

Ivan IV laid greater stress on the unlimited, or indeed limitless nature of the tsar's power in his further claim to 'reward or punish' according to his will and in total disregard of the duty implicit in the classical sixteenth-century definitions of sovereignty of ruling according to divine and natural law.[11]

Ivan IV was not so concerned to assert the title of *samoderzhets* in foreign relations as that of *tsar'*.[12] Under his successors the emphasis was rather on independence from foreign overlordship than on the absolute power of the ruler in the internal field. Boris Godunov made the word *samoderzhets* part of the official title of the ruler, to underline his more shaky authority.[13] But there is no ultimate incompatibility between an elected *tsar'* and a sovereign *tsar'* (William III of England provides another example!). What matters is the extent of the legal, enforceable, limitations on the ruler's power. Vasilii Shuiskii was also called *samoderzhets* because there was no incompatibility between sovereignty and the kind of self-limitations placed on his power by his own oath, namely not to punish without trial, i.e., not to rule in an un-Christian manner. To sum up therefore: by the end of the sixteenth century the term *samoderzhets* was used in Russian to express not only independence from a foreign overlord (be he Tartar khan, Byzantine vasileus or Western emperor),

11. With all due deference to so great an authority, I am somewhat perplexed by Professor Szeftel's remark ('The Title', p. 67) that 'At no time from the appearance of the title *Samoderzhets* in Muscovy was it interpreted in the sense of absolutism', particularly since he then concludes that Ivan IV's famous phrase: 'Kako zhe i samoderzhets naritsaietsia ashche ne sam stroit?' meant only that Ivan emphasized his prerogative to choose his councillors without any limitation and even to govern without consulting anyone. Surely sovereignty implies political absolutism to a greater or lesser degree? Bodin defined internal sovereignty as 'the power to make law binding on all his [the ruler's] subjects in general without the consent of any superior, equal or inferior' (*Six Books of the Commonwealth*, tr. and selected by M.J. Tooley [Oxford: Basil Blackwell, 1967], ch. 10, p. 43). To argue that Ivan IV had 'immense power over persons but not over the system' as Kliuchevskii did seems a little odd for a man who set up a rival tsar and divided the country into *oprichnina* and *zemshchina*. But in any case if we discard comparisons with Byzantine autocracy and look to monarchical absolutism as defined and practised in the West, was not the absolute monarch Philip II far more limited by institutions than Ivan IV? Absolute monarchy, or sovereignty in internal affairs, is a relative concept. It refers to the nature and source of power, not to the capacity to use it. An absolute monarch has the theoretical power to override both men and institutions though in practice he may have neither the ability to override the first, nor the strength to override the second. In 'The Title', n. 28, Professor Szeftel refers to the article by J. Raba, 'The Authority of the Muscovite Ruler at the Dawn of the Modern Era', quoted above in fn. 2, in which the author puts forward the argument that 'at the beginning of the modern era, a specifically Russian form of government was evolved. Autocratic absolutism was born – a kind of absolute monarchy in which society delegates all creative prerogatives to the supreme ruler as the sole holder of formal authority'. Professor Szeftel disagrees with this view. So do I, but for a different reason, namely that to my mind' there is no such thing as 'autocratic absolutism' (which is a tautology), but merely 'absolute monarchies' of varying degrees of effectiveness, according to the density of the social and political institutions existing in a given country, and the coercive power of the ruler.

12. Binner, 'Zur Datierung', p. 61. Binner also suggests that inclusion of *samoderzhets* in the tsar's title in occasional letters to Sweden was designed to stress the sovereign nature of Ivan IV's *hereditary* rule as distinct from the elective position of Swedish and Polish kings, whose power was limited by estates (pp. 59ff.).

13. The absence of any sense of the Greek origin of the word *samoderzhets* in the West is suggested by the variety of the efforts made to translate it. Boris Godunov was described as 'governor', 'upholder' in English correspondence. Elsewhere he is described as *Selbsterhalter* (German), and *Selsbehoeder* or *selferhoeder* (Dutch). See *ibid.*, p. 66.

but also the concept of internal sovereignty as expounded by say Jean Bodin: an independent ruler, enjoying sole power in internal government, unlimited by men or institutions, responsible for his actions only to God, and under God the sole source of law for his subjects. Under Ivan IV, the concept had been associated with a particularly arbitrary, and indeed sadistic use of the supreme power; but such abuse was not inherent in the concept of *samoderzhavie* itself, since a sovereign was expected to use his power with moderation, and with an eye to the divine will.

In the seventeenth century the Romanov monarchs enjoyed the theoretical plenitude of sovereign absolute power in internal affairs, though they might be limited in practice by the need to find support for their policies in the Assemblies of the Land.[14] But these Assemblies of elected or selected representatives of the social estates had no rights they could assert against the tsar, and put forward no theoretical justification for such claims. By the end of the seventeenth century the Russian political system corresponded closely, in terms of the nature of the political power of the ruler, with royal absolutism as incarnated in the monarchy of Louis XIV or the restored absolute monarchies of Denmark (1666) and Sweden (1693).

Western rulers found the theoretical justification for the concept of sovereignty in a monarchy as the independent and unrestricted power of one ruler, under God, in the works of Bodin, Hobbes or Pufendorf. In Russia, it was not until the reign of Peter I that it was found necessary to formulate clearly the full range of powers now claimed by the tsar, in part because of the increasing contacts between Russia and Europe. Understandably enough, it was in the Military Code, published both in Russian and in German (for the many foreign officers in Russian service), that this definition was first proclaimed: 'His Majesty is a Sovereign monarch, who is responsible to no one for his actions, but has the power to rule his state and his lands as a Christian lord [*gosudar'*] according to his will and good understanding.' For 'sovereign', the Russian text uses *samovlastnyi*, but the original German draft of the law from which the Russian text was translated was *ein souverainer Monarch*.[15] In 1722 the main ideologue of early Russian eighteenth-century absolutism, Archbishop Feofan Prokopovich, influenced in part by Hobbes, expounded the political basis of the Petrine Empire. The *Pravda voli Monarshei*[16] based itself on the contract between ruler and people, by which all power is ceded irrevocably to the sovereign, who has absolute authority and is above the laws of the state. In

14. See, however, the differing emphasis given by Szeftel, 'The Title', p. 68, and H.J. Torke, *Die Staatsbedingte Gesellschaft in Moskauer Reich* (Leiden: E.J. Brill, 1974), *passim* and ch. 6 in particular.
15. *Polnoe Sobranie Zakonov Rossiiskoi imperii* [hereafter *PSZ*]; First series, 45 vols. (St Petersburg: Tip II Otd. Sobst. E.I.V. Kantseliarii, 1830), V, No. 3006, 30 March 1716, Ustav Voinskii, Artikul No. 20. The Russian *Tsar' i samoderzhets* in the title of Peter I is translated *Czaar aller Reussen und Selbsterhalter*, M. Szeftel ('The Form of the Russian Government Prior to the Constitutional Reforms of 1905–06', in *Essays in Russian and Soviet History in Honor of G.T. Robinson*, ed. J.S. Curtiss [Leiden: E.J. Brill, 1963]) points out that the claim to absolute sovereignty expressed here is the literal translation of the decision of the Swedish Riksdag in 1693 (p. 106, n. 2).
16. *PSZ*, V, No. 3151.

this work, Feofan uses both *samoderzhavie* and *monarkhiia*, and identifies the two concepts explicitly. Other eighteenth-century Russian political writers, such as V.N. Tatishchev, used the term *monarkhiia*, not *samoderzhavie*, when speaking of the Russian form of government.[17]

Reference to the glossaries, dictionaries and lexicons of the eighteenth century shows that an enormous confusion prevailed over the meaning of words and their correct translation. Compilers were bound by few rules since there was no dictionary of the Russian language until the Academy Dictionary, edited by Princess Dashkova, was published in the 1780s.[18] A traveller's lexicon in French, German, Latin, and Russian, published in 1764, gives the following entry for monarch and monarchy:

> *Monarchie* (Fr.) = *Monarchie, eine Herrschaft* (Ger.), *Monarchia* (Lat.), *Monarkhiia, gosudarstvo* (Rus.)
> *Monarque* (Fr.) = *Ein König, Monarch* (Ger.), *Monarcha, Rex* (Lat.), *Monarkh, Korol', gosudar', imperator, tsesar'* (Rus.)

Here the words *Herrschaft* and *gosudarstvo* might be considered out of place under *monarchie*; and *gosudar', imperator*, and *tsesar'* are certainly out of place under *monarque*.[19] But the Academy Dictionary is no more precise, indeed it introduces fresh complications:

> *Monarkh = gosudar', samoderzhets*
> *Monarkhiia = edinoderzhavie, samoderzhavie, edinovlastie.*

Here the correct *edinoderzhavie* appears only under *monarkhiia*, not under *monarkh*, while strictly speaking neither *gosudar'* nor *samoderzhets* are correct for *monarkh*.

Eighteenth-century usage showed conclusively the identification of Western 'sovereignty', *souveraineté*, or *souveränität* with *samoderzhavie*. 'On est' suveren ili samoderzhavnyi iako gertsog Shlesvigskii' dates from 1717;[20] 'Samoderschetz veut dire Conservateur ou Souverain'[21] from 1757. More unusual is the translation 'Sole-Monarch' (*edinoderzhavie*?) in the Manifesto issued in 1763 inviting foreigners to settle in Russia.[22]

The confusion which prevailed is illustrated in a number of dictionaries and lexicons of the mid-eighteenth century. The lexicon for travellers of 1764 quoted above[23] gives, translating from the French:

17. See R.L. Daniels, 'V.N. Tatishchev and the Succession Crisis of 1730', *Slavonic and East European Review*, 49, No. 117 (Oct. 1971), 550–59.
18. *Slovar' Akademii Rossiiskoi*, 5 vols. (St Petersburg: Imp. Akademii nauk, 1789–94).
19. *Novyi voiazhirovyi leksikon na frantsuzskom, nemetskom, latinskom, i rossiiskom iazykakh*, 2 vols. (St Petersburg: Imp. Akademii nauk, 1755–64).
20. E.E. Birzhakova, L.A. Voinova, L.L. Kutina, *Ocherki po istoricheskoi leksikologii russkogo iazyka XVIII veka. Iazykovye kontakty i zaimstvovaniia* (Leningrad: Nauka, 1972), p. 131.
21. Baron Strahlenberg [Stralenberg], *Description historique de l'empire russien*, 2 vols. (Amsterdam and Paris: Desaint and Saillant, 1757), I, 238.
22. English translation quoted from R. Bartlett, *Human Capital: The Settlement of Foreigners in Russia* (Cambridge: Cambridge Univ. Press, 1979), pp. 237ff.
23. See n. 19.

Souverain: der höchste Oberherr, Summus, Supremus, supremus dominus, somoderzhets (sic), *samoderzhavnyi, samovlastnyi gosudar'.*
Un prince souverain: ein unumschränkter Fürst, supremus princeps, samovlastnyi kniaz', vladetel', prints.
Souveraineté: droit de pouvoir souverain, die Oberherrlichkeit, die volle Macht, unumschränkte Gewalt, samovlastie, derzhavstvo, samoderzhavstvo.

An etymological lexicon published in 1771 in Moscow by F. Hölterhof gives German equivalents as follows:[24]

Samoderzhets: der Selbstherrscher, Monarch
Samoderzhavstvovat': monarchisch regieren
Samoderzhavie: die monarchische Regierung, die unumschränkte Macht
Samoderzhavnyi: unumschränkt, souverain.

So far, the compilers take *samoderzhavie* to translate both 'monarchy', i.e. rule by one person (*edinoderzhavie*), and unlimited, absolute power: *unumschränkte Macht*; thus monarchy and unlimited power are treated as synonymous. A later edition of Hölterhof's lexicon identifies *samoderzhavie* with *samovlastie*, though there is a subtle difference of meaning in Russian. *Samovlastie* hints at the way in which absolute power is actually used and conveys a suggestion of arbitrariness. *Samoderzhets* in this edition is given in Latin as 'quis habet supremum dominium'. Can one perhaps read a subtle compliment into the translation of *samoderzhitsa* as 'quae supremo domino gaudet'?[25]

P. Alekseev's Ecclesiastical Dictionary gives under Gk. *monarkh:* R. *edinonachal'nik:* and under Gk. *monarkhiia*: R. *edinonachalie, monarkhicheskaia vlast', t.e. samoderzhavnaia, bezpredel'naia, neogranichennaia.*[26] This is the first time the Russian *neogranichennaia* (unlimited) has appeared in the texts consulted, though the concept has appeared in German (*unumschränkt*).[27] An English/Russian dictionary published on the Cadet Corps press in 1784 gives: 'sovereign' = *samoderzhavnyi, samovlastnyi.*[28]

Much the most authoritative dictionary, however, is the French/Russian–Russian/French dictionary compiled 'par une société de gens de lettres' with the encouragement and patronage of the Empress Catherine, of which the first edition of the French/Russian appeared in 1786.[29] Both translations and examples of usage are given in this dictionary. Thus we find:

24. Francis Geltergof [Hölterhof], *Rossiiskii Tsellarius ili etimologicheskoi rossiiskoi leksikon kupno s pribavleniem inostrannykh v rossiiskom iazyke vo upotreblenie priniatykh slov takoi s sokrashchennoiu rossiiskoiu etimologiiu* (Moscow: Pechatano pri Imp. Moskovskom universitete, 1771).
25. F. Geltergof, *Rossiiskoi leksikon po alfavitu s nemetskim i latinskim perevodom*, 2 vols. (Moscow: Pechatano pri Imp. Moskovskom universitete, 1778).
26. Alekseev, *loc. cit.*
27. See fn. No. 24 above.
28. P.I. Zhdanov, *A New Dictionary, English and Russian–Novyi slovar' angliiskio i russkoi* (St Petersburg: Pechatano pri Imp. Morskom kadetskom korpuse, 1784).
29. *Dictionnaire Complet Framçois et Russe*, composé sur la dernière édition de celui de l'Académie Françoise par une société de gens de lettres, 2nd ed., 2 vols. (St Petersbourg: de l'imprimerie Impériale, 1798).

Monarchie [as a regime] = *edinonachalie, edinonachalstvo, edinovlastie, edinoderzhavie, samoderzhavie, monarkhiia ili monarkhicheskoe pravlenie.*

But for *monarchie* as a kingdom or state the following are given:

monarkhiia, gosudarstvo upravliaemoe monarkhom, edinovlastnikom samoderzhavtsem.

As an example of usage the dictionary gives: 'vivre sous un gouvernement monarchique' = 'zhit' pod samoderzhavnym pravleniem'. *Monarkh*, among many other translations, is of course given as *samoderzhets*. As for *souverain* (adj.), it is translated

odnovladetel'nyi, samovlastnyi, samoderzhavnyi, nezavisimyi, neogranichennyi.

But *souverain* (noun) is *samovlastnyi gosudar', samoderzhavets, samoderzhets* and *souveraineté* is *samovlastie, samoderzhavie, gosudareva neogranichennaia, bezpredel'naia vlast'*. Under *pouvoir absolu* we also find *samoderzhavie* and *vys'shaia vlast'*.

There is no entry in this French/Russian dictionary for *autocrate*, or *autocratie*,[30] but a Russian/French/German dictionary published in 1792 has the following:

samoderzhavie: la souveraineté, die monarchische Gewalt, Monarchie . . .
samoderzhets: l'Autocrateur, der Selbstherrscher . . .
samoderzhavstvovat': régner en souverain, ein Selbstherrscher seyn.[31]

A German/Russian dictionary of 1795 gives:

der Souverain: gosudar', samoderzhets
die Souverainität: samoderzhavie, samovlastie

while the Russian/German part of the dictionary which appeared in 1798 gives:[32]

samovlastie: die unumschränkte Gewalt, Souverainetät [sic]
samoderzhavie: die unumschränkte Macht, Souverainität
samoderzhets: selbstherrschend, ein unumschränkter Monarch.

To conclude this survey of dictionaries, a Russian/French/German dictionary published by the same author in Moscow in 1799 introduced the word *autocrate*. While *samoderzhavie* is given as: *la souveraineté, die Selbstherrschung, Souverainität, samoderzhets* is: *l'autocrate, der Selbstherrscher.*[33]

Finally, what does the Russian Academy Dictionary of the Language say? For *samoderzhets* it gives: 'nazvanie pridanoe gosudariam samovlastno

30. According to Littré (*Dictionnaire de la Langue française*, 4 vols. [Paris: Hachette, 1885]), *autocrate* signifies 'souverain, souveraine dont la puissance n'est soumise à aucun control legal'. The emperor of Russia is given as an example.

31. *Ruchnoi rossiiskoi slovar' s nemetskimi i frantsuzskimi perevodami* (Moscow: Vol'naia tipografiia pri Teatre, 1792).

32. Johann Heym [Geim], *Deutsch-russisches Wörterbuch:* Part I, *Deutsch-Russisch*; Part II, *Russisch-Deutsch* (Riga und Leipzig: J.F. Hartknoch, 1795–98). Heym was a professor at Moscow University.

33. *Novyi rossiisko-frantzuzsko-nemetskii slovar'*, sochinennyi po slovariu rossiiskoi akademii Ivanom Geimom, 3 vols. (Moscow: Pechatano pri Imp. Moskovskom universitete, 1799).

upravliaiushchim kakim libo gosudarstvam'; while *samoderzhavie* is regarded as identical with *samovlastnyi*, but is also applied to a person 'zakonodatel'nuiu vlast' v sebe zakliuchaiushchim', which is the usual attribute of a sovereign ruler.

This brief survey shows clearly that there was still very little precision in the use of Russian words, and in many ways it is German which provides the translations closest in spirit to the Russian original because the words can be built up in the same way. Far the best translation of *samoderzhets* is *Selbstherrscher*, just as *eigenmächtig* faithfully reflects *samovlastle*.

The most interesting examples of the difficulty of transposing Russian political terminology into Western languages are provided by the many editions of Catherine's *Great Instruction*, or *Bol'shoi Nakaz*, which she prepared for the meeting of the Legislative Commission of 1767. Here we have a semantic problem of some importance for the understanding of Catherine's political doctrine. To begin with, which of the many, slightly divergent, texts most truly expresses her thought and intentions?

There are good reasons for giving priority to the French texts, in case of any discrepancy in translation, because the main sources from which Catherine copied her maxims were written in French (Montesquieu's *Esprit des Lois*, and a French translation by Abbé Morellet of Beccaria's *Delle delitte e delle pene*). Moreover, Catherine's own draft of her *Nakaz* was written in French, a language she knew infinitely better than Russian; it was later translated into Russian by her literary secretary, G. Kozitskii. It is therefore fair to assume that the French text of the *Nakaz* was the most faithful expression of her ideas.[34]

The key issue here is Catherine's use of the word *souveraineté* and her acceptance of its translation into Russian as *samoderzhavie*.

If Catherine needed a definition of the concept, she found it at hand in one of her main source books, namely the *Grande Encyclopédie* of Denis Diderot and d'Alembert.[35] *Souverains*, states Diderot in the Encyclopedia, 'sont ceux à qui la volonté des peuples a conféré le pouvoir necéssaire pour gouverner la société'. Peoples have sometimes limited the powers they granted to sovereigns, sometimes they have granted them legislative and executive power. 'C'est là ce qu'on appelle souveraineté absolue', a sovereignty which is however limited by the obligation to maintain the fundamental laws of a state, namely its religion, the order of the succession, and constitution. 'Lorsqu'un souverain absolu', warns the author of this entry, 's'arroge le droit de changer

34. There are at least three French texts. According to N.D. Chechulin, the most authoritative writer on the subject, one manuscript version was sent to Voltaire in 1768, of which a fair copy still existed in 1907 in the Russian archives. This text was closer to the original Montesquieu than the printed text in which some editorial changes were made drawing the French further from the Russian when it was prepared for printing. The first French text to be published appeared in 1769 as *Instruction de sa Majesté Impériale Catherine II pour la commission chargée de dresser le projet d'un nouveau Code de Loix* (St Petersbourg: Imp. de l'Académie des sciences, 1769). It is not quite identical with the parallel Russian/French text printed in *PSZ*, XVII, No. 12949, 30 July 1767, which in turn was reproduced by N.D. Chechulin in his *Nakaz imperatritsy Ekateriny II dannyi kommissii o sochinenii proekta novago ulozheniia* (St Petersburg: Tip. Imp. Akademii nauk, 1907), pp. 1–166.

35. D. Diderot, d'Alembert *et al.*

à sa volonté les loix fondamentales de son pays; lorsqu'il prétend un pouvoir arbitraire sur la personne et les personnes de son peuple, il devient un despote.'

It will be observed that the emphasis in this definition is no longer that of Hobbes, or even of Bodin. Diderot is not concerned with sovereignty in terms of the independence of a state, of the relations between two rulers, but with the nature of the power of a ruler in internal affairs. In the first place he stresses the popular origin of sovereignty, in accordance with a sound medieval tradition. Secondly he distinguishes between different degrees of sovereignty: some sovereigns have limited powers; others, notably absolute rulers, have both legislative and executive powers. Even the latter, however, are bound to observe the fundamental laws of the state if they are not to be regarded as mere tyrants.

The concept of fundamental laws owed a great deal to the elaboration given to it by Montesquieu in *L'Esprit des Lois*.[36] It was extremely influential in Russia since it was the existence of such laws in Russia which would enable Catherine to shed the image of a despotism and graduate into the more respectable circle of monarchies. Hence the concept of 'sovereignty' as expounded by Bodin and Hobbes was modified by Catherine in Russia to conform to the new emphasis on respect for the fundamental laws of a nation and on moderation in the use of power.

This new conception of sovereignty or *samoderzhavie* is adopted explicitly by Catherine throughout the *Nakaz*. It is instructive to observe how the word was translated in the various languages in which her treatise was published.

Chapter II article 9 states:
Russian: Государь есть самодержавный.[37]
French: Le monarque de Russie est souverain.
Latin: Quis imperat est monarcha.
German: Der Regent ist selbstherrschend.
English: The sovereign is absolute (Dukes, ditto).[38]
Italian: Il sovrano de questo impero gode di un autorita senza limiti; egli e indipendente.[39]

36. See *L'Esprit des Lois*, 2 vols. (Paris: Garnier Frères, 1961), I, 19ff; 60ff; p. 67.
37. The most recent survey of the various editions is in W.E. Butler, 'The Nakaz of Catherine the Great', *The American Book Collector*, 16, No. 5 (1966), 19–21. The present quotations in Russian, German and Latin are taken from the four-language edition printed by the Academy of Sciences in 1770. The French text reproduces the 1769 French edition.
38. The English text is quoted from the translation by M. Tatishcheff which was published as: *The Grand Instruction to the Commissioners appointed to Frame a New Code of Laws for the Russian Empire: composed by H.I.M. Catherine II* (London: T. Jefferys, 1768). A slightly different MS translation, possibly prepared for George Macartney, the British envoy to Russia at the time, has recently been found in the Library of Congress, and published in *Russia under Catherine the Great*. vol. II, *Catherine the Great, Instruction (Nakaz) to the Legislative Commission*, translated and introduced by P. Dukes (Newtonville: ORP, 1978).
39. The quotation is from the *Istruzione emanata da Caterina Seconda, imperatrice e legislatrice di tutta la Russia*, [hereafter Florence 1769] (Firenze: Stamperia bonducciana, 1769), translated from the French edition of 1769.

(This last edition specifically spells out the two meanings of sovereignty: internal supremacy, external independence.)

Italian: Il signore ne e sovrano assoluto.[40]
Greek: *Ὁ τῆς Ῥωσσίας Μονάρχης εἶνα Ὑπέρτατος* (the monarch of Russia is supreme).[41]
Greek: *Ὁ βασιλεῦς τῆς Ῥωσσικῆς Μοναρχίας εἶναι παντεξόυσιος Αὐτοκράτωρ* (the King (*basileus*) of the Russian monarchy is an all powerful Autocrat).[42]

It will be noted that the texts in the four-language edition, French, Latin, German, and Russian, are fairly close to each other. The Latin text subsumes the concept of sovereignty in the verb *imperat*; the German gives the neutral 'Regent' to describe the person of the ruler while the concept of sovereignty is included in *beherrschend*. The English, Italian and Greek versions mostly depart from the pattern except for the Bulgaris 1771 Greek version which states: 'the monarch of Russia is supreme', and the Pisa 1769 text: 'il signore ne e sovrano e assoluto'.

A few more examples may be noted:

Chapter II article 13 runs as follows:
Russian: Какий предлог самодержавнаго правления?
Latin: Quae finis rectionis Monarchicae?
German: Was ist aber der Endzweck einer souverainen Regierung?
French: Quel est l'objet de la souveraineté?[43]
English: What is the true end of monarchy?[44]
English: What is the Object of Absolute Government?[45]
Italian: Quale è adunque l'oggetto di un governo assoluto?[46]
Italian: Qual è lo scopo della Potenza sovrana?[47]

40. *Istruzione di Sua/Maesta Cesarea Caterina II Imperatrice delle Russie alla deputazione sopra il piano di un nuovo codice di leggi* [hereafter Pisa 1769] (Pisa: 1769). I must thank my student Miss Pia Pera for photocopies of the relevant portions of these Italian editions.
41. Quoted from the two column Russian-Greek edition printed in 1770 or 1771 in St Petersburg by the Academy of Sciences Press, and translated by Evgenii Bulgaris, the future Archbishop of Ekaterinoslav [hereafter Bulgaris 1771].
42. Quoted from a Greek translation published in Venice in 1770. The translator is still unknown today but since this edition was dedicated to Aleksei Orlov (as incidentally was Pisa 1769), it is suggested that it may have emanated from Ionian Greek circles which supported the Russians in the hope of achieving Greek liberation from the Ottoman Turks, during the 1769–70 Mediterranean campaign of the Russian fleet. (This edition is not mentioned in Butler, 'The Nakaz'.) A Romanian translation was prepared in 1773 for the Metropolitan Gabriel of Moldavia (from the Bulgaris Greek) at the request of Field Marshal P.A. Rumiantsev (not in Butler, 'The Nakaz') by a certain Toma Dimitriu. (See Ariadne Cioran Camariano, 'Traducerile în limba greacă si Romînă a "Nacazului' (învătătura] Ecaterinei a II-a"', *Studii. Revista de Istorie*, 11 [1958], 123–32. I owe this reference to Dr Richard Clogg.) The Romanian edition formed part of Catherine's propaganda campaign among the orthodox peoples subjected to the Turks.
43. Quoted from the four-language edition.
44. Tatishcheff edition.
45. Dukes edition.
46. Florence edition.
47. Pisa edition.

Greek: *Τίς οὖν ἡ ἰδέα μιᾶς ἀηολύτου Διοικήσεως*[48] (What is the idea of absolute government? The word incidentally was coined to mean absolute as distinct from relative.)

Greek: *Ποῖος εἶναι τάχα ὁ σκοπὸς μιᾶς ὑπερτάτης ἐξουσίας*[49] (Of what kind is the scope of supreme power? But note that in article 10 the Russian *prostrannye gosudarstva* is translated *Μία εὐμεγεθης βασιλεια* in the Venice edition and *Μία μεγάλη αὐτοκρατορία* in the Bulgaris edition.)

The answer to the above question is given as follows in article 15 of the *Nakaz*:

Russian: Самодержавных правлении намерение и конец есть . . .
Latin: Monarchici regiminis scopus et finis est . . .
German: Das Augenmerk und der Endzweck souverainer Regierung ist . . .
French: L'objet et le but d'un gouvernement monarchique est . . .[50]
English: The Intention and the End of Monarchy, is . . .[51]
English: The Intention and End of Absolute Government is . . .[52]
Italian: L'oggetto diretto e il fine dei governi assoluti e la gloria dei cittadini, dello stato e del sovrano.[53]
Italian: L'intenzione e il fine dei governi assoluti e la gloria dei cittadini, dell' impero e del sovrano.[54]
Greek: *Ἡ ἰδέα καὶ τὸ τέλος τῆς Μοναρχικῆς Διοικήσεως . . .*[55] (The idea and the end of monarchical government.)
Greek: *Ὁ σκοηὸς, καὶ τὸ τέλος τῶν Μονοκρετιῶν εἶναι ἡ δόξα τῶν Πολιτῶν, της Βασιλείας καὶ τοῦ Βασιλέως.*[56] (The scope and end of monarchies is the glory of the citizens, of the kingdom, and of the king.)

In many other articles throughout Catherine's *Nakaz*, the word *samoderzhavie* is translated by *monarchie* in contexts which make it perfectly clear that the two concepts were regarded as interchangeable. One of the most striking is article 511 which states 'Samoderzhavstvo razrushaetsia eshche togda, kogda gosudar' dumaet chto on bol'she svoiu vlast'iu pokazhet, ezhe li on peremenit poriadok veshchei. . . .' In French the article runs: 'La monarchie se perd encore lorqu'un prince croit qui'il montre plus sa puissance. . . .'[57]

It is evident from the above examples that the word *samoderzhavie* was used in the eighteenth century to express a far greater range of political concepts than is the case today. It had moved well away from the original meaning of

48. Bulgaris edition.
49. Venice edition.
50. Four-language edition.
51. Tatishcheff edition.
52. Dukes edition.
53. Florence edition.
54. Pisa edition.
55. Bulgaris edition.
56. Venice edition.
57. St Petersburg four-language edition.

independence from an overlord, and the emphasis was by now on the supreme authority of a ruler in internal affairs: 'le droit de commander en dernier ressort dans une société', as the *Encyclopédie* put it.[58] *Samoderzhavie* was translated as sovereignty, monarchy, absolute monarchy, unlimited monarchy. Moreover all these concepts were understood in the context of the forms of government in existence at that time throughout Europe. The kings of France, Spain and Prussia were *samoderzhavnyie*. So was the king of England though he was a 'king in parliament'. The kings of Sweden and Poland were not *samoderzhavnyi*, or sovereign. They did not enjoy the right to declare war or make peace, nor the right of supreme justice inherent in a true sovereign who 'comme tel n'est tenu de rendre compte à personne ici bas de sa conduite'.[59] The efforts of King Adolf Frederick of Sweden in the 1750s and 1760s to overthrow the constitutional limitations on the royal power imposed in 1720 are described in current Russian diplomatic correspondence as 'vvedenie samoderzhavstva' or in French as 'la restauration de la souveraineté'.[60] *Samoderzhavie* was therefore clearly not regarded as a uniquely Russian form of government; it was a word used to describe the most common form of government in Europe at the time. Catherine, in article 15 of the *Nakaz*, speaks of *samoderzhavnye pravleniia* in the plural, not in the singular, implying that there were many such governments in existence.

Rarely in the eighteenth century was the term 'autocrat' or the word 'autocracy' used.[61] It is not found in Russian dictionaries until the very end of the century. Voltaire once addressed Catherine as 'l'admirable autocratrice'.[62] One of the German translators of the *Nakaz*, the historian August Ludwig Schlözer, inserts the Greek word *αὐτοκράτορ* after the translation of chapter II article 9: 'der Beherrscher desselben ist unumschränkt'.[63] The Greek translations naturally use the word more often. The title of Catherine in the Latin version of the *Nakaz*

58. Entry *souveraineté*.
59. *Ibid.*
60. See Swedish Royal Archives, Russian Microfilms reel 51, Osterman to Panin, 8/19 Oct. 1762; E. Amburger, *Russland und Schweden 1762–1772* (Berlin: Verlag Dr Emil Ebering, 1934), p. 69 and *passim*.
61. See for instance G. Vernadsky *et al.*, comps., *A Source Book for Russian History from Early Times to 1917*, 3 vols. (New Haven and London: Yale Univ. Press, 1972). Vernadsky, in a note on the translation of the *Nakaz*, states that 'the present translation borrows somewhat from the English translation of 1768 but it incorporates extensive revisions both to modernize the English and to bring it closer to the Russian version'. The changes introduced by Vernadsky include: Chapter 2, article 13: 'what is the purpose of autocracy'; article 15: 'The intention and the aim of autocracies is . . .'. This seems to me a most mistaken policy since modernizing the English falsifies the meaning of the original, and does not bring it closer to the eighteenth-century Russian original, but only to the twentieth-century distortion of the meaning of the Russian original.
62. W.F. Reddaway, ed., *Documents of Catherine the Great*, The Correspondence with Voltaire and the *Instruction* of 1767 in the English text of 1768 (Cambridge: Cambridge Univ. Press, 1931), p. 201, Voltaire to Catherine 6 October 1774. *Autocratrice* was also incorporated in the title of Catherine in ratifications of treaties, e.g. the Treaty of Verela of 1791. See *Consolidated Treaty Series*, ed. C. Parry, LI (Dobbs Ferry, N.Y.: Oceana Publications, 1971), pp. 43, 251.
63. J.J. Haigold ([A.L. Schlözer] *Neuverändertes Russland oder Leben Catharina der Zweyten Kayserin von Russland*, erster Theil, dritte Auflage [Riga und Mietau: J.F. Hartknoch, 1771]), published a German translation of the *Nakaz* and the Russian original in parallel columns.

is given as 'Autocratorissae omnium Rossiarum' – an invented Latin word modelled on the Greek. In English the word 'autocracy' figures in the Oxford English Dictionary as '1) obs. self-sustained or independent power'. Oddly enough the example given here is: 'The king of Sweden . . . had prospered to an autocracy, a self subsistence, and so needed no participants . . . in the hazard.' In the second sense, that of absolute government, the first example given dates from 1855. The word 'autocrat' as a 'monarch who rules with uncontrolled sway' dates back to the 'Corsican autocrat' in 1803. Thus when autocrat came to be applied to a particularly authoritarian form of government, it was not necessarily the *tsar'* of Russia who sprang to mind.

Gosudar'

Thus far 'autocracy'. What of *gosudar'*? If 'autocrat' or *samoderzhets* was used to translate the Western concept of 'sovereign', to what did *gosudar'* correspond? It is usually taken to mean sovereign by modern historians, yet surely the word is one of several Russian variants for the slightly different concept of 'lordship', *seigneurie, Herrschaft*? Would not this translation simplify some of the problems of interpretation faced by historians?

M. Szeftel in 'The Title of the Muscovite Monarch' goes into the history of the word (which he translates as 'sovereign'),[64] and discusses the various schools of thought on the evolution of the concept and its introduction into the titulature of the tsar. There was a very thin dividing line between the three forms *gospodin, gospodar,* and *gosudar'*, and efforts have been made to suggest that one form, namely *gospodin*, belonged to the sphere of private relations, while the form *gosudar'* belonged to the sphere of public relations. As long as *gosudar'* is associated with 'sovereign' clearly much hinges on these arguments: for instance it can be argued that *gosudar'* could not be used in foreign relations until Muscovy was free from the overlordship of the Tartars. But in fact *gosudar'* was used as early as the mid-fifteenth century in internal affairs.

If we take up a second suggestion put forward by M. Szeftel: that *gosudar'* 'could have been simply a translation of the Latin *dominus* by those princes whose contact with Latin terminology was constant', many difficulties disappear. *Gosudar'* as *dominus* or *seigneur* implies merely lord and master. Hence when Ivan III asserted his right to be *gosudar'* over Novgorod the Great, he was claiming *seigneurie*, not the wider-ranging sovereignty; he was dealing with an overmighty subject (in his view), not with an independent power.[65] It is noteworthy that the title *gosudar'* is used systematically by the grand duke of Moscow first in conjunction with Novgorod and Pskov, city republics

64. Szeftel, 'The Title', pp. 62ff.

65. It was not at all unusual in sixteenth-century Europe for a ruler to be bound by different constitutional relationships with different parts of his dominions. The classical example is Philip II of Spain, King of Castile but also Señor de Vizcaya, one of the Basque provinces. Baron Strahlenberg, n. 21, p. 238, translates *gosudar' Pskovskii* as *Seigneur de Plescow*.

over which the ruler of Moscow had to exert his overlordship by force. Subsequently it was extended to the whole of the Russian land.[66]

It appears probable that with the passage of time a word which originally meant 'lord' became associated with the idea of sovereignty, because it was used in conjunction with *samoderzhets*. ('Lord' and *seigneur* do not mean 'sovereign' in English and French, though *Herr* and *Herrschaft* come close to it in German.) Its use in a generalized way to signify either a sovereign or a prince belonging to a ruling house, but not actually a ruler, is found in the Russian translation of Marmontel's *Bélisaire*.[67]

Nevertheless, the fact that *gosudar'* did not mean *samoderzhets* may explain why the title of *Velikii Gosudar'* could be given to Patriarch Filaret and Patriarch Nikon. They were not sovereigns, but they could be granted quite exceptional prerogatives as 'lords'.

Subsequently, in eighteenth-century court etiquette *gosudar'* became the usual formula for addressing the tsar when speaking or writing to him, as the king of England is addressed as 'Sir'. Catherine II, both in correspondence and in conversation with friends, was addressed as *Matushka gosudarynia*, and gentlemen wrote to each other as *milostivyi gosudar'*, 'Dear Sir'.

III

If the arguments put forward here are well founded, if the formula *gosudar' i samoderzhets* should be translated 'lord and sovereign', how and when did the word 'autocrat' come to be so systematically and uniquely associated with the Russian form of government? Three reasons suggest themselves. First, the word *samoderzhets* forms part of the official titulature of the ruler of Russia, while its equivalent, 'sovereign', is not added to the titulature of other European rulers, who may not have felt so strongly at any stage in their historical evolution the need to emphasize the moment when external sovereignty was achieved.

Second, greater familiarity with the Russian language in the nineteenth century led to a renewed realization of the Greek origin of the word, and to an assumption by Western historians that 'autocrat' represented a more faithful and accurate translation of the Russian *samoderzhets*, while leaving the actual content of the word 'autocrat' rather vague. It was also a way of suggesting that Russia was different.

Third, since 'autocrat' became the usual appellation of the ruler of Russia at a time – in the second quarter of the nineteenth century – when the rigidly

66. On the evolution of *gosudar'* and *gosudarstvo*, see Stökl, 'Die Begriffe Reich', pp. 104–18. In the form *gosudarstvo*, state, the link with lordship was lost by the beginning of the seventeenth century.
67. I have used M. [J.F.] Marmontel, *Bélisaire*, nouvelle edition corrigée et augmentée (Paris: chez Merlin, 1769), and Velizer, *Sochinenie Gospodina Marmontella chlena frantsuzskoi akademii*, pereveden na Volge, 3rd printing (Moscow: Pechatana pri Imp. Moskovskom universitete, 1785). Chapter 9, on the nature of absolute monarchy, was translated by Catherine. The Pisa 1769 translation of the *Nakaz* also translated *gosudar'* as *il signore, seigneur*.

absolutist nature of the regime stood out in particularly glaring contrast with the increasing number of European constitutional monarchies, so the previously vague concept of autocracy acquired particularly authoritarian, even arbitrary overtones, and came to be associated almost entirely with Russia. Within Russia, too, *samoderzhavie* came to be regarded as a peculiarly Russian phenomenon, and the word was used increasingly in ordinary speech and writing to refer to 'the government'. This usage has been translated into English, for example, where phrases such as 'the policies of the autocracy' are frequently found.[68] Little by little the concept lost all remaining vestiges of connection with the original idea of independence from a suzerain. As a result a new word had to be coined in Russian to express the concept of sovereignty in relations with other states. It was, as so frequently happened, borrowed from German: *suveren* and *suverenitet*. These foreign loan words are used to express 'sovereignty' to this day.[69] Is it too late now for us to shake off the habit of referring to the Russian tsarist regime as 'the autocracy'?

68. Nowhere is this more clearly seen than in the debate over the Fundamental Law of 1906. Could the *tsar'* remain an autocrat in a constitutional monarchy? If *samoderzhavnyi* is taken to mean sovereign, then the example of the United Kingdom, Spain and other nineteenth-century monarchies showed that he could. For a full discussion of this topic and its history, see M. Szeftel, *The Russian Constitution of April 23, 1906: Political Institution of the Duma Monarchy*, Studies presented to the International Commission for the history of representative and parliamentary institutions (Brussels: Ed. de la Lib. Encyclopédique, 1976).
69. In V. Dal' (*Tolkovyi slovar' zhivago veliko-russkago iazyka*, 2nd ed., 4 vols. [1880–82: rept. Moscow: Gos. izd-vo inostrannykh natsional'nykh slovarei, 1995], IV: P–V), there is no entry for *suveren*. But see *suveren*, 'nositel' verkhovnoi vlasti', and *suverenitet*, 'nezavisimost' i samostoiatel'nost' gosudarstva v ego vnutrennykh i vneshnikh delakh' in the 3rd edition of 1903–09. The following quotation from J. and W. Grimm *Deutsches Wörterbuch* 15 vols. in 24 (Leipzig: S. Hirzel, 1854–1913), is also apposite: '*Selbstherrschaft* . . . ich glaube wir können ein gutes deutsches Wort an die Stelle des fremden Wortes *Volkssouveränetät* [sic] setzen, nämlich das Wort *Selbstherrschaft*'.

CHAPTER THREE

Portrait of an eighteenth-century Russian statesman: Prince Dmitry Mikhaylovich Golitsyn

In this essay I present some reflections on an aspect of Russian history which has always intrigued me, namely the frequency with which political liberty has been sacrificed for the achievement of other, seemingly more pressing, goals such as the strengthening of the state, or social reform, or the interests of a particular social group. I would also like in the process to try to fill out and give depth to the portrait of one of the leading eighteenth-century Russian statesmen about whose role there is still much controversy, namely Prince Dmitry Mikhaylovich Golitsyn. Why have I chosen him? Because he was one of those rare people in Russian history who endeavoured in some way or another to limit the absolute power of the ruler, and paid the penalty.

The subordination of political liberty to other goals occurred already in Muscovite Russia and both Russian and Soviet historians have justified the appalling cruelties of Ivan the Terrible by the need to centralize and unify the state, and to destroy the independent power base on the land of the hereditary aristocracy of birth, that is to say the descendants of sovereign princely houses or of ancient boyar families. Contemporary Western historians do not accept that Ivan actually succeeded in destroying the hereditary aristocracy and the boyar class, which continued long after his reign to be the political élite in Russia, from which tsars were bound to choose their chief ministers. But the political power of this aristocracy was never consolidated since it failed to achieve the inheritance of rank, let alone of position in the state. During the brief reign of Fyodor Alekseyevich (1676–82) and the regency of his sister Sophia (1682–89), Muscovy seemed to incline culturally and even politically towards the example of Poland, but Peter the Great put a stop to such trifling, and turned Russia firmly away from the aristocratic, Catholic, Polonized south to the *Polizeistaat* of the German, Protestant, and indeed Pietistic north.[1] The

Isabel de Madariaga is Professor of Russian Studies at the School of Slavonic and East European Studies, University of London. This paper was delivered as Professor de Madariaga's inaugural address on 11 May 1983.

1. J. Keep, 'The Muscovite Elite and the Approach to Pluralism' (*Slavonic and East European Review*, vol. 48, 1970, pp. 201–31); L. Lewitter, 'Peter the Great, Poland and the Westernization of

ruthless dynamism of Peter may have served to strengthen the conviction that administrative and social reform could only be successfully undertaken by means of the absolute power of the tsar. For many of Peter's contemporaries and successors, change, in the sense of the introduction of a more modern attitude to the exploitation of the human and material resources of Russia, could only be brought about by coercion. This confidence in the power of the tsar to put desirable policies into effect continued throughout imperial Russia – it continues today, though for tsar read party; only the goals change.

In the nineteenth century the 'peculiar' institution of Russia, the existence of which barely aroused comment in the early eighteenth century, began to dominate the thinking of administrators, reformers, and idealists as the influence of the Enlightenment spread through the élite and society as a whole. Under the impact of the French Revolution and the Napoleonic wars two successive generations of young people placed social reform before political liberty and gave priority to the emancipation of the serfs. One need only recall the determination of the young friends of Alexander I to reject all political liberalization so that they might use the power of their friend the tsar to put through the reforms they projected. Similarly among the Decembrists, Pestel' wanted a dictatorship to replace imperial absolutism. More striking still is the attitude of a man who for most of his life was a genuine liberal, namely Nikolay Turgenev. Arguing, sometime between 1810 and 1820, with Admiral Mordvinov, a much-respected relic of the Catherinian age and a fervent admirer of the English political system who declaimed against 'l'immensité du pouvoir imperial', Turgenev exclaimed: 'Moi je m'accomoderai assez de ce pouvoir pourvu qu'il fût employé à delivrer le pays de la monstrueuse exploitation de l'homme par l'homme.'[2] Thus political liberty was always regarded as expendable – in the interests of the centralization of Russia under Ivan the Terrible, of the modernization of Russia under Peter the Great and his successors, and of the emancipation of the serfs in the nineteenth century.

Yet there were always men who reacted against the all-inclusive claims of the absolute ruler or the absolute state, and Russia was not totally insulated against events in other countries. Prince Kurbsky fled to the constitutional political climate of Lithuania; the boyars who invited a Polish prince to become tsar in the Time of Troubles were familiar with Polish constitutional structure and appreciated the political role of the aristocracy in the Polish-Lithuanian Commonwealth. And the members of the Supreme Privy Council led by Prince Dmitry Mikhaylovich Golitsyn who, on the death of Peter II and the extinction of the male Romanov line in January 1730, offered the throne to a woman with no legal claim, Anna of Courland, niece of Peter the Great, imposing on her a number of conditions which would effectively have

Russia' (*Journal of the History of Ideas*, xix, Lancaster, Pennsylvania, October 1958, pp. 493–506). On the connection between Pietism and Absolutism, see the comparative study by M. Fulbrook, 'Religion, Revolution and Absolutist Rule in Germany and in England' (*European Studies Review*, 12, No. 3, July 1982, pp. 290–301), and seminar paper at London School of Economics.

2. N.I. Tourguénieff, *La Russie et les russes*, 3 vols, Paris, 1847, i, pp. 123–4.

turned Russia into a limited monarchy, were familiar with political theories and historical events in the West – but a different West from the West which Peter the Great was busily translating into the Russian context.

What were Dmitry Golitsyn's political aims? What influences was he subjected to? It is not easy to reconstruct the political personality of an eighteenth-century Russian, to make him stand out against the background. It is particularly difficult in Golitsyn's case because there are no biographies; his papers and his library were dispersed after his disgrace. It is difficult to find a portrait of him,[3] he seems almost to have become an unperson, only briefly mentioned in Novikov's *Drevnyaya rossiyskaya vivliofika*.[4] Moreover there is a great dearth of memoirs and letters by prominent Russians until well into the eighteenth century. Many of them were illiterate, and a leading Soviet scholar has recently remarked that after years working in the archives he had not yet found a document written in his own hand by Peter the Great's principal friend and collaborator, Generalissimus Prince A.D. Menshikov.[5] Private papers were usually destroyed as a precautionary measure, and one of the first people to write his memoirs, the diplomat Prince B. Kurakin, felt obliged to ward off accusations of vainglory by pointing out that he was following a practice common among European nobles.[6]

In order to trace Dmitry Golitsyn's political portrait, I shall bring together his own service career, and his policy in the different posts he filled in so far as it can be reconstructed, the opinion in which he was held by contemporaries, the general European setting, and finally what we actually know of his attempt to enact a 'Glorious Revolution' in Russia in 1730.

Golitsyn was born in 1663, fourteenth in descent from Grand Prince Gedimin of Lithuania, and offspring of six successive generations of boyars, the highest court rank in Muscovy. He grew up to manhood in the reigns of Tsar Alexis, Tsar Fyodor and the Regent Sophia, whose lover and minister, Prince V.V. Golitsyn, one of the first great Russian Westernizers, was his first cousin. Dmitry Golitsyn's younger brother Mikhail was a drummerboy in Peter's toy regiment. Little is known of Dmitry's early career, but he survived unscathed the crisis in which Peter I overthrew his sister the regent and exiled Vasily Golitsyn. By 1694 he was a captain in Peter's favourite regiment of the Preobrazhensky

3. There is a portrait in *Ocherki po istorii SSSR, Period feodalizma, Rossiya vo vtoroy chetverti XVIII veka*, Moscow, 1957, p. 251, said to be an engraving by A. Afanas'yev. Professor B.I. Krasnobayev of Moscow University has kindly made inquiries for me in Moscow at the Tret'yakovskaya gallery, and informs me that this is probably a late nineteenth-century imaginary portrait, and the wig belongs to the wrong period. A quite different portrait is reproduced with the article by D.A. Korsakov in 'Sud nad kn. D.M. Golitsynym' (*Drevnyaya i novaya Rossiya*, October 1879, pp. 20–63).

4. Golitsyn is described as a man of great intelligence and strength of character, but no mention is made of the plan of 1730. *Drevnyaya rossiyskaya vivliofika*, ed. by N. Novikov, Moscow, 1791. M.M. Shcherbatov, in his *Corruption of Morals in Russia*, ed. A. Lentin, Cambridge, 1969, pp. 175–95, attributes the initiative in 1730 entirely to the Dolgoruky family and merely remarks that 'Prince Dmitry Mikhaylovich, the most intelligent man of the age' was banished (p. 187).

5. S.P. Luppov, *Kniga v Rossii v pervoy chetverti XVIII veka*, Leningrad, 1973, p. 230.

6. *Arkhiv knyazya F.A. Kurakina*, ed. M.I. Semevsky, 3 vols, St Petersburg, 1890, I, p. 246.

Guards, and therefore presumably in the young tsar's good graces. At the age of thirty-four he was chosen in 1697 to go with a group of other aristocrats to study navigation abroad. Prince Dmitry's party was sent to Venice and spent some eighteen months in Italy. These very mature naval apprentices – all in their mid-thirties – spent much time at sea and learnt sailing by sailing in the best Wackford Squeers tradition. But they also visited Rome and Naples, and studied, as another of them, Prince Kurakin, has recorded, mathematics, navigation, astronomy, mechanics, defensive and offensive fortifications and Italian and received a certificate signed by the Doge of Venice to that effect.[7] We can assume that Golitsyn felt some interest in the political life and in the luxurious and sophisticated cultural life of the Venetian Republic – it was the great age of Vivaldi. After a brief diplomatic and military career, Golitsyn was appointed in 1707 voyevoda and later governor of Kiev and lieutenant of Smolensk. This was an extremely sensitive post, since the governor had to deal with supplies to the armed forces before and after the battle of Poltava, in 1709, and to steer his way through the upheaval in the Ukraine caused by the defection of Hetman Mazeppa to Charles XII of Sweden.

Kiev until 1654 had formed part of Catholic Poland, and was wide open to Latin, Roman, and Catholic influence. The whole area was permeated with traditional Polish political culture and the law was based on the various Lithuanian Statutes. In the early eighteenth century Kiev was the intellectual capital of Russia. Graduates of the Kievan Academy filled the highest ecclesiastical posts, and were responsible for most of the translations from the classics, from French, or from Polish, which were published on the best printing presses in Russia, at Kiev and Chernigov.[8] We may fairly assume that Golitsyn learnt a lot about Polish political culture during his eleven years as governor in Kiev. We know that he gathered a number of scholars around him to indulge in intellectual discourse, and that sometimes on his own initiative, sometimes at Peter's request, he arranged for translations of important works to be made by students at the Academy. Among those which have survived in manuscript from his library were translations of Aristotle's *Politics*, Grotius's *De jure pacis et belli*, Pufendorf's *De jure naturae et gentium*, the *Political Testament* of Richelieu and Locke's *Treatise on Civil Government.*[9]

During his stay in Kiev Golitsyn knew Feofan Prokopovich, who as bishop of Pskov was to become the architect of Peter's church reform, and author of the *Spiritual Regulations*. But in later life a degree of hostility grew up between them. Feofan Prokopovich was a forceful exponent of the supremacy of the state over the church, of which Peter had heard so much good from the lips

7. Ibid., p. 255. See also M. Okenfuss, 'Russian Students in Europe in the Age of Peter the Great' in J. Garrard, ed., *The Eighteenth Century in Russia*, Oxford, 1973, pp. 131–48.
8. M.N. Bantysh Kamensky, *Istoriya Maloy Rossii*, 3rd edn, 3 vols, Moscow, 1842, p. 229.
9. A. Lappo-Danilevsky, 'L'Idée de l'Etat et son évolution en Russie, depuis les troubles du XVIIe siècle jusqu' aux reformes du XVIIIe' in P. Vinogradoff, ed., *Essays in Legal History*, Oxford, 1913, pp. 372ff.; P. Pekarsky, *Nauka i literatura v Rossii pri Petre Velikom*, 2 vols, St Petersburg, 1862, I, p. 257 discusses some of the activities of Golitsyn as governor of Kiev, and his reputation as a *rachitel' premudrosti* (patron of wisdom).

of the English Bishop Burnet, a view Golitsyn did not share. In later years, Golitsyn agreed – with some reservations – to the publication in 1728 of the work by Metropolitan Stefan Yavorsky, entitled *The Rock of Faith*, a hitherto banned and extremely controversial attack on Protestantism and, incidentally, on Feofan Prokopovich, and a veiled exposition of the Catholic doctrine of the two powers, of the superiority of the spiritual power of the church over secular authority.[10]

Golitsyn's correspondence with the Hetman of the Ukraine, Skoropadsky, appointed by Peter I after the defeat of the traitor Mazeppa, shows him to be efficient, tactful towards Ukrainian sensibilities and respectful of their liberties.[11] His letters are, incidentally, written in incisive Russian, free from bureaucratic jargon – though it must be said that some letters to Menshikov show him to be perfectly capable of self-abasement and flattery of the all powerful *patron* as Menshikov was called.[12] The Golitsyn family had estates in the Ukraine and was popular there, and one may perhaps see a gesture of sympathy towards Ukrainian traditions in the restoration of the hetmanate in 1728 after it had been abolished by Peter in 1722. In common with most of the high ranks of the armed forces and the bureaucracy, Golitsyn signed the condemnation for treason of Peter's son, Aleksey, in 1717. In 1719 he was appointed to Peter's new College of Revenues, an appointment which put him in touch with Heinrich Fick.

Fick was a Holsteiner, who had been sent by Peter on a clandestine mission into Sweden to study Swedish administrative structures and procedures. He succeeded in smuggling out quantities of printed and manuscript materials, some of them sewn into his wife's skirts, because these matters were regarded as state secrets in Sweden. Later Fick played an important part in the preparation of Peter's administrative reforms, and was appointed one of the councillors on the board of the College of Revenues. Many of the Swedish documents he brought were translated for Golitsyn, and the two men became friends, so much so that the condescension of the haughty Golitsyn towards the obscure Holsteiner aroused comment. Fick wrote several memoranda on the structure of the Russian government, using his knowledge of past and present Swedish constitutional forms, and recommended setting up an efficient policy-making body which he called by the prophetic name of Supreme Privy Council (Hohes Geheimes Conseil), possibly modelled on the Swedish Council or Riksråd.[13] In 1723 Dmitry Golitsyn was marginally implicated in the disgrace of Baron Shafirov, the Vice-Chancellor, placed under house arrest and fined. He must

10. I. Chistovich, 'Feofan Prokopovich i ego vremya' in *Sbornik statey chitannykh v Otdelenii russkogo yazyka i slovesnosti Imperatorskoy Akademii nauk*, vol. IV, St Petersburg, 1868, pp. 607ff.
11. M. Sudyenko, *Materialy dlya otechestvennoy istorii*, vol. 2, Kiev, 1855, *Pis'ma k getmanu Skoropadskomu*, *passim*.
12. S.M. Solov'yov, *Istoriya Rossii s drevneyshikh vremyon*, 17 vols, reprinted Moscow, 1963, vol. IX, pp. 632–3.
13. C. Petersen, *Peter the Great's Administrative and Judicial Reforms*, Stockholm, 1981, pp. 71ff. See also P.M. Milyukov, *Gosudarstvennoye khozyaystvo v Rossii, v pervoy chetverti 18–go stoletiya i reforma Petra Velikogo*, St Petersburg, 1892, p. 675.

have found it deeply humiliating to owe his release to the intercession of Peter's wife Catherine, the servant-girl who had passed through several hands before she became Peter's mistress and, after his death, the Empress Catherine I.[14] In 1726 Golitsyn was appointed to the Supreme Privy Council which took over the government of Russia during the reign of Peter's widow, and acted as a Regency Council for Peter II.

What was Golitsyn like as a man? All the foreign envoys in Russia during the 1720s speak highly of him. Rondeau, the English resident, describes him as 'possessed of singular abilities improved by art and experience' and as 'having an active mind, of deep foresight and penetration, with a solid judgement surpassing all men in the knowledge of the Russian laws, and a manly eloquence, of a bold and enterprising genius, full of ambition and artifice, remarkably sober but in his temper cruel and implacable. The clergy and common people have him in the highest veneration; but he is rather feared than beloved by the lower nobility. In short no man is more capable than he, nor any more inclined to raise and conduct a rebellion in the Russian empire.'[15] The Swedish envoy, H. Cedercreutz, describes him as 'coarse and hard but understanding and just . . . and the one who understands domestic affairs best of all'.[16] The Spanish envoy, the Duke of Liria, added that he was 'a man of good understanding, subtle mind, insufferable vanity and unequalled arrogance'.[17] Certainly Golitsyn behaved like an old-style aristocrat, maintaining traditions common throughout Europe at the time. Since he was the head of the family, his younger brothers, including the Field Marshal, Mikhail Mikhaylovich the elder, the most distinguished Russian soldier of the age, did not presume to sit in his presence until invited. Prayers were said in his house every day, and even the tsar was kept waiting until they were over if he called while the prince was at prayer.[18] Prince Golitsyn's portraits show him however in stylish western dress, with a sharp thin face, bold nose, and no trace of the old boyar about him.[19]

More to the point, Dmitry Golitsyn had one of the best private libraries of eighteenth-century Russia, of which two incomplete lists have survived. It was a library of some 2,600 books, composed of political, economic, historical and legal works, in which literature, poetry and science played a less important part. It included, of course, the classics: Tacitus, Livy, Suetonius. There were histories of Henri IV, Louis XIII, Elizabeth of England; travellers' accounts of Russia such as those by Olearius, Possevino, and Perry. There

14. F.W. von Bergholz, *Dnevnik kameryunkera F.V. Berkhol' tsa, 1721–25*, translated by I.F. Ammon, 3 vols, Moscow, 1860, II, p. 33.
15. *Sbornik Imperatorskogo russkogo istoricheskogo obshchestva* (quoted in future as *SIRIO*), vol. 66, St Petersburg, p. 159: C. Rondeau, Appendix to letter of 26 February 1730 (OS) to Lord Townshend.
16. Petersen, *op. cit.*, p. 77, n. 159.
17. James Fitzjames Stuart, Duke of Liria, 'Diario del Viaje a Moscovia del Duque de Liria y Xerica' in *Colección de documentos inéditos para la historia de España*, vol. 93, Madrid, 1889, p. 364.
18. See *Mémoires du Prince Pierre Dolgoroukow*, 2 vols, I, Cherbuliez, Geneva, 1867, II, H. Georg, Geneva, 1871. The value of Dolgorukov's *Mémoires* as a historical source is discussed in D.A. Korsakov, *Votsareniye imperatritsy Anny Ioannovny*, Kazan', 1880, pp. xxxvi.
19. But see above, n. 3.

were works on diplomacy, collections of treaties, handbooks of court ceremonial. Golitsyn subscribed to nearly all the periodicals published in France and Holland, notably *Le Journal des Savants*, *Les Nouvelles de la République des Lettres*, the journal of the freethinker Pierre Bayle, *La Clef du Cabinet des Princes de l'Europe*, *Le Mercure Historique et Politique*. On a lighter note, we may add that he had twenty books on gardening, for he was one of the first owners of succession houses in Russia.[20]

The bulk of Golitsyn's collection was in French, a more congenial language than German. Next in number came Russian books, totalling 682, of which more than half are dismissed by the Soviet historian Luppov as of no interest since they deal with religion.[21] They include St Augustine's *City of God*, and the *Imitation of Christ* of Thomas à Kempis. The secular works include Prince Kurbsky's *Letters* to Ivan the Terrible, and his *History of Muscovy*.

More interesting for my present purpose is the content of the political library of Dmitry Golitsyn. The list is of course not complete, so unfortunately we cannot deduce any preferences from it, we can only obtain a general picture of the range of his interests. He possessed the complete works of Machiavelli in Italian, doubtless picked up in Italy, and also the more rare *Ragguagli del Parnaso* of the Italian satirist, Trajano Boccalini.[22] In this work, published in 1613, parts of which were later seized on by the Rosicrucian Enlightenment in Central Europe,[23] the community of statesmen, scholars, and wise men gathered in Parnassus and ruled over by Apollo meet to discuss the woes of the world and how to set them right. The satire is biting and can be read with pleasure even today. The villain of the piece is usually the Spanish monarch (Boccalini was profoundly opposed to Spanish hegemony in Italy),

20. N.N. Golitsyn, 'Novyye dannyye o biblioteke D.M. Golitsyna (verkhovnika)', in *Chteniya v Imperatorskom Obshchestve istorii i drevnostey rossiyskikh pri Moskovskom universitete*, 1900, No. 4, pp. 1–16.

21. Luppov, *op. cit.*, p. 219. See also V. Yu. Poresh, 'Knyaz′ D.M. Golitsyn (verkhovnik) i frantsuzskiye knigi ego biblioteki' in A.I. Kopanev, S.P. Luppov *et al.*, *Knigopechataniye i knizhnyye sobraniya v Rossii do serediny XIX v.: Sbornik nauchnykh trudov*, Leningrad, 1979, pp. 98–111. I am grateful to Dr W. Ryan for drawing my attention to this article. References to the presence of specific works in Golitsyn's library are all drawn from one or other of the articles by N.N. Golitsyn (see n. 20), Luppov and Poresh.

22. T. Boccalini, *Ragguagli del Parnaso*, Venice, 1612–13. See L. Galeotti, 'Trajano Boccalini e il suo tempo' in *Archivio storico italiano*, nuova serie, tomo primo, parte 2ª, Florence, 1855, pp. 119–62. The *Ragguagli* are divided into the first and the second 'centuries', each containing 100 'advertisements' and a posthumous third part entitled *Pietra del paragone politico* (1615) of thirty-one advertisements. I have used the English translation of 1656: *I Ragguagli di Parnasso or Advertisements from Parnassus in Two Centuries with the Politick Touchstone written originally in Italian by that famous Roman Trajano Boccalini and now put into English by the Right Honourable Henry Earl of Monmouth*, London, printed for *Humphrey Moseley* at the Prince's Arms in *St Paul's* church-yard and *Thomas Heath* in Russel-Street near the Piazza of Covent Garden, 1656. The *Ragguagli* were an important source for James Harrington's *Oceana*.

23. On the translations of Boccalini, see Luigi Firpo, *Traduzioni dei Ragguagli di Traiano Boccalini*, Florence, 1965. A German translation of one of the advertisements, in which Apollo proposes a general reformation of the world (I, no. 77, pp. 146–62 in the Monmouth translation) was published with the first edition of the Rosicrucian manifesto known as the *Fama Fraternitatis* (see F. Yates, *The Rosicrucian Enlightenment*, London, 1975, pp. 72ff., and for the full text, Appendix, pp. 279ff.).

but the ruler of Muscovy did not come off very well on the only occasion in which he took part in the debates on Parnassus. He was accused of leaving his subjects to be brought up in gross ignorance and scoffed at for having banished the liberal arts from Muscovy, leaving only reading and writing. He replied that the hideous fire to which learning gives rise had determined him not to allow so scandalous a cockle to be sown in his dominions. For 'learning did infinitely hinder good government of states and the prince might with more ease command a million of idiots'.[24]

Golitsyn was particularly interested in the history of the rise and fall of institutions, in changes of regimes and governments, in what, in his own time, was known as 'revolutions'. A few titles illustrate this topic: *De la naissance, durée et chute des états* (Paris, 1588); *Histoire de la dernière révolution de Perse*; Fontenelle, *Histoire des révolutions de Suède* (1696); *Histoire de la rebellion et des guerres civiles en Angleterre.*[25] He had a large collection of works on Polish history and constitutional structure, and on English political theory and party politics, sometimes in French translations difficult to identify. Locke was well represented; but it is more surprising to find Algernon Sidney's *Discourse on Government* in the French translation of 1702.[26] The History of Whigs and Tories[27] by Rapin-Thoyras was there as well as that by Emmanuel de Cize.[28] Three works dealt with the power of Parliament: in matters of religion as in Andrew Marvell's *Relation de l'accroissement de la Papauté et du gouvernment absolu en Angleterre*;[29] in foreign affairs, as in C. Davenant's *Essay upon the Ballance of Power*,[30] which attacked the right of the king to decide on war and peace without Parliament; and in matters of the succession, such as *Histoire du droit des parlements de la*

24. *Ragguagli*, Monmouth translation, p. 446. A translation of the *Pietra del paragone politico* entitled *Kamen' opyta politicheskogo* figured among manuscript translations in Golitsyn's library. See N.A. Popov, *Tatishchev i ego vremya*, Moscow, 1961, pp. 94–5.

25. Poresh, *op. cit.*, p. 109 gives no further details of the first work nor is the second identifiable. I have not been able to find a work by Fontenelle on revolutions in Sweden. The history of the English Civil War, by 'Edwards', is evidently the *Histoire de la rebellion et des guerres civiles en Angleterre depuis 1641 jusqu'au rétablissement du roi Charles II par Edward Comte de Clarendon*, 6 vols, The Hague, 1704, 1709.

26. *Discours sur le gouvernement* par Algernon Sidney Fils de Robert Comte de Leicester et ambassadeur de la republique d'Angleterre près de Charles Gustave roi de Suède, traduit de l'anglois par P.A. Samson. A la Haye chez Louis et Henri van Dole, 1702.

27. Paul Rapin-Thoyras, *Dissertation sur les Whigs et les Torys*, A la Haye chez Charles Le Vier, libraire dans le Spuystraet, 1717.

28. Emmanuel de Cize, *Histoire du Whigisme et du Torisme* composée par Mr de Cize cy-devant officier au service d'Angleterre. A Leipzig, imprimée par Andre Zeidler et se trouve à Amsterdam chez Jean Frederic Bernard, 1717. This work was dedicated to Count Flemming who was Chief Minister to Augustus of Saxony-Poland, which may explain why it came to Golitsyn's notice.

29. *Relation de l'accroissement de la Papauté et du gouvernement absolu en Angleterre particulièrement depuis la longue prorogation de novembre 1675.* Traduit en français de la copie anglaise, Hamburg, 1680. Translated from A. Marvell, *An Account of the Growth of Popery and Arbitrary Government in England, more particularly from the Long Prorogation of November 1675 ending the 15th of February 1676 till the Last Meeting of Parliament, the 16th of July 1677*, Amsterdam, 1677. I must thank Mr Graham Gibbs for his help in tracing some of these English works.

30. C. Davenant, *Essays upon I the Ballance of Power; II The Right of Making War, Peace and Alliance; III Universal Monarchy*, London, printed for James Knapton at the *Crown* in *St Paul's* churchyard, 1701.

Grande Bretagne touchant la succession à la couronne.[31] Golitsyn also possessed a copy of a work published anonymously in a French translation in 1714, *Traité du pouvoir des rois de la Grande Bretagne.*[32] This work was an extremely forceful exposition of the contract theory of government: '. . . no government is lawful but what is founded upon Compact and Agreement between those chosen to govern and those who condescend to be governed'; 'The Power that is lodged in the Crown is only a trust and nothing more . . .'. It is also a powerful attack on the doctrine of passive obedience which 'is a Treasonable Doctrine by being an Encouragement to Rebellion, Usurpation and Tyranny'. It defends the right of Parliament to alter the succession, defends elective monarchy and

31. *Histoire du droit des parlements de la Grande Bretagne touchant à la succession à la couronne* (1715). I have found no work with exactly this title in the catalogue of the British Library, in Ascoli (see n. 32) or in W. Morgan, *A Bibliography of British History, 1700–1715*, 5 vols, Bloomington, Indiana, 1934. But it may be either a translation of the anonymous work (by Sir John Willes) entitled *The Present Constitution and the Protestant Succession Vindicated*, in answer to a book by G. Harbin, or the book by G. Harbin which appeared in French as *Histoire succincte de la Succession à la Couronne de Grande Bretagne depuis le commencement de la monarchie jusqu'à present*, 1714.

32. The full title of this work is: *Traité du pouvoir des rois de la Grande Bretagne, où l'on fait voir quel a été de tout temps le gouvernement monarchique et où l'on justifie par les autorités des anciens et des modernes les principes qui ont causé la revolution en 1689*. Traduit de l'anglais, Amsterdam, 1714, chez Jean Frederick Bernard. According to G. Ascoli, *La Grande Bretagne devant l'opinion française au XVII*[e] *Siècle*, 3 vols, Paris, 1930, II, pp. 247, its author was either J. Dunton or Daniel Defoe, but I was unable to find a probable English original in the lists of their works. I have not been able to find a copy of the French version, which does not figure in the catalogue of the Bibliothèque nationale, but some quotations from the French text show it to be the anonymous English work entitled *Vox Populi Vox Dei*: 'being true maxims of Government, proving I that all Kings, Governours and Forms of Government proceed from the People II The Nature of our Constitution is fairly stated with the Original Contract between King and People and a Journal of the late Revolution III That Resisting a Tyrannical Power is allow'd by Scripture and Reason IV That the Children of Israel did often resist and turn Out their Evil Princes and that God Almighty did approve of Resistance V That the Primitive Christians did often resist their Tyrannical Emperors, and that Bishop Athanasius, St Chrysostom, Luther and Melancthon did approve of Resistance VI that the Protestants in all Ages did resist their evil and destructive Princes VII Together with a Historical Account of the depriving of Kings for their Evil Government in Israel, France, Spain, Scotland &c and in England before and since the Conquest VIII That Absolute Passive-Obedience is a Damnable and Treasonable Doctrine, By contradicting the glorious Attributes of God, and incouraging of Rebellion, Usurpation and Tyranny. To which no answer will be made or can be made without Treason, not to be behind Mr. Lesley or any Jacobite in Assurance.' London, printed for the author and are to be sold by *T. Harrison* at the West Corner of the *Royal Exchange* in *Cornhill*, where is to be sold above Two Hundred and Forty sorts of Penny, Two-penny and Three-penny sermons, with good allowance to them that buy a quantity for Charity; where is likewise Sold the finest *Brasil* Snuff for Colour and Flavour, and all other sorts of Snuff at very reasonable Rates 1709 Price Three Pence.

This work is also known under the title: *The Judgment of Whole Kingdoms and Nations Concerning the Rights, Power and Prerogative of Kings and the Rights, Privileges and Properties of the People*, London, 1710. According to C. Robbins, *The Eighteenth-Century Commonwealthman*, Cambridge, Mass., 1959, p. 80, n. 47, eleven editions appeared before 1717, the tenth edition 'corrected' was published again in 1771 and a further edition appeared in Philadelphia in 1773. According to Morgan, *op. cit.*, II, p. 69, there is a marginal note in the copy belonging to the library at Bloomington, Indiana, to the effect that this work has been attributed 'to Lord Somers, J. Dunton, Charles Powey, Daniel Defoe and T. Harrison (the publisher). Harrison is the most likely.' But C. Robbins, *op. cit.*, p. 79, attributes it definitely to Lord Somers. For its influence on Diderot, see Denis Diderot, *Oeuvres politiques*, ed. by Paul Vernière, Paris, 1963, pp. 9–20; Vernière quotes from the French text of *Du Pouvoir* on pp. 10, n. 2, 11, n. 1, 13, n. 1, and 15, n. 1. The English equivalents are on pp. 4, 35 and 11 of *Vox Populi.*

declares that 'Absolute Monarchy is inconsistent with Civil Society'. It was this work which was one of the sources of Diderot's article on 'Autorité politique' in the *Encyclopédie*, and which nearly led to its being banned in 1753. Clearly it could be regarded as highly seditious in a Russian context, and its presence in Golitsyn's library casts a revealing light on his interest in the literature of limited monarchy.

The section of Golitsyn's library dealing with French political thought included of course the major exponents of the French theory of sovereignty, such as Bodin and Loyseau, and of French absolutism, such as Cardin Le Bret.[33] His interest in economic affairs may account for the presence of one of the most unusual early seventeenth-century French works, namely the *Traicté de l'œconomie politique* by the poet Antoine de Montchrétien,[34] said, incidentally, to be the first occasion on which the phrase *économie politique* is used in its modern sense. It is a work with an astonishingly modern ring, favouring the setting up of schools, the division of labour, more equal taxation, reciprocal free trade and protection for necessities. Among later French exponents of the *Polizeistaat*, there was the great work by Nicolas de la Mare, *Traité de la police*.[35]

As one might expect, Golitsyn's library contained many sixteenth- and seventeenth-century works on heraldry, genealogy and on the estate of the nobility, its origins and its rights.[36] The most original is the *Trois traictez*[37] by Florentin Thierriat. He quotes Plato to explain natural inequality of birth: some men are of gold, others of silver, yet others of lead. The three metals represent those who command, those who advise (presumably with silver tongues) and those who remain bound down to the soil. Unlike most authors on this difficult subject, Thierriat does actually tackle the awkward problem of the origins of nobility, the moment when base clay was first transmuted into gold. Some authors, he explains, argue that nobility proceeds from the creation of the angels. Others state that the first nobles were Cain and Abel, but Cain lost his nobility when he killed his brother. The angels kept nobility alive during the flood, when it was transmitted by Noah to Shem, Ham and Japhet, but Ham

33. There are several editions of Cardin Le Bret's *De la Souveraineté*, and it is not clear which was in D.M. Golitsyn's library. On him see G. Picot, *Cardin Le Bret (1558–1655) et la Souveraineté*, Société d'impression typographique, Nancy, 1948. In general, see H. Sée, *Les Idées politiques en France au XVIIe siècle*, Paris, 1923.

34. *Traicté de l'oeconomie politique dedié en 1615 au Roy et à la Reyne mère du Roy*, ed. Th. Funck Brentano, Paris, 1889.

35. Nicolas de la Mare, *Traité de la police*, 4 vols, Paris, 1713.

36. E.g. Phillip Jacob Spener, *Insignium seu Operis Heraldici pars generalis quae circa insignia, horum, originem, scuta eorumque partitiones, metalla, colores, figuras, galeas, apices aliasque scutorum appendices et consectaria studioso historiarum et vitae civilis nosse proficuum visum et.* Francofortie ad Moenum Sumptibus Joannis Davidis Zunneri, Anno MDCXC.

37. Florentin de Thierriat, *Trois Traictez scavoir 1) De la Noblesse de Race; 2) De la Noblesse Civille; 3) Des Immunitez des Ignobles esquesl toutes les questions touchant les exemptions, Immunitez & autres Droicts des Nobles et Ignobles sont redigées en un bel Ordre et decidées par la Conference du Droit Civil, Romain, des Saincts Canons, Ordonnances Royaux, Arrests des Cours Souveraines, Coustumes particulieres des Provinces de France, selon les opinions des Iurisconsultes tants anciens que modernes*, Dediez à Prince Henry, fils de M. François fils de Lorraine Comte de Vaudemont etc. A Paris chez Lucas Bruneau rue S. Jean de Latran à la Salamandre, D.DCVI.

lost his by his evil life, and his descendants became slaves. Nobility, Thierriat explains, 'plus elle vieillit plus elle est excellente'. The origin of the best nobility is lost in the mists of time. Thierriat is also very picturesque on the rights of nobles who must be better treated in gaol and have more sumptuous funerals than the ignoble. Nobles can of course indulge in intellectual pursuits, though sculpture and painting are somewhat more menial than poetry. But mere versifiers, rhymesters with a shameful Muse, are classed as ignoble, together with executioners. Ploughing is also permissible because Adam ploughed.

For a man belonging to a country in which the aristocracy seemed to be suffering from dilution by promotion in accordance with Peter's Table of Ranks, it must have been of some comfort to see how widespread ennoblement by promotion was. Nearly all the manuals in Golitsyn's library which I have been able to consult stress the basic division between the nobility of birth – *de race* – and nobility by royal grant or promotion. As Gilles de la Roque put it in 1678: 'celuy qui est annobli acquiert la noblesse mais non pas la race',[38] a phrase which almost echoes the contemporary Russian saying: 'tsar' zhaluyet chinom no ne rodom'. Jacques de Caillières in *La Fortune des gens de qualité* (1664)[39] argues from a different point of view that a monarchy is better for the nobility than an aristocracy, for aristocrats owe their fortune to their birth alone; if they rise it is because of the antiquity of their race, rather than by virtue. Whereas in a monarchy kings can raise whom they please, and by rewarding courageous actions they encourage their subjects to compete in virtue. Gilles de la Roque, from whom I quoted earlier, states that in Dauphiné twenty years' service in specific offices automatically entitled the office-holder to ennoblement. It is perhaps this possibility of ennoblement on the grounds of office which explains why the English aristocracy looked down on the French nobility as a service class.[40]

38. Gilles André de la Roque, *Traité de la Noblesse, de ses differentes espèces, de son origine, du Gentilhomme de Nom et d'Armes, des Bannerets, des Bacheliers, des Ecuyers et de leurs differences: Du Gentilhomme de Quatre Lignes; du Noble de Race: de la Noblesse paternelle et de la maternelle; de la Noblesse par Adoption; de l'Origine des Fiefs; Que les premiers nobles ont esté faits l'investiture qu'ils en ont reçue: De la Noblesse par Chevalerie; des Anoblissements par lettres et de leurs differences; Des Charges et des Privilèges qui anoblissent: Des Derogeances à la Noblesse: Des Rehabilitations: Des Dignités Ecclesiastiques et Seculieres; Des Ordres de Chevalerie: De la Noblesse d'Angleterre, d'Espagne, de Portugal, d'Allemagne, de Hongrie, d'Italie, de Pologne, de Suede, de Danemark, des Pais-Bas etc.* A Paris chez Etienne Michelet, ruë Saint Jacques à l'Image Saint Paul près la Fontaine Saint Severin, MDCLXXVIII.

39. J. de Caillères, *La Fortune des gens de qualité et des gentilshommes particuliers – Enseignant l'art de vivre a la Cour suivant les maximes de la Politique et de la Morale*, A Paris chez Estienne Loyson, au Palais à l'entrée de la Galerie des Prisonniers, au Nom de Jesus, M.DC.LXIV.

40. Gilles de la Roque, *op. cit.* See also J.G.A. Pocock, *The Machiavellian Moment*, Princeton, N.J., 1975, p. 413. Among Golitsyn's books was also one of the many editions of R.P. François Menestrier de la Compagnie de Jesus, *Le Blason de la noblesse ou les preuves de noblesse de toutes les nations de l'Europe*. The edition I have used is that of 1683, A Paris, chez Robert J.B. de la Caille, rue St Jacques, aux trois Cailles, MDCLXXXIII. Menestrier discusses the nobles of all European countries except Muscovy. He quotes a Spanish saying which with typical realism defines nobility in a nutshell:

Las letras y las armas dan Nobleza
Consérvala el valor y la riqueza.

Not one of these French treatises on the nobility goes into the question of the role and the rights of the noble order in the state, that is to say the political function of an élite. This is typical of the general French outlook at the time, which moved only slowly away from the idea that noble privilege consisted in being exempt from government duties to the idea that noble privilege consisted in monopolizing political power in the state. The transition has been dated to the personal rule of Louis XIV which aroused the aristocracy to the dangers of personal despotism.[41] Since we have no complete lists of Golitsyn's library we cannot tell whether he was familiar with the thought of the circles around Fénélon and the Duke of Burgundy. However, Fénélon's *Télémaque* is listed among his books and also a work entitled 'l'Éducation des dames'. This might possibly be Fénélon's *De l'éducation des filles*, but it is scathingly dismissed by the nineteenth-century author of the article in which it is mentioned, who obviously misunderstood its nature; 'this section', he explains, 'does not interest us'.[42]

I would like now to turn briefly to the European background and to the political consequences of succession crises. It would be a mistake to assume that thrones were everywhere and always inherited according to immutable laws of primogeniture. Expediency had frequently overruled law and custom, and where there was no Salic Law, the succession of women often gave rise to legal uncertainty. During the period running from 1688 to 1730 there were several distinct deviations from the norm, involving women. There was first of all the expulsion of James II of England and the offer of the throne by Parliament to his daughter Mary, jointly with her husband. But the Commons, or, in the picturesque language of an earlier Russian envoy to England, 'starosty mirskikh lyudey vsekh gorodov',[43] had insisted that they ought first to 'secure the rights, laws and liberties of the nation', and imposed on the rulers thirteen points or 'conditions', known in English as the Bill of Rights. These covered the rights of Parliament and parliamentary control over the armed forces, justice, and taxation.

Chronologically, the next episode which might have attracted the attention of Golitsyn occurred in connection with the succession not of a woman but of a minor, with a regency. I refer to the accession of Louis XV of France, and the curiously futile attempt of a group of French aristocrats to put into effect that form of government by aristocratic councils which had been preached in the coterie surrounding the Duke of Burgundy, and which goes under the name of Polysynodie. It failed dismally, but the principle might still be valid. The men, not the measures, had been found wanting.

41. On political trends among French nobles at this period I have drawn on R. Mettam, *The Role of the Higher Aristocracy in France under Louis XIV* (Unpublished Ph.D. Thesis, University of Cambridge) and a seminar paper on 'From Social Élite to Political Élite' given at the Institute of Historical Research, London University, in May 1982.

42. N.N. Golitsyn, *op. cit.*

43. Quoted from a dispatch by A. Vinnius in E.P. Karnovich, 'Zamysly verkhovnikov i chelobitchikov v 1730 godu' (*Otechestvennyye zapiski*, St Petersburg, 1872, vol. CXIX, otd. I, pp. 209–37, 485–516, at pp. 224–5).

Then, in 1718, just over the border from Russia, Charles XII of Sweden was killed on the battlefield. On the extinction of the male line of the Vasas, the order of succession became uncertain. The Swedish governing class, in this case the army, reacting against the despotism of Charles XII, promptly proclaimed his younger sister Ulrike Eleonora, Princess of Hesse, instead of the son of his deceased elder sister, the Duke of Holstein. As soon as Ulrike Eleonora received the news from her husband who was with the Swedish army on the Norwegian border, she irrupted into the Council Chamber in Stockholm and declared that the armed forces had proclaimed her queen. The Council accepted her, on condition that she gave up 'the hated sovereignty', as Swedish absolutism was described in the current vocabulary. Indeed, in order to forestall any move by the Duke of Holstein, Ulrike Eleonora agreed even to abandon any *hereditary* claim to the throne, and to rely only on her election by the Estates as Queen of Sweden. Her declaration of 26 December 1718 was soon followed by her abdication in favour of her husband Frederick of Hesse, and finally, in May 1720, the new Swedish 'form of government' was sworn by Frederick: it consisted of forty-eight conditions, which set out the terms of his rule.[44] One other case of doubtful succession must have made a strong impact in Russia, namely the efforts of the Holy Roman Emperor, Charles VI, to secure the Habsburg inheritance to his daughter Maria Theresia, first cousin of the young tsar Peter II, by means of the Pragmatic Sanction, to which Russia acceded in 1726. Here, too, 'in-house' legislation and international treaties were being called in to modify the existing order in favour of the succession of a woman.[45]

The drama of the Russian succession crises of 1725, 1727 and 1730 must be seen against this background. Twice the opportunity had been taken of the choice of a queen, whose title was not incontrovertible, to impose limitations on the power of the crown. Would the lesson be learnt in Russia?

The death of Peter I in 1725 led to a significant weakening of the central power and the Supreme Privy Council proceeded to fill the vacuum. Soon the foreign envoys sensed a diminution in the absolute power of the crown. They began to detect the existence of a so-called 'Old Russian' or 'boyar' party, which sought to 'reduce the despotic power of the crown' or 'to model itself on the Swedes' or on 'the English system'.[46] This suspicion was reinforced when it was observed that in the oath of allegiance of the privy councillors

44. See in general C. Nordman, *Grandeur et liberté de la Suède (1660–1972)*, Editions Nauwelaerts, Paris/Louvain, 1971. For a contemporary account, see *An Account of Sweden*, 4th edn, 1728, printer for Tho Longman at the sign of the Ship in Paternoster row. The full text of the Constitution of May 1720 is in British Library Kings MS, 187, Swedish Act of Government. See also P.H. Mallet, *Forme du Gouvernement de Suède, avec quelques autres pièces concernant le droit public de ce royaume traduits en françois sur les originaux Suèdois Imprimés pour la dernière fois à Stockholm en 1755, par ordre des Etats*. A Copenhague, à Genève chez les Freres Philibert MDCCLVI, de l'imprimerie de Ludolphe-Henri Lillïe.

45. The death of Charles II of Spain in 1700 opened up a disputed succession through the female line. The question was ultimately decided by war, not by law or treaties.

46. *SIRIO*, vol. 64, pp. 172ff.: Campredon (French envoy) to the King, 3 January 1726, p. 187; 15 January 1726, pp. 199ff.

to Catherine I, she was not called 'samoderzhitsa' or sovereign.[47] There is also a great deal of evidence that the Supreme Privy Council tried to lighten the burden of Peter's heritage; it set up a special commission under Dmitry Golitsyn to re-examine Peter's taxation policy together with representatives of the nobility and the towns. It dismantled the expensive local government system.[48] The restoration of the Hetmanate in the Ukraine and attempts to restore the patriarchate are further evidence of a reversal of Peter's policies. Most revealing is the breach opened by the Supreme Privy Council in Peter's system of precedence, the Table of Ranks, by decreeing that members of the Supreme Privy Council should take precedence over full generals, that is to say that civilians should take precedence over the military. Membership of a political institution was for the first time to confer a higher status than service rank.[49]

Membership of the Supreme Privy Council had moreover under Peter II become almost totally aristocratic. Only Count Osterman, in charge of foreign affairs, remained of those who had risen under Peter I. This was not entirely due to disagreements over policy, but to the personal choice of the young Peter II, and to his decision to eliminate all those who had taken a leading part in the condemnation of his father for treason in 1717. The young emperor had filled the Council with members of the aristocratic Dolgoruky family, one of whom was to play a part second only to that of Dmitry Golitsyn in the crisis. This was Vasily Lukich Dolgoruky, who had spent most of his life in diplomatic posts abroad, in France, Poland, Denmark, and Sweden, and who was therefore well acquainted with modern political literature, and with the operation of limited monarchy in Poland and Sweden.

However, it would be misleading to assume that the 'Old Russian' party wished for a total rejection of Peter's westernizing programme. Field Marshal Mikhail Golitsyn, who acted with his brother throughout, confided to the Swedish envoy during the crisis that absolutism had never been so powerful anywhere as in Russia; people were executed, exiled or robbed of their estates without any warning. This was not to happen in the future, he added. On the contrary unnecessary expenses and taxes would be reduced, trade would be encouraged, and everyone would be given security for his possessions. The

47. *Polnoye sobraniye zakonov imperii rossiyskoy* (quoted in future as *PSZ*), vol. VII, No. 4842, February 1726, forma prisyagi. On the translation of 'samoderzhaviye' as sovereignty, and not autocracy, see my article 'Autocracy and Sovereignty' (*Canadian–American Slavic Studies*, vol. 16, Nos 3–4, Tempe, 1983, pp. 369–87).

48. Yu. V. Got'ye, *Istoriya oblastnogo upravleniya v Rossii ot Petra I do Yekateriny II*, 2 vols, Moscow, I, 1913, II, 1941; I, pp. 18–48. On the administration of the Supreme Privy Council see E.V. Anisimov, 'Materialy Kommissii D.M. Golitsyna o podati (1727–1730 gg.)' (*Istoricheskiye zapiski*, vol. 91, Moscow, 1973, pp. 338–50).

49. *PSZ*, vol. VIII, No. 5245, 26 February 1728. The *ukaz* gives precedence for life to privy councillors who are members of the Supreme Privy Council. But it also decrees that the automatic precedence given to the military ranks over civil rank should be abolished and replaced by precedence according to date of appointment across all services, army, navy, bureaucracy and court. See also *SIRIO*, vol. 75, pp. 309ff., Magnan to Morville, 10 February 1729.

emphasis in this programme is on restricting the arbitrary use of power, not on a change of policy.[50]

It is extremely unlikely that Dmitry Golitsyn had a ready-prepared plan. No one expected a young and healthy fourteen-year-old to die on his wedding day. When the crisis came, in January 1730, reliable contemporary evidence ascribes the initiative to Dmitry Golitsyn in the following words: 'We must make things easier for ourselves . . . we must have more freedom.' After which he and Vasily Lukich Dolgoruky feverishly dictated to the Secretary of the Supreme Privy Council the conditions they wished to impose on Anna of Courland.[51] The similarity between these conditions and those imposed on Ulrike Eleonora of Sweden has been conclusively proved by Paul Milyukov.[52] But they are also politically obvious: they deprived the ruler of all control over peace and war, the armed forces, taxation, promotion, appointments and rewards, and the succession to the throne. In all these fields she would be powerless to act without the consent of the Supreme Privy Council. As in Sweden the choice of person was endorsed by a full gathering of the political élite, the group of people in the first four ranks of the Table of Ranks, both military and civil, usually known as the *Generalitet*, but not the ecclesiastical hierarchy, who were pointedly excluded by Golitsyn. But there the resemblance with the Swedish situation stops. Unlike in Sweden, the conditions were kept secret at first, so that when news of Anna's acceptance of the throne arrived in Moscow, they could be presented as having been spontaneously offered by her. And when on 2 February the conditions were made public, Moscow burst into a ferment of activity, for the crucial question had been posed by a timid voice from the crowd: 'What sort of government will there be in future?'[53] This was precisely the question to which the Supreme Privy Council had no answer. No plan for a constitutional structure has ever been found among Golitsyn's papers, and reports that he proposed to establish a supreme council of aristocrats supplemented by a chamber of elected nobles and a chamber of urban representatives are drawn from the gossip current among foreign envoys and have not been substantiated. The draft of the oath to be taken by the higher ranks in the empire to the new empress outlines a

50. Quoted by the Swedish envoy Ditmar in a dispatch to Stockholm of 19 February 1730, in H. Hjärne, 'Ryska konstitutionsprojekt år 1730 after svenska förebilder' (*Historisk Tidskrift*, IV, Stockholm, 1884, pp. 189–272, at p. 235). I am grateful to Professor Hatton for translating this article for me.

51. Korsakov, *op. cit.*, pp. 5ff.

52. P.N. Milyukov, 'Verkhovniki i shlyakhetstvo' in *Iz istorii russkoy intelligentsii, Sbornik statey i etyudov*, St Petersburg, 1903, pp. 1–51, who drew on the study by Hjärne noted in footnote 50. There is no space here to go into the historiography of the 'Verkhovniki', which still gives rise to considerable controversy. The Swedish influence has of late been rejected in Soviet historiography (see G.A. Protasov, *Konditsii i proekty 1730 g.*, Avtoreferat dissertatsii, Moscow Oblast' Pedagogical Institute, Moscow, 1955, p. 8). However, the similarity in form and in external circumstances is undoubtedly there. For a recent discussion with a full bibliography, see D.A. Ransel, 'Political Perceptions of the Russian Nobility: the Constitutional Crisis of 1730' (*Laurentian University Review*, No. 3, Sudbury, Ont., 1972, pp. 20–38).

53. Korsakov, *op. cit.*, p. 121.

number of concessions on *policies* favourable to the various social groups, but says nothing about the sort of institutions which might be established.[54]

Thus the example of Sweden could be followed only to a limited extent: a woman with only a tenuous right to the throne could be put forward. And partly because her right was tenuous, and partly because she was a woman, her exercise of full sovereignty could be prevented. But the form of government adopted in Sweden could be integrated into a living system of political and social institutions with a long tradition: the Riksråd and the four-chamber Riksdag. A brief word about the Swedish constitutional structure may not come amiss here. It derived from the mid-fourteenth-century Land Law, which laid down that the elective king was to be advised by a Council appointed by him, but which was not the king's council but the Council of the Realm, the Riksråd.[55] Its function was to see that both king and subjects fulfilled their pledges to each other. In the event of the demise of the crown, the royal authority would revert to the Riksråd, which would exercise residual sovereignty, and elect a fresh sovereign. It is noteworthy that the Council antedated the consolidation of the Riksdag. In ensuing years the Council maintained its role with varying degrees of effectiveness even after Sweden became a hereditary monarchy in 1544. It reached a new apogee with the form of government of 1634, introduced for the minority of Queen Christina, and subsequently again during the minority of Charles XI.

In Russia there were no such institutions. The Russian Senate (the Swedish Council was often called Senate) was an administrative policy-coordinating body appointed by the tsar with no *ex-officio* membership. Above all there were no formally constituted Estates, no *Stände*, no local assemblies of the nobility, no council of the Church.

It was this lack of formal Estates which proved the stumbling block not only to Golitsyn but to all the various groups of nobles who now rushed to devise and put forward their own proposals for a new form of government in Russia. It was easy to suggest a Supreme Council of 12, or 20, or 200, the

54. G.A. Protasov in '"Konditsii" 1730 i ikh prodolzheniye' (*Uchonyye zapiski Tambovskogo gosudarstvennogo pedagogicheskogo instituta*, No. xv, Tambov, 1957, pp. 215–31) argues that one of the documents in the archives usually attributed to an opposition group of nobles should in fact be attributed to the Supreme Privy Council. This is entitled, 'Sposoby kotorymi, kak vidittsa, poryadochneye i tverzhe mozhno sochinit′ i utverdit′ izvestnoye tol′ vazhnoye i poleznoye vsemu narodu i gosudarstvu delo'. If so it does represent an attempt by the Supreme Privy Council to set up a constituent body composed of twenty to thirty chosen from the nobility, with written instructions from their electors. Up to six deputies from the church, the armed forces and the Synod would attend to discuss matters of concern to them, also duly mandated. Presidents and representatives of colleges could attend for other relevant issues. Drafts would be submitted to the full assembly together with the Senate and subsequently would be referred to the Supreme Privy Council, for examination in a joint session with the Senate and the noble assembly, and when approved a draft would be sent to the Empress 'with a request that she should confirm it'. This document, which has not been printed in full, is of fundamental importance to an understanding of the policy of the Supreme Privy Council if Protasov is right about its provenance.
55. On the Swedish constitution, see 'On Swedish History in General', 'On Aristocratic Constitutionalism in Swedish History 1520–1720' and 'Charles XI' in M. Roberts, *Essays in Swedish History*, London, 1967, *passim*.

members of which should be selected by the nobility. But what was the electorate to consist of? The *Generalitet*? The nobility as a whole? Both Golitsyn, and his friends, and the bulk of the high nobility proved far more fertile in improvising proposals for limiting the power of the new empress than in defining the nature and ensuring the legitimacy of the bodies to which the limiting was to be entrusted. The only existing political institution, the Supreme Privy Council, failed to achieve this legitimacy.

It has been argued by the Russian historian Lappo-Danilevsky that the sources of Dmitry Golitsyn's policy are to be found in the theories of Samuel Pufendorf on the distinction drawn between sovereign power and absolute power, and on the establishment of a Council to limit the power of the crown in specific areas. Basing himself on a marginal mark in Golitsyn's copy of Pufendorf, Lappo-Danilevsky argues that he chose to emphasize not the first social contract between individuals, made in order to constitute civil society, but the second contract drawn up between civil society itself and the ruler. This choice explains why Golitsyn, allegedly deliberately, rejected the idea of calling a national assembly to devise a form of government – the first form of social contract – and preferred to assign this role to a Council, already empowered to negotiate a civil contract with the ruler.[56]

This seems to me a very anachronistic interpretation. It is true that representative bodies in the *ancien régime* have frequently been called upon to adjust the existing balance between political institutions – though one should point out that both the Swedish and the English systems were not purely representative in that the heads of noble families attended in person. But not until the American Revolution was a genuinely representative assembly specifically called upon to devise a whole new form of government to replace one which had been discarded, and the revolutionary nature of such an undertaking is starkly emphasized in that most revolutionary act of the French Revolution, the oath of the tennis court, when the body elected as the last States General of the *ancien régime* turned itself into the first European constituent assembly.

In Russia a representative assembly had twice been called upon to choose a successor to the throne on the extinction of the ruling line – in 1598 and in 1613. But it did not use the opportunity to define or limit the power of the crown, let alone re-structure the government. And strangely enough, neither in the original documents nor in the extensive literature on the crisis of 1730 is the *Zemskiy Sobor*, the Russian Assembly of the Land, so much as mentioned. The Supreme Privy Council regarded itself as acting in the name of the people in offering the crown to Anna, as is clear from the letter the councillors wrote to her, in the name of the civil and spiritual ranks of the Empire, thus rendering it superfluous to summon a *Zemskiy Sobor*.[57]

56. Lappo-Danilevsky, *op. cit.*, pp. 378–80.
57. One feature of the conditions imposed on Anna recalls the Swedish model above all, namely the demand that she should not appoint a successor. Peter the Great's law of succession had been repealed by Peter II as part of the campaign to rehabilitate his father. The Supreme Privy Councillors clearly intended to use the extinction of the dynasty to inaugurate an elective monarchy, in the

With what justification could the Supreme Privy Council be regarded as speaking for the *pays légal* of Russia? The nobility did not constitute an organized social Estate. Yet Dmitry Golitsyn once remarked to a foreign diplomat that 'les ordres de l'état de la Russie sont le conseil privé, le sénat et le généralat'.[58] We come back here to the interesting concept of the *Generalitet*, the first four ranks in the Table of Ranks, which subsumed the Senate and usually the presidents of the colleges, from the point of view of personnel. In the existing Russian social system there was no means of defining membership of an upper and lower nobility other than by rank in the Table of Ranks, which did not, of course, coincide with birth. Where there is no genuine political aristocracy, a service aristocracy can substitute for it. This is obviously what Dmitry Golitsyn was prepared to accept and use. The *Generalitet*, composed at the time of some 126 people if one excluded foreigners, formed a social group with common values and interests which could provide the basic personnel for the new legislative and executive bodies. The higher ranks of the nobility below the *Generalitet*, and the Holy Synod, could be drawn into consultation when their interests were affected.[59]

One may wonder whether the role reserved to the Council by Golitsyn does not go back to the political discussions around 1681 in the circle of his cousin V.V. Golitsyn, on the establishment of a consultative chamber or *palata* of twelve members 'to remain permanently in our tsarist majesty's command and exercise civil justice conscientiously and discerningly', a mixed administrative and judicial chamber which may have been modelled on the sixteen-man Council in the Polish Commonwealth.[60] In this connection we should remember the nostalgia with which Prince Boris Kurakin speaks of the reign of Sophia: in terms reminiscent of Talleyrand's lament for the *ancien régime*, he declaimed: 'never was there such a wise government in the Russian state . . . the whole state was brought to great and flourishing wealth . . . and "polites" [*sic*] reigned among the high nobility and the courtiers in the Polish manner . . .'.[61] Such a chamber, council, or *palata* composed of people at the very top of the Table of Ranks, who could be regarded as the *pays légal* of Russia, was also mooted by Catherine II in her draft plans for the reform of Russian central government in 1788–89.[62] Clearly no one in Russia thought of associating any

style of Sweden until 1544 and again after 1720, arrogating to themselves the right to choose the monarch. It should be remembered that in the political thought of the age, a hereditary monarchy was regarded as an absolute monarchy (even in Sweden), and only an elective monarchy guaranteed the freedom of the subjects.

58. Westphalen (Danish envoy) to the King of Denmark, 22 January/2 February 1730, quoted in Korsakov, *op. cit.*, pp. 69ff.

59. For an excellent study of the *generalitet* of 1730, see B. Meehan Waters, *Autocracy and Aristocracy*, New Brunswick, 1982. If one includes foreigners, the top four ranks of the *generalitet*, i.e. Major-General, Lt.-General, full general (in Russian *generalanshef*) and Field Marshal, and their civilian equivalents, numbered 179 people in 1730.

60. Keep, *op. cit.*, p. 229.

61. *Arkhiv Knyazya F.A. Kurakina*, I, p. 244.

62. M. Raeff, 'The Empress and the Vinerian Professor' (*Oxford Slavonic Papers*, New Series, vol. VII, 1974, pp. 18–40).

kind of States General or *Zemskiy Sobor* with the government. The whole Russian tradition was in favour of administrative institutions with legislative or judicial functions.

But when Golitsyn attempted to limit the absolute power of the ruler, the nobility proved too deeply divided. Most of the articulate élite favoured some form of limitation of the power of the crown. None of the alternative projects put forward during the crisis suggests abandoning the conditions imposed on Anna. But many of the nobles distrusted what appeared to be the monopoly of power reserved to themselves by the two aristocratic families which happened at the time to dominate the Supreme Privy Council. The dispute thus centred much more on the composition of the institution which was to do the limiting than on the institution itself. But there were also many adherents of undiluted absolutism among the great families excluded by the Golitsyns and the Dolgorukys, as well as among survivors of the regime of Peter the Great and above all among the minor nobles. Many believed that the strength of the Russian state would be dissipated, that its greatness would wither away, that it might even break up, without the strong hand of an absolute ruler at the helm. Archbishop Feofan Prokopovich, bitterly offended by Golitsyn's open contempt for him as the man who had engineered the accession of Catherine I, worked on the feelings of the minor nobility who had everything to gain from the maintenance of the Table of Ranks and the absolute power of the crown.[63] As in Sweden when absolutism was introduced in 1680, the minor nobility preferred the despotism of one to the despotism, as they saw it, of many. When the crisis came to a head, they begged Anna to assume full sovereign powers, whereupon she graciously condescended to tear up the conditions she had signed with her own hand.

That night a blood-red *aurora borealis* such as had never been seen before spread ominously over the sky. 'The banquet was ready,' said Golitsyn, 'but the guests were unworthy. I know that I will be the sacrifice. Let it be so.'[64] By the end of the year the Dolgorukys were languishing in exile, and in 1736 the survivors were executed. Dmitry Golitsyn himself was arrested in 1737, having laid himself open to charges of bending regulations in his favour in a law suit over an inheritance. Sentenced to death for having expressed doubts about the validity of human as distinct from divine justice, the sentence was commuted to incarceration in the fortress of Schlüsselburg and confiscation of all his property. Special orders were dispatched to Moscow to seek out his books and particularly to lay hands on the works of Machiavelli and Boccalini which had evidently led him astray.[65]

63. The importance of the role of Feofan Prokopovich both at the time and in subsequent historiography has been well brought out by J. Cracraft in 'The Succession Crisis of 1730: A View from the Inside' (*Canadian–American Slavic Studies*, vol. 12, No. 1, Spring, 1978, pp. 61–85).
64. Korsakov, *op. cit.*, p. 278.
65. I.E. Zabelin, 'Materialy dlya russkogo indeksa librorum prohibitorum. Perepiska o knigakh D.M. Golitsyna Makhiavelevoy i Bokalinovoy' (*Bibliograficheskiye zapiski*, No. 11, 1861, pp. 319–24). I am grateful to Dr Branch for securing a copy of this article for me.

Yet, in 1737, for men of Golitsyn's rank, Schlüsselburg was not the Gulag Archipelago. On his departure for the grim fortress, Golitsyn was allowed to take with him three servants and a cook, silver dishes for himself and earthenware for them, kitchen equipment, linen, bedding, and clothing, twenty-eight geese, eighty-five chickens, butter, pigs, dried fish, mead, flour of several kinds, four icons, and a bible. He died after four months, at the age of seventy-five, and was buried within the walls of the fort.[66]

Historians have swung from one extreme to another in their interpretation of his aims. In the eighteenth century, probably under the influence of Feofan Prokopovich's extremely hostile account of what he described as a plot to introduce, not what the Greeks called an aristocracy, but an 'oppressive and violent tyranny, which the Greeks call oligarchy', Golitsyn was regarded as selfish and backward-looking. The first historian to write a really scholarly study, D.A. Korsakov, in 1880, was both balanced and judicious, but misled by his belief in the existence of a Golitsyn plan. The kadet historian and politician P. Milyukov, another influential interpreter, particularly conscious of Swedish influence, saw him as a proto-constitutionalist, and portrayed the whole episode in the light of the constitutional struggles of early twentieth-century Russia. More recent German and particularly American scholarship has tended, with some exceptions, to swing back to the view of Golitsyn as a narrow oligarch and to justify the minor nobility's rejection of what would have been only an enlarged despotism.[67]

The trouble is that the comparison with Sweden is usually posed in the wrong terms. If we assume that Golitsyn was influenced not by the Swedish form of government of 1720, but the seventeenth-century constitutional structure, then the pieces fall into place.[68] The high nobility had monopolized the Council and the high positions of the government in the seventeenth century, but in 1680 they fell before the combined onslaught of the king on the one hand and the lower nobility, together with the non-noble Estates, on the other.[69] The *verkhovniki* of Sweden lost their political power, the Council now became the King's Council, instead of the Council of the Realm, and Sweden advanced further on the course that was to provide a model for Peter the Great. There was moreover a greater degree of similarity between the social composition of the nobility in Sweden and in Russia than is usually admitted. While Magnus de la Gardie had 222 servants, there was a numerous and growing service class

66. 'Sud nad Knyazem D.M. Golitsynym (1736–1740 gg.)' in D.A. Korsakov, *Iz zhizni russkikh deyateley XVIII veka*, Kazan', 1881, pp. 229–82.
67. See Ransel, *op. cit.*, for an extensive survey of recent trends. Ransel himself considers that the *verkhovniki* were narrowly oligarchic in their aims, and so does Meehan Waters, *op. cit.*, pp. 132ff.
68. Protasov, *op. cit.*, argues forcefully that there was no resemblance between the 'konditsii' of 1730 and the forty-five articles of the Swedish form of government of May 1720. He forgets, however, that the real parallel is with the conditions imposed on Ulrike Eleanora in December 1718. He also overlooks the fact that the very use of the formula 'forma pravleniya' (form of government) is foreign. It has no precedent in Russian.
69. Roberts, *op. cit.* I have also benefited from a seminar paper by Dr Upton, given at the Institute of Historical Research in May 1983, in which he underlined the fragility of the aristocratic interpretation of the seventeenth-century Swedish constitution.

of bureaucrats and officers who lived on their salaries, as well as a great pressure for ennoblement.[70] In 1680, in Sweden, the lower nobility and the crown combined against the high aristocracy, but in 1720 the high and the low nobility combined against the crown. In Russia in 1730 as in Sweden in 1680, the crown and the lower nobles combined against the aristocracy. Historically sometimes one class, sometimes another has proved the more reliable protagonist of limited monarchy.

Historians who dismiss Golitsyn as a narrow oligarch underestimate the nature of his problem, the difficulty of creating institutions with a political dimension. It was too late now for the state to create representative institutions from above and too early for them to be created by revolution from below. In Soviet historiography Golitsyn is portrayed as a reactionary; a modern French historian speaks of him as a proto-slavophile.[71] I would disagree with both these judgements. As a man of his time Golitsyn thought in terms of the institutions of the *ancien régime*, of orders, estates and councils, not of constituent assemblies. He was a revolutionary in the sense in which that word was used in England in 1688 and in Sweden in 1718–20. He was not a slavophile. The church played no part in his political programme, nor did any Muscovite political institution. He wanted the Russian aristocracy to play the role aristocracies played in Europe. He was a proto-Westernizer, a *'zapadnik' avant la lettre*, the direct ancestor of S.E. Desnitsky, of Speransky, of the Decembrist Nikita Murav'yov, indeed of P.M. Milyukov himself, who tried to do justice – perhaps a little more than justice – to Golitsyn's vision of a more civilized and freer polity in Russia. In the long gallery of Russian reformers he belongs with the Sakharovs, not the Solzhenitsyns.[72]

70. The author of the *Anecdotes de Suède* illustrates this social climbing: 'les filles des Comtes vouloient être traitées de *Demoiselles*; au lieu que celles des Barons se devaient contenter du nom de Vierges'.

71. Simone Blanc, *Un Disciple de Pierre le Grand dans la Russie du XVIIIe siècle: V.N. Tatishchev, 1686–1750*, 2 vols, Université de Lille III, 1972; see vol. I, p. 246: 'un slavophile avant la lettre' is to my mind the only misjudgement in a sensitive analysis of the aims of Golitsyn in contrast with those of Tatishchev.

72. As a footnote one might add that both the leaders of the movement to restore absolute power to the Empress Anna, Prince A.N. Cherkassky and Prince G.D. Yusupov, came from Tatar princely families absorbed by Russia in the seventeenth century. The shadow of Ghengis Khan?

CHAPTER FOUR

The eighteenth-century origin of Russian civil rights

I

I have for a long time been interested in the form and the extent of the civil rights granted by Catherine II in the Charters of 1785 to the Nobles and the Towns, and outlined in the unpromulgated Charter of 1787 to the State Peasants, as well as in the models upon which Catherine may have drawn in her rather unusual formulation. My interest was further aroused in the context of a conference sponsored by Professor Olga Crisp and Dr Linda Edmondson some years ago designed to compare the civil rights in late tsarist Russia with those enjoyed in early Bolshevik Russia.[1] I was asked to examine the extent to which the concept of civil rights had existed, in theory and in practice, earlier, notably in the eighteenth century.

In some countries, for instance England, the definition of some civil rights attached to the individual and their enforcement in law had reached a degree of legal precision at a relatively early date. According to English legal tradition, the rights of freeborn Englishmen antedated their legal enactment which, when and if it occurred, served merely to give them form. These rights belonged to the common law, and to this day there is no English Bill of Civil Rights. Magna Carta itself, in its 1217 version, scarcely deals with the subject except to state that no freeman shall be taken and judged except by his peers and by the law of the land. But, interestingly enough, Magna Carta does set down a number of limitations on the king's right to interfere with the property rights of the barons. The importance of Magna Carta lay not so much in what it said as in what English freemen of whatever class believed it said.[2] This gave it a far wider resonance within England and through the ages and eventually in Europe and America than similar charters, such as the Golden Bull, issued at more or less the same time in other parts of Europe.

1. The project resulted in a book, *Civil Rights in Imperial Russia*, Clarendon Press, Oxford, 1989, edited by Crisp and Edmundson, which was limited to the study of some civil rights in the nineteenth century and up to 1917.
2. G. Hindley, *The Book of Magna Carta*, Guild Publishing, London, 1990, p. 211.

I cannot, however, think of any European *constitutional* document in the seventeenth and early eighteenth centuries which clearly sets out the range of civil rights enjoyed by the individual. Charles I's 'Answer to the nineteen propositions' of Parliament, of 18 June 1642, speaks of the 'regulated monarchy having the power to . . . preserve the laws in their force and the subjects in their liberties and properties', but there is no systematic exposition of individual liberties.[3] The English Bill of Rights of 1689 is called an 'Act for declaring the rights and liberties of the subject and settling the succession of the crown'. Most of the clauses state what the crown *cannot* or should not do, not what rights the subject have. The right of subjects to petition the king is indeed stated in so many words, but most of the other rights are defined indirectly, for example 'that excessive bail ought not to be required', or that 'election of members to parliament ought to be free'. Clearly, therefore, the enactment of civil rights in positive law was still in its infancy in England, where most of the civil rights we expect to enjoy today, such as 'trial by jury' or 'immunity from fines and forfeitures before conviction', were part of the common law of the land and needed no statutory enactment, and 'where the most substantial bulwarks of liberty were constructed not so much by the legislature as by the judges in individual court cases'.[4]

In the history of the evolution of the various concepts of civil rights, we must note the important distinction between collective rights and individual rights. And we must further face the problem whether either collective or individual civil rights can exist as 'rights' in the real sense of the word in an absolute regime. These two questions are of particular relevance to the situation in Russia, since whether individual or collective rights predominate varies according to the political culture of a given polity and the Russian ruler was an absolute monarch. Most writers, whether nineteenth-century Russian or twentieth-century Western, on the development of the concept of civil rights in Russia have stressed the native emphasis on the collectivity rather than on the individual. The subjects of law were not individuals but the *rod* or clan, which answered for the deeds of the individual. Even after the clan structure was transformed and Russia became a territorial state, the responsibility of the group for the actions of the individual, the *krugovaya poruka*, or system of collective responsibility for individual behaviour, continued to operate at all levels of society, from the payment of taxes or fines by merchants to the recruit levy on peasants.[5]

3. J.P. Kenyon, *The Stuart Constitution*, Cambridge University Press, 1966, pp. 21–33.
4. E.N. Williams, *The Eighteenth-Century Constitution*, Cambridge University Press, 1960, No. 10, the Bill of Rights, *passim*, and p. 423.
5. The *krugovaya poruka*, or collective guarantee, an extremely ancient system of ensuring collective responsibility for past misdeeds or future behaviour, had to a great extent fallen out of use for the nobility by the eighteenth century, but it remained in force for other social groups. A similar institution, the 'frankpledge', existed in England in Saxon times and particularly in Norman times. Every freeman had to be enrolled in a 'pledge' which would be responsible for bringing him to justice if he committed a crime.

The failure to conceive of rights as attached to a person in law in Russia as late as the twentieth century is reflected in the St Petersburg 1909 edition of one of the standard histories of Russian law, Vladimirsky Budanov's *Obzor istorii russkogo prava*. The concept of *litso*, persona, Vladimirsky Budanov explains, is the foundation of civil law. Yet there was no word for *persona* in old Russian law, for *litso* was the word used of a slave. The *litso* only slowly emerged out of the family or rod, or commune, but the rights of the *litso* were then subordinated to the state. In Vladimirsky Budanov's work there is no section on *lichnyye prava* or personal rights, either in the section on civil law or in the section on criminal law. There is no mention of the right to trial before sentence, to trial by one's peers, to freedom of speech. It was only in the reign of Catherine II, Vladimirsky Budanov concludes, that the limits between the power and activities of persons and state power began to be defined, and the idea of the individual emerged from the collective background. Catherine expressed this new approach in article 243 of her *Great Instruction*: 'Would you *prevent* crimes? Order it so, That the Laws might rather favour every *Individual*, than any particular Rank of Citizens in the Community.'[6]

I would like now to turn briefly to the objection which may be raised to the whole idea of the existence of collective or individual civil rights in an absolute monarchy, since they are by definition exercised against the state. It seems to me that there are a number of modern civil rights which in practice are no more incompatible with an absolute monarchy (in Montesquieu's use of the word) than with a liberal democracy. These would be mainly personal rights, like, for instance, no arrest without charge, no conviction without trial according to the law of the land, no confiscation of property without due legal process. These are less potentially subversive of absolute authority than rights which regulate positive human activity, such as freedom of speech, movement and association. I would not include freedom of religion or freedom of the press among rights compatible with an absolute monarchy, though a limited toleration would not be incompatible with the rule of a confident monarch during a period of civil tranquillity. Not even in mature England were the various religions equal before the law. And no absolute monarch could grant the right to participate in decision-making or in the means of enforcement of the law.

Normally an absolute ruler would behave as if such civil rights as he had enacted (though he may not have thought of them as such) were guaranteed as fundamental laws of the land, which he would not think of tampering with – like say the Salic law in France. In emergencies, of which he would be the sole judge, he could always suspend the exercise of the rights he had granted. So could the English Parliament, which suspended Habeas Corpus in 1794 and

6. See article 243 of Catherine's *Great Instruction* or *Nakaz*. I am using the 1768 English translation edited by W.F. Reddaway, Cambridge University Press, 1931. However, even in England the individual did not always emerge from the collectivity. For instance the Hundred Court could be amerced if any person guilty of homicide escaped; and it had to make good damage to hayricks, barns and houses if these were burnt in riots etc., up to 1811. (See S. and B. Webb, *English Local Government from the Revolution to the Municipal Corporation Act. The Parish and the County*, London, 1924, p. 308, n. 1).

introduced other restrictions on civil liberties in the 1790s. Let us not forget that civil rights have been regularly suspended in liberal democracies. In Spain, during the Second Republic in 1931–36, my days were punctuated by the words 'suspender las garantías constitucionales', something governments of all political colours threatened to do or did. If the sovereign parliament in a democracy so wishes it can behave just as arbitrarily as an absolute monarch.

The seventeenth-century Russian legal code of 1649 had granted certain rights – to own property, to trade, retail or wholesale – to various specified groups. Duties were also imposed on groups, and penalties for failure to fulfil them were enforced by the system of *krugovaya poruka*, i.e. security given for other people's behaviour. The rights of private property were well secured against theft, but not against confiscation by the state.[7]

In the period between the Code of 1649 and the death of Peter I, well over 8,000 laws were enacted; they were frequently contradictory or overlapping. Since I have not read them all, I cannot say that the rights of individuals are nowhere mentioned, but I do not recollect any historian drawing attention to any law covering what has here been called civil rights. Inevitably, given the increasing westernization of the Russian intellectual climate, the ideas and formulations of theorists such as Grotius, Hobbes, Pufendorf and Locke, and in general the exponents of natural law philosophy, began to circulate to some extent among the elite, but as between Hobbes and Pufendorf on the one hand, and Locke on the other, the choice was fairly clear. In any case, however well acquainted Russian rulers might have been with current political thought, the enactment of civil rights for their subjects was the least of their concerns.[8]

Yet in the course of the eighteenth century some Russian nobles did at times try to secure civil and indeed political rights for their social estate, most notably in the succession crisis of 1730. The *Verkhovniki* and other noble groups were clearly influenced by political events elsewhere in Europe, notably the Bill of Rights in England, and the Swedish constitution of 1720 (*forma pravleniya*) and earlier Swedish forms of government. The conditions imposed on Anna Ioanovna in 1730, however, included only one of those rights which have usually been comprised under the general rubric of 'civil rights', namely personal security, the undertaking not to 'deprive the nobility of life, property, and honour, without trial'. But in the many projects drafted by various groups of nobles during the crisis we find formulations in modern terminology of a programme of political rights without precedent in Russian legal or constitutional history.[9]

As the eighteenth century advanced, new trends in political thought began to be influential in Russia. Voltaire and Montesquieu aroused Russian interest

7. The Lithuanian Statute which operated in parts of Russia saw a much more rapid development of private rights *vis-à-vis* state rights, thanks to the influence of Roman and Germanic law.
8. For an interesting survey see Summer Benson, 'The Role of Western Political Thought in Petrine Russia', *Canadian-American Slavic Studies*, 8, No. 2, Summer 1974, pp. 254–73.
9. See M. Raeff, *Plans for Political Reform in Imperial Russia, 1730–1905*, Prentice Hall, Inc., Englewood Cliffs, New Jersey, 1966, for the texts of some of the documents which circulated at the time, and see my 'Portrait of an Eighteenth-Century Russian Statesman: Prince Dmitry Mikhaylovich Golitsyn', *Slavonic and East European Review*, 62, No. 1, January 1984, pp. 36–60.

in English institutions, a trend reinforced when Catherine herself drew attention to the work of William Blackstone (himself deeply indebted to Montesquieu). Possibly the single greatest catalyst was Diderot's *Grande Encyclopédie*, which provided easily comprehensible digests of ideas and definitions, many of them of English origin (for instance the English court of equity, which provoked Diderot to an outburst of rapture, urging other nations to copy it[10]).

The plans and proposals of the *Verkhovniki* were not made public at the time, though copies certainly circulated among the aristocracy. They would have been regarded as highly treasonable by Anna Ioanovna's government, but the ideas of 1730 survived and were handed down verbally among magnates descended from the same families. The same demands for no arrest without trial, immunity from corporal punishment, no confiscation of property except for debt, recur in the discussion of the rights of the nobility in the Legislative Commission of 1754–62, in discussions surrounding the Manifesto on the Freedom of the Nobility of 1762 and in the Commission of 1763, set up by Catherine II to revise Peter III's manifesto. But they are not really conceived of as individual rights, i.e. rights pertaining to all individuals, but rather as rights attached to the nobility as a social group.[11]

The next important discussion of concepts of civil rights came with Catherine II's *Great Instruction* in 1767. It contains no programmatic formulation of civil rights, but their existence, sometimes as individual rights, is implicit in many of its articles. The phrase 'civil liberty' occurs frequently, for example in article 67, but it is not defined except in very general terms: 'social or civil liberty consists not in doing everyone as he pleases', or 'civil liberty is a tranquillity of mind arising from the opinion that every individual of the whole society enjoys his personal security . . .' (article 39). Article 114 states, for instance, 'In states under a moderate government where equal attention is paid to the Life, the Property and the Honour of the meanest citizen, no one can lose his Honour, or Property, without a long and strict examination into the truth . . .'; articles 127 and 128 stress the need for the right to choose one's judges, and to be able to choose judges in the same rank as oneself, i.e. one's peers.[12]

There is no time nor is it necessary to go into a careful analysis of Catherine's approach to public and private law. She was no lawyer, but she followed the

10. See entry 'équité' in the *Encyclopédie*, 'cette cour de chancellerie [the English equity court] est un des plus beaux établissements qu'il y'ait en Angleterre et des plus dignes d'étre imite par les nations civilisées'. The speed with which Catherine seized on and made use of new ideas is quite remarkable, notably those of Beccaria. Blackstone was not translated into French until 1774–76, by which time he had replaced Montesquieu as Catherine's bedside book. She used the translation by Damiens de Gomicourt, *Commentaires sur les lois Anglaises* de M. Blackstone, traduits de l'anglois, sur la quatrième édition d'Oxford, J.L. de Boubers, Bruxelles, 1774–76, 5 vols 8.

11. The most scholarly and recent study of the Legislative Commissions of the 1750s and 1760s and the manifesto of 1762 is to be found in various works by O.A. Omelchenko, notably *Kodifikatsiya prava v Rossii v period absolyutnoy monarkhii, vtoraya polovina XVIII veka*, Vsesoyuznyy yuridicheskiy zaochnyy institut, Moscow, 1989, and his *Zakonnaya monarkhia Yekateriny II*, Moscow, Iurist, 1993, both of which draw on much hitherto unpublished material.

12. Catherine II, the *Great Instruction*, see n. 6.

basic principle of drawing a clear line between the sphere of civil law, i.e. matters affecting relations between citizens such as property, and state law. 'State law', as she put it in the special instruction to the Procurator General delivered at the time of the convening of the Legislative Commission, 'confirms their freedom, civil law confirms their property.'[13] Her use of the word 'citizen' also introduced a new approach to the relation between state and individual, rather than state and *sostoyaniye* or 'status'.[14]

Unpublished or unofficial documents of the time as well as the official records of the Legislative Commission confirm that the whole question of civil rights was now confronted in a way which came much closer to the political literature of the West and even to some of its constitutional documents. The draft projects of codes of laws for the nobles, the townsmen, the cossacks and even the peasants, drawn up in the subcommissions of the Legislative Commission between 1767 and 1774, used a more sophisticated language than the language of 1649.

An important source of some of this new sophistication may have been the Scottish trained Ukrainian jurist, S.E. Desnitsky. Desnitsky had been sent to Glasgow to study jurisprudence in 1761, where he attended lectures by Adam Smith, John Millar and other luminaries of the Scottish Enlightenment. He returned to Russia in 1767, and in February 1768 he submitted 'a plan for the establishment of the Legislative, Judicial and Executive Power in the Russian empire' to Catherine through A.P. Shuvalov, the director of the Journals of the Legislative Commission, to whom he was acting as legal adviser.[15] Desnitsky did not draw up a specific charter of civil rights in this document, but it included suggestions for the reform of the judiciary, including trial by jury.[16] He may also have influenced the form and content of a draft plan by A.P. Shuvalov for the reform of the laws of the Russian state which was re-worked by Catherine herself into an 'Instruction for the procedure for the conclusion of the Commission for the drafting of a new code', forwarded to the Commission on 8 April 1768. Catherine's Instruction on the procedure of the Commission clearly envisaged the drafting of some sort of statement defining the structure of the Russian government, for she divided the laws

13. General prokurorskiy nakaz, No. 11, *Polnoye sobraniye zakonov imperii rossiskoy* (*PSZ*), St Petersburg, 1830, vol. 18, No. 12950, 30 July 1767. The word *sobstvennost'* was used for the first time for property in this *nakaz*, according to G. Vernadsky, *Obzor istorii prava russkogo gosudarstva XVII-XIX vv*, Prague, 1924, p. 116.

14. The word '*sosloviye*' was not used in Russia in the eighteenth century; it does not figure in the Academy dictionary. See W. Philip, 'Zur Frage nach der Existenz altrussische Stande', *Forschungen zur osteuropäische Geschichte*, 27, 1980, pp. 64–73, and Ch. Schmidt, 'Über die Bezeichnung der Stände (sostojanie-sosolovije) in Russland seit dem 18. Jahrhundert', *Jahrbücher für Geschichte Osteuropas*, NF, 38, 1990, pp. 199–211.

15. Omelchenko, *Zakonnaya monarkhiya*, pp. 140, 144.

16. See S.E. Desnitsky, 'Predstavleniye o uchrezhdenii zakonodatel'noy, suditel' noy i nakazatel'noy vlasti v Rossiiskoy imperii' in S.V. Paparigopoulo and S.A. Pokrovsky, *Yuridicheskiye proizvedeniya progressivnykh russkikh mysliteley*, Moscow, 1959, pp. 99–142 and A.H. Brown, 'The Father of Russian Jurisprudence: The Legal Thought of S.E. Desnitsky' in *Russian Law – Historical and Political Perspectives*, ed. W.E. Butler, A.W. Sijthoff, Leyden, 1977, pp. 117–42.

into 'general laws' dealing with the state, and 'particular' laws which dealt with matters concerning the individual citizen. General laws regulated matters concerning the state, particular laws gave legal form to matters concerning the legal status of citizens.[17]

The growing influence of Blackstone on her thinking is attested by Catherine herself in a letter to her *souffre douleur*, Melchior von Grimm. By 1774 his *Comentaries on the Laws of England* had become one of her principal sources.[18] It is extremely unlikely that she was unacquainted with the public and published allocutions of S.E. Desnitsky, who had taught in Moscow University since 1767, and was formally appointed to a chair in Russia law in 1773. (Catherine spent most of 1775 in Moscow.) Desnitsky was of course perfectly familiar with the work of Blackstone and there are many echoes of the English lawyer's thought in the plan he had put forward to Catherine in 1768. It is probably through him that the Empress first heard of the existence of Blackstone. Desnitsky was profoundly influenced by the English jurist's formulation that 'rights consist . . . in a number of private immunities which are no other . . . than the residuum of *natural liberty* which is not required by the laws of society to be sacrificed to public convenience'. In other words they were civil privileges which society had agreed to provide *in lieu* of natural liberties which had been sacrificed. 'These are personal security, personal liberty, private property.'[19]

The unaccustomed labour of attempting to formulate legal concepts in the very large number of draft projects prepared by Catherine herself, her advisers and the deputies to the Legislative Commission, undoubtedly helped to educate a goodly proportion of Russian elite society in political thought, and Desnitsky, who was the first professor to lecture in the Russian language, served to reach a wider public. But to my knowledge there is as yet no *model* on which the Empress and her advisers could draw.

The first influential public constitutional statement of civil rights that I can think of is surely the Virginia Bill of Rights of 12 June 1776, which states, in terms much more sensible than the Declaration of Independence of 4 July, that 'all men are by nature equally free and independent and have certain inherent rights of which they may not divest themselves. These are the enjoyment of life and liberty with the means of acquiring and possessing property and pursuing and obtaining happiness and safety.'[20] Further articles echo the English Bill of Rights, but specify civil rights quite clearly, e.g. the right to demand the cause and nature of an accusation, the right to a speedy trial by

17. *Nachertaniye o privedenii k okonchaniyu Komissii proekta novogo ulozheniya*, PSZ, vol. 18, No. 13095, 8 April 1968.

18. Catherine to Melchior von Grimm, 4 August 1776, *Sbornik imperatorskogo russkogo istoricheskogo obshchestva* (*SIRIO*), 23, p. 52.

19. Blackstone, *Commentaries*, I, p. 125. It is noteworthy that Desnitsky was appointed to teach Russian law at Moscow University almost at the same time as Blackstone was appointed to teach English common law at Oxford University, hitherto neglected subjects in both universities.

20. For text see R.R. Palmer, *The Age of Democratic Revolution*, Oxford University Press, 1959, I, p. 418.

jury, or, as in article 8, 'no man may be deprived of his liberty, except by the law of the land and the judgment of his peers'. Article 12 is to my knowledge quite new: 'that the freedom of the press is one of the great bulwarks of liberty and should never be restrained but by despotick government'. (The English Bill of Rights only mentions freedom of speech in Parliament, which had not been guaranteed under the Stuarts.) Article 16 demands total freedom of religion. It may well be that this Virginian Bill of Rights served as one of the models for the way in which Russian ideas on civil rights were formulated in 1785.

Bearing in mind her interest in Blackstone, it is not unlikely that Catherine was aware of the public allocution by Desnitsky, delivered in Moscow University and published in 1778, entitled *Yuridicheskoye razsuzhdeniye o pol'ze znaniya otechestvennogo zakonoiskusstva i o nadobnom vozobnovleniya onogo v gosudarstvennykh vysokopokrovitel'stvuyemykh uchilishchakh* ('A juridical discourse on the usefulness of knowledge of the jurisprudence of one's country and of its necessary renewal in state schools under high protection'). To this speech he appended the table of contents of a proposed textbook on Russian law which he thought could be used for teaching in the university. He lists the first part of the contents as follows:

I. heading of the book of Russian personal rights ['personal'nyye prava'][21]
   1) the rights of persons i) in a natural state and having the right to defend
   a) their personal security
   b) their personal freedom
   c) their personal property and estates.
   ii) in an *acquired* situation in which they have rights as public persons, i.e. as for instance
A) the Power [there follows a list of the agencies of state starting with]
   1) the supreme legislative power of the monarch
   2) the executive: corporations such as the Academy; 'political corporations' such as the *kuptsy* [merchants] and *meshchane* [townspeople], contractors, and finally
   3) persons in a private situation having rights such as A) ancestral nobles, nobles promoted through military service, nobles promoted through civil service.

Desnitsky goes on to list others entitled to personal rights such as *raznochiutsy* (people not legally ascribed to any particular order), serfs, slaves and lords, servants and masters, husbands and wives etc.[22]

This outline is interesting because I think it is the first time as far as I can establish that a definition of personal civil rights appeared in print, in a published document in Russia couched in contemporary legal and political language. The demands of the *Verkhovniki* and others in 1730 did not appear in print.

21. Note the use of the word 'personal'nyye' not '*lichniyye*'.
22. Paparigopoulo and Pokrovsky, *Yuridicheskiye*, pp. 225ff., at 240.

At this point the particular formulation of civil rights in the Charter to the Nobles, and the Charter to the Towns of 1785, and in the unpromulgated Charter to the State Peasants of 1787 should be examined.[23] Though already in earlier legislation different rights had been granted to different strata of the population, and different penalties exacted for the same crime according to status, it was Catherine who systematized this process in 1785, in spite of what she had written in her *Instruction*. The civil rights which she enacted were granted to individuals within social groups (which had replaced the rod) and not to individuals as such. Moreover, while the actual civil rights (as distinct from the corporate rights) granted to the nobles were the same and treated all the nobles as one single homogeneous class, the civil rights granted to the urban social group differentiated between various status and income levels.

The Charter to the Nobles of 1785 was issued as a permanent or fundamental law of the Russian empire (*na vechnyye vremena*).[24] It is entitled 'o lichnykh preimushchestvakh dvoryan' ('on the personal privileges of nobles', though I have seen *preimushchevstva* translated as 'prerogatives', when it refers to the *preimushchestva* of the crown).

The articles specifically concerned with civil rights are numbers 8–13. Article 8 reads 'Bez suda da ne lishitsya blagorodnyy dvoryanskogo dostoinstva' ('the well born shall not be deprived of his noble rank without a trial'). The same convoluted form is used in the remaining articles. Article 9 states that 'without trial [the well-born] shall not be deprived of his honour' and articles 10 and 11 make similar provision for his life and his property (*imeniye*, not *sobstvennost'*) respectively. Article 12 states that the well-born shall not be tried except by his equals. Equally important for the nobles was article 15, again expressed in somewhat convoluted form: 'telesnoye nakazaniye da ne kosnetsya do blagorodnogo' ('corporal punishment shall not concern a noble'). Article 36 stated that the well-born noble did not pay personal taxes, namely the poll-tax, the equivalent of the taille in France, which had come to be regarded as humiliating in France as well as in Russia.[25] Noble status was declared to be hereditary, a non-noble wife acquired it on marriage to a noble, but a noblewoman did not lose it on marrying beneath her.[26] The property rights of nobles were also confirmed including the right to buy 'villages', i.e. serfs. The

23. The published version of the draft Charter to the State Peasants is dated 1787, but according to Omelchenko, *Zakonnaya monarkhiya*, Catherine worked on it at the same time as she worked on the other two charters of 1785.

24. Omelchenko has also pointed out that Catherine was particularly concerned at this time with the idea of introducing 'fundamental laws'.

25. M. Marion, *Dictionnaire des Institutions de la France au XVIIe et XVIIIe siècles*, Paris, 1923, p. 397.

26. M. Ostrogorsky, *The Rights of Women*, Swan Sonnenschein and Co, London, 1893, points out that in Russia women have been able to exercise rights more easily when they were attached to property or office than to citizenship, and that women's rights over property, whether they were married or not, were extensive. See also the unpublished Ph. D. thesis by Michelle Marrese, 'A Woman's Kingdom: Women and the Control of Property in Russia, 1700–1861', Northwestern University, 1995.

corporate rights included the calling of noble assemblies every three years, the right to petition the Empress, and the election of a number of noble officials in the local administration and assessors to law courts for nobles. The noble corporation was not to be made responsible or tried for crimes committed by individual nobles, thus ending the collective responsibility of nobles for the crimes committed by one of them.[27]

The personal civil rights granted to the townspeople were set out and phrased in similar form in section D of the Charter to the Towns issued on the same day as the Charter to the Nobles. The status of the *kuptsy* (merchants) and of the *meshchanstvo* (the middling sort of people), like that of the nobles, was defined as hereditary, and was passed to a wife if her status was the same or lower than that of her husband, and to his children. Article 83, 'meshchanin bez suda da ne lishitsya dobrogo imeni, ili zhizn' ili imeniya' ('a townsman shall not be deprived of his good name, or life or property without trial'), and article 84, a townsman is to be judged by a court of townspeople, echo the Charter to the Nobles. Perhaps because the status of the petty bourgeoisie was less well established, article 87 repeats that it is strictly forbidden to take away or destroy the property of a *meshchanin* without trial and sentence of the proper court. Members of the first and second merchant guilds were not to suffer corporal punishment, nor to pay the poll-tax (which had been replaced by a tax of 1 per cent on capital in 1774), and all townsmen were freed from the heavy burden of petty government services which had weighed on them so heavily in the past.[28]

The unpromulgated Charter to the State Peasants offers a striking illustration of the abstract nature of Catherine's thought and her passion for symmetry. She divided the registered state peasants into six groups (similar to the divisions she had applied to the nobles and the townspeople). The top two levels, the *stateynyye* (or men of substance), which included wealthy peasants owning from 500 to 1,000, 1,000 to 5,000 and 5,000 to 10,000 roubles, and the *pervomestnyye*, who had served the village well as elected officials in the past, were freed from corporal punishment. The *stateynyye* would pay 1 per cent of their capital in lieu of the poll-tax and could purchase substitutes for the recruit levy. Registered *poselyane*, or villagers, could travel freely into and out of towns, without a passport in normal healthy times. Part D of the draft stated that a peasant conferred his status on his wife and children; that he could not be deprived of his property without trial by his peers, namely the *nizhnaya rasprava* and the *nizhniy zemskiy sud*,[29] tribunals set up by the Statute

27. This was the formal death blow to the concept of the *krugovaya poruka* among nobles, but it may not have been immediately realized by officials.
28. PSZ, XXII, No. 16188, 21 April 1785.
29. It is frequently asserted that the *nizhniy zemskiy sud* was not a court. Catherine intended it to be one. As there has never been a single study of the operation of such a court, it is impossible to know how it functioned. But an interesting case is quoted in the *Zhurnal zakonodatel'stva na 1817 god.* published by the Commission for the Compilation of Laws, vol. II, No. 132, p. 109, 2 May 1817, in which three *odnodvortsy* complained against a *zemskiy ispravnik*, who had sent them illegally out of turn as recruits to please a local landowner with whom they were carrying on a

of 1775 to which peasants elected assessors. Prosecutions could not be brought after ten years. Foreigners and *inovernyye* could practice their religion freely.[30]

II

I now propose to examine briefly the extent and evolution of some civil rights in Catherine's reign in the following fields:

1) personal freedom and freedom of movement (what Blackstone calls loco-motion, with a hyphen)
2) the right to life, liberty and property and immunity from corporal punishment
3) freedom to practice one's religion
4) freedom of association
5) freedom of expression

as far as these civil liberties were enjoyed by those categories of people who were, as Russian lawyers put it, entitled to rights, i.e. *usloviya pravosposobnosti*, in this context mainly nobles and townspeople.

Personal freedom and freedom of movement

Since 1762, Russian nobles enjoyed freedom from service and hence freedom of 'loco-motion' within Russia and the right to travel abroad and enter the service of foreign powers, provided they returned if summoned in time of war. The penalty for not returning in 1762 was confiscation of property. I have not been able to find evidence of whether a noble needed a passport for internal travel – a passport for foreign travel was obligatory, presumably delivered by the Heraldmaster's Office or the local governor.

The terms of the Manifesto of 1762 seem to have been mainly observed during the reign of Catherine. Nobles entered and left service (N.I. Novikov, A. Radishchev and many others), travelled abroad and do not seem even to have been compelled to serve in time of war if they were not already in the armed forces – and even then. In the reign of Paul I, however, considerable pressure was put on the nobility to serve in the armed forces, and the spirit of Peter III's manifesto was evidently frequently breached. Alexander I reverted to his grandmother's policy.

---

lawsuit over land. The complaint went right up to Alexander I, who confirmed the decision of the lower court that the lawsuit be speeded up, the *zemskiy ispravnik* be charged before the court with all severity and attention be paid to the dereliction of duty on the part of the local authorities. Finally the three *odnodvortsy* were to be returned, and replaced by the three recruits whose turn it was; one of them had disappeared since he was last heard of in hospital. If he could not be found, the 2,000 ruble fine imposed on the guilty was to be paid as compensation to his family – but if the soldier did return from the dead he was to stay in the army.

30. *SIRIO*, 20, pp. 447ff. 'Proekt imperatritys Yekateriny ob ustroistve svobodnykh sel'skikh obyvateley'. See also R.P. Bartlett, 'Catherine II's Draft Charter to the State Peasantry', *Canadian-American Slavic Studies*, 23, No. 1, 1989, pp. 36–57.

The personal freedom and freedom of movement of the townspeople (*kuptsy* and *meshchanstvo*) had been limited under the Code of 1649, and even more under Peter I. They were bound to the town by the collective guarantee for payment of taxes, and the collective obligation to perform a number of services for the state, as well as the collective obligation to provide recruits for the army. The collective responsibility for the payment of taxes was broken in 1774 when the members of the first or richest guild were freed from the poll-tax and assessed to pay 1 per cent of their declared capital. Collective responsibility for misdeeds and the performance of town services was removed by the Charter of 1785, but nothing was said about the right to loco-motion, which, one must assume, continued to be dependent on the issue of a passport by the town duma.

It should be noted incidentally that freedom of 'loco-motion' was also relative in England at the time. Whereas nobles and the gentry were free to travel abroad and take service, the emigration of craftsmen and artisans was strictly forbidden. Thus many British naval officers entered Russian service without difficulty, but masons, blacksmiths, plasterers etc., attempting to seek employment in Russia, could be subjected to prosecution and fines.[31]

The right to life, liberty and property, and immunity from corporal punishment

The security of the individual had been increased in 1762 by the abolition of the Secret Chancery and the *slovo i delo* procedure by Peter III, who transferred the secret police to a secret department in the Senate directly under his control – a policy maintained by Catherine II.[32]

Broadly speaking, what is included under this heading is that no one will be deprived of life, liberty and property, except by the verdict of a trial by his or her peers according to the law of the land in a properly constituted court. Such a court, with assessors elected by members of one's own social estate, together with the 'Conscience Court' also with assessors elected from one's own estate, was one of the innovations of Catherine's Statute of Local Administration of 1775. The *guberniya* Conscience Court was, *inter alia*, charged with carrying out Catherine's adaptation of the practice derived from England of obliging the authorities to inform a prisoner within three days of his arrest of what were the charges against him, and to release him on bail, or to 'produce his

31. For the latest brief discussion of the rights of British subjects see A.G. Cross, *By the Banks of the Neva*, Cambridge University Press, 1996, pp. 241ff. The extremely complicated passport regulations governing the lives, residence, social status, work, etc. of all classes of Russian society have been studied by M. Mathews, *The Passport Society, Controlling Movement in Russia and the USSR*, Westview Press, Oxford, 1993. Only a few pages deal with the eighteenth century, but they are enough to illustrate the economic disadvantages of the control of movement, of which serfdom was of course the most glaring example.

32. It is frequently stated that Peter III abolished the Secret Chancery and that Catherine II restored it. This is not the case. Peter III abolished the Secret Chancery but transferred some of its security functions, and its director, S. Sheshkovsky, to a privy office (*taynaya ekspeditsiya*) which he set up in the Senate. See V. Samoilov, 'Vozniknoveniye taynoy ekspeditsii pri senate', *Voprosy istorii*, No. 6, 1948, pp. 79–81.

body' (habeas corpus). It is impossible to state with any degree of scholarly accuracy how effective these institutions were, because we know very little about the administration of justice after 1775, and how these courts operated. Memoirs, like those of Derzhavin, Mertvago, Dmitriyev and Vinsky,[33] are quoted again and again, but they provide a very limited view, and Dr J. Hartley is the only person I know who has actually studied the records of some of the conscience courts.[34]

The property rights of the individual, as against those of the rod, had never been regarded with so much respect and veneration in Russia as for instance in England,[35] where property was viewed as the foundation of liberty. Property was treated differently according to whether it was inherited (*rodovoy*), granted, acquired by purchase, or by a wife's dowry. The state usually confiscated all property until the middle of the century in the course of the various factional fights and treason trials, but after Catherine's accession, property was usually passed on to the heirs in the rare cases of treason. Property seems to have become more secure in her reign in the sense that confiscation for political reasons almost disappeared (it is not possible to say that it never took place) and confiscation for other causes such as debt took place by court order.

To what extent the property of townspeople was subject to arbitrary confiscation, before and after the Statute of 1775, is a moot point. Until a far more thorough examination of court verdicts has been undertaken one can draw no conclusions.

Again, during the reign of Paul I, noble and merchant immunity from corporal punishment became a dead letter, thus underlining the fragility of the status of a fundamental law in Russia. Alexander reversed his father's policy.

Freedom to practice one's religion

Freedom of religion was inconceivable in Russia where Orthodoxy was a state religion which defined whether a person was a Russian subject. Nevertheless, some concessions had had to be made to the many foreigners in Russian service from the days of Tsar Alexis, and the strictly controlled practice of their religion was allowed to Catholics and Protestants but no proselytising. This degree of toleration was viewed askance by the Orthodox hierarchy, which also continued to persecute Old Believers, and indulged in forceful

33. G. Derzhavin, *Sochineniya*, ed. Ya Grot, St Petersburg, 1864–78, vol. V; D.B. Mertvago, 'Zapiski Dmitriya Borisovicha Mertvago', *Russkiy Arkhiv*, Supplement, 1867; I.I. Dmitriyev, *Vzglyad na moyu zhizn*', Oriental Research Partners, Reprint, 1974.
34. J.M. Hartley, 'Catherine's Conscience Court – an English Equity Court?' in *Russia and the West in the Eighteenth Century*, Proceedings of the Second International Conference of the Study Group on Eighteenth Century Russia, 17–22 July 1981, Oriental Research Partners, 1983. Some of the weakneses of the conscience courts can be attributed to the failure to define their relationship with other courts. For an example see *Zhurnal zakonodatel'stva*, No. 165, 8 June 1817.
35. The absence of political rights for dissenters and of basic property rights for Catholics in the United Kingdom should be borne in mind.

missionary activity among Moslems and Pagans. The small number of Jews were expelled in 1742, and Jews were not allowed to settle in Russia, though some settlements survived in the Ukraine and in Livonia. The problem acquired new dimensions with the partitions of Poland, when Russia acquired large numbers of Catholic and Jewish subjects, who under the terms of the first partition had been guaranteed the practice of their religion.

Catherine regarded freedom to practice one's religion as essential in a multinational empire, but in common with her fellow sovereigns throughout Europe she believed that religion should be practiced under broad state supervision. She issued no general patent of toleration but all the non-Orthodox religious communities which came under her sway – Uniat, Catholic, Moslem, Protestant and Jewish – were organized in such a way as to leave matters of faith under the heads of the religious communities, and the control of buildings, appointments and financial arrangements in the hands of state-appointed councils. In theory there was no discrimination on religious grounds in state service for nobles – at any rate as between Christian religions – and in elective municipal posts. Until the 1790s Jews were treated fairly, but heavier taxation introduced then discriminated against them, and the introduction of the Pale of Settlement in 1794 reduced their freedom of movement. The Orthodox Church continued to be the state church, and attendance at church was compulsory,[36] though it was no longer enforced on Old Believers who were on the whole left to their own devices under the benevolent eye of Prince G.A. Potemkin. It continued to be a crime to attempt to convert someone from Orthodoxy to another religion. Improper behaviour in church was dealt with under the Police Ordinance of 1782. The practice of non-Orthodox religions was less free in the reigns of Alexander I and Nicholas I.

Freedom of expression

The idea of freedom of expression in the abstract was not conceived of until the reign of Catherine II, who set out her views in her *Great Instruction*: 'The Law cannot subject words to capital punishment', she wrote in article 481, and continued in article 483: 'Writings contain Things, which are more durable than Words; but if they do not lead to the crime of High Treason, they cannot of themselves constitute the essence of High Treason'.

Until 1783 censorship was exercised by a combination of intervention from the Empress, who did occasionally act to tone down harsh and offensive personal attacks in works submitted to her, and the self-censoring of the printing presses, all of which were operated by government institutions such as the Synod, the Senate, the Academy of Sciences, the Cadet Corps etc. Works were censored for offences against religion (*zakon*), the ruler and public decency. As

36. Attendance at church was compulsory in England until at least 1740. See S. and B. Webb, *English Local Government*, p. 469.

the contemporary German historian, August Ludwig Schlözer put it, 'Catherine defined the concept of state secret, legalized the enormous difference between treasonable spying and learned research'.[37]

The role of censorship in the life of the journals which proliferated between 1768 and 1774 has not yet been fully elucidated, since the identity of all the editors and the censors is not known for certain and their activities cannot be followed. Books imported from abroad were subjected to the approval of the Academy of Sciences or the University of Moscow. Censorship does not seem to have been a major issue in the period 1762–83. But a new phase opened in 1783 with the *ukaz* which allowed anyone to set up a printing press, provided the local police were informed. Censorship was now lodged with the heads of the police boards (*uprava blagochiniya*) set up in 1782 in the towns, who seem to have taken their responsibilities very lightly. The police official who read Radishchev's *Journey from Petersburg to Moscow* is said to have thought it was a travelogue.

During 1789–90 a surprising amount of material on the French Revolution was published (as previously on the American Revolution) in the gazettes, but the watershed seemed to have been the Polish revolt of 1791 followed by the execution of Louis XVI in 1793. Censorship became much more severe, the content of the gazettes was politically slanted, and finally on 16 September 1796 the first decree instituting censorship throughout the empire was issued. Private printing presses were closed and censorship offices were set up in a number of cities for pre-publication censorship and the control of imports. Alexander I repealed the *ukaz* on his accession, yet in his reign censorship gradually became both more haphazard and more rigorous. It may not be suprising that *Les Aphrodites ou Fragments pour servir à l'histoire du plaisir*, published in Russia in 1793, was banned in 1818, but it is really astonishing to find that H. Storch's *Cours d'économie politique qui a servi à l'instruction des Grand ducs Nicolas et Michel* was banned in 1823, the year of its publication in French in France.

Freedom of association

According to the Soviet author, A.D. Stepansky, it was in the reign of Catherine II that the legal norms for setting up what we would call private societies and what he calls social organizations were laid down in the Police Ordinance of 1782. Article 64 states that the Police Boards were to keep societies of all kinds which had been legally set up within their legal limits, and were to respect their constitutions and rules according to law, and give them what assistance was necessary. The *Ustav* did not state how to obtain this legal status and it appears that each case was treated on its merits, and usually referred to the emperor for a final decision. Article 208 of the *Ustav* forbade setting up such

37. Quoted in K. Papmehl, *Freedom of Expression in Eighteenth Century Russia*, Martinus Nijhoff, The Hague, 1971.

societies without permission and article 250 set out the penalties for doing so. According to Stepansky this was the first and last general regulation in Russia allowing the foundation of a private society (but not a secret society). We do not in fact know how this permission worked, and who needed it. The masonic societies evidently did without any permission, but what about literary groups such as Arzamas? (Some Western authors, however, take issue with Stepanov and regard this article 64 as a means of ensuring government control over private societies.[38])

Thus the legal definition of a number of civil rights in major legislation did begin in the fourth quarter of the eighteenth century. The drafting clearly did not take account of many of the legal implications of such a policy, and must have given rise to many difficulties of interpretation, which have not been studied. Moreover, interpretation of the law is one of the issues on which Catherine parted company with the English model, for she did not believe in 'judge-made law', the right (and duty) of judges to interpret the law, or even in making verdicts public, in common with such good authorities as Diderot. It is up to scholars now to take advantage of the greater access to Russian archives in order to study the procedures and verdicts of the courts at all levels to discover how far these rights were observed in real life, in what circumstances and how long for.

Catherine herself continued at any rate until the Second Turkish War to ponder over questions of legal reform, both of the structure of government and of civil society. To a greater extent than any of her predecessors, and most of her successors, she thought over ways and means to associate members of the various social groups, to which she had herself given legal form, with policy-making, and thus establishing a number of rights for them. First analysed in any detail by Marc Raeff in 1974, her extensive notes from Blackstone's *Commentaries* occupy 386 folio pages. She also based her work on her secretary A. Khrapovitsky's translations into French of crucial English constitutional documents, such as the Bill of Rights of 1689, the Habeas Corpus Amendment Act of 1679, and of course Magna Carta. All these notes illustrate the general trend of her thought.[39] Her drafts of plans for the actual reorganization of Russian government have now been further studied by O. Omelchenko, who has published some of them, such as 'O uzakoneniyakh voobshche' (on legislation in general) in full. None of these plans were carried to a conclusion, but they reflect the seriousness of Catherine's approach, and in many cases the extent of the influence of Blackstone on her thought. In her 'o uzakoneniyakh',

38. A.D. Stepansky, 'Materialy legal'nykh obshchesvtennykh organizatsii tsarskoy Rossii (seredina XVIII veka- Fevral' 1917)' in *Arkheograficheskiy Ezhegodnik za 1978*, Nauka, Moscow, 1979, pp. 69–80.
39. See M. Raeff, 'The Empress and the Vinerian Professor: Catherine II's Projects of Government Reform and Blackstone's Commentaries', *Oxford Slavonic Papers*, NS, VII, 1974, pp. 18–41, and O.A. Omelchenko, 'Idei konstitutsionnogo zakona i vseobshchey zakonnosti' v pravovoy politike prosveshchennogo absolyutizma v Rossii: neizvesntyy proekt Yekateriny II 'o uzakoneniyakh voobshche' in *Problemy pravovoy i politicheskoy ideologii – sbornik nauchnykh trudov*, Vsesoyuzniy yuridicheskiy zaochniy institut, Moscow, 1989, pp. 70–109.

for instance, Catherine lists a number of actions by the authorities which she considers to be illegal, in itself a novelty in Russian legal thought, and her condemnation is clearly derived from the English Bill of Rights, from which she quotes: 'let no one be deprived of his honour, or his status [*sostoyaniye*], or his property or his life without trial'.

PART TWO

Social and Administrative Problems

CHAPTER FIVE

Penal policy in the age of Catherine II

HISTORICAL BACKGROUND

Before embarking on a study of Russian penal policy in the second half of the eighteenth century, it is essential to give some idea of the legal and penal traditions Catherine II inherited, which are strikingly different from the Germanic and Roman traditions of the West. Kievan Rus knew a patriarchal approach to law, suitable to a society based on clans. There were laws, but no jurisprudence, no systematic development of native or borrowed legal science. The first Russian code, the *Russkaya Pravda*, was a compendium of customary law, incorporating features common to all early societies such as the right to revenge, the payment of weregild for death or mutilation. It was reinforced by princely regulations and judicial decisions, and by references to Byzantine jurisprudence. Already before the Mongol conquest, authority was being concentrated in the hands of the princes, particularly in relation to the punishment of serious crimes such as brigandage.[1]

The Mongol conquest acted as a brake on native development in the legal as in so many other spheres.[2] The increasing authority of princes, as agents of the Tartars, and the poverty resulting from Tartar devastation, both contributed to the grim process of gradual enserfment of all classes of the population to the state. Punishment, rather than payment, became the normal answer to crimes against persons or property. With the emergence of Moscow in the 1480s as the heir to the Golden Horde, the legal link with Kievan customary law seemed to be broken, and Byzantine influence, fostered by the Church, grew within the psychological framework of the Mongol acceptance of great physical pain.

1. G.S. Fel'dshteyn, *Glavnyye techeniya v istorii nauki ugolovnogo prava v Rossii*, Yaroslavl', 1909, pp. 16–71; cf. also A.G. Timofeyev, *Istoriya telesnykh nakazaniy v russkom prave*, St Petersburg, 1897, pp. 52–3.
2. Yet the argument that the Mongols are responsible for the cruelty of Russian punishments is refuted by the fact that the Lithuanian Statute listed a very large variety of very cruel punishments. But the knut was unknown, and in general the nobles had achieved immunity from corporal punishment for their order. On the other hand, the fact that corporal punishment was not regarded as dishonouring among the Mongols may have affected Russian attitudes. See G. Vernadsky, *The Mongols and Russia*, New Haven, 1953, p. 356; Timofeyev, *op. cit.*, p. 55 and n. 2.

The law codes, or *sudebniki*, of 1497 and 1550 were mainly concerned with procedural matters, drawing on Byzantine precedent; but Russian practice probably continued to be based on customary law in the localities, supplemented by a variety of orders issued by the various *prikazy* (administrative offices). In 1649 a new code was promulgated, endorsed by an Assembly of the Land. It lacked any theoretical foundation and adopted a purely pragmatic approach to specific crimes according to a practical estimate of their frequency and harmfulness.[3] The new code drew on earlier Russian *sudebniki*, the decisions of *prikazy*, individual laws, laws borrowed from Byzantium and the Lithuanian Statute, adapted to the Russian needs of the moment. The code embraced civil, criminal, and military law indiscriminately, and provided the basic framework for Russian judicial life until the promulgation of the *Svod Zakonov* of 1832. The code also dealt with a number of procedural matters, laying down where cases were to be heard, and confirming the existing Muscovite confusion between administrative and judiciary instances.

A second deeply significant aspect of the Code of 1649 was its impact on the social structure of Russia. By formulating the service obligations of all classes of society, it completed the total enserfment of the peasantry. In a society in which all were servants and none were free, fear was the only means of preserving public order, and was induced by the universality, for all social estates, of painful punishment. The Code of 1649 prescribed the death penalty for 36 offences. It prescribed the knut ('beat cruelly' or 'beat without any mercy') more than any other form of corporal punishment. In theory many forms of physical mutilation could be inflicted, though the cutting off of hands and feet was gradually phased out when exile to Siberia became a usual punishment. The punishment for the murder of a husband was burying the woman alive up to the shoulders until she died. It was repealed in the 1680s, but is known to have been carried out as late as 1730.[4] The Code of 1649 only mentioned a few of the methods of capital punishment employed, but there seems to have been an endless variety. However, in the second half of the century practice seems to have grown gradually less harsh than the law.

THE REFORMS OF PETER I

With the advent of Peter I a new phase opened in Russian criminal law and practice. The violence and all-pervasiveness of his reform programme provoked an equally violent reaction. The number of offences for which the death penalty was inflicted and the forms which it took increased enormously.[5] In addition the codification of the laws governing various branches of Russian military and civil life provided a new framework for the penal policy of the government;

3. Fel'dshteyn, *op. cit.*, pp. 30ff.
4. In 1730 a woman was buried up to the neck on 21 August and died on 22 September. See A. Skinder, 'Zhivaya zhenshchina vrytaya v zemlyu v 1730', *Russkaya Starina*, 25, 1879, p. 398. For the same crime women were burned alive in England.
5. Timofeyev, *op. cit.*, p. 74.

members of the different social estates or of different functional categories were subject to their own laws. Thus the clergy, after an initial period of confusion at the beginning of Peter's reign, in theory came under the jurisdiction of the Holy Synod, in accordance with the Spiritual Regulations which governed the Church, but in practice the secular authorities tended to invade ecclesiastical jurisdiction with impunity.[6] The General Regulations not only laid down procedure in the bureaucracy but also established the penalties for failure to carry out orders, inefficiency, bribery, corruption, etc., and those accused of offences against the Regulations would be tried and sentenced by the employing body itself, namely a College or, in the provinces, the governor or voyevoda. The Navy, of course, ruled its own officers and sailors. But by far the most important for Russia was the Military Code, which subsumed all previous partial Petrine codes. Borrowed mainly from Sweden, the articles of the Military Code were not integrated with Russian law based on the Code of 1649 and subsequent ukazy.

Since all the nobles who were not physically incapacitated served in the armed forces for a great part of their life, the whole social estate fell under the jurisdiction of the Military Code – and to a lesser extent the Naval Code. Even when nobles had been transferred to the civil branch, and worked in the bureaucracy, as officers they remained subject to the Military Code even for civil offences, or for criminal offences which had nothing to do with the armed forces. Possibly because the code was applied to all serving officers, i.e. in practice to all nobles, its provisions were taken over and applied in civil cases. The military concept of a disciplined, hierarchically organized society was imposed on civil society, and in the absence of a civil code, the Military Code was used in civil courts to determine guilt and pass sentence in matters which had nothing to do with the armed forces, such as the trial of elderly women accused of murdering their serfs.

The Military Code and the Naval Code took over from their foreign models a whole series of new offences and new punishments, such as breaking on the wheel, quartering, shooting (*arkebuzirovaniye*). The death penalty was mentioned in 122 cases; mutilation of various kinds could be imposed in 11 cases; running the gauntlet (*spitzruten*) in 41 cases.[7] Burning alive was reserved for idolaters and sorcerers.

The social consequences of this form of codification were enormous. To begin with, it perpetuated the exclusion of almost half the population – the serfs – from the state's civil and criminal jurisdiction except in cases of really

6. For the clerical estate see G. Freeze, *The Russian Levites. Parish Clergy in the Eighteenth Century*, Harvard University Press, 1977, *passim*. For the Military Code, see Claes Peterson, *Peter the Great's Administrative and Judicial Reforms*, Stockholm, 1979, pp. 340ff. It should be remembered that all criminal codes in use at the time were very cruel.

7. It is difficult to find exact English equivalents for the immense variety of instruments of punishment. The knut ranked as the most severe. See A. Filippov, *O nakazanii po zakonodatel' stvu Petra Velikogo v svyazi s reformoyu*, Moscow, 1891, pp. 334ff. After 1711 serfs were no longer subjected to being beaten on the calves (*pravezh*) in place of their masters, condemned for debt. P. Maykov, *O svode zakonov rossiyskoy imperii*, St Petersburg, 1905, p. 10 n. 2.

serious crime such as murder, brigandage, robbery, treason etc. Most of the offences committed by serfs, small-scale misdemeanours, offences against religious practice, brawling and drunkenness, were dealt with by landowners directly or in estate courts run by stewards and peasant elders, or in the case of possessional serfs by factory or mine owners. (State peasants similarly came under the jurisdiction of communal institutions responsible to local government authorities such as the voyevodas.) Landowners were free to treat their serfs as they chose, though not to sentence them to death or to kill them. Nor, in principle, were they to use the knut. But since there was no control over their activities, they were able to use a whole arsenal of instruments of torture and punishment culminating in the death of the unfortunate victim. The more responsible landowners drafted veritable codes for the economic and legal administration of their estates.[8]

PUNISHMENTS

Broadly, punishments had been consolidated by Peter's reign into three types of penalties: the death penalty in various forms; 'political death', i.e. exile and hard labour and '*shel 'movaniye*' (dishonour); and corporal punishment, fines and prison. It was of course possible to be punished under several of these headings for one crime. Apart from the criminal activities listed in the Military Code, burning alive was reserved for apostasy from orthodoxy, conversion to Judaism etc. Executions took place in public and the remains were prominently displayed. It was typical of all the Petrine codes that punishment was prescribed without any evaluation of the seriousness of a given crime; and in the case of corporal punishment without ever specifying the number of lashes to be inflicted.

The death penalty

The death penalty was abolished officially in mid-century. When Elizabeth Petrovna seized the throne in 1741, she had already determined never to confirm a death sentence. In 1744 she ordered that all such sentences should be forwarded to her, as a result of which a vast number had accumulated by 1751 waiting for her to take a decision. In 1753 the Senate issued an ukaz stating that death sentences should be commuted to the knut, nostril clipping, branding and hard labour.[9] This was approved by Elizabeth who subsequently, on 20 September 1754, issued an ukaz, of a temporary nature, which abolished the death penalty until the introduction of a new code.[10]

8. See the study of 47 different codes in V.A. Aleksandrov, *Sel'skaya obshchina v Rossii, (XVII–nachalo XIX v)*, Moscow, 1976.
9. See M.F. Vladimirsky Budanov, *Obzor istorii russkogo prava*, Kiev, 1909, p. 371 and *passim* for the description of this event.
10. *Polnoye sobraniye zakonov Rossiyskoy imperii* (*PSZ*), St Petersburg, 1830, XII, No. 9293; see also 9312; without Senate confirmation the death penalty was not to be carried out.

This measure was not, however, by any means as humanitarian as it seems on the surface. For the punishment which came to be used where before the death sentence had been inflicted, namely the knut, could very easily kill. It was not a matter of the number of lashes, but of the manner of their delivery. A victim could survive one hundred, or die after three.[11] It was moreover a completely arbitrary punishment. Death depended on the caprice of the executioner, since the number of lashes was almost never stated. The norm was up to 40 for men, but up to 100 was said to be possible, sometimes spread over several days, particularly when used in the process of torture during an investigation.

Corporal punishment

Already at the end of the seventeenth century, contact with the West had led to a self-protective reaction among the elite of the aristocracy and the *d'yaki* or senior officials against the pain and the dishonour implicit in corporal punishment. Dishonour had not been a factor in the Muscovite attitude to punishment, but the concept crept in with the influx of Western military officers who brought with them some elements of Western military ethos and notions of chivalry. Peter seized on this new means of disciplining his officer class, even though it was bound to increase the gulf between the nobles and the rest of the population. He deliberately introduced and cultivated the idea that corporal punishment, notably the knut, was dishonouring, hence an officer who had been subjected to it lost his status as an officer and could no longer serve. Eventually it was replaced to a great extent in the army by the dreaded *spitzruten* (running the gauntlet), which could kill, but as a punishment inflicted by a man's own fellows, and not by an executioner, was less dishonourable.[12] *Shel'movaniye* was the most severe form of dishonourable punishment and entailed the expulsion of the criminal from the society of all good men. The victim of this punishment was reduced to the status of an outlaw: he could not give evidence, he could not petition against ill-treatment or assault. He was usually also sent into exile with hard labour, and suffered political death. 'Political death' was never defined specifically in Petrine legislation and the Senate first attempted a definition in 1753 when the Empress Elisabeth

11. The English traveller, Archdeacon William Coxe, reports seeing the administration of 333 lashes after which the man walked away. This must be a misprint, since it seems hardly likely that anyone could survive such a number, nor that any spectator could last out the time taken (several hours). *Travels into Poland, Russian, Sweden and Denmark*, London, 1784, I, p. 77.

12. Note that orders of chivalry were first introduced into Russia by Peter I. There is no Russian word conveying the social status of 'knight'; the French 'kaval'er' was used. The display of a naked body on the scaffold and the scars of the knut soon came to be regarded as incompatible with the honour of an officer or even of a soldier. Hence those sentenced to hard labour in perpetuity were beaten with the knut, but those who might possibly return to service were subjected to *spitzruten*. When Peter was asked what to do about galley slaves who had reached the end of their sentence, he replied that if they had been beaten with the knut the flag was to be waved over them to remove the stain before they were returned to service. Filippov, *op. cit.*, p. 273.

Petrovna asked to be told what it was and for what crimes it was prescribed. The Senate explained that in contrast to natural death, it was the fate of a criminal brought to the gallows on the scaffold, and subsequently suffering the knut, nostril clipping and exile.[13] The significance of this formula was underlined by the fact that between 1720 and 1753 it enabled a wife, if she wished, to marry again, for her husband was 'as dead'.[14] Political death was usually accompanied by confiscation of property.

Exile

The Petrine system also inherited and continued the practice of exiling convicts to settlement or hard labour in Siberia, or elsewhere, for a period, or in perpetuity; in the case of settlement, with their wives and children under three if they so wished. But in Peter's reign hard labour included the galleys (from which the Russian word *katorga* derives), the building of St Petersburg, Kronstadt, Azov, ship building, fortifications, endless construction projects for which convicts and conscripts were both used. Those exiled for settlement in Siberia included one peculiar category, namely criminals who had already purged their penalty, or accused who had not been perfectly cleared, whom the communities to which they belonged did not wish to receive again. This was frequently the case in peasant communes, as a result of which a man theoretically innocent might be sent off to exile.[15]

Prison

Prison was too wasteful of manpower and money to play a large part in the Petrine penal system. Prisons were mainly places in which people were kept for short sentences, or while awaiting trial. Where it was necessary to sentence for longer terms, as with the prisoners of the security organs, the convicted were usually sent to the great fortresses of St Peter and Paul and Schlüsselburg, or to other forts or to monasteries. In all prisons, and in convoys of convicts, shackles and fetters, irons, chains, and metal collars were used both as a means of punishment and for security reasons. They were also frequently used on estates by landowners.

THE SECURITY SYSTEM

One further institution owes its origin and development to Peter – what became known in the course of the first half of the century as the Secret

13. The phrase 'political death' was used for the first time in 1723. For a discussion of 'loss of rights' in a country in which no one had any rights see Filippov, *op. cit.*, pp. 365ff., and n. 3. Loss of rights amounted in the end to loss of property and *chin*, or to the loss of the right to serve in a form leading to the granting of a *chin*.
14. Filippov, *op. cit.*, p. 369. After 1753 the Synod's permission was necessary for remarriage.
15. See Alan Wood, 'The Use and Abuse of Administrative Exile to Siberia', *Irish Slavonic Studies*, 6, 1985, pp. 65–81.

Chancery. It developed out of the Preobrazhensky Prikaz, the body set up to run Peter's first Guards Regiments. From the revolt of the strel'tsy onwards, it investigated all cases of 'anti-government' thought and action described as political, ranging from criticism of ukazy to claims that Peter was antichrist – with the notable exception of the trial of Aleksey Petrovich. The functions of the Secret Chancery were carried on after Peter's death by a number of intermediate organizations until the setting up in April 1731 of the Chancery of Secret Investigation. The cry of *slovo i delo gosudarevo* ('word and deed of the lord') was enough to launch an inquisition in which the accused, the delator and the witnesses were all tortured. The description of the way the Secret Chancery functioned given by the lawyer Goryushkin, who joined it at the age of 12, leaves one in no doubt that it was a worthy ancestor of the GPU or the NKVD, though its resources were strikingly small by comparison – a staff of 32 and a budget of 3360 rpa.[16] Orders issued by the Secret Chancery had to be obeyed throughout the country and overrode orders issued by other state institutions. Both soldiers and civilians passed through its hands: punishment for the former (if guilty, or if guilty of a false denunciation) was usually *spitzruten*; for the latter it was the knut until 1742, when the whip replaced it. The Chancery survived until 1762, when it was abolished by Peter III, and its functions transferred to a special 'secret expedition' of the Senate. The practice of denunciation by means of the formula *slovo i delo gosudarevo* was also now forbidden.[17]

THE PROCURACY AND COURT PROCEDURE

This sketch of the Russian penal system would not be complete without reference to two other features: the first is the institution of the procuracy. The Procurator General was the tsar's agent (*oko gosudarevo*) in the Senate, its secretary, the controller of its agenda, and the head of a network of procurators throughout the country. The function of the procurators was to supervise the legality of the action taken by officials at all levels. As an institution it suffered from the fact that its members (who of course had no legal training) were often junior in military rank to the officials, also officers, the legality of whose actions they were supposed to superintend. Nevertheless, the Procurator General

16. A special Commission was set up to try Aleksey Petrovich, which subsequently survived for a while. For the Preobrazhensky Prikaz see the classic work by N.B. Golikova, *Politicheskiye protsessy pri Petre*, Moscow, 1957. See also by the same author 'Organy politicheskogo syska i ikh razvitiye v XVII–XVIII vv' in *Absolyutizm v Rossii*, ed. N.M. Druzhinin, Moscow, 1964, pp. 243–80.

17. V.V. Samoylov, 'Vozniknoveniye taynoy ekspeditsii pri Senate', *Voprosy Istorii*, 6, 1948, pp. 79ff. I find the statement by J.L.H. Keep that Russia was unique among eighteenth-century European states in having a specific governmental institution for the repression of political 'crimes' somewhat surprising. The lieutenant de la police in Paris had political functions, spelled out in a memorandum prepared by Berryer. See M. Le Clère, *Histoire de la Police*, Paris, 1964, pp. 41ff. For Keep see his 'The Secret Chancellery; the Guards and the Dynastic Crisis of 1740–1741', *Forschungen zur osteuropäischen Geschichte*, 25, 1978, pp. 169–93.

had the ear of the tsar, and the procurators throughout the country provided an alternative channel through which glaring injustices might achieve *glasnost'*.

The second feature is court procedure, and the means of procuring evidence. In Muscovy, the accusatorial system (*sud*), had coexisted with the inquisitorial system (*rozysk*). In the belief, typical of eighteenth-century *Polizeiwissenschaft*, that state supervision and control would eliminate corruption and chicanery, Peter I at first developed the inquisitorial process in the so-called 'Short Presentation of Trials' which was promulgated as part of the Military Code in 1716. Borrowed from Swedish sources, the Short Presentation prescribed a completely inquisitorial procedure, in which the state was the prosecutor, proceedings were conducted in strict secrecy, based on written materials, with legally established formal proofs, including primarily a confession which could be extracted by torture. The sentence was simply pronounced by the judge according to his lights. It does not appear that the Short Presentation was intended for use in civil proceedings.[18]

However, the administrative reforms of the 1720s led Peter to promulgate an 'Ukaz on the Form of Trials' in 1723 (again based on Swedish practice), reviving the accusatorial system in which there was no state prosecutor, but a plaintiff and a defendant, appearing before a neutral judge. But serious crimes against the state, such as *lèse majesté*, treason, robbery, brigandage, murder or revolt were to be tried by inquisitorial procedure, if the criminal was actually caught in the act. If actual proofs were not conclusive, however, then the accusatorial procedure was to be employed until sufficient proofs had been accumulated to transfer the case to the inquisitorial procedure. Both systems evidently thus operated in eighteenth-century Russia, and it is likely that there was some confusion in practice. This may explain the complaints in several of the instructions submitted by noble deputies to Catherine II's Legislative Commission in 1767 against the practice of dealing with brigandage by means of the accusatory procedure. The nobles complained that, since the initiative in collecting evidence and prosecuting was left to them, and they frequently lived a long way from the administrative centre, the prosecution limped along, nothing was done, the criminals were either released or escaped and returned to revenge themselves on those who had denounced them or caught them in the first place.[19]

THE DEVELOPMENT OF RUSSIAN JURISPRUDENCE

We have to realize the total absence of a native school of jurisprudence – and of trained lawyers – in Russia. From the beginning of the eighteenth century,

18. See Peterson, *op. cit.*, pp. 339ff; see also R. Wortman, 'Peter the Great and Court Procedure', *Canadian-American Slavic Studies*, 8, No. 2, Summer 1974, pp. 303–10.
19. *Sbornik Imperatorskogo russkogo istoricheskago obshchestva* (*SIRIO*), vol. 14, p. 291, Nakaz of the nobles of Belozersk; *ibid.*, p. 99, Nakaz of the nobles of Nizhniy Lomov, asking that all criminal matters should be dealt with by the inquisitorial procedure; *SIRIO*, vol. 8, p. 531, Nakaz of the nobles of Suzdal; p. 356, Nakaz of the nobles of Voronezh.

when Russians first attempted to codify the law under Peter I, they came under the influence of theories of natural law totally at variance with their own historical experience. Peter tried to import lawyers and to set up schools of law. But his view of a lawyer was someone who knew procedure, and was probably dishonest. The bulk of the teaching and the textbooks introduced into Russia concentrated on *how* to administer justice, not on the nature of justice and law. A second trend developed with the influence of natural law theory, following the ideas of Christian Wolff, and of the German jurist, Nettelbladt, who was very influential in Moscow University, and his disciple, Ph. H. Dilthey. The gulf between natural law theory and Russian positive law proved difficult to bridge. Strube de Pyrmont attempted to reconcile *pravo*, the law of nature, with *zakon*, positive law. The German professor, K.G. Langer, who created the first real school of Russian law, combined the historical context with natural law, and in regard to criminal law, the history of individual and social conditions.[20]

CATHERINE II AND THE NAKAZ

This was the background against which Catherine began to operate, bringing in a number of fresh ideas and a more rational approach, with varying fortune, perseverance and consistency. In attributing initiatives to her, it must be taken for granted that she represented a new trend towards rationality and humanity which had developed among the aristocracy and the military and bureaucratic elite, even if it found little response in the country at large. There is in fact very little evidence of the existence of any public debate on the subject of criminal law reform at this time, of the kind which had already begun to take place elsewhere, particularly after the publication of Beccaria's *Delle delitte e delle pene*. The book itself was not published in Russian translation until 1803, but the court aristocracy was of course familiar with the French translation.

The first outward sign of a new course was the *Great Instruction* or *Nakaz*, prepared for the Legislative Commission of 1767 by Catherine herself. She had drawn largely on Montesquieu, whose condemnation of torture she echoed. But the main influence in the field of penal policy was that of Beccaria, whose book Catherine read in 1765 in Morellet's translation. As usual with her, Catherine was less interested in the theoretical approach than in the pragmatic utilitarian approach. Hence she discarded Beccaria's theory of the social contract, and went straight to those aspects of his book which stated in compelling terms the need to regard the punishment of crime not as divine retribution, but as a means of guaranteeing and preserving society. Her borrowing concerned the criminal law as such, and the penal system, which she regarded as quite separate from the organization of the courts. She introduced into Russia the concept of *nullum crimen sine lege*, and *nulla poena sine lege*; she

20. Fel'dshteyn, *op. cit.*, pp. 151ff.

argued that law should be a deterrent, that prevention was better than cure, that the punishment should fit the crime, and that a distinction should be drawn between crimes, moral offences and misdemeanours.

The right to punish and the nature of punishment were very carefully analysed in the *Nakaz*. The right to punish resides in the legislator, i.e. the ruler; punishment should be quick, certain, unavoidable and appropriate. It should not reflect the need to terrorize people by the threat of painful punishment, it should not imply retribution so much as deterrence. Cruel punishments blunted sensibilities, and the death penalty was in normal times unnecessary. The *Nakaz* also gave an evaluation of other methods besides corporal punishment, such as banishment, deportation, fines, and imprisonment. The Empress distinguished between custody pending trial, and prison as a penal sentence. Offences against religion were viewed as offences against public order, not as sacrilege, and Catherine proclaimed a 'prudent' toleration in religion.

All punishments which mutilated the human body were loudly condemned, and in article 194 Catherine declared that since no man is guilty until he has been condemned by a court, it is quite unjustifiable to use torture, which was a form of punishment, in order to procure a confession of guilt. 'The innocent ought not to be tortured', and 'in the Eye of the Law every person is innocent whose crime is not yet proved'.[21]

The *Nakaz* is not a consistent document, and Catherine was not a lawyer. In a somewhat confused and even contradictory manner, she draws both on natural law theory and on historical tradition, though barely on Russian positive law. It is possible that she was influenced by K.G. Langer's *Slovo o nachale i rasprostraneniyi polozhitel'nykh zakonov*, published in 1766. Perhaps more incongruous than any other divergence between the *Nakaz* and Russian reality was Catherine's statement that the law should be designed for individuals, which implied the defining of a border between the rights and duties of the individual and the rights of the community or the state, and the existence of the *litso*, or person, as a bearer of rights, as distinct from the community to which he belonged, and to which he was bound by the collective guarantee (*krugovaya poruka*).[22]

THE INFLUENCE OF THE NAKAZ

In the context of Russian society of the 1760s, this was a startling programme to hear from the pen of the ruler. It was too out of tune with the general trend of

21. On the many editions of the *Nakaz* see W.E. Butler, 'The Nakaz of Catherine the Great', *American Book Collector*, 16, No. 5, January 1966, pp. 19ff., and for the Roumanian edition, Ariadne Cioran Camariano, 'Traducerile în limba greacà si Romînà a "Nacazului" învoîtátura Ecaterinei a II-a', *Studii, Revista de Istorie*, 11, 1958, pp. 123–32. For the Italian versions, see F. Venturi, *Settecento Riformatore La prima crisi dell'Antico Regime (1768–1776)*, Turin, 1979, III, pp. 80–1. For Beccaria's influence, Fel'dshteyn is even more detailed and searching than the standard account in N.D. Chechulin, *Nakaz imperatritsy Yekateriny II dannyy kommissii po sochineniyu proekta novogo ulozheniya*, Moscow, 1907.

22. Fel'dshteyn, *op. cit.*, p. 60 and n. 2; Vladimirsky Budanov, *op. cit.*, p. 315, and also article 243 of the *Nakaz*.

legal theory and practice in Russia to have an immediate effect on jurisprudence (though none of the exponents of natural law theory fared any better). But the *Nakaz* had a considerable influence in a number of ways. In the first place it introduced into Russian intellectual life the most advanced contemporary ideas on the subject of criminal law, and prepared the ground for the writings of a whole school of publicists, such as F. Ushakov and A. Radishchev, who advocated abolition of the death penalty, and later nineteenth-century writers on criminal law who also drew upon Catherine's maxims.[23]

Secondly, the *Nakaz* exercised a beneficient effect in an unexpected way on Russian practice. It was not a code, it had no legal validity, and could not be used in the courts to bolster a judicial decision. Yet it became the standard against which legislation and judicial decisions were measured. For instance, almost since her accession, Catherine had taken steps to limit the use of torture, not daring to abolish such a time-honoured practice at one fell swoop.[24] In ukazy of 11 and 23 February 1763, she ordered that torture should only be used with great caution, and not if the accused had already confessed. If torture was permissible in law, it should not be used without reference to the local voyevoda in the provincial chanceries.[25] These two ukazy led to a considerable outcry, which found its expression in the debates in the Legislative Commission. In the instructions put forward by noble deputies to the Commission in 1767, there were repeated demands for the repeal of Catherine's ukazy of 11 and 23 February 1763 limiting torture, on the grounds that they made it impossible to convict dangerous criminals and discover their accomplices.[26]

Yet in 1767, after the publication of the *Nakaz*, Catherine went even further. In an ukaz of 13 November she issued an order to the Senate to the effect that in matters in which torture could be used according to existing law, investigations should be conducted on the basis of Chapter X of the Nakaz (the chapter almost entirely lifted from Beccaria) which condemned torture roundly. This same order was repeated in an ukaz of 8 November 1774, which ordered categorically that no form of torture should be used in guberniya courts, by implication not even whipping and beating, and that the principles of the *Nakaz* should be followed.[27] The same principles were extended to

23. *Ibid.*, pp. 214ff.
24. See N.M. Korkunov, *Z.A. Goryushkin, Rossiyski zakonoiskusnik*, St Petersburg, 1895 for Goryushkin's horrifying description of his service in the Moscow sysknyy prikaz, which he entered at the age of 12.
25. *PSZ*, XVI, No. 11750; see also No. 11759 of 17 February 1763.
26. *SIRIO*, vol. 14, p. 479, the Nakaz of the nobles of Chukhlomskiy uezd refers specifically to Catherine's ukazy and demands that people be tortured as before in order to ensure discovery of their accomplices; p. 291, Nakaz of the nobles of Belozersk, demanding the full severity of the Code of 1649, and the use of torture; *SIRIO* vol. 8, p. 531, Nakaz of the nobles of Suzdal, pointing to the uselessness of 'admonishing' criminals *(uveshchevat')*.
27. M.M. Gernet, *Istoriya tsarskoy tyur'my*, I., p. 99. It is curious that this order was issued when the repressions against the Pugachevshchina were in full swing. Was it meant to influence the work of repression? Or was it meant to prevent confusion between the ordinary civil courts and the special courts?

military courts in 1782.[28] In general, in cases where humane judges and officers wished to reduce a penalty, the safe method, which was widely adopted, was to quote the *Nakaz*. Thus, the *Nakaz* was interpreted as positive law in many cases, and in many more it provided the intellectual climate in which decisions were taken. In judicial decisions, existing law was interpreted in the spirit of the *Nakaz*, or sometimes, where necessary, a new law was issued. In 1770, for instance, there was an epidemic of minor thefts in Belgorod among young *odnodvortsy*, anxious to evade military service; the penalty, in accordance with the Code of 1649, was the knut. The guberniya chancery thought this penalty excessive, and proposed instead a whipping and inscription in the army. The proposal went to the Senate in full session, which decided against the Code of 1649 and in favour of the *Nakaz* as the basic principle of legislation. As a result a general law on theft, applicable to all except the nobility and the priestly caste, was issued on 27 February 1773. It quoted articles 205 and 240 from the *Nakaz*, and laid down that for thefts worth less than 20r, the guilty were to be whipped and sent to the army, and in the case of serfs and state peasants the owners or communes would receive a recruit quittance. Those guilty of thefts valued at more than 20r would be punished as previously (i.e. the knut) unless they were also fit to serve in the army, in which case they would be whipped.

The *Nakaz* was only quoted once in a judicial decision in the reign of Paul I, but it was frequently referred to in the reign of Alexander. M. Klochkov, who has studied the matter in the records of the Senate, concludes that some 41 articles are referred to in various judgments, mainly from Chapters IX, X and XV, stressing the general principles of discretion in making arrests on slender grounds, the need to go carefully into the evidence, acquitting where proof is not sufficient or where there is any doubt, the rejection of torture, making the punishment fit the crime, and reducing it where possible.[29]

The Legislative Commission of 1767–74 led to no new Russian code of laws, though, as we shall see, many of the principles of the *Nakaz* trickled through into areas of the criminal law which were partly codified, into ukazy dealing with specific issues, and into the major re-structuring of administrative institutions such as the Statute of 1775, or of social estates such as the Charters to the Nobles and to the Towns of 1785.

An example which predates the *Nakaz* deals with the definition of criminal responsibility. In Russian law the age of majority varied according to the

28. *PSZ*, XXI, No. 15313 of 1 January 1782, referring to a secret ukaz of 13 November 1767 which is not in *PSZ*. Torture was not to be applied where it was allowed in the Military and Naval Codes, without reference to the College of War and the Admiralty College.

29. See M. Klochkov, *Nakaz imperatritsy Yekateriny II v sudebnoy praktike* in *Sbornik statey v chest' Matveya Kuz'micha Lyubavskogo*, Petrograd, 1917, pp. 1–18; see also A.V. Florovsky, on Friedrich Andreae, *Beiträge zur Geschichte Katharinas II*, Berlin, 1912, review in *Zhurnal Ministerstva Narodnogo Prosveshcheniya*, March 1914, pp. 188–97. Florovsky notes the existence among the papers of Prince M.M. Shcherbatov in the Imperial Public Library of a list of decisions taken by the Senate based on the *Nakaz*. He argues that the *Polnoye Sobraniye Zakonov* does not fully reflect the influence of the *Nakaz*, since it was quoted much more frequently in ukazy dealing with religious toleration, illegitimate children, or the procedure to be followed on arrest etc. It was also frequently cited in petitions addressed to the Empress. For the ukaz of 25 February 1773, see *PSZ*, XIX, No. 13951.

context but in criminal law it had already been established as 17 as far back as 1742.[30] Minors could not be sentenced to the knut, only to whipping and confinement in a monastery. The whole concept was refined in the ukaz of 2 March 1765: those under 17 guilty of crimes for which the death penalty or the knut was prescribed by law were to be referred to the Senate for decision (the whole question had been opened up because of the murder of two girls by a girl of 14). Youths of 15–17 could be whipped, from 10–15 birched, and children under 10 were to be handed over to their parents or to their landowner.[31]

In 1781 there was a further attempt at codifying the specific forms of theft which were now divided into three kinds: *grabezh* (armed robbery against a person), *krazha* (theft from unattended premises) and *moshenichestvo* (fraud), and into two groups, of more or less value than 20r. If the value was above 20r, the offences were to be proceeded with according to existing law. But in the case of theft of less than 20r in value, the offender was to be punished by confinement in a workhouse (see below), and the value of the theft was to be worked off with an increment of 6 per cent. In the case of a second offence, the criminal was to be sentenced to two lashes of the whip, and to work off the sum stolen with an increment of 12 per cent; a third offence incurred the punishment of three lashes of the whip and an increment of 18 per cent. Fraud was treated in a similar way by starting with 24 hours on bread and water. There are two interesting features about this ukaz, apart from its attempt to lay down a general law for the treatment of minor thefts: first, no first offenders of *any* social estate receive corporal punishment; and in the case of second and third offenders, for the first time to my knowledge, the number of lashes of the whip is specified – and they are very few by contemporary standards anywhere.[32]

THE STATUTE OF LOCAL ADMINISTRATION OF 1775

The approach to law of the *Nakaz* found an echo in the great Statute of Local Administration of 1775, which set up a whole new network of civil and criminal courts, separated for the first time, and divided on an estate basis. The new structure of the courts provided for appeals from the lower to the next court in the case of a sentence to death, *shel'movaniye*, or deprivation of rights (political death), the knut or the whip; the reviewing court then passed it to the guberniya criminal chamber which again reviewed, confirmed or amended the sentence, and passed it to the governor for confirmation. Until 1784 the governor was entitled to confirm such sentences except in the case of nobles which had to be passed to the Senate; after 1784 all such sentences, whatever the social estate of the accused, had to be forwarded to the Senate in crimes arising from

30. *PSZ*, XI, No. 8601.
31. *PSZ*, XVII, No. 12412, 2 March 1765.
32. *PSZ*, XXI, No. 15147, 3 April 1781, further defined in 3 April 1787. Not until 1807 was an order issued to always specify the number of lashes.

or committed in the course of duty. Ordinary crimes were treated as before.[33] Finally, the Senate could forward to the Empress cases in which it had not been able to reach agreement, or had been unable to find a relevant law.

The Statute did not introduce any novelties in the field of criminal law, though it clarified the appeals procedure and laid down a series of fines for frivolous appeals against sentences and for various forms of dereliction of duty (the proceeds payable for the maintenance of schools). In theory at any rate, the fact that sentences involving really harsh punishments had to be forwarded to the Senate was in the interests of the offender, since in almost all known cases the Senate invariably took a more lenient view of the offence than the lower courts which may not have had the courage to go against local public opinion, or to move away from the letter of the law.

The major innovation of the Statute from the judicial point of view was the establishment of the *sovestnyy sud* or Courts of Conscience. There has been a good deal of debate in the literature about the sources on which Catherine drew for this institution, which include the *Grande Encyclopédie* (Équite, Droit), the English equity or chancery court, and the Ukrainian *treteyskiy sud* (court of arbitration). In the present context what matters is not so much its origins as the power given to it and the way it functioned. According to the definition in the Statute, the Conscience Court was set up in order to attenuate the severity of the law and to take circumstances into account in pronouncing judgment. It could act as a court of arbitration in civil cases, but in criminal cases its jurisdiction extended to offences committed by lunatics, minors, and cases concerning sorcery. It was also to the Court of Conscience that an offender imprisoned for more than three days, without being formally charged with a specific crime, could appeal for release on bail (except in cases of *lèse majesté*, treason, murder, theft and brigandage). Unfortunately there appear to exist only two studies of the functioning of conscience courts, published in 1909 and 1983, and far too little is therefore known about how they operated. But a surprising number of serious crimes such as murder came before those courts when there was no question of insanity. This suggests that cases were going before the Conscience Court because its procedure was speedier. In 1780 the Smolensk Conscience Court, set up after 1775, had already dealt with 18 criminal cases and settled 700 civil cases.[34] The St Petersburg court heard 2,016 cases between 1780 and 1793.[35] The courts certainly heard cases dealing with minors and sexual offenders as well. Sentences were usually more lenient than in other courts: a 14-year-old girl in Tula who had kept silent about the murder of her mistress by house serfs was not sentenced to corporal punishment, but to a month in the workhouse; a serf who had accidentally killed another serf was

33. *PSZ*, XXII, No. 16022, 17 June 1784.

34. *SIRIO*, vol. 1, p. 384.

35. In her ground-breaking study of the conscience courts of the guberniya of St Petersburg, Kaluga and Archangel, Dr Hartley mentions only one earlier work, by N.N. Knorring, a study of the Conscience Court of the guberniya of Tula. See her 'Catherine's Conscience Court – An English Equity Court?' in A.G. Cross, ed., *Russia and the West in the Eighteenth Century*, Oriental Research Partners, Newtonville, Mass., 1983, pp. 306–18.

freed and sent home because he had already been held under guard for a long time. Known cases of appeal for release on bail are extremely rare. Three have been noted by Dr Hartley and I have found one in 1817.[36] But it must be stressed again that until a thorough study of the cases that went before these courts, and of their verdicts, is made, judgment on their efficacy must be suspended. One may only note that Catherine herself seems to have placed great faith in them.[37]

THE POLICE ORDINANCE OF 1782

The Police Ordinance of 1782 was in its way too a codification of penal procedure within its own framework. The *Nakaz* is here less in evidence than the *Traité de la Police* of Nicolas de la Mare, and the traditional *Polizeiordnungen* typical of seventeenth- and eighteenth-century Germany.[38] Detailed and very wide-ranging regulations were laid down in the Ordinance for the maintenance of cleanliness, good order and decency in the towns. An offence against morality was now treated under a specific regulation as a breach of the law. Penalties for infringement of these regulations, which could be summarily inflicted by the police, were laid down in a short penal code, articles 191–274 of the Ordinance. If a serious crime had been committed, the police board, composed of a provost, a criminal and a civil assessor and two councillors, could arrest and send the accused to detention in a prison attached to a court for investigation. If it was merely a misdemeanour the police could inflict summary punishment, which amounted to detention for one to four days, fines, detention in houses of correction or workhouses, heating the water in the public baths for those over the age of seven who dared to penetrate the baths of the opposite sex. The police board was now authorized to deal summarily with theft and fraud of less than 20r in value. There was no nation-wide police service or organization; each town had its own semi-appointed, semi-elected constables and wardens, under the direction of the *gorodnichi* or town provost, and under the overall authority of the governor. According to one visitor, the St Petersburg Police Administration dealt with some 20,000 cases in the course of a year, and some 10,000 prisoners passed through its hands.[39]

THE RIGHTS OF THE ESTATES

All forms of physical mutilation had been phased out without any specific legislation by mid-century, as had burning and burying alive, but not nostril

36. Hartley, *op. cit.*, p. 310; see also *Zhurnal Zakonodatel'stva na 1817 god*, St Petersburg, 1819. No. 167, 8 June 1817.
37. See her remark to her secretary in *Dnevnik Khrapovitskogo*, St Petersburg, 1874, p. 54.
38. *PSZ*, XXI, No. 15379, 8 April 1982; for the latest exposition see M. Raeff, *The Well-Ordered Police State. Social and Institutional Change through Law in the Germanies and Russia, 1600–1800*, Yale University Press, 1983.
39. *Archivo del General Miranda* II., Caracas, 1929, p. 466. Miranda also states that there was a separate police court for the German population of the capital.

clipping and branding for men, which were not regarded as a punishment but as a means of preventing escape.[40] And ever since the beginning of the century when the idea that corporal punishment dishonoured the status, then the person, of a noble and rendered him unfit to serve as an officer had first dawned, the Russian nobility had striven to secure immunity from physically degrading punishment. Little by little in the 1740s and 1750s the practice of flogging nobles began to decline, even though the whip, the knut and batogi remained in use for other social groups. Even so, the whip had replaced the knut for many offences from mid-century, particularly offences against property, among other reasons because the whip did not prevent the offender from performing military service afterwards.[41] By the 1760s the penalty of whipping was always commuted in the case of nobles; yet the privilege of immunity from corporal punishment is not mentioned in the manifesto freeing the nobility from service issued by Peter III in February 1762.[42] The demand does however surface in the discussion in the commission set up by Catherine II in 1763 to decide whether to confirm or amend the manifesto.[43] In the event it was not formally confirmed but, *de facto*, nobles were no longer subjected to corporal punishment. Pressure had also been mounting within the clerical estate for some time to raise the esteem in which they were held, and in 1767 the Synod at last agreed that the ecclesiastical authorities should no longer sentence offending clerics to corporal punishment. But they were still subject to the full rigours of the law for crimes which went before the ordinary civil courts, and they were only too often regarded by noble landowners as little better than peasants and treated accordingly. Not until the last year of Catherine's reign, in 1796, did priests obtain full immunity from corporal punishment.[44]

The Charters to the Nobility and the Towns of 1785 were landmarks in the codification, theoretically 'for ever', of the judicial, personal and property rights of the nobles and townspeople, and provided legal norms for the operation of the law courts. The principle of individual responsibility for criminal acts was enunciated, and family property was now no longer subject to confiscation. Nobles, merchants of the first guild in the towns, and the category of urban citizens known as 'distinguished' were henceforth legally immune from corporal punishment. This immunity was lifted by Paul for nobles, priests and townspeople but finally restored by Alexander I in 1801.[45]

40. Even *shel'movaniye* was modified in 1766, and turned into 'deprivation of the rights of status' (*Lisheniye vsekh prav sostoyaniya*). See N.D. Sergeevsky, *Russkoye ugolovnoye pravo chast' obshchaya*, St Petersburg, 1913 (10th edn), pp. 190ff.

41. Timofeyev, *op. cit.*, p. 96, p. 197.

42. Contrary to what is stated in Freeze, *op. cit.*, p. 70.

43. In 1764 Catherine forbade any form of corporal punishment of any one including servants in the school attached to the Academy of Sciences, so that 'the children should not see any example of severity'. *PSZ*, XVI, No. 12275, 4 November 1764.

44. Freeze, *op. cit.*, pp. 70–1.

45. In the unpromulgated Charter to the State Peasants, dating from 1787, the first and second categories of rich peasants with the unlikely fortune of above 10,000 rubles, or between 1,000 and 10,000r. were also to be given immunity from corporal punishment. See *SIRIO*, vol. 20, pp. 447ff., 'Proekt imperatritsy Yekateriny II ob ustroistve svobodnykh sel'skikh obyvateley'.

However, the rest of the population continued to be subject to the knut (for really serious crimes) and the whip. The former seems to have been administered much more rarely. John Howard, the English prison reformer, saw a man suffer 60 lashes, from which he later seems to have died, and a woman 25.[46] Miranda saw the administration of 11 lashes.[47] An ukaz of 1812 ordered that the number of lashes must be specified in the sentence; the norm then was between 10 and 100, usually under 50. In 1768 Catherine had also abolished the custom of seizing on a passer-by in the street, and hoisting the victim on to his back for the executioner to administer the flogging. This task was in future to be carried out by convicts.[48] The only alleviation to the fate of those condemned to corporal punishment was the frequent amnesties which punctuated Catherine's reign.[49]

THE PENAL SYSTEM UNDER CATHERINE II

The continued existence of a security organ such as the Secret Expedition in the Senate, directly under the Procurator General, Prince A.A. Vyazemsky, reflects the regime's need to root out any trace of seditious intention. Most of the recorded cases in Catherine's reign are trivial – reluctance in a peasant society to accept the legitimacy of a woman's rule, incautious exclamations in a moment of drunken euphoria, claims to be Peter III – and were often treated without undue severity. But there were a number of serious cases in which the sentences were harsh, notably cases of intellectual dissent such as that of Radishchev, or of masonic links with the Grand Duke Paul, as in the case of N.I. Novikov, or criticism of the basic social structure of Russia as in the case of F. Krechetov. The first was sentenced to exile in a very distant backwater in Siberia; the two latter to incarceration in state prisons.[50]

The question remains to what extent torture was used in the Secret Expedition. There is no doubt that Catherine tried to abolish it. There are too many private letters and instructions to her senior servants, never meant for publication, but to be obeyed, which support this view. But how far could she control the actions of her subordinates in St Petersburg, let alone throughout the

46. J. Howard, *The State of the Prisons in England and Wales with Preliminary Observations and an Account of some Foreign Prisons and Hospitals*, London, 1792 (4th edn), pp. 75ff. The knut was abolished in 1845.
47. Miranda, *op. cit.*, p. 469.
48. *PSZ*, XVII, No. 13108, 28 April 1768.
49. I have found no mention in any ukaz of Catherine's reign of the sentencing of convicts to the galleys, though galleys were still extensively used in the Russian fleet, both in the Baltic and in the Black Sea. It appears, according to contemporary reports, that the galleys were manned by sailors who were landed and put into camps at night.
50. Catherine certainly followed the work of the Secret Expedition and sometimes issued orders to it directly. See for instance her order to N.P. Arkharov, the Chief of Police in St Petersburg, sending a list of ten people, clearly officers, who were banished to live on their estates and not allowed to visit the capitals or the imperial residences. 'Iz bumag N.P. Arkharova', *Russkiy Arkhiv*, 1864, cols. 420–76.

country? It is generally assumed that S.S. Sheshkovsky, the head of the Secret Expedition which had replaced the Secret Chancery, used torture extensively. There is no evidence to support this. All the stories told about Sheshkovsky rely on the formula 'they say', or assert that Sheshkovsky made his victims swear that they would never reveal what had happened within the four walls of his rooms in the Procurator General's palace. However, there is no reason to believe that such an oath would be kept, particularly after Sheshkovsky's retirement in 1792, or in the case of highly placed personages. There is only one piece of concrete evidence, namely a report by Prince A.A. Vyazemsky to the Empress, on a soldier who had been arrested for declaring that Peter III had been seen in the Crimea, and that Russian troops were awaiting him like a father. Vyazemsky reported that the soldier had been interrogated *s pristrastiyem*, i.e. with coercion, but he added 'not as before, but with a beating with batogi'. Catherine confirmed Vyazemsky's proposal that since the soldier had evidently been drunk, and what he said invented and false, the beating should count as his punishment, and he should be released and sent back to his service.[51]

It appears from Vyazemsky's report that though the horrifying tortures of old were no longer used, beating and whipping, or the threat of torture, were still regarded as a legitimate means of extracting confessions. However, there is no record of torture of *any* kind being used in the cases of prominent nobles like Radishchev, Novikov or Knyazhnin, nor in the case of Mirovich or Pugachev. It is of course a fair assumption that *pristrastiye* was less likely to be used against members of the elite and in the capital.[52] Sheshkovsky is also reported to have been used by Catherine to give a whipping to court ladies who had made offensive personal remarks about her, but again, these stories are conflicting and there is no evidence to support them.

State prisoners were usually incarcerated in the Peter and Paul fortress in St Petersburg, in the grim castle of Schlüsselburg, or in some monastery prisons. The young Ukrainian, G. Vinsky, has given a vivid description of the months he spent in the Peter and Paul fortress, where he was *not* incidentally tortured, before his release to settlement in Orenburg guberniya with loss of noble rank.[53] In a somewhat different genre is the account of Julian Niemcewicz of the period he spent there as a prisoner of war, when his servant crossed the Neva every day to the Marble Palace where Koscsziusko was held, to collect the five-course dinner and wine prepared for him.[54] What happened to the unfortunates held in the unlit and overheated cells Vinsky was held in at first we do not know. Novikov was confined in Schüsselburg, in a cell which he was allowed to share with his personal physician and his personal serf, there to

51. 'Iz bumag general prokurora knyazya A.A. Vyazemskogo', *Russkiy Arkhiv*, 1878, II, col. 478.
52. Catherine's constant repetition of her orders against the use of torture does tend to suggest that she was not very confident of their being obeyed.
53. See G. Vinsky, *Moe vremya*, introduction by I. de Madariaga, Oriental Research Partners, Newtonville, Mass., 1974.
54. Julian Ursin Niemcewicz, *Notes sur ma captivité à St Petersbourg en 1794, 1795, et 1796*, Paris, 1843, p. 152. Niemcewicz was allowed books, pen and paper, and of course his servant. He suffered above all from lack of air and exercise.

attend to his wants. Noble inmates of both institutions were usually held with some consideration for their rank, and larger allowances of food and drink.

The Secret Expedition was ultimately also responsible for the investigation of serious uprisings such as the attempt by Mirovich to free the ex-emperor Ivan VI, the plague riot in Moscow in 1771, or the Pugachev Revolt. In the former, Mirovich was eventually sentenced to death by beheading (as befitting an officer). Pugachev was sentenced to death by quartering, but on the special and secret instructions of the Empress, he was beheaded first; four others were executed with him. However, the repression throughout the country seems to have been exceptionally severe. General Peter Panin is reported to have sentenced 326 people to death (though it is not clear whether the sentences were carried out) and to have authorized physical mutilation such as the cutting off of ears, which had not been in use for some time.[55]

We can have some idea of the number of people sentenced to prisons or banishment by the Secret Expedition from its records when it was finally abolished by Alexander I in 1801. A list of inmates of Schlüsselburg which unfortunately includes both prisoners and 'already freed' gives 49 names, many of which of course had been sent there by the arbitrary Paul I. A man and a woman for instance were confined because of their 'wilful acquaintance and its subsequent consequences'. Of the 49, 46 were men and 22 were officers up to the rank of Major-General. In many cases the offences had little to do with security, but concerned illegal seizure of land, gambling, forging passports etc.[56] When Novikov had been freed in 1796, together with his physician and his serf, there were only five other prisoners. A second incomplete list of people detained in prison or living in towns or the country under surveillance, dated 12 March 1801, totals 695 people. These included, however, over 300 sentenced to hard labour in Dünamunde, Nerchinsk or Perm. In St Petersburg, in 1788, there were 133 prisoners.[57]

MONASTERY PRISONS

The English travellers, Archdeacon Coxe and prison reformer John Howard, travelled extensively in Russia and visited many prisons. But they did not see Dünamunde or Keksholm, or any monastery prisons, otherwise Howard might not have written: 'I found no traces of any such prisons or dungeons as were common formerly in the castles of England and in several foreign

55. J. Alexander, *Autocratic Politics in a National Crisis – The Imperial Russian Government and Pugachev's Revolt*, Bloomington, Indiana, 1969, pp. 171ff.

56. Gernet, *op. cit.*, pp. 253–4.

57. Gernet, *op. cit.*, pp. 253–4; pp. 206–7; pp. 118–19. This figure includes 41 in Tobol'sk, the classic place of exile for those living under surveillance. There were also 19 in the Peter and Paul fortress in St Petersburg, 49 in Schlüsselburg, 14 in the Solovetsky monastery, 18 in the Spasoefimskoye monastery. One should note that these figures reflect the large number of detentions under Paul I, and secondly, it is unlikely that they all came under the Secret Expedition, notably in the case of the two monastery prisons. Of the 133, 14 were nobles, 27 were peasants, 21 were under investigation and seven were women. Gernet does not specify which St Petersburg prison he refers to.

countries . . .'.[58] Not only were there plenty of dungeons in these two state prisons, but also in the monasteries which served as prisons for members of the clerical estate, and for certain state prisoners as well as the criminally insane. The most fearsome of all was the monastery on the Solovetsky Islands in the White Sea (Solovki – the regime changes but not the names of the prisons) where cells were carved out of the thick walls, and prisoners could be held in the dark, incommunicado, allowed only to hear but not to see religious services. The regime varied according to the status of the prisoner: the last hetman of the Zaporozhian Cossacks was for instance confined in Solovki, but was allowed one ruble per day from his own funds, and brought all his own clothing and linen with him. In 1786 there were 15 prisoners, four of whom were mad, and at least five of whom were nobles, one a peasant, one a serf and one a soldier. As frequently happened, the abbot did not know why the prisoners had been sent, nor how long for.[59]

The Spaso-Efimskoye monastery in Suzdal was more clearly intended for the insane and some steps were taken to humanize their treatment. They were not to be kept in shackles, and could go to church services. If they began to rave they were to be kept apart from other prisoners. A report of 1777 suggests that these brave words were not being observed, and that the guards frequently ill-treated the prisoners. Of the 27 held in that year, there were 11 chancery clerks, six military of various ranks, four clerics, two peasants, two foreigners, one merchant and one student.[60] There were other such prisons, notably the Ivanovskoye, Novodevichiy and Voznesenskiy for women. It was in the first of these that a special underground cell was prepared for Darya Saltykova, the 29-year-old noblewoman who was convicted of torturing to death at least 38 of her serfs, and who was sentenced to life imprisonment in total darkness. After 11 years she was moved to a cell above ground, and could be seen at times at the window gesticulating wildly at passers-by. Rumour goes that she bore a son in gaol. She died in 1801, by which time her gaolers did not remember what she had been sentenced for.[61]

ORDINARY PRISONS

There was no nation-wide prison administration or prison service. In towns prisons were attached to the voyevoda's office, or after 1775 to the *gubernskoye pravleniye* for civilians. They were traditionally composed of a number of smaller buildings surrounded by turreted walls or palisades. The rooms were small, ill lit, heated by stoves. Prisons were well supplied with handcuffs,

58. Howard, *op. cit.*, p. 93.
59. Gernet, *op. cit.*, p. 270. Only one prisoner was specifically incarcerated on the order of the Procurator General.
60. Gernet, *op. cit.*, p. 282.
61. See G. Studenkin, 'Saltychikha, 1730–1801', *Russkaya Starina*, 10, 1878, pp. 487–56. One hundred and thirty-eight women and girls had disappeared from the estate, presumed murdered. Saltykova was convicted of the 38 cases which could be proved.

shackles, fetters, chains and blocks. Civil prisons were guarded by detachments of garrison troops, no longer fit for active service, and gaolers were selected from among them. Military personnel had their own (e.g. at Butyrki in Moscow). Prisoners were maintained at state expense (in theory) at a cost ranging between 1 and 3 kopeks p.d., though members of the higher classes could supplement this, while the poor, particularly in the provinces, might be reduced to begging for alms in the streets, which were then distributed by the gaolers. Provincial prisons were of even lower standard than in Moscow, as for instance in Tambov, where Derzhavin, as governor, protested in 1780 at the inhuman conditions in which prisoners were held in semi-basement cells, with no light or heat.[62]

In 1763 prisoners were placed under the overall supervision of the governors, who were to report on the number of undecided cases to the Senate.[63] The general disorder in prison administration is reflected in a report by the Procurator General A.A. Vyazemsky, of 24 December 1767,[64] in which he described the crumbling buildings in the Moscow prison and the accumulation of up to 300 convicts awaiting transport to Siberia and held up by lack of a convoy. The prisoners were crowded and ill fed, and even the guards had no room. The Senate issued an instruction that not more than three men were to be fitted into a square sazhen, i.e., seven ft. sq. or 1.83m^2, and took steps to improve the food supply. But this referred only to the capital. In 1775 a further more general effort was made to tighten up the regulations for food and clothing supplies.[65]

In the Statute of 1775 Catherine attempted to devise an integrated penal system. It consisted of a series of prisons in which people were kept prior to sentencing or while waiting to be transported to exile or hard labour; houses of correction for minor crimes and disorders, and workhouses to provide employment for the indigent and opportunities for purging minor offences against property.

All prisons were now placed under the board of administration in a guberniya (*gubernskoye pravleniye*) and were to be visited and inspected once a week by the local procurator. The statute provided for the setting up in each guberniya of workhouses and houses of correction, for which elaborate instructions were laid down. The houses of correction were for the temporary detention of people whose way of life was antisocial by contemporary standards. Landowners could send their serfs, though not if they had been previously subjected to corporal punishment since a person should not be punished twice for the same offence.[66] People who wasted their substance, refused to work, led a dissolute life, could be sent, as well as disobedient children, at the request of masters, parents or the Boards of Social Welfare, but only with a court order.

62. Gernet, *op. cit.*, pp. 311–13.
63. *PSZ*, XVI, No. 11750, 10 February 1763.
64. *PSZ*, VXIII, No. 13040.
65. *PSZ*, XX, No. 14260, 2 March 1775.
66. *PSZ*, XXI, No. 15486, 3 August 1782.

Breaches of discipline in the houses of correction could be punished by not more than three lashes with a birch. The owners, masters, parents, etc. had to provide for the keep of the inmates.

The workhouses were established for people with no visible means of subsistence and eventually used as places of detention for people sentenced to work off penalties for theft etc. Inmates were fed and clothed at state expense, and worked at breaking stones or spinning. The workhouses and houses of correction were placed under the Boards of Social Welfare set up by the Statute of 1775. Given a conscientious official this provided for some regular supervision.

CATHERINE'S PLAN FOR PRISON REFORM

Catherine herself had shown considerable interest in the modernization of prisons to which article 166 of the *Nakaz* refers. Sometime in the 1770s she drafted a plan for the reform of prisons. As usual she went into considerable detail, ranging from the type and construction to the size of rooms. The plan provided for the separation of civil and criminal prisons, and the division of the criminal prison into separate buildings or accommodation for prisoners pending investigation, prisoners sentenced to prison terms, and prisoners awaiting transport to hard labour or exile. Men and women were also to be kept separate. Prisoners were to be fed and clothed according to their status, the poor at state expense. The duties of the gaoler were spelled out in detail, as well as the procedure to be adopted on the reception and release of prisoners. Provision was made for a hospital and medical attention.

There are two interesting features about this project: one is the fact that corporal punishment is nowhere mentioned. Infringements of prison discipline are to be punished by transfer to a punishment cell (*temnitsa*). Secondly the gaoler is made personally reponsible for reporting to the Conscience Court if a prisoner is not informed within three days of the charge against him, under threat of losing his job. The provisions of the project in terms of health, hygiene and welfare are humane by eighteenth-century standards, though there is of course no attempt at reformation or education of prisoners, nor any mention of religious instruction or the building of a prison chapel. The draft was never promulgated but Catherine sent it in 1788 to the St Petersburg guberniya procurator, who was in charge of the local prisons, asking him to compare it with existing regulations and prisons. The procurator apparently cut it by 33 per cent – but Gernet, who gives us this information, most tantalizingly stops there.[67] However, the draft clearly was known since it

67. For Catherine's draft, see M. Filippov, 'Tyur'my v Rossii. Sobstvenno-ruchnyy proekt imperatritsy Yekateriny II, 1787', *Russkaya Starina*, 8, 1873, pp. 60–86. See also Gernet, *op. cit.*, I., pp. 110–12, and for the most recent study, A.G. Cross, 'The Philanthropist, the Travelling Tutor and the Empress: British Visitors and Catherine's Plans for Penal and Medical Reform', paper delivered at the Indiana Conference of the XVIII Century Group, 1984, in *Russia and the World of the Eighteenth century*, ed. R.P. Bartlett, A.G. Cross, K. Rasmussen, Slavica Publishers Iuc., Columbus, Ohio, 1988, pp. 214–28. I am indebted to Professor Cross for allowing me to see an advance copy of his paper.

exercised some influence on the building of new prisons in St Petersburg and Moscow, and it was certainly known to the architect, M. Kazakov, who built a new prison near Butyrki in 1800.[68]

Most of the information we have about eighteenth-century Russian prisons comes from William Coxe and John Howard, who visited Russia in 1778 and 1782 respectively, and saw many of the same prisons. In Moscow Coxe visited the Kaluga prison, where there was room for 800, but there were only 97 prisoners at the time, a convoy of 248 having only just left for Siberia. Howard also saw the prison when it had been remodelled according to Catherine's plans. The separation between those detained pending trial and the sentenced was now carefully maintained, as well as the separation of the sexes. There were 47 inmates, included one noble confined for whipping his serfs to death.

The different estates were treated differently. Howard saw men in chains and chained to the walls, but the women did not wear irons. When Miranda visited the same prison in 1787, there were 267 prisoners. He confirms the separation of the sexes, and thought the prison and the hospital fairly clean. Both Coxe and Howard saw the military prison at Butyrki, which, although harsh, seemed not unhealthy, since the inmates were allowed to move about in the open air during the day. The prison contained 48 people in 1778, 120 prisoners in 1781 as well as 55 inmates in the prison hospital. The St Petersburg House of Correction was visited by Howard in 1781. This elegant modern building was again constructed on the new lines. The central block is faintly reminiscent of Jeremy Bentham's ideas on prison construction, about which Catherine may have known.[69] In general, the English visitors commented on the absence of gaol fever, which they attributed to the diet of kvass and rye bread, and in some cases to the open air. Apart from these prisons in more favoured localities, however, and nearer to government supervision, there remained throughout Russia the usual appalling mixture of crowded, stuffy and dark prisons, typical of the age throughout Europe.[70]

THE EXILE SYSTEM

Russian penal policy continued to use exile to hard labour or to settlement, in Siberia or elsewhere, during the reign of Catherine. This entailed a very high mortality rate and a great deal of brutality and hardship during the process of assembling the convoys and transporting them to their destination, in many cases as far as the silver mines of Nerchinsk on the Chinese border. The system of exile had moreover become confused since 1760 with a parallel policy, inaugurated as a means of increasing the Russian population of Siberia.

68. Gernet, *op. cit.*, p. 118, reproducing a plan of the prison.
69. See A.G. Cross, *op. cit.*, for the contacts in 1778 between Jeremy Bentham, the Rev. J. Forster, chaplain to the Duchess of Kingston during her stay in Russia, and Vasily Petrov, the Empress's librarian. Bentham sent copies of his publications to Forster for the Empress. This may have included his 'A View of the Hard Labour Bill . . .' which has very detailed suggestions for the construction of prisons, though it does not yet mention the panopticon.
70. Coxe, *op. cit.*, *passim*; Howard, *op. cit.*, *passim*; Gernet, *op. cit.*, *passim*.

An ukaz of 1760 had authorized landowners, the church, state peasants, and merchant communities to banish to Siberia for settlement a member of these communities whom for any reason they wished to get rid of. Landowners, and all the other communities, would receive a recruit quittance for men of military age. The exiles were to be allowed to take with them their wives and small children, and the clothing and travel allowances to be provided by landowners, town, or village communities were strictly laid down.

Such a system was wide open to abuses at the despatching and at the receiving end. In the villages, whether serf or state, peasants combined to send into exile some sort of scapegoat who would then reduce their own quota of recruits for the army. There could be massive connivance between rich peasants, village elders, and sometimes landowners, in the choice of the unfortunate exile. But the real difficulty arose when people banished to settlement in this way found themselves lumped together with people sentenced by the courts to settlement or hard labour in Siberia, and were transported in the same harsh conditions. In the present state of research it is impossible to establish the numbers actually sent under these two procedures; the figure of 20,000 sent by landowners up to 1773 is not substantiated by a careful study of the evidence. We know that in 1773 more than 4,000 were sent for settlement (but not only by landowners), and 200 convicts were waiting for transport in Kazan, but we do not know over how many years they had accumulated.[71] Coxe estimated that the annual number of convicts exiled to Siberia, both to settlement and hard labour, was in the region of 500, which seems likely.[72] Landowners had, in addition, since 1765 the power to send insubordinate serfs to hard labour in the Admiralty, without any form of trial. John Howard saw a number of them in Kronstadt in 1781.[73]

THE EXTENT OF CODIFICATION IN THE REIGN OF CATHERINE II

Catherine's hope that the Legislative Commission of 1767 would lead to the drafting of a new code of laws foundered on a number of obstacles. She did not herself specify them, but it is likely that they included the unsuitability of an assembly of representatives of disparate interest groups of unequal weight and totally untrained in law (except for a few deputies from the nobility and the towns in the Baltic Provinces); the demands of war; and finally the pressure for immediate piecemeal reform as a result of the Pugachev revolt. However, Catherine's new approach to legislation led her to promulgate a number of major laws which codified areas of social and economic activity and public order. Among these must be considered not only the Statute on Local Administration of 1775, the Police Ordinance of 1782, and the Charters of 1785, but also the Maritime Code of 1781, the Banking Code of 1786, the Statute of

71. See my article 'Catherine II and the Serfs: A Reconsideration of some Problems', *Slavonic and East European Review*, 3, No. 126, January 1974, pp. 34–62; see also Aleksandrov, *op. cit.*, pp. 279ff.
72. See my article cited above, and Coxe, *op. cit.*, p. 77.
73. Howard, *op. cit.*, pp. 90–1.

National Schools of that same year, and the codes which regulated production and trade in alcohol and salt. All these laws laid down norms for state and public activity and prescribed the penalties for breaches of these norms. The system therefore presented no break with the Petrine, and indeed Muscovite practice of establishing separate codes for different functional and social groups. Under Catherine officials continued to be judged according to Peter's General Regulations; but if they were school teachers, they now came under the jurisdiction of the Commission for National Schools, and were not, as members of other social groups, judged in accordance with the Code of 1649 as amended by later ukazy.

Catherine drastically reformed the system of courts, bringing justice nearer to the localities, and associating the different free estates (including the state peasants) with the courts in response to the principle of 'trial by one's peers'. She also enacted a number of personal rights for the nobility and the townspeople. Nevertheless, half the population, namely the serfs, remained under the jurisdiction of the landowners for ordinary misdemeanours, ranging from failure to obey the orders of a steward to lack of decorum in church. But the law still strongly asserted its direct relationship with the serf in major crime, and as labour, taxpayer and soldier. Hence, whereas disputes over land went before civil courts, harbouring runaway serfs, or selling someone else's serf as a recruit to the army, was a criminal offence, as was theft of more value than 20 rubles.[74]

Does this concern with serfs signify that the law was simply an instrument of the ruling class? Insofar as the serf was a form of property, the sanctity of which the state guaranteed to a greater extent than that of any other form of property, it might appear that the law served merely the interests of the nobility. This would be a misleading simplification, for serfdom, i.e. the adscription to the soil, the ultimate control of labour, was fundamental to the economic and military power of the state. In general, offences against property, not entailing violence against the person, were far more mildly treated in Russian law, whatever the poverty or status of the criminal, and particularly in the case of a minor, than in English law.

CONCLUSION

In general a number of trends can be detected in the last quarter of the eighteenth century. Not only was there an increasing interest in humanitarianism as such, as a feature of a more cultured society, but there was a movement away from painful punishment towards payment, whether in cash or in loss of status, as befitted a more prosperous society. The debates on the reform

74. See the interesting case of the widow of General Ettingsher, who was sentenced to one month in prison for the double offence of flogging a serf too harshly, and for having taken action herself in a case which should have gone to the courts. Catherine ordered the Senate to have a care to protect the judicial power from private encroachments. *PSZ*, XIX, No. 13516, 16 October 1770, and XIX, No. 13578, 13 February 1772.

of criminal law, and on the utility of the death penalty in other countries, notably in revolutionary France, were echoed in Russia, though I have found no specific mention of the *Leopoldina*.[75] The government was usually in advance of public opinion throughout the country, but there were already many high officials who were deeply influenced by the new ideas and endeavoured to put them into practice. There was also a distinct trend away from collective responsibility for crimes towards the concept of the responsibility of the individual, which is nowhere more clearly stated than in the two Charters of 1785.

There was also a new concern with legality, *zakonnost'*, the rule of law, the achievement of uniformity and predictability in the administration of the law, and the elimination of private judgment. This was central to Catherine's attitude to law as expressed in article 153 of the *Nakaz*: 'Nothing is so dangerous as this general Axiom: the Spirit of the Laws ought to be considered and not the Letter'. Such an approach was in many ways alien to Russians who throughout their history seem to have been more concerned with equity than with justice.[76] This may in part explain the early popularity of the Courts of Conscience, which could judge according to the rules of equity, and their decline in the nineteenth century when the presence of more lawyers enabled the courts to function more efficiently.

Zakonnost' was also fostered by a steady encouragement of the study of law at the University of Moscow, where the Scottish trained S.I. Desnitsky was appointed to teach Russian law in 1768 – the first professor of Russian law to teach in Russian – and where Z.A. Goryushkin was appointed to teach practical law in 1786, as well as serving on the Moscow criminal court, where he distinguished himself by his defence of legality and humanity, basing himself frequently on arguments drawn from Catherine's *Nakaz*. He was extremely influential not only through his written works, but as a teacher of law and legal procedure in which he worked by the dramatization of specific cases.[77] Catherine also subsidized the despatch of young Russians to study abroad (such as Radishchev) and endeavoured to attract foreign lawyers to Russian service, such as Charles de Villiers, who came, and Beccaria, who did not. This same period also saw the publication of an increasing number of legal textbooks, dictionaries, handbooks, collections of laws, and even the first Russian legal periodical, the *Teatr sudovedeniya*, in 1791.

75. For an account of the views of a number of important writers, e.g. V.N. Tatishchev, I.N. Boltin, Prince M.M. Schcherbatov and many others, see Fel'dshteyn, *op. cit.*, *passim*. See also the articles by W.E. Butler, 'Foreign Impressions of Russian Law to 1800: Some Reflections', and A.H. Brown, 'The Father of Russian Jurisprudence: the Legal Thought of S.E. Desnitskii' in *Russian Law: Historical and Political Perspectives*, ed. W.E. Butler, Leyden, 1977, pp. 65–92 and 94–117.

76. See for instance A.N. Radishchev in *Viaggio da Pietroburgo a Mosca*, ed. F. Venturi, Bari, 1972. 'Zajcovo', pp. 126ff. See also I.V. Lopukhin, *Zapiski*, ORP reprint, 1976, pp. 142–4; Metropolitan Gavriil too argued the need to 'follow the spirit, not the letter' as a means of individualizing the punishment in relation to the criminal. See Fel'dshteyn, *op. cit.*, p. 245.

77. See Korsakov, *op. cit.*, in which Goryushkin describes his battle for justice to the booksellers tried in 1792 as a result of the Novikov affair, in which sentences were reduced from the knut, exile, and nostril clipping to loss of status as a merchant.

However, there are many shadows on this picture. There was no systematic supervision of the new legislation, which depended on the intelligence and humanity of the local governors and judges. Though the general cultural level had improved, particularly in the higher reaches of government service, nevertheless there were still primitive brutes in positions of such power as to render miserable the life of the common people, and even quite distinguished bureaucrats, such as Governor General Bruce of Moscow or the poet Gavriil Derzhavin, were very lacking in understanding of the rule of law.[78] Penal policy was still based on status, offences being punished differently according to the 'estate' of the offender. There was thus in all likelihood a huge discrepancy between theory and practice. We do not know precisely how great it was, because so much work remains to be done in this field of Russian history. Regrettably, most of the works published merely repeat known facts from each other. There is not a single modern study of the operation of a court of law, even of the Senate in its judicial capacity as the final court of appeal, based on records, following verdicts through to their final confirmation. There are no statistical studies of criminality based on court records, comparable to the work of scholars in England and France.[79] It is possible that in Russia, as elsewhere, the actual numbers who suffered at the hands of the law were somewhat fewer than has been assumed, since the state seems to have left the prosecution of offences to a great extent to the initiative of the plaintiffs, under the accusatorial procedure, and expense proved a deterrent factor. For the time being the study of the actual operation of the criminal law in eighteenth-century Russia is in its infancy.[80] It is assumed, on the basis of memoir literature, that judges were corrupt, that torture continued to be inflicted and prisoners abused. No doubt this is to a very large extent true. The abyss between intent and achievement is everywhere vast, and the enlightened ideas harboured by a small court elite took a long time to penetrate into the outer reaches of Russia. But for historians, assumptions are not enough.

78. See Lopukhin, *Zapiski*, for Bruce, and Derzhavin, 'Zapiski', in *Sochineniya*, *passim*.
79. For England, see the work of Sharpe, Beattie, and the school of E.P. Thompson and Douglas Hay; for France see Y. and N. Castan, J. Ruff and S. Reinhardt; for Spain, see Ruth Pike.
80. For instance, there is no doubt that Catherine systematically reduced the severe punishments inflicted on women, but there has been no study of their actual incidence.

CHAPTER SIX

Catherine II and the serfs: a reconsideration of some problems

I

It is a commonplace of the historiography of Russia that the age of Catherine II saw the high point of serfdom. The origins of this judgment on serfdom in the latter half of the eighteenth century in general and on Catherine's policy towards serfdom in particular must be sought in the work of V.I. Semevsky, by far the most thorough historian to have tackled the subject.[1] His work was the first major study of the peasantry in any reign to be published in Russia, for in spite of the devotion of both Slavophiles and Westerners to the peasantry little work had previously been done on the subject. Semevsky himself was close to the populists in ideology and sympathies,[2] and the emphasis he places on the peasant commune has attracted criticism from Soviet historians.[3]

The high regard in which Semevsky's scholarship is rightly held has tended, in the West at any rate, to act as a brake on fresh thinking on the subject. His conclusion that in the age of Catherine serfdom 'was intensified both in depth and in extent' is repeated uncritically by almost all authors dealing with eighteenth-century Russia or serfdom.[4] In the Soviet Union, attention has been devoted mainly to the study of the peasantry *before* the outbreak of the Pugachev revolt,[5]

This article is based on a paper originally presented at the History Seminar of the School of Slavonic and East European Studies.

1. V.I. Semevsky, *Krest'yane v tsarstvovaniye Yekateriny II*, 2 vols., St Petersburg, 1903.
2. See M.B. Petrovich, 'V.I. Semevsky, Russian Social Historian' in *Essays in Russian and Soviet History in honor of G.R. Robinson*, ed. J. Sheldon Curtiss, Leiden, 1965.
3. See e.g. M.T. Belyavsky, *Krest'yanskiy vopros v Rossii nakanune vosstaniya E.I. Pugachova*, Moscow, 1965, pp. 20–1 (hereafter called *Krest'yanskiy vopros*).
4. Cf. Semevsky, *op. cit.*, I, p. xxvi. And see e.g. Jerome Blum, *Lord and Peasant in Russia from the Ninth to the Nineteenth Century*, Princeton, N.J., 1961, p. 424.
5. With the notable exception of the articles by N. Rubinshteyn, 'K kharakteristike votchinnogo rezhima: krest'yanskogo dvizheniya v kontse 70kh gg. XVIII veka' (*Istoricheskiye zapiski*, XL, Moscow, 1952, pp. 140ff.); and 'Krest'yanskoye dvizheniye v Rossii vo vtoroy polovine XVIII veka' (*Voprosy istorii*, XI, Moscow, November 1956, pp. 35ff.). But see e.g. P.K. Alefirenko, *Krest'yanskoye dvizheniye i krest'yanskiy vopros v Rossii v 30–50kh godakh XVIII veka*, AN SSSR, 1958; S.I. Volkov, *Krest'yans dvortsovykh vladeniy podmoskov'ya v seredine XVIII v.*, Moscow, 1959; E.I. Indova, *Dvortsovoye khozyaystvo v Rossii, pervaya polovina XVIII veka*, Moscow, 1964; Belyavsky,

which tends to be viewed as a reaction against their increasing exploitation in the ten years of Catherine's reign before the revolt took place.[6] Moreover, Soviet historians have, for obvious reasons, concentrated on the economic exploitation of the peasantry and the class war rather than on the systematic study of the legal aspects of the institution of serfdom which, in their view, are bound to be manipulated by the landowning class in the interests of maintaining its economic and hence its political supremacy.

Yet if the first limitation on the exploitation of the serf's labour is usually said to date from the ukaz of 5 April 1797,[7] the first legal limitations on enserfment and self-enserfment date from the age of Catherine II. According to decrees issued in the reigns of Peter I and his successors, the children of church servants who could not find clerical employment were to be 'assigned to a proprietor'. Orphans, foundlings and illegitimate children were enserfed to those who took them in. Free people who had hired themselves out as servants were, according to the census law of 1746, assigned to their masters. All these and many other ways of enserfing people were cut short by various *ukazy* issued by Catherine II, culminating in the manifesto of 17 March 1775 which prohibited a serf who had once been freed from becoming a serf again.[8]

It would seem, therefore, that Semevsky's broad generalisation regarding the depth and the extent of serfdom in the age of Catherine could, after the passage of much time, be examined more closely.[9] What does 'depth and extent' actually mean? Does 'depth' mean that the economic exploitation of the serf reached its highest point in the eighteenth century? There is some dispute on this point among Soviet economic historians, some of whom suggest that economic exploitation of serf labour reached its apogee in the nineteenth century, with the enormous development of the production of grain for export.[10] Does 'extent' mean that the proportion of serfs to the non-serf population of Russia increased substantially in the years 1762–96? Yet V.M. Kabuzan, in his study of population growth and movement in Russia, notes that it is precisely

---

op. cit. and 'Nakazy krest'yan vostochnoy Sibiri v ulozhennuyu kommissiyu 1767–68gg' in *Novoye o proshlom nashey strany*, in honour of M.N. Tikhomirov, Moscow, 1967. In this work Belyavsky remarks (p. 344) that since Semevsky first used these *nakazy* they had not been looked at again by scholars until 1961. See also Belyavsky, 'Novyye dokumenty ob obsuzhdeniy krest'yanskogo voprosa v 1766–68 godakh' in *Arkheograficheskiy yezhegodnik za 1958*, Moscow, 1960 (hereafter called Belyavsky, 'Novyye dokumenty').

6. See among non-Soviet authors who express this view P. Avrich, *Russian Rebels 1600–1800*, London, 1973, pp. 224–5.

7. *Polnoye sobraniye zakonov Rossiyskoy imperii, XXIV*, No. 17,909 (hereafter called *PSZ*).

8. For an analysis of these decrees see M.F. Vladimirsky-Budanov, *Obzor istorii russkogo prava*, St Petersburg, 1900, pp. 235ff. And see *PSZ*, XX, Nos 14,275, 14,294 and 15,070 of 17 March and 6 April 1775 and 5 October 1780.

9. It is, for instance, frequently stated that one of the causes of the Pugachev revolt was the enormous grants of state peasants made by Catherine to her favourites. The latest statement of this view is in Avrich, *op. cit.*, p. 225, who moreover locates these grants in provinces 'to be affected by the Pugachev revolt'. See below, pp. 143–9 for evidence that (a) state peasants were not given away and (b) most of the grants took place *after* the Pugachev revolt.

10. See the discussions between P.G. Ryndzyunsky, I.D. Koval'chenko, N.L. Rubinshteyn and A.M. Anfimov in *Istoriya SSSR*, No. 2, 1961, pp. 48–70; No. 1, 1962, pp. 65–87; No. 2, 1963, pp. 141–60.

TABLE 1

Data	Total male population in area of 1st census	Serfs as % of total male population	Serfs as % of peasantry
1719–21	6,345,101	62.80	69.64
1744–46	7,399,546	63.24	69.87
1762–64	8,436,779	52.17	55.36
1782–84	10,469,767	48.77	53.02
1795–96	11,352,774	49.49	54.18
1811	12,983,379	47.74	52.13

TABLE 2

Date	Total male population	Serfs as % of total male population	Serfs as % of peasantry
1762–64*	614,993	72.89	76.48
1782–84	640,567	71.97	76.16
1795–96	761,340	81.09	89.52
1811	767,357	80.64	88.27

* Figures for 1772 included in census of 1762–64.

in the years 1772–82 that one can place the beginning of the downward trend in the proportion of serfs to the total population and to the peasantry. Though the numbers of serfs increased in absolute terms, the relative weight of the serf population began now to decline.[11] In order to illustrate this movement it is necessary to distinguish between the population figures for the area included in the censuses of 1719–21, 1742–44 and 1762–64, and the figures for the considerably enlarged Russian empire of 1796, which comprised many newly incorporated areas in which the proportion of serfs was very high. Table 1 above gives the figures in the eighteenth-century censuses and in 1811 for the area comprised in the first census of 1719–21.

The percentage of serfs to the total male population would present quite a different picture if one were to include the figures for the guberniya of Mogilev and Vitebsk, acquired at the first partition of Poland (see Table 2) or the figures for the three Baltic provinces, Vyborg, Livland and Estonia (see Table 3).

In the western territories incorporated into the Russian empire after the second and third partitions of Poland, the total male population was 1,257,738; serfs formed 72.38 per cent of the total male population and 83.55 per cent of the peasant population. In Right Bank Ukraine the total population was

11. See V.M. Kabuzan, *Izmeneniya v razmeshchenii naseleniya Rossii v XVIII – pervoy polovine XIX v.*, Moscow, 1971, pp. 11–12.

TABLE 3

Date	Total male population	Serfs as % of total male population	Serfs as % of peasantry
		Vyborg	
1762–64	79,249	?	?
1782–84	93,234	23.77	25.58
1795–96	92,904	32.66	33.70
1811	100,453	29.83	30.63
		Livland	
1762–64	190,962	93.33	100.00
1782–84	266,624	71.51	77.91
1795–96	270,790	74.98	80.91
1811	282,051	74.45	80.09
		Estonia	
1762–64	83,192	?	?
1782–84	101,152	84.57	93.16
1795–96	107,601	85.75	95.72
1811	113,057	85.65	93.07

1,737,609; serfs numbered 72.26 per cent of the total and 85.23 per cent of the peasant population.[12]

Did serfdom spread to new areas where it was previously unknown? The ukaz of 3 May 1783 did not in fact introduce serfdom into Little Russia – it merely put the final confirmation on a process of binding the peasant to the soil which had been going on for some time. The *numbers* of peasants in bondage do not seem to have increased, though the *form* of the bondage became more severe (see Table 4).[13]

12. All the above tables have been extracted from the appendixes to Kabuzan's work cited in note 11. There have been various attempts to analyse the causes of the gradual decline in the percentage of serfs to total peasantry. Explanations range from the drift into the state peasantry, the recruit levies (the armed forces were not included in the censuses), flight, economic exploitation, hence malnutrition and a higher mortality and lower rate of reproduction. But it is in fact impossible on the existing data to determine whether the net rate of growth by reproduction was higher in one group than the other. Kabuzan, in appendix I does not attempt to do so. From the data he gives it would be possible to work out the rate of change in numbers, but not the causes, some of which might be due to changes of status or internal migration.

13. The extension of the Russian type of serfdom to Little Russia and eventually in 1796 to New Russia is a long and very complicated story which deserves separate treatment and will not be entered into here. The social and political background of the Ukraine was quite different from that of Russia, and it is unfortunate that it is not given more thorough treatment. See, however, V.A. Myakotin, 'Prikrepleniye krest'yanstva levoberezhnoy Ukrainy XVII–XVIII vv.' in *Godishnik Sofiiskiya universitet*, Istoriko-filologicheski fakultet, Sofia, 1932, and by the same author, *Ocherki sotsial'noy istorii Ukrainy XVII–XVIII vv.*, I, vypusk 3, Prague, 1923 and also *PSZ*, XXI, No. 15,724, 3 May 1783. As regards New Russia, see the observations of E.I. Druzhinina in *Severnoye Prichernomor'ye 1775–1800*, Moscow, 1959, pp. 195–6 on the law of 12 December 1796

TABLE 4
Left Bank Ukraine

Date	Total male population	Serfs as % of total male population	Serfs as % of peasantry
1719–21	909,651	39.10	43.28
1744–46	1,156,165	48.86	42.18
1762–64	1,342,221	52.69	54.41
1782–84	1,689,823	43.32	45.56
1795–96	1,696,284	42.68	46.11
1811	1,832,727	44.62	47.14

'The trade in peasants reached its peak – as did so many of the cruellest aspects of Russian serfdom – during the reign of Catherine II.'[14] On what evidence is this statement based? Peter I is reputed to have disliked the practice as such, and the break up of families in particular. Yet it was legalised in his reign[15] and doubtless flourished with every recruit levy. The sale of individuals continued until 1843.[16] No actual figures have been published on which a comparative judgment can be based in terms of numbers sold in different periods. But whether larger or smaller, this *de facto* if not *de jure* slave trade stands out of course ever more glaringly as a moral issue, the higher the cultural level of society. It is in the latter half of the eighteenth century that this moral aspect intrudes, both with regard to owners buying and selling without regard to the humans involved, and with regard to the serfs, many of whom were by now large-scale entrepreneurs, skilled artisans or genuine creative artists or scholars, unfitted for the life of the village and suffering intensely from their lack of freedom. Yet the trade continued.[17]

Finally were the legal powers which landowners had over their serfs greatly increased in Catherine's reign, and specifically before the Pugachev revolt? Some aspects of these problems will be explored below.

which prohibited the free movement of peasants in this area: 'Did the ukaz of 12 December signify the direct enserfment of all the free settlers living on landowners' land? This conclusion is sometimes drawn by historians, but it cannot be considered well founded.' And, *ibid.*, n. 30, in which Druzhinina points out that these peasants, though now fixed to the land, kept their personal freedom.

14. Blum, *op. cit.*, p. 424. Blum states that 'in 1771 she [Catherine] decided that the spectacle of human beings on the block should be banned, and ordered that the serfs of bankrupt seignieurs could not be sold at public auction'. Blum misses the point. Catherine ordered – very peremptorily – that serfs without land should not be auctioned, i.e. settled estates could be sold in this way but not individual serfs. See her two orders of 5 August 1771 in *Sbornik Imperatorskogo Russkogo istoricheskogo obshchestva* (hereafter called *SIRIO*), XII, St Petersburg, 1771, p. 143.

15. Ukazy of 1701, 1705 and 1720 (which imposed a tax of 10 per cent of the price in roubles or 3 altyn per head whichever was the higher on sales without land), confirmed in 1773 (*PSZ*, XIX, No. 13,950, 21 February 1773).

16. Vladimirsky-Budanov, *op. cit.*, p. 236.

17. See Bertha Malnick, 'Russian Serf Theatres' (*Slavonic and East European Review*, XXX, 75, June 1952, pp. 393ff.) for the trade in serf actors.

II

In approaching the question of the legal powers of landowners over their serfs, it is necessary to know first what did a particular law actually say; secondly what was its specific purpose, what policy did it seek to enforce; thirdly how well or badly was the law enforced, and if the text of the law laid itself open to doubt, how was it in practice interpreted.

The purpose which the law was designed to serve is especially important. Students of Russian social history have very often approached the subject in terms of the different social estates, and studied each of these in isolation. Such studies tear from each ukaz the paragraph relevant to the 'estate' which is being examined, be it the nobility or the peasantry or the *kuptsy*, but fail to study the ukaz as a whole, as the expression of the government's policy in relation to a problem seen as a whole, in terms of *all* estates. In the stratified society of the *ancien régime*, social estates and social groups did not exist in isolation, but formed a veritable mosaic. One piece could not be removed without changing the whole picture, influencing the relationship and the balance between the other pieces. This was all the more true of a society like Russia in which bondage played such a large part. The clearest illustration of this interrelationship is given by the manifesto freeing the nobility from compulsory service in 1762. It said nothing at all about the serfs; but it fundamentally altered the relationship, in fact if not in law, between the serf and the serf owner, and the serf and the state. The balance was gone. Thus though many laws deal specifically with the privileges or the burdens of particular *sosloviye*, some cannot be properly understood if they are not taken as a whole, as the expression of government policy in terms of all estates.

A case in point is the ukaz which is usually briefly referred to in studies of serfdom as empowering the landowners to exile serfs to Siberia. The ukaz was enacted in the reign of Elizabeth Petrovna on 13 December 1760[18] and its title reads as follows: 'On the reception for settlement in Siberia of landowners' peasants, court peasants, synodal peasants, church peasants, monastery peasants, merchants and state peasants with recruit quittances and on the payment by the treasury for wives and children of both sexes of such peasants according to the rates set out in this ukaz.' The object of the ukaz is clearly to promote the settlement of Siberia, and it defines the application of the policy to the different *sosloviya* or estates. In the first section, landowners are informed that they are permitted to send to Siberia for settlement (*na poseleniye*) such of their peasants who are considered to be unsatisfactory as they wish, with their wives and such younger children as they wish; the state would give a recruit quittance for each adult male and would buy children under five years for ten roubles and between five and fifteen for twenty roubles. The ukaz goes on to specify the allowance which the landowners must supply for the journey. The same offer is then made to the court, synodal, state peasants and merchants, enabling

18. *PSZ*, XV, No. 11,116 (Senatskiy). The final titles of ukazy were of course given in the nineteenth century, when they were codified.

them to get rid of unwanted members of their communities in exchange for recruit quittances. In their case, however, the ukaz specified certain procedures which must be followed in order to prevent abuses; notably that in each *volost'* or village the elected representatives and *starosty* of the peasants must produce a written sentence (*prigovor*), certified by the village *pop*, that the chosen peasants were indeed ill-behaved. This sentence had then to go for confirmation from monasteries to the College of Economy, from church estates to the eparchies, from the *kuptsy* to the *Magistraty*, from court peasants to the Court Chancellery and from state peasants 'tozhe cherez ikh komandu'.

The whole phrasing of the ukaz, together with the powers conferred on communities in other estates, shows that this policy was not conceived of as part of a programme designed to strengthen the power of the landowner over his serf, but as part of a policy of assisted emigration to Siberia of members of all estates except the nobility. Landowners were allowed to send their serfs. Other social groups were allowed, with suitable safeguards, to eliminate one of their equals whom they regarded as a burden on the community or wished to get rid of for any reason. In no case was any kind of judicial procedure involved. Except in the case of the landowners, the community acted according to its lights. We know that the merchants made use of this power: an ukaz of 15 October 1773[19] referred specifically to the previous ukaz of 1760 which enabled *kuptsy* to make use of the right in the same way as *pomeshchiki* to 'send useless and harmful people to settlement in exchange for recruit quittances . . .'. It noted that in order to prevent abuses the *Magistraty* were supposed to certify the sentences of the *mirskiy skhod* or town assembly which was authorised to sign the sentence. But, continued the ukaz of 1773, 'it has been brought to our attention' that the judges (*sud'i*) elected to the *Magistraty* and *Ratushi* have appropriated such powers to themselves that they 'send whomsoever they wish whenever they wish', moved by caprice and prejudice, 'and without the consent of the town assembly'. Thus they were exiling to settlement people who by 'their status, property and the size of their trade are useful members of society'. New regulations were now introduced to correct these vices, notably that the decision (*prigovor*) was to be reached by the town assembly without the presence of members of the *Magistrat* or *Ratusha*; the *prigovor* must contain an account of the reasons for sending someone to settlement and must be signed by the assembly's *starosty* who must then submit it to the *Magistraty* and *Ratushi*; if these agreed that the sentences were according to the law and the facts correct, the sentence was to be forwarded to the governor who had the right of final approval. If the *Magistraty* wished to exile someone to settlement they must put his name before the town assembly,

19. *PSZ*, XIX, No. 14,045, 'O pravilakh osuzhdeniya kuptsov na poseleniye i otdachu v rekruty'. An ukaz of 11 July 1767 (*PSZ*, XVIII, No. 12,937) refers to a *kupets* who had been exiled to settlement without his wife. The ukaz states that his wife must be sent to him, and if the 'kupechestvo wishes', his children may also be sent, provided the *kuptsy* pay the allowances laid down in the law of 1760.

who would act in accordance with the procedure described above. Whether in fact this change made much difference would of course depend a great deal on local circumstances. But it is possible that by strengthening the role of the town assembly as a kind of tribunal on the merits of a case, and by introducing the governor as a final arbiter, the activities of the *Magistraty* in this field were placed under some kind of public control, and their power to exile their business rivals was limited.[20]

It is usually asserted that the nobles used the power to exile serfs to Siberia very widely,[21] but the fact that other social groups in the community enjoyed and used this power is rarely mentioned. The actual operation of the system of settlement needs much more research. How many people, and *from which estate*, were actually dispatched to Siberia? We know from the harrowing accounts by Count Sievers and others of the appalling conditions in which convoys of exiles made the journey; and there are many reports of landowners' misuse of the law in order to get rid of the old and the unfit.[22] But unfortunately these reports mostly give round figures of those included in the convoys, without distinguishing between convicts (*kolodniki*), i.e. those sentenced by the courts to hard labour or settlement, and those sent by landowners or other communities to settlement under the law of 1760. Analysis of the recruit quittances might prove helpful but so far this has not been done.[23] Again, according to reports of eye-witnesses and governors it is clear that landowners and other communities often refused to send the wives and children of those exiled to settlement, thus undermining the original object of the law of 1760 which was to populate Siberia.[24]

The way the ukaz of 1760 worked is complicated by the fact that the landowners' power to exile to settlement in Siberia became entangled with an ill-defined power to send serfs to hard labour. The relevant ukaz is dated 15 January 1765, and is entitled 'On the reception by the Admiralty College of

20. The power of urban communities to exile one of their members by administrative order survived until 1900, and that of peasant communities even longer. As an illustration of how the system worked in the late nineteenth century it is worth quoting the following: On the average in the years 1887–96, the villages exiled 2,639 criminals per annum who had served their sentences, but whom the villages refused to re-register as members of the communes, and 2,083 people for bad behaviour, a total of 4,722. In the same period the average number of people sentenced to Siberian exile by the courts was 3,328 (not including political offenders sentenced to internment). Thus the village communities did not hesitate to make use of this power as late as 1900. See A. Löwenstimm, 'Die Deportation nach Siberien vor und nach dem Gesetz vom 12 Juni 1900' (*Zeitschrift für die Gesammte Strafrechtswissenschaft*, XXIV, Berlin, 1903, p. 87). I am much indebted to Dr R. Beerman, of the Institute of Soviet and East European Studies in the University of Glasgow, for drawing my attention to this article.

21. V.M. Kabuzan and S.M. Troitsky, 'Dvizheniye naseleniya Sibiri v XVIII v.' in *Sibir' XVII–XVIII vv., Materialy po istorii Sibiri. Sibir' perioda feodalizma*, vyp. 1, Novosibirsk, 1962, p. 149.

22. See Semevsky, *op. cit.*, I, pp. 179–82, 187.

23. *Ibid.*, I, p. 180, n. 1. In 1771, a total of 7,823 recruit quittances were presented, i.e. over 11 per cent of a total levy expected to raise 69,825 men. But this figure included 'a certain number of harmful [*porochnyye*] people . . . and others sentenced to settlement by communities of state peasants . . . though *probably* [my italics] the majority were serfs exiled for insolent behaviour'.

24. *Ibid.*, pp. 181–3.

serfs sent by their landlords for correction (*smireniye*) and on their employment in heavy labour'.[25] In its printed version the ukaz states that if landowners, for the better correction of insubordinate serfs, wished to send them to heavy labour, the Admiralty College could receive and employ them for what periods the landlords might define (no recruit quittance was offered). Thus the landlords are not given – if one takes the actual text of the ukaz – a blanket power to send their serfs to hard labour in Siberia and then claim them back.[26] But the question remains: were the powers granted in the two ukazy, that of 1760 and that of 1765, jumbled together? Were landowners on the strength of the ukaz of 1765 able to sentence serfs to hard labour in Siberia in practice if not in law? Were the reception centres empowered to receive serfs sentenced by landowners in this way, or did they only receive serfs sent for settlement?

Semevsky argues that in practice landowners did now send serfs to hard labour in Siberia and claim them back. But the evidence he adduces is slender. He quotes a report from the Governor of Siberia, Chicherin, dated 15 January 1768, in which Chicherin complains that many of those sent for settlement were old and unfit. But Semevsky assumes that these were serfs sent by landowners, whereas Chicherin mentions both settlers and *kolodniki*.[27] And in any case the word *kolodniki* was used of those convicted by the courts, not of serfs sent by landowners. In a later report, of November 1771, Chicherin again complained of the numbers sent – more than he could settle. He pointed out an additional abuse, namely that many of those sent for settlement had been specially bought by landowners in order to obtain recruit quittances, and he again stressed that many were too young, too old or unfit, and unaccompanied by their wives. The total sent in 1771 had reached 6,000 settlers and a further 4,000 were on the way.[28] But when Chicherin gives figures, he again

25. *PSZ*, XVII, No. 12,311. According to Semevsky, *op. cit.*, p. 185, n. 2, in the Senate Archives the ukaz was entitled 'On the reception of landowners' servants in the hard labour office [*katorzhnyy dvor*]'.
26. As stated by e.g. Blum, *op. cit.*, p. 431; M.T. Florinsky, *Russia: A History and an Interpretation*, I, New York, 1955, pp. 572–3. The phrasing of the ukaz leads one to wonder whether it reflects a temporary labour shortage in the dockyards, which might not be unconnected with the fact that the Empress was interested in naval development. She did in fact review the fleet in June 1765, and her comments on its deplorable state are in a letter to N.I. Panin, of 8 June 1765, *SIRIO*, X, pp. 23–4.
27. Semevsky, *op. cit.*, I, p. 185 and n. 2: 'Those sent for "bad behaviour" on the basis [of this ukaz] were now sent also to hard labour in Siberia'. No evidence is adduced.
28. It is not clear whether this means the total sent in the one year 1771, or the total 'received' by 1771. By 1763 according to Semevsky, *op. cit.*, p. 185, n. 1, 1,664 men, with their families totalling 2,848 people, had been sent 'by landowners, monasteries and other places for bad behaviour in exchange for recruit quittances'. According to a Senate report, 402 men had been sent in 1767, and this was regarded as a large number (*PSZ*, XIX, No. 13,475, 16 June 1770). From other sources, Semevsky gives the information that *until* 1772, a total of 20,515 of both sexes had been settled, though he considers that a far larger number had actually been sent by landowners, basing himself on Chicherin's figures. Mortality in the convoys of settlers and convicts was very high during the two-year journey, sometimes as much as 50 per cent, particularly among those who travelled by water to Kazan'. Chicherin pointed out that in convoys from Orenburg to Siberia mortality was only 2 per cent (*op. cit.*, pp. 186–8).

does not distinguish between those sentenced to hard labour or exile by the courts, and those sent for settlement by landowners or communities.

Chicherin's report of November 1771 was considered by the Senate, probably sometime early in 1773, which recommended that since the exile to settlement of serfs by landowners in exchange for recruit quittances was open to so many abuses it should be stopped 'until a further ukaz' was issued and a fresh plan for the colonisation of Siberia drawn up.[29] The report of the Senate was submitted to Catherine who commented on it in May 1773: 'I find for various reasons that it is very inconvenient to repeal the present law, though it has given rise to inhuman abuses, unless a new and better arrangement is made in advance'.[30] The Senate's report was then submitted to Catherine's Council of State, which agreed with the measures proposed by the Senate.[31] These took some time to be enacted, and were possibly hastened by the outbreak of the Pugachev revolt, news of which reached the capital in October 1773. An ukaz of 30 November 1773 ordered a complete halt to the sending of convicts or exiles to settlement in Siberia. Convicts already on the way, or sentenced to settlement, were to be directed elsewhere in European Russia. Those 'sent from different places to settlement in Siberia', of which there were now some 4,000 waiting in Kazan′, were to be sent home (no mention was made of the return of recruit quittances); and until a further ukaz, no one was to be 'accepted' for settlement in Siberia.[32]

The question remains: did this ukaz in fact take away the power of landowners, and others, to send unwanted serfs or members of their communities to Siberia for settlement? And did it stop landowners from sending serfs to hard labour in Siberia if they had ever in fact done so? Typically, the ukaz does not refer to the power of the landowner to send his serfs to Siberia; it removes the power of local government institutions to 'receive' people sent for settlement. Eighteen months later an ukaz of 31 March 1775 restored the power of these bodies to 'receive' convicts sentenced by the courts to settlement in Orenburg and Siberia, but made no mention of serfs sent by landowners *na poseleniye*.[33] The first reference to the fact that the law of 1760 was still regarded as valid occurred in 1787: the Treasury Court (*Kazennaya palata*) of Tobol′sk had protested that among convicts sent by the courts and serfs sent by landowners for settlement some were unfit and too old (between 65 and 76 years). The Senate therefore issued an ukaz reaffirming the provisions of the law of 1760, and stating that only those under 45 were to be sent.[34] According to Semevsky, since there was never any formal repeal of the law of

29. *Ibid.*, p. 188.
30. Belyavsky, *Krest′yanskiy vopros*, pp. 289–9.
31. *Arkhiv Gosudarstvennogo Soveta*, II, St Petersburg, 1869, p. 359.
32. *PSZ*, XIX, No. 14,077, 30 November 1773. Belyavsky, *Krest′yanskiy vopros*, pp. 268–9, does not mention this ukaz.
33. *PSZ*, XX, No. 14,286, 31 March 1775.
34. *PSZ*, XXI, No. 16,602, December 1787. Only two serfs sent for settlement are specifically mentioned as being too old, the others were therefore convicts.

30 November 1773 prohibiting the 'reception' of serfs sent for settlement by landowners, the ukaz of 1787 was thus the first official 'reinstatement' of the power to do so,[35] though evidently serfs were being sent before 1787, judging by the complaints of the Tobol'sk Treasury Court. But what was now the procedure? Did the Statute of Local Administration of 1775 alter in any way the procedure by which landowners could sentence serfs to settlement? Semevsky quotes an interesting case from 1795. A landowner, basing himself not on the law of 1760, but on his rights as a noble, asked his local Governing Board (*gubernskoye pravleniye*) to send four of his serfs to exile in Siberia or the Kuban' (without recruit quittances). His request was not fulfilled, and he complained to the Senate against the Orel and Smolensk Lieutenancy Board (*namestnicheskoye pravleniye*). The landowner considered it beneath him to have to appear in court to justify his sentence on serfs for laziness and drunkenness; but the Senate declared that the serfs must be sentenced by a court, though of course the evidence given by the landowner would be conclusive.[36]

Whatever the law or the practice in the 1780s and 1790s, a new manifesto was issued by Paul I in October 1799, which casts fresh light on the way in which the power of exiling to Siberia was regarded by the state and which further regulated procedure. With the object of colonising lands on the borders of China, the manifesto announced a plan to settle some 10,000 people, starting in September 1800. Settlers were to be recruited from two categories: retired soldiers, who were to be called state settlers (*gosurdarstvennyye poselyane*); and criminals sentenced to exile but not to hard labour, who were to be called exiles (*ssylochnyye*). In addition, Paul 'graciously' granted landowners the right to send serfs for settlement with a recruit quittance if they were no older than forty-five. The landowner must also send the wife, and must provide a wage (*zhalovaniye*), shoes, clothes and food supplies for a year. On arrival the settler would be allotted thirty desyatins of land per male soul, and would be free of taxes for 10 years.[37] The programme of settlement was halted in 1802 in an ukaz which again, without revoking the *power* of the landowner to send serfs to settlement, forbade the further *reception* of serfs sent in this way. The number of settlers was more than could be absorbed and the programme of emigration was limited to the sending of exiles sentenced by the courts.[38] In both these ukazy it is clear that the landowners' power to send serfs for settlement is envisaged from the point of view of its utility in regard to the colonisation of Siberia and not as part of a programme of strengthening or weakening the landowner's control over his serfs, though, of course, it had the incidental result of strengthening it.

The confusion created by the various eighteenth-century ukazy under which landowners claimed the power to exile to Siberia with a recruit quittance, to

35. Semevsky, *op. cit.*, I, p. 189.
36. *Ibid.*, n. 1.
37. *PSZ*, XXV, No. 19,157, 17 October 1799. The area to be settled lay between Lake Baikal, the Upper Angar, Nerchinsk and Kiakhta.
38. *PSZ*, XXVII, No. 20,119, 23 January 1802.

exile serfs to Siberia without a recruit quittance,[39] and to sentence serfs to hard labour in Admiralty establishments, and maybe in Siberia too, without recruit quittances, was partly cleared up in 1809. The power to sentence to hard labour in Admiralty establishments, granted in 1765, was then considered to have been specifically revoked by the Statute on Local Administration of 1775 and subsequent legislation, which had enacted the setting up of workhouses and houses of correction for the punishment of people who behaved badly; hard labour was reserved for genuine criminals, by implication for offences which had to go before the courts.[40] The principles which Alexander I believed operated in Russia were further enunciated in a personal ukaz in 1811. This ukaz arose again because of a specific incident: two serfs had absented themselves for a short period without permission from their estate, and had then surrendered themselves voluntarily to the Lower Land Court. They had been sentenced by the Tver′ Criminal Court to hard labour. The Governor General, Prince George of Holstein Oldenburg, had refused to carry out the sentence and laid the facts before the Emperor. Alexander now issued a long ukaz, in which he explained that according to Russian law there were three categories of crime, according to the severity of the punishment incurred. The first, including murder, brigandage, riot, etc., involved the penalty of 'civil death', i.e. hard labour. The second, including theft of over 100 roubles, incurred sentence to exile to Siberia or to service in the army. The third (minor thefts, drunkenness, 'wilfulness', *svoyevol′stvo*) involved 'light punishment' (*lyogkoye nakazaniye*) and return to the previous dwelling, or confinement in workhouses or houses of correction, 'to which landowners' peasants can also be sent without trial, at the wish of the landowners, but not without an explanation of their reasons'. Paragraph 3 of the second part of the ukaz runs as follows: '*On the wishes of landowners:* In deciding the affairs of criminals the law prevails; there is no place here for what the landowner wishes or does not wish'. Paragraph 4 repeats that landowners' serfs sent for settlement in Siberia as 'state settlers' must be accompanied by their wives.[41] The ukaz is interesting in that it serves to confirm that an effort was made to distinguish clearly between the landowners' right to exile a serf to settlement, which did not turn the serf into a criminal but into a state settler, and the courts' exclusive right

39. The situation was further complicated by the fact that according to an ukaz of 1763, if an accused person persisted in denial of his guilt and could find no one to stand as his guarantor, and an inquiry (*povaln′yy obysk*) among witnesses showed him to be unreliable, he could be sent for settlement to Siberia (*PSZ*, XVI, No. 11,750, 10 February 1763); and if a landowner did not wish to receive back serfs convicted by the courts or even serfs acquitted, and with a good local reputation, then they too could be sent to Siberia, without recruit quittances (*PSZ*, XXXVIII, No. 28,954, 3 March 1822, referring to serfs who had been acquitted for lack of evidence on the charge of attempting to poison their owners). In the same way, throughout the nineteenth century peasant communities could refuse to take back peasants convicted of offences, when they were released, and sent them to Siberia instead (cf. n. 20 above). The rights of landowners to send serfs to settlement without going through the courts and by applying directly to the local government boards, and the right to send people over 45, were granted by Alexander I in the 1820s. See V.I. Semevsky, *Krest′yanskiy vopros v XVIII veke i pervoy chetverti XIX veka*, I, St Petersburg, 1888, pp. 497–8.

40. *PSZ*, XXX, No. 23,530, 10 March 1809.

41. *PSZ*, XXXI, No. 24,707, 5 July 1811.

to sentence to hard labour. Again it assumes that the act of 1775 had codified the powers of landowners over their serfs, which were limited from then onwards to sentencing them to detention in the houses of correction and the workhouses.[42] From this brief survey of the relevant legislation, it is evident that it was extremely confusing and that it could be and was interpreted in a number of ways. All the more need, therefore, to study the verdicts of the local courts and analyse the way in which the various ukazy were in fact applied.

Looking at the problem from the receiving end, existing studies are not very enlightening. According to Soviet historians much work remains to be done on the movement of population in Siberia in the eighteenth century.[43] There was a striking growth in the total Russian (as distinct from native) population of Siberia between the third census (1762) and the fourth (1782), from 261,000 to 389,000, which is attributed to the numbers of exiled settlers and fugitives.[44] No analysis has been made (nor perhaps can it be made on existing data) of which proved the bigger source. The contribution of natural growth to the rising population of Siberia is unknown and no quantitative assessment has been made of the importance of government sponsored resettlement of fugitive serfs or peasants returned from the West, and of ex-soldiers.[45] Part of the difficulty in interpreting the data from the Siberian end arises from the fact that the settler did not necessarily enter in Siberia into the status or *sostoyaniye* he occupied before. Many probably registered as *posadskiye lyudi* or *meshchane*, or even as *kuptsy*.[46] Some returned to Russia.[47] At any rate, in the present state of knowledge we have no way of establishing how often the different communities made use of the power of exile. Since the community was given a recruit

42. In 1782 an ukaz had already laid down that houses of correction were not to accept serfs sent by landowners for punishment if they had already been punished (presumably beaten or fined) for the offence, since they should not be punished twice for the same offence: *PSZ*, XXI, No. 15,486, 3 August 1782.

43. Kabuzan and Troitsky, *op. cit.*

44. Kabuzan and Troitsky state on p. 149 of their article that 'the data in table 4 (p. 150) show that the great mass of exiled settlers were serfs [*krepostnyye krest'yane*]'. Table 4 however (entitled numbers of settlers, resettled retired soldiers and exiled settlers in the 3rd and 4th *reviziya* in male souls) divides the various categories in the three guberniya analysed (Tobol'sk, Kolyvan and Irkutsk) into 'peasants', 'retired soldiers and officers', and 'exiled soldiers and officers', and does not state that these 'peasants' were serfs.

45. Cf. *PSZ*, XV, No. 11,714, 27 November 1762, and No. 11,815, manifesto of 13 May 1763, offering fugitives who had fled before 4 December 1762 and were returning from Poland-Lithuania permission to settle on state lands 'where they wish' and tax exemption for 6 years. If serfs, their owners would receive recruit quittances. According to Belyavsky, *Krest'yanskiy vopros*, p. 42, at the end of 1766 there were some 12,000 ex-fugitives returned from Poland among Siberian 'assigned' peasants.

46. Kabuzan and Troitsky, *op. cit.* According to the tables on p. 146, there were 223,676 peasants in 1762, and 318,061 in 1782; there were 24,261 *kuptsy* and registered towndwellers in 1762 and 27,241 in 1782.

47. In 1784 the Senate decided that landowners' serfs exiled to Siberia, for whom owners had received recruit quittances, and who subsequently returned to European Russia, should become state peasants and be granted state lands. If, however, they were returned to their landowners the recruit quittance which had originally been given would be taken back. In the same way, those exiled by other groups could return to their previous dwelling places, but in that case the recruit quittances given to village and urban communities would be withdrawn (*seleniya* and *grazhdanskiye obshchestva*): *PSZ*, XXII, No. 16,090, 14 November 1784.

quittance, this power could be a formidable weapon in the hands of the unscrupulous.[48]

III

A second ukaz of Catherine's reign on which further research is needed, both as regards its origin and its application, is the one dated 22 August 1767 on the right of serfs to complain against their masters. Two separate issues were here combined into one ukaz. The first is the right to petition the ruler in person; the second is the right of the serf to complain against the landowner. Already, on 4 March 1762, Peter III had issued a personal ukaz, in which he recalled that since 1700 there had been many ukazy (fifteen are quoted) forbidding petitioners to address themselves directly to the Emperor in person and enjoining them to present their petitions through the established government offices. Since these ukazy were being disobeyed, Peter now repeated the order, threatening harsh punishment for all, whatever their *chin* or rank, who approached him in person. Only if petitioners wished to appeal against the verdict of a court, i.e. if they had already been through the proper channels, could they address themselves directly to the Emperor – and in this case, should the appeal go against them, they would be severely punished.[49] Barely a fortnight after her accession Catherine repeated this ukaz almost word for word.[50] However, a much more precise formulation than the brief ukazy mentioned above was promulgated in an ukaz of 19 January 1765.[51]

This ukaz is directly related to previous ukazy on this subject, and points out that in spite of them, people still dared to send petitions directly to the Empress. Should they continue to do so instead of going through the proper channels, the ukaz specified the various penalties to be applied to the different classes of society for first, second, third and fourth offences, differentiating also between men, women and those under twenty in the case of nobles with a *chin* or nobles without a *chin*. The maximum penalty for a fourth offence for a noble with a *chin* was to be deprived of his *chin* for ever;[52] in the case of

48. Loewenstimm, *op. cit.*, p. 105, points out that peasant communities made use of this power to exile a peasant whose land they coveted, and the procedure was open to many abuses.
49. *PSZ*, XV, No. 11,459.
50. *PSZ*, XV, No. 11,606, 12 July 1762; confirmed again on 2 December 1762 (*PSZ*, XV, No. 11,718). This latter ukaz particularly reflects the conflict between the patriarchal and the bureaucratic conceptions of tsardom. Catherine's explanation of her refusal to receive petitions in person is that, as the sovereign, she must not be swayed by considerations of a personal nature, but must be equally just and merciful to all. A further ukaz of 23 June 1763 (*PSZ*, XV, No. 11,868) laid down an elaborate procedure to be followed in the presentation of petitions, including appeals against decisions of the courts which could go directly to the Empress. The rights of the serfs to complain is not mentioned at all in these ukazy.
51. *PSZ*, XVI, No. 12,316.
52. Eighteenth-century Russian ideas of what constituted more or less severe punishment did not of course correspond strictly to contemporary ones. Wives of nobles with a *chin* for instance were punished by a year's detention in the local government office (*prisutstvennoye mesto*) for a third offence, but a fourth offence incurred the far more dire penalty of perpetual banishment to their estates without permission to visit either capital. Those under age were sentenced to one month's arrest in all cases.

nobles without a *chin* the maximum penalty for a fourth offence was to be sent as a private soldier to the army in perpetuity.

In the present context, of most relevance is the final category of non-nobles with no *chin*, i.e. *kuptsy*, *meshchane*, *raznochintsy*, and all kinds of peasants of both sexes. For a first offence they were all sentenced to one month's hard labour; for a second offence to public punishment (presumably corporal, but no instrument was mentioned) and hard labour for a year, after which they would be returned to their dwelling place; for a third offence, to a public whipping (*plet'mi*) and perpetual exile to settlement in Nerchinsk. No penalty was specified for a fourth offence. Should any of these third offenders be serfs, continued the ukaz, their owners were to be given recruit quittances, since the landowners were in no way guilty of any offence.[53]

There is of course a striking difference between the penalties inflicted on those with a *chin* – whether they were noble or not – and on nobles, and the penalties on those who had neither *chin* nor noble rank. But within this second category, *kuptsy*, townspeople and peasants of all kinds were treated equally. However, it is also quite clear from this ukaz that the serf, provided he submitted his petition through the proper government offices, was committing no offence; and only in the case of a third attempt to present a petition directly to the Empress would he incur the penalty of public whipping and exile to Nerchinsk. The ukaz in no way specified what petitions should be about.

The ukaz of 1765 thus implicity allowed the serf to submit petitions through the proper channels. But his right to complain against his owner is governed by the relevant provision of the Code (*Ulozheniye*) of 1649. This is to be found in chapter 2, article 13 and suffers from all the obscurity usual in seventeenth-century Russian legal drafting. It reads as follows: 'And should people denounce those whom they serve, or if they are peasants those to whom they are peasants, concerning the health of the sovereign or other treasonable matter, and there is nothing with which to accuse them [the masters], then do not believe them; and inflict on them a cruel punishment, beating them mercilessly with the knut and give them up to those whose people or peasants they are. And except in those great affairs do not believe any such denunciators.'[54] The implications of this paragraph are that denunciations by serfs of their masters on great affairs of state were not to be believed unless there was some evidence; and on other matters serfs should not be listened to at all. The article in the Code clearly therefore forbade serfs to apply to any court or government office for redress against their masters. The ukaz of 1765 does not mention the article in the Code at all, either to confirm, expand or repeal it. The two issues were evidently not regarded as related.

The next relevant ukaz only adds to the confusion. It combines the article from the Code of 1649 and the ukaz of 1765, and proclaims them both to be

53. 'yesli ch'i krepostnyye . . .' is the phrase used.

54. Cf. 'Sobornoye ulozheniye tsarya Alekseya Mikhaylovicha 1649 goda', in *Pamyatniki russkogo prava*, ed. K.A. Sofronenko, VI, Moscow, 1957, pp. 29, 34.

valid. This is the frequently quoted Senate ukaz of 22 August 1767.[55] It is entitled 'On serfs and landowners' people remaining in subordination to their masters and on not handing petitions personally to the Empress', i.e. the compilers of the *Sobraniye* did not recognise (or chose not to recognise) its importance in the consolidation of the landowners' power over his serfs. Here again the background needs to be sketched in. In May 1767 the serfs on the estates of the Olsuf'yev family had submitted a petition to the Empress 'in person' while she was touring the provinces, asking that they should 'no longer belong to landowners'. They had been moved thereto by an episode connected with the summoning of the Legislative Commission. When the manifesto of December 1766 calling for the election of deputies was read out to them, they insisted that the 'true' version was being concealed from them. For a consideration, the village *pop* then read the 'full' text and said that the peasants too could elect deputies.[56] The disturbances assumed such proportions that they were put down as usual by a military detachment. In July 1767 peasants on three other estates submitted petitions directly to the Empress, complaining that they were unable to pay the very heavy dues in cash and kind exacted by the landowners.[57] Catherine forwarded these petitions to the Senate in July 1767, and pointed out that the increasing number of petitions indicated rising peasant discontent, which might have harmful consequences. She invited the Senate to propose means by which this evil could be averted. The Senate thereupon reported its advice to the Empress: the most convenient way of putting an end to groundless denunciations by the peasants *until a new law was drafted by the Legislative Commission* [my italics] was to issue a printed ukaz to the effect that serfs should on no account submit petitions against their landowners except on the issues allowed in the Code of 1649 and earlier ukazy; those who dared to do so should be punished with the knut. As for the peasants involved in the present riots, they should be interrogated 'under torture' to discover who had drafted their petitions, and subsequently whipped and returned to their landowners. Nevertheless the Senate observed that landowners might give the peasants just cause for complaint. It therefore proposed that a number of senators should in these particular cases 'admonish' the landowners concerned.[58]

55. *PSZ*, XVII, No. 12,966.
56. Belyavsky, *Krest'yanskiy vopros*, p. 77.
57. In her journey along the Volga to Kazan', Catherine received some 600 petitions, and it is commonly stated that the bulk of these were from serfs, complaining of the exactions of their landowners (cf. Solov'yev, *Istoriya Rossii s drevneyshikh vremyon*, Moscow, 1965 edn, XIV, p. 54; Belyavsky, *Krest'yanskiy vopros*, pp. 78, 153). According to Catherine's own account, most of the 600 petitions she received were from soldier farmers (*pakhotnyye soldaty*) and newly baptised (i.e. non-Russian) state peasants, complaining of shortage of land, 'except for a few unfounded petitions from serfs complaining of their owners' exactions, which were returned to them with the instruction not to submit such petitions in future'. Cf. *SIRIO*, X, p. 216, 22 June 1767.
58. Semevsky, *Krest'yane*, I, p. 374. The senators chosen to do the admonishing were R.L. Vorontsov, A.A. Vyazemsky, and P.I. Panin. We have no information as to whether and how they carried out their duties. See also Solov'yev, *op. cit.*, who quotes the journals of the Senate on six different dates, the last of which, 11 July 1767, is presumably the date of this report of the Senate to the Empress.

The ukaz, as eventually published on 22 August 1767, left out all references to torture. It started by repeating word for word the ukaz of 1765 which implicitly allowed serfs to 'petition' provided they did so through the proper channels. It condemned the serfs of the three landowners for their presumption in attempting to hand petitions directly to the Empress, contrary to that ukaz, and for submitting petitions forbidden by chapter 2 article 13 of the Code of 1649. It deplored the fact that such crimes arose from 'rumours spread by ill-intentioned people spreading invented stories about changes in the laws and collecting money on this pretext from the peasants by promising to procure them advantages'. The ukaz went on to enjoin peasants to obey their masters under threat of penalties as provided in previous laws: 'And should there be people and peasants who after the promulgation of this ukaz do not remain in the proper subordination to their landowners, and dare to submit forbidden [*nedozvolennyye*] petitions, contrary to chapter 2, point 13 of the Code, and above all into the hands of the Empress herself, such petitioners and those who draft the petitions will be punished with the knut and sent straight to hard labour in Nerchinsk with recruit quittances for their landowners.' To make sure that the law was known it was to be read in church on Sundays and feastdays for a month, and thereafter annually.

Semevsky, in analysing this episode, argues that in spite of the provisions of the Code of 1649, *in practice*, before 1767, denunciations by serfs of the exactions or cruelties of landowners were accepted in government offices, and that serfs only incurred punishment if they attempted to place petitions directly in the hands of the ruler.[59] But the only evidence of previous practice he adduces is the case of the notorious Saltychikha. The first twenty-one denunciations were however ignored or stifled by these government offices, and only the twenty-second, delivered personally to Catherine II in the summer of 1762, led eventually to an investigation and to the unravelling of the whole story.[60] However, in sentences of 25 June 1762 and 26 July 1762, the Senate condemned serfs who had petitioned against their landowners, basing its condemnation specifically on the provisions of the Code of 1649.[61] Thus there is evidence that the provisions of the Code were interpreted as forbidding all complaints against landowners before the ukaz of 1767. On the other hand, in a number of cases occurring between 1763 and 1764, though the complaints were not followed up, the peasants were merely sent back to their villages without punishment or got off with a whipping.[62]

Semevsky does, however, rightly point out the total contradiction between the law of 1765, sentencing serfs to one month's hard labour for the first offence of petitioning the Empress in person, and the Code, which forbade *all* denunciations except for treason, under threat of the knut. Both provisions

59. Semevsky, *Krest'yane*, I, p. 370.
60. *Ibid.*, p. 225.
61. Cf. V.M. Gribovsky, *Materialy dlya istorii vysshego suda i nadzora v pervuyu polovinu tsarstvovaniya imperatritsy Yekateriny II*, St Petersburg, 1901, p. 234, n. 129.
62. Semevsky, *Krest'yane*, I, pp. 371–2.

were repeated in the ukaz, but evidently the Code took precedence over the ukaz of 1765. The question which needs to be solved is to what extent the ukaz of 1767 actually changed existing practice, and to what extent the provisions of the Code had been applied earlier in the century.

One further point needs elucidation: the reference, in the Senate's report to the Empress, to the temporary nature of this ukaz, until the Legislative Commission should have produced a new law.[63] No specific law dealing with the subject was in fact promulgated.[64] But was the Statute on Local Administration of 1775 meant to supersede this law in any way? Were the institutions set up by that statute meant to channel complaints through the *zemskiy ispravnik* to the courts? Two lines of approach might be helpful in analysing this problem. First of all a study should be made of cases of peasants complaining against their landowners after 1775; were verdicts in such cases based on the law of 1767? Secondly, in the known cases of prosecution of landowners for cruelty to serfs after 1775, on whose denunciation were the cases taken up?

There is no systematic analysis of court verdicts after 1775, but Semevsky provides a few indications. In 1775 (probably before the Statute) a petition had been submitted personally to the Grand Duke Paul by serfs who addressed him as 'sovereign' and 'Majesty'. They were sentenced to the knut and Nerchinsk. Of the serfs involved in two other cases of petitioning the Empress directly, some were sentenced to the knut, but not all, and hard labour in Nerchinsk was commuted to 'working for their keep'. Other cases mentioned by Semevsky after 1775 are less clear, because 'petitioning' became involved with outright refusal to obey a landowner and with revolt, and hence the serfs were sentenced for the latter offence rather than the former.[65]

In the cases of cruelty to serfs recorded by Semevsky, some occurred after 1767, but Semevsky does not explain always how they came to be taken up in the first place. The Statute of 1775 enjoined governors to act as the defenders of the oppressed, as the advocates of those who could not speak for themselves, whose duty it was to put an end to tyranny and cruelty. Much would of course depend on the governor in these circumstances. When

63. The words italicised are not in Solov'yev, *op. cit.*, p. 54; Semevsky moreover is not quoting literally from the Senate report at this point, Semevsky, *Krest'yane*, I, p. 374.

64. In the draft project of laws for the third estate prepared by Baron Ungern Sternberg for the Sub-Commission on the Different Estates of the Legislative Commission, provision is made for a *zemskiy sud*, or Land Court, to which an elected serf elder, *alone*, could address complaints against a landowner. But the investigation of the complaint, the 'admonishing' of the landowner, and if he failed to reform his ways, the eventual decision to petition the Empress to appoint a trustee for the estate, was to be dealt with by the nobility of the uyezd in its corporate capacity under the Marshal, not by a law court. The draft project actually prepared by the Sub-Commission merely states that 'when serfs are tyrannised over by their landowners, or when their own property is unjustly taken from them by their landowners . . . they have the right to be defended in the established places (*v uchrezhdyonnykh mestakh*). Cf. *SIRIO*, XXXVI, pp. 270–1, and 283.

65. Semevsky, *Krest'yane*, I, pp. 444ff. In the Semevsky Archives in the Moscow section of the archives of the AN SSSR are copies of petitions by serfs complaining of ill-treatment by their owners and of decisions by the Senate on matters concerning serfs. Unfortunately the author of the article describing this archive gives no further details. See S.I. Volkov, 'Fond V.I. Semevskogo' (*Arkheograficheskiy yezhegodnik za 1958 g*, Moscow, 1960, p. 251).

A.P. Mel'gunov (whose wife was a niece of the Saltychikha) was governor of Yaroslavl', 'several nobles' were sent to Siberia for cruel behaviour to their serfs.[66] Saltykov, Governor General of Vladimir and Kostroma, was also reputed to listen to serf complaints. When, in 1785, some serfs complained to him of their owners' cruelty, he ordered the Lower Land Court to interrogate witnesses in the neighbouring estates.[67] Indeed it is clear that the *zemskiy ispravnik* and the Lower Land Courts played a considerable part in the putting down of peasant disturbances after 1775, and often took charge of the operations of military detachments sent to quell the riots or to restore serfs to their 'obedience'. Peasants on trial for taking part in such disturbances sometimes passed through the three local instances, the Lower Land Court, the District Court and the Guberniya Criminal Court.

Of course there was always widespread evasion of the law – all law, even when it was clearly formulated. But long study of the documents of this period conveys an impression, which further research might confirm or disprove, that after 1775 the repression of peasant disturbances was less arbitrary, though perhaps no less effective. It was also, in some cases, accompanied by efforts to induce landowners to reduce excessive money or labour dues and to behave with more humanity. But it was a brutal age (not only in Russia)[68] and the process of training a new generation of bureaucrats in the procedures of a *civil*, as distinct from a military, service was a slow one. Mel'gunov, one of the more active governors, found it very difficult to make his staff understand that they should not beat people – or each other – and to make the elected and appointed officials accept the need to follow the established procedures and apply the law.[69] Curiously enough there is evidence that in 1787 the law of

66. 'Razskazy ot Yaroslavskoy stariny', in *Russkiy arkhiv*, Moscow, 1876, pp. 314ff., on p. 329. (But would sentences have to be confirmed by the Senate?) Semevsky, in *Krest'yane*, I, pp. 208ff. lists twenty cases of cruelty to serfs. It is often assumed that these were the only cases which came before the courts (indeed, according to Blum, *op. cit.*, p. 439, only 'six serf owners are known to have been punished'). But Semevsky lists separately six further cases of landowners sentenced for the murder (usually when drunk) of serfs, and moreover speaks always of 'cases known to him' and mentioned in personal ukazy of the Empress or in the Senate Archives (*ibid.*, p. 229, and n. 2).
67. *Ibid.*, pp. 222–3; Semevsky also quotes a case in 1780 of a scribe who drafted a petition for some serfs; all were arrested and interrogated in the *taynaya ekspeditsiya* by Sheshkovsky. What happened to the peasants he does not state, but the scribe was sent to a house of correction (*ibid.*, p. 378). It may be that some of the records of peasants arrested under the law of 1767 for petitioning the Empress in person are to be found in the *taynaya ekspeditsiya*.
68. Semevsky, with his frequent comparisons with contemporary practice elsewhere in eastern and even western Europe, is more balanced than many who have written after him. But one might add that if there was no law to prevent a landowner ill-treating a serf, there was also no law to stop a serf or a state peasant from ill-treating and brutalising his wife, his children, his daughter-in-law (often only too vulnerable) or his employees if he had any. The power of the *pater familias* throughout society was vast, and often exercised in a brutal, if not perverted, manner.
69. Cf. L. Trefoleyev, 'A.P. Mel'gunov: General-Gubernator yekaterininskikh vremyon' in *Russkiy arkhiv*, 1865, pp. 873–919; Mel'gunov frequently fined judges for delays or improper procedure (i.e. taking cases to the wrong courts). In one case he rebuked the Vologda Criminal Court for sentencing two serfs guilty of stealing corn to the knut, nostril clipping, and Siberia, in disregard of the provisions of the manifesto of 28 June 1787 (*PSZ*, XXII, No. 16,551) which in article 7 stated that 'criminals . . . at present sentenced to corporal punishment are to be freed from it and sent for settlement'.

1765 was still regarded as valid, taken by itself. When Catherine II was starting out on her journey to the Crimea, a special *obryad* for her progress through the Governor-Generalship of Khar′kov was issued by the Governor General, Vasily Chertkov. The *obryad* dealt with such ordinary matters as instructing the inhabitants to clean the streets, wear their best clothes and whisk beggars out of sight. Then, referring to the proper maintenance of public order, the *obryad* repeated word for word the ukaz of 19 January 1765, including all the various punishments set out for the different ranks of society should they dare to present petitions directly to the Empress, instead of through the proper channels. The reference to the serfs remained exactly as in the ukaz of 1765, and no mention was made at all of the additional gloss put upon it by the ukaz of 1767. Indeed earlier ukazy were referred to, which specified the particular government officials who would be in the Empress's suite and to whom petitions could be handed.[70] The *obryad* cannot have been an unknown and obscure document; on the occasion of the Empress's journey there must have been correspondence between the Governor General and the Senate, possibly with the Empress herself (the Governors General were authorised *ex officio* to correspond directly with the Empress). Did anyone try to put Vasily Chertkov right and point out to him that the law of 1765 had been superseded?

IV

Yet a further general statement about the extension of serfdom in terms of the increase in the number of serfs at the expense of the number of state peasants needs to be re-examined. This is the view that large numbers of state peasants were turned into serfs as a result of grants of land made by Catherine II to her favourites and to government servants.[71] The figure invariably quoted – 800,000 adult peasants of both sexes – stems from the calculations made by V.I. Semevsky, which he gives in his *Krest′yane v tsarstvovaniye Yekateriny II*. Semevsky does, however, point out that most of these grants of settled land were in fact made from lands taken by Russia from Poland in the three partitions.[72] In an article published much earlier, Semevsky gave an account of the investigation which led him to this conclusion.[73]

With his usual thoroughness, Semevsky went through all the imperial ukazy of Catherine's reign, referring to land grants, and found only a short gap for the period March–April 1764. He also made use of a secret land survey,

70. The *obryad* is printed in P. Bartenev, *Osmnadtsatyy vek*, Moscow, 1869, I, p. 306.
71. To quote only two such statements, see e.g. Belyavsky, 'Novyye dokumenty', p. 387, 'massive distributions of state peasants . . .' were made 'to private owners'; and see the statement by M. Raeff, which goes even further and attributes the failure of the government's revenue from taxes to rise in the late eighteenth century to 'Catherine's generous gifts to private individuals of large tracts of state lands and a great number of state peasants': (M. Raeff, *Michael Speransky, Statesman of Imperial Russia, 1772–1839*, The Hague, 1957, p. 83).
72. Semevsky, *Krest′yane*, I, p. 228.
73. *Ibid.*, 'Razdacha naselyonnykh imeniy pri Yekaterine II' (*Otechestvennyye zapiski*, VIII, St Petersburg, 1877, pp. 204–27).

prepared on the instructions of the Procurator General, Prince A.A. Vyazemsky, in 1773, which listed, though incompletely, the number of dvoryane and the numbers of serfs they owned. These and other sources enabled Semevsky to trace the details of all but 18 of the 383 known grants of settled land.

Semevsky then proceeded to analyse the sources from which these grants were made. There were first of all the court and sovereign's peasants from which grants of at least 58,500 serfs were made, mainly before 1772.[74] Secondly there was the Chancery of Confiscated Lands. The Chancery administered lands confiscated in previous reigns from state criminals, also lands which reverted to the crown on the extinction of the family, or lands confiscated for poll tax arrears, or for debt. The supply of confiscated lands was not large at Catherine's accession but it increased enormously with the partitions of Poland. Not only were estates confiscated from prominent Polish opponents of Russian policy, but royal private estates, crown lands and lands belonging to the Catholic hierarchy, to monasteries and cathedral chapters, and to Uniat establishments were all swept into this category.

Great Russian state peasants, states Semevsky, only very rarely were granted to private owners (he quotes only one instance). But non-Russian state peasants, i.e. those settled on crown lands in the Baltic Provinces, or on state lands or military fiefs in Little Russia (*mayetnosti*, *uryadovyye* and *rangovyye* lands), or on crown lands in Poland (*koronne starostwa*), were widely distributed. It was of course the case that these lands were normally granted to private owners on leases of longer or shorter duration, and the peasants were therefore in closer direct contact with the 'landlord' lessee than the Russian state peasant ever was with a landowner. Finally, the new category of 'economic' peasants, formed when the estates of the Orthodox Church were secularised in 1764, was very rarely touched, and in the four cases when 'economic' peasants were granted to private owners, the number was made up from other sources (Semevsky does not state which).

It is clear from Semevsky's analysis that the Great Russian state peasantry were not regarded as an inexhaustible source from which grants could be made and that court and sovereign's peasants were not touched if it could be avoided. Indeed the government was hard put to it at times to find lands, and estates were occasionally purchased in order to make grants. In 1793, on the occasion of the anniversary of peace with Turkey, grants to fifteen people were announced, but the recipients had to wait until 1795 for the land since it was simply not available.

Semevsky divides Catherine's reign into three periods with regard to grants of land: (1) 1762–72, during which period the government had to 'search for estates in Great Russia and Little Russia, where most of the land had been given

74. Court peasants were given away more freely under Catherine's predecessors, says Semevsky (*ibid.*, p. 210, n. 3).

away in previous reigns'; (2) 1773 to mid-1795, when the government made use of lands in Belorussia acquired in the first partition of Poland; (3) 1795–96, when lands in Lithuania and South-Western Russia (i.e. ex-Polish lands) became available.

In the first period, to 1772, there were seventy-one grants of land totalling 66,243 male souls. Of these the bulk were court and sovereign's peasants, 5,897 were in Livonia or Little Russia.[75] In three cases the numbers are unknown.[76]

In the second period, 1772 to mid-1795, 216 grants were made, amounting to 182,730 male souls on known facts. No details were available for fourteen grants including one – presumably large – grant to G.A. Potemkin. Hence Semevsky estimates the total at 202,730. Of these, 10,084 were in the Baltic Provinces and 192,646 'mainly in Belorussia', where, by 1795, very little land suitable for distribution remained.

In the third period, mid-1795 to 28 June 1796 (OS) when Catherine signed her last land grant, 96 grants were made totalling 130,000 male souls. Of these 18,420 were in the Baltic Provinces, Curland and Little Russia, and the remainder (121,580) mainly in territories newly acquired as a result of the second and third partitions. Thus the total distributed from 1762 to 1796 amounts to 398,973 male souls, or in round figures, 400,000. Of these 314,226 came from ex-Polish territories, 34,401 from the Baltic Provinces and Little Russia and some 60,000 from other sources.[77]

The nature, purpose, location and timing of these land grants raise a number of questions. Was there first of all any policy behind these awards, and did this policy vary throughout the period? The practice of rewarding favourites and officials in this way had of course a long history in Russia. Peter I used it freely,[78] and so did his successors. The avidity of the nobility was hard to satisfy and Elizabeth Petrovna was led to issue an ukaz declaring that in future grants were to be made from confiscated lands and demands for grants of court estates were not to be forwarded to her.[79] In a serf-owning society, where the government was permanently short of currency, and a settled estate

75. Semevsky calculates that one Little Russian *dvor* contained four male souls; one *khata*, one male soul; one Livonian *haken* comprised on average thirty male souls. Semevsky's total figure of 400,000 male souls might have to be raised, to take into account the figures given by Kabuzan: 6.8 souls per *dvor* and 3 souls per *khata* in Little Russia (*op. cit.*, p. 179, note d).

76. By the end of this period shortage of land in Great Russia was such, that if the unity of the large court estates was to be preserved, grants of court and confiscated lands had to be made in small parcels dotted about different uyezdy (*ibid.*, p. 216).

77. The usual figure, 800,000, is reached by doubling the number of male souls to include wives and female children. Semevsky states (*ibid.*, p. 206) that he had drawn up a full chronological list of all those who received grants of settled land in Catherine's reign including information on the number of souls, location, nature of the source of the grant, reason for the grant, and source of his evidence for all this information. He hoped, he wrote, to publish it. It has not been published yet, but it has survived among his papers and it is to be hoped that it will be (Cf. S.I. Volkov, 'Fond V.I. Semevskogo', p. 256 (see above, n. 65)).

78. Between 1682 and 1711 Peter gave away 43,655 homesteads.

79. *PSZ*, XV, No. 10,957, 23 May 1759.

was both the external mark of social status and the basic means of livelihood of the nobility, such a grant was the most, if not the only, acceptable reward for service to the state – it was the Russian equivalent of the 'pensions' granted on one or more lives elsewhere.[80]

The timing of Catherine's grants raises, however, some interesting questions. Of the 66,243 male souls granted between 1762 and 1772, 18,725 were given at once as rewards to the participants in the *coup d'état* of 28 June 1762 (OS), and hence in the next ten years only some 48,000 were distributed. Yet this is precisely the period when Catherine is portrayed as attempting to woo the nobility in order to increase the stability of her hold on the throne. One might therefore have expected these years to coincide with the largest land grants, or at least the most numerous individual grants. But there were only seventy-one all told. It would be fair to deduce from this that the policy of granting settled land was not regarded as a means of conciliating a discontented or 'oppositional' nobility, but in a much more straightforward and narrow way, as a means of attaching and rewarding specific government servants chosen from a fairly small group. A detailed analysis, based on Semevsky's information, might cast an interesting light on who the people worth attaching – or rewarding – were.

By 1772 the amount of land available was exhausted and only the acquisition of Belorussia enabled the government to continue the policy of grants without raiding the reserves of court, state or economic peasants. Would grants have been lavished on such a scale had these lands not become available? According to the historian Lektonen, the need for more settled land outside the existing boundaries of Russia, in order to satisfy the desires of the nobility, was one of the factors which contributed to the first partition of Poland.[81] But once these lands had become available, the policy of granting settled estates should be viewed in the context of Russian policy towards non-Russian lands. Grants had been, and continued to be, made primarily from estates in lands outside the borders of Great Russia proper, i.e. in Little Russia, Livonia and Estonia, Belorussia and later Poland and Curland. Certainly the amount of confiscated settled land available after the first partition was considerable.[82] In addition the Russian government could dispose of the crown

80. Occasionally nobles preferred to receive a grant in cash, usually if they were badly in debt. Princess Dashkova for instance asked for 24,000 roubles instead of an estate, as her reward for her part in Catherine's *coup d'état*, in order to pay off her husband's debts.

81. U.L. Lektonen, *Die polnischen Provinzen Russlands unter Katharina II in den Jahren 1772–1782*, Berlin, 1907, p. 504. It might be added that Count Z. Chernyshev, who had favoured partition, and had been appointed Governor General of the two new gubernii of Mogilev and Pskov, was the recipient of a grant of 5,304 souls in the guberniya of Mogilev in 1773. Cf. E.P. Zakalinskaya, *Votchinnyye khozyaystva Mogilevskoy gubernii vo vtoroy polovine XVIII veka*, Mogilev, 1958, p. 27. (I owe this reference to the kindness of Professor Ian Christie.)

82. Lands confiscated from Polish landlords who failed to take the oath of allegiance or to sell their property within the time limit enacted by Catherine came to 95,097 souls in the two guberniya. (See *Belorussiya v epokhu feodalizma*, III, Academy of Sciences of Belorussia, Minsk, 1961, pp. 41–2, Report of the Governor General on confiscated estates, 1 June 1773, hereafter called *Belorussiya*). Several very large estates belonging to magnates such as Prince K. Radziwill (7,805 and 16,280) and Prince A. Sapieha (18,602) fell into the Russian net.

lands leased to Polish landlords.[83] Does the way in which the lands were disposed of give any indication of Catherine's policy in relation to the nobility? The lands were not disposed of all at once. In 1774, twelve grants were made; the number rose to thirty-seven in 1775, reflecting both the end of the Russo-Turkish War (a grant of 7,129 souls to Field-Marshal P.A. Rumyantsev), and the end of the Pugachev revolt (2,463 to the widow of General A. Bibikov). In 1776, eighteen grants of land were made,[84] including two large grants, one to P. Zavadovsky (the favourite) and one to Count Z. Chernyshev.[85] In the years 1776–79 the number of grants dropped drastically to an average of ten per annum (including incidentally the grant of 14,247 souls to Prince G.A. Potemkin in 1776, and of 11,821 souls to S.T. Zorich in 1777, both favourites). The total number of grants made in Belorussia between 1773 and 1779 according to Lektonen was 107.[86] Semevsky gave the figure of 216 grants for the period 1772 to mid-1795, so that a further 109 grants were spread over the period 1779–1795.

From the data provided by Lektonen, it is clear that some twenty grants of large estates (above 1,000 souls) were made in 1772–79, mainly to favourites and prominent public servants, and to court servants close to the Empress herself.[87] Many of the large confiscated estates were, however, divided into smaller parcels of some 200–300 serfs and distributed among some eighty-seven recipients.[88] About these recipients much less is known at present. All of them were Russians except one: the smallest estate, of sixty-five serfs, was allotted to a deserving Pole.

It is evident, from what is known, that large grants were reserved to those who were already associated with the Empress's policies and helped her to carry them out, whether as favourites or as government servants. The circle of recipients was a very narrow one. The smaller grants may have been conditioned by two factors. The first, already mentioned, was the inability of the Russian government with its primitive financial system and relatively small resources to reward deserving servants in any other way than by grants of

83. There were 125 crown *starostwa* with 148,857 souls granted on varying kinds of leases to private owners. Most of these were left in the possession of Polish landlords, if they had taken the oath of allegiance (Lektonen, *op. cit.*, p. 498). Zakalinskaya estimates that in Mogilev guberniya some 25–30 per cent of the landlords were now Russians, and they held the largest estates. (This figure does *not*, however, refer to the total proportion of land or souls held.) (Zakalinskaya, *op. cit.*, p. 37).

84. Lektonen, *op. cit.*, p. 508.

85. Zakalinskaya, *op. cit.*, p. 27.

86. *Ibid.* and Lektonen, *op. cit.*, p. 508. Lektonen mentions annual grants of four to six estates in these years, plus twenty-one grants for which no dates are available.

87. Apart from those already mentioned, grants were made to N.I. Panin, Head of the College of Foreign Affairs and Tutor to the Grand Duke Paul (3,900 souls); A.M. Golitsyn, Vice Chancellor (3,152); Count I.A. Osterman (foreign affairs) (2,840); Prince A.A. Vyazemsky, Procurator General (1,520); A.A. Bezborodko, the Empress's secretary (1,222); I.P. Yelagin, senator, one time secretary and friend of Catherine's (3,712); G. Koz'min, secretary (1,918); Vasil'chikov, favourite (2,927); Dr Kruse, the Grand Duke's physician (1,528), etc.

88. Lektonen, *op. cit.*, pp. 508–9; in 1773–74, 10 large estates were divided into 118 small ones; grants were made of 8 estates of 6–800 serfs; 10 over 500; 3 over 400; 16 over 300; 28 over 200; 21 over 100; 1 under 100.

land. The second factor may well have been the conscious desire to 'russify' the newly annexed territories by introducing a number of Russian landowners. After the first partition the Russian government made no attack on Polish institutions and the Polish language in civil government; there was not a vast displacement of Polish landowners. But 1773 is a key date in the preparation of the Local Government Statute of 1775. The remodelling of the guberniyi was already under consideration, and indeed the new institutions were tried out in Belorussia before they were – in their final form – promulgated for the whole of Russia in 1775. Since the nobility were to play an important part in local government, and to elect many of its functionaries, the introduction of Russian landowners would serve to strengthen Russian influence.[89]

In 1793 fifteen awards were made in September but these were in the nature of promises since the land was simply not available, even in Belorussia. Once the second and third partitions of Poland had been completed, distribution went more briskly, since far more Polish landowners were displaced, and far more land was confiscated. Here too, however, the same principle was followed in making awards: the large awards went primarily to military leaders (Rumyantsev, Suvorov, Saltykov, etc.), to prominent government servants (Osterman, Sievers), favourites (Zubov, the nieces of Potemkin) and smaller grants of 100–400 serfs were made to officers and bureaucrats.[90] Aristocratic cupidity and government policy here probably went hand in hand. The nobility carried out administrative and judicial functions in Poland. They would have to be replaced either by a Russian administration or by Russian landowners. Russian landowners may have appeared to present a cheaper and more reliable way of extending Russian control into the annexed areas than an expensive and corrupt bureaucracy. Moreover, within the general Russian conception of local administration at that time, the landowners had a definite role to play. It was nowhere envisaged that they might be replaced by a network of government agents. Indeed it was difficult enough for the government to find trained cadres to deal with the more pressing problems of financial and judicial administration. It was scarcely equipped to take over control of large areas often of alien language, religion and tradition.

Finally, is the total number of grants made in the thirty-four years of Catherine's reign enough to warrant the assertion that policy had changed in any way in this field throughout the century? It would seem rather that

89. On 16 January 1773, for instance, Catherine authorised the nobles and towns of Belorussia to elect deputies to the Legislative Commission. Cf. *Belorussiya*, p. 36. Semevsky observes that the names of landowners in Belorussia in the survey of 1777 are almost exclusively Polish. The few Russian names to be found are almost all identifiable as the recipients of government grants (Semevsky, *Krest'yane*, I, p. 205).

90. Cf. *Belorussiya*, pp. 75, 85. Reports of estates granted of 18 August 1795 and March 1797. Unfortunately these lists are incomplete. The first lists thirty-seven grants made in Belorussia out of sixty-four, but provides no information on where and to whom the remaining grants were made. The second list deals only with the new guberniya of Lithuania (previously Vil'na and Slonim). It is thus not possible to correlate the data in these lists with the information provided by Semevsky. Incidentally, the Empress's physician, Dr Roggerson, a Scot, was awarded a total of 1,580 serfs in Minsk guberniya, including 308 confiscated from the Bishop of Vil'na.

Catherine continued to reward public (or private) service in the traditional way. Very large grants were made from Peter I onwards to favourites, military leaders and high government officials, and smaller grants to those lower on the social scale. The reluctance to give away court peasants, shown by both Elizabeth and Catherine, and the refusal to give state peasants, might be explained on moral grounds – the desire not to enserf the relatively free. But financial motives may well have played a larger part; the crown had no desire to deprive itself of the *obrok* paid directly by the state peasants. Forcing ex-Polish serfs (or crown peasants) to exchange a Polish landowner for a Russian one posed fewer moral problems, and the crown lost potential, not actual revenue thereby.

The nature of Catherine's policy in the field of serfdom is crucial to the elucidation of a second important aspect of her reign, namely the problem of the extent of her political dependence on the nobility. It is a general assumption among historians that in order to secure her hold on the throne she had usurped she was forced, willingly according to some, unwillingly according to others, to conciliate the nobility by granting them increased powers over their serfs. In my view, however, the specific relationship crown/noble/serf should be analysed in the wider context of other problems facing the crown, notably public order, finance, economic development, public administration, and war. Only such an approach enables one to assess the options open to the government at any one time, and to estimate the field for manoeuvre. It would also explain some of the very contradictory features in Catherine's policies, the discrepancies between expressed ideals and actual achievements. The timing of particular policies should also be examined, both in relation to domestic and foreign events, and in relation to the evolution of Catherine's own opinions and those who were closest to her at any one moment.

The three topics analysed here have been chosen merely to illustrate the fact that some of the interpretations of Catherine's policies have been based on inadequate evidence: the power to exile to Siberia for settlement had been granted to all estates, but we know very little about how it was used. The law of 1767 was extremely confused, and may even have been intended as a temporary measure. We do not know how it was applied after 1775. Large numbers of state peasants were not turned into private serfs. Many other aspects of Catherine's policy in this field still require detailed treatment: for instance the law enacted by Peter III and confirmed by Catherine, which prohibited the further purchase by non-nobles of serf villages for industrial enterprises.[91] Much more research is needed on the formation and implementation of government policy before a balanced conclusion can be drawn on the nature of the political partnership between crown and nobility.

91. *PSZ*, XV, No. 11,490, 29 March 1762, confirmed on 8 August 1762 (*ibid.*, No. 11,638).

CHAPTER SEVEN

*Freemasonry in eighteenth-century Russian society**

Interest in gnostic, hermetic, alchemical, esoteric and mystical lore has provided a constant undercurrent to European intellectual life.[1] In the eighteenth century one of the forms in which it sometimes manifested itself was freemasonry. The masonic movement was not primarily a challenge to political orthodoxy, as it became in the French Revolution and in the nineteenth and twentieth centuries – with the notable exception of the 'Illuminati' of Bavaria, founded by Adam Weishaupt in 1776, and disbanded by the Elector in 1784. The masons represented rather a challenge to religious orthodoxy coming from people whose faith in revealed religion had been shaken by the rational certainties of the Enlightenment and who were trying to build a bridge between science and religion.

There were many strands in freemasonry. In very broad terms one can divide members of the movement into those concerned with self-knowledge and self-improvement, a rational philanthropy, and the manifestation of the brotherhood of man, above and beyond the distinctions of caste, and those who sought to discover the ultimate meaning of life and death by means of esoteric study and mystical contemplation, supported by the resort to magical, alchemical and hermetic science.

There was a long tradition of magic and astrology in Russia, and in spite of the barriers to foreign contamination set up by the Orthodox Church, occult literature was not unknown. The pseudo-Aristotelian *Secretum Secretorum*, with its alchemical, astrological and onomantic elements, was known in Russia probably by the end of the fifteenth century, and certainly by the early sixteenth century, and there were copies in the libraries of Tsar Mikhail Fedorovich, Patriarch Nikon and Tsarevich Aleksei, while Tsar Aleksei Mikhailovich was

* I am very grateful to Dr W.F. Ryan, Librarian of the Warburg Institute in London, for directing me to many essential works used in this article.

1. See B. Walker, *Gnosticism, Its History and Influence*, Northampton, 1983, and F. Yates, *The Occult Philosophy in the Elizabethan Age*, London, 1979 and *The Rosicrucian Enlightenment*, London and Boston, 1972.

evidently familiar with it.[2] An exposition of Ramon Lull's *Ars Magna* and a translation of his *Ars brevis* had been produced in Russia in the late seventeenth century and circulated widely in manuscript. Parts of the *Ars Magna* were reproduced by A. Denisov, of the priestless Old Believer Community, at the beginning of the eighteenth century.[3] Among 'portraits' of Hellenic sages to be found in Russian art of the sixteenth and seventeenth centuries were representations of 'Hermes Trismegistus'.[4] John Dee's *Monas Hieroglyphica* (already known in Russia in the sixteenth century) formed part of the library of Simeon Polotsky in the reign of Tsar Aleksei.[5]

The religious turmoil of seventeenth-century Russia prepared the way for the limited penetration of hermetic science, and elements of gnosticism in the small intellectual elite around the tsars, and for the much more widespread practice of astrology, magic and divination both at court and in the population at large. But there was no prehistory in Russia of one of the most important sources of freemasonry, namely the old tradition of medieval craftsmanship, as expressed in the guilds, which was said to have survived in England among the workers who rebuilt London after the great fire of 1666. Nor was there any precedent for a third alleged source, namely the Order of the Temple, founded in the twelfth century by crusaders in the Holy Land, a movement in which Russia took no part.

The spread of freemasonry in Russia has to be viewed as part of the process of 'Westernization' originally embarked on by Peter I. One of the features of Russian intellectual life in the eighteenth century is the extraordinary concentration into a very short space of time of the influence of powerful trends coming from the West. Whereas in the West intellectual and religious experience had been growing and deepening throughout some five centuries, and was given an extremely powerful fillip by the Renaissance and the Reformation, all these trends manifested themselves almost at the same time in Russia. Among Peter I's closest friends and collaborators was the Russian-born Scot, James Bruce, who was interested in the occult and indeed had the reputation of being a magician, from whose mouth flames might spurt when he spoke.[6] Peter himself introduced the Renaissance courtly spectacle into Russia,

2. See most recently W.F. Ryan, 'The Secret of Secrets and the Muscovite Autocracy', in *Pseudo-Aristotle. The Secret of Secrets, Sources and Influences*, ed. W.F. Ryan and C.B. Schmitt, Warburg Institute Surveys, IX, London, 1982, pp. 114–23.

3. See the two articles by A. Kh. Gorfunkel', 'Velikaya nauka Raimunda Liullia i ee chitateli', *XVIII vek*, No. 5, 1962, pp. 336–48, and 'Andrey Belobotsky – poet i filosof kontsa XVII – nachala XVIII v.' in *Trudy otdela drevnerusskoi literatury*, XVIII, ANSSR, 1962, pp. 188–213. Gorfunkel' identifies the translator of Lull as A. Kh. Belobotsky who, in his view, is the same person as the much better known Yan Belobodsky. As many as 55 ms copies of the *Ars magna* have survived, dating from the late seventeenth century right through to the early nineteenth century. Some belonged to non-noble owners. Gorfunkel' also published an article on 'Giordano Bruno in Russia', in *Rivista di Filosofia*, vol. LII, No. 4, October 1961, pp. 461–76.

4. Ryan, *op. cit.*, p. 122, n. 35.

5. On Aleksey's interest in the occult see P. Longworth, *Alexis Tsar of all the Russias*, London, 1984, pp. 205–6.

6. For Bruce's importance as a scientist in Russia, see V. Boss, *Newton in Russia – The Early Influence, 1698–1796*, Harvard University Press, 1972.

secularizing what had previously been religious elements in court culture. He patronized the allegorical use of myths, and one of the emblem books used as a source for such spectacles was published in his reign in Russia, namely *Symbola et Emblemata*, which became virtually Peter's 'bedside book'.[7]

The general consensus is that the first grand master of Russian freemasonry was the Scot, James Keith, a Jacobite who had entered Russian service in 1728, and whose cousin, Lord Kintore, was at one time grand master of English masonry.[8] Keith's lodge was founded in 1741–42 but he left Russia to enter Prussian service in 1747. There is not much reliable evidence about the Russian masonic movement during the reign of Elizabeth (1741–61). The Empress's favourite, I.I. Shuvalov, was reputed to be one of the leading masons, and Baron Theodor Heinrich Tschoudy, the author of the ritual of *The Flaming Star*, was his secretary and protégé in the 1760s. Public opinion, particularly among the less educated and among women, was extremely hostile, in the belief that masons indulged in all sorts of unspeakable rites. The aunt of the poet Derzhavin would not allow him to go near I.I. Shuvalov, then curator of Moscow University, on the grounds that the masons were 'apostates, heretics, blasphemers, given over to Antichrist' and able to kill their enemies thousands of versts away.[9] Much of the hostility to freemasonry undoubtedly derived from the Church, always inimical to religious convictions not buttressed by ecclesiastical authority. A contemporary manuscript poem runs: 'Frank-masons, your laws are full of lies, and your mystery consists in counting up to 666', the number of the beast in the Apocalypse, and of great significance in gnostic tradition and among the Old Believers in the seventeenth century.[10] But by the 1750s and 1760s masonic motifs and symbols were already much in evidence in poetry, prose and drama published in periodicals and reviews, and many high government servants belonged to lodges.[11]

7. S.L. Baehr, 'The Iconography of Happiness in Eighteenth-Century Russian Courtly Spectacle', in *Great Britain and Russia in the Eighteenth Century*, ed. A.G. Cross, Oriental Research Partners, 1979, pp. 109–23.

8. Eighteenth-century Russian freemasonry has been extensively studied in pre-revolutionary Russia and a reasonably up-to-date bibliography will be found in P. Bourychkine, *Bibliographie sur la franc-maçonnerie en Russie, complétée et mise au point par Tatiana Bakounine*, Paris, 1967. See also the unpublished Ph.D dissertation by In-Ho L. Ryu, 'Freemasonry under Catherine the Great – A Reinterpretation', Harvard University, 1966. Very little has been published in the Soviet Union but A.G. Cross's 'British Freemasons in Russia in the Age of Catherine the Great', *Oxford Slavonic Papers*, NS, No. 4, 1971, pp. 43–72, contains important new material.

9. Tschoudy was in Russia off and on from 1753 to 1760 and acted as the private secretary of I.I. Shuvalov; he used the name of Chevalier de Lussy, and Comte de Puttelange, and published the first French language periodical in Russia, *Le chaméleon littéraire*, in 1759. His masonic ritual seems to have been very influential. See also *Sochineniya Derzhavina*, ed. Ya. Grot., St Petersburg, 1876, vol. VI, pp. 427–8; for examples of anti-masonic verses, see S.V. Yeshevsky, *Sochineniya po russkoy istorii*, Moscow, 1900, pp. 173ff. and I.F. Martynov, 'Ranniye masonskiye stikhi i pesni v sobranii biblioteki akademii nauk SSSR' in *Russia and the World of the Eighteenth Century*, ed. R.P. Bartlett, A.G. Cross and Karen Rasmussen, Columbus, Ohio, 1988, pp. 437–45.

10. G.V. Vernadsky, *Russkoye masonstvo v tsarstvovaniye Yekateriny II*, Petrograd, 1917, p. 7; *Revelations, 13*, 18.

11. Vernadsky, *op. cit.*, pp. 5ff.; A. Levitsky, 'Masonic Elements in Russian Eighteenth Century Poetry', in *Russia and the World of the Eighteenth Century*, pp. 419–36.

During his six-month reign Peter III is said to have become a mason, but freemasonry at this time cannot be identified with any political orientation. Many of Peter III's adherents were freemasons, but so were many of Catherine's supporters. Many of the high government servants Catherine inherited from Elizabeth, such as the senator Roman Vorontsov, General Z.G. Chernyshev (an old flame of hers), Nikita Panin, senator and governor of the Grand Duke Paul, and her secretary Adam Olsuf'yev, were masons of more or less standing and she seems to have been indifferent to their activities.

The movement really took off in Russia in Catherine's reign in large part for two reasons. One was the lively intellectual intercourse with Western culture, primarily French, German, English, and to a lesser degree Italian, which characterized her reign. The second was the manifesto issued by Peter III in February 1762, freeing the nobility from compulsory service. This gave the class with most pretensions to culture the leisure to travel, study, read and write, and to indulge, if its members so wished, in all kinds of private social activities.

As in many countries the various masonic trends were often in rivalry with each other, and their relationships are by no means easy to disentangle. The early Russian masonry was limited to the three degrees of the Johannine English system. An English lodge, *Parfaite Union*, the members of which were all English, was founded in 1771. One of Catherine's supporters while she was yet Grand Duchess, Ivan Perfil'yevich Yelagin, became one of the most important masons in her reign. He was at one time one of Catherine's secretaries, then director of court spectacles and a senator. A mason already in the early 1760s, he is one of the relatively few Russian masons to have left an account of his progression through various masonic systems and degrees, as well as a large collection of manuscript constitutions, rituals, cathechisms, correspondence with lodges in Russia and other countries, and his own masonic writings which have mainly remained unpublished.[12]

Yelagin founded the Russian Grand Provincial lodge in 1771 which was followed by a number of lodges based on the English system. He was in correspondence with the English Grand Lodge, which sent him a diploma signed by the English Grand Master, the Duke of Beaufort. Yelagin agreed in turn to send reports to England, and three guineas for every new lodge opened.[13] He eventually controlled some 14 lodges in St Petersburg, Moscow and the provinces.

But masons often felt that the more degrees there were, the more likely some great ultimate truth would be revealed at the end. Thus many Russians now joined the so-called strict observance masonry, brought to Russia from Germany in 1771 by the German Baron P.B. Reichel. The Reichel system introduced a more developed mystical strand, and more complex and abstruse

12. A.G. Cross, *op. cit.*; 'Zapiska o masonstve I.P. Yelagina', *Russkiy Arkhiv*, 1864, pp. 592ff.; cf. A.N. Pypin, *Russkoye masonstvo XVIII i pervaya chetvert' XIX v.*, Petrograd, 1916, pp. 92–115.
13. A.G. Cross, *op. cit.*, p. 45.

degrees. Reichel inaugurated the lodge Apollo in 1771, which depended on the Grand Lodge of Zinnendorf in Berlin, and soon controlled eight lodges, including one in Riga and one in Reval, presumably operating in German. (The publisher and future Rosicrucian, Nikolai Ivanovich Novikov, was a member of Reichel's Latona lodge.[14]) Many of the members of Yelagin's lodges now went over to Reichel's system and by 1776 Yelagin agreed to merge his lodges with those of Reichel; he became Grand Master of the new united Grand Provincial Lodge, and Nikita Panin, Catherine's Foreign Minister, became his deputy. The new lodge depended not on England, but on Berlin, and the English lodges in Russia were also ordered by the Grand National Lodge of England to accept the authority of the Yelagin/Reichel system.[15]

Ever seeking for more certain illumination, some of the masons in the now united Reichel/Yelagin system began to correspond with Swedish masons, who practised the ritual of the Order of the Temple under their Grand Master, the Duke of Sudermania, brother of the King of Sweden. The Order of the Temple was a system of strict observance which was widespread all over continental Europe; it was composed of ten degrees, three Johannine, two Scottish or Saint Andrew, and five knightly degrees.[16] Its attraction lay in its mythical connection both with the construction of the temple of Solomon and with the Templars in the crusades, who had allegedly survived the destruction of the Order by Philippe le Bel in the fourteenth century. The Order of the Temple was perhaps particularly attractive to Russians: not only did it adopt splendid robes and dramatic cloaks, but its members were known as knights, using the Latin *eques*. Since Russia had no medieval history of chivalry and knighthood (orders of knighthood were only introduced by Peter the Great, using the imported French word *Kaval'er*) the Templars appealed particularly to the aristocracy and the nobles.[17] The contacts between Russian and Swedish masonry were inaugurated in 1776 by Prince A.B. Kurakin, a friend of the Grand Duke Paul, nephew and ward of Nikita Panin, and already a mason. He was asked by the Yelagin/Reichel lodge to seek out the higher degrees in use in Sweden and bring them back. Swedish masonry was openly recognized in Russia with the visit of the King, Gustavus III, in 1777 when a brilliant gathering of masons was held in his honour in the lodge Apollo.[18]

The first Swedish lodge, the Phoenix, was set up in St Petersburg in 1778. But Yelagin and other prominent public servants like Nikita Panin saw the political disadvantages in joining a system directly under the control of a member of the Swedish royal family and viewed askance by the Empress. For Catherine had suffered a serious diplomatic setback when Gustavus III, with French support, restored a modified form of absolutism in Sweden in a *coup d'état* in 1772. Most of the lodges under Yelagin's direction refused to join

14. Vernadsky, *op. cit.*, p. 33.
15. Cross, *op. cit.*, p. 53.
16. Vernadsky, *op. cit.*, p. 37.
17. Pierre Chevallier, *Histoire de la franc-maçonnerie française, 1725–1799*, Paris, 1974, p. 87.
18. A.N. Pypin, *Russkoye masonstvo XVIII i pervaya chetvert' XIX v.*, Petrograd, 1916, p. 154.

the Swedish Grand National Lodge, which was finally established under the direction of Prince G.P. Gagarin, who received his patent from the Duke of Sudermania in May 1780.[19] The Swedish system was strictly hierarchical and above the generally known degrees there was a secret and 'invisible chapter' or directorium on which an official appointed by the Swedish Grand Master sat; among the officials there was also a 'prelate', which explains to some extent the suspicion which many contemporaries and later historians felt that the system was modelled on, and influenced by, the Jesuits. At its height in the early 1780s the Swedish system in Russia controlled 14 lodges in St Petersburg and Moscow and a few in the provinces. But the Swedish Grand National Lodge in St Petersburg was dissolved when she moved Gagarin to an official post in Moscow, where he started up a new Swedish provincial lodge.

By the early 1780s, therefore, there were two systems rivalling for control of Russian masonry: the Reichel/Yelagin and the Swedish systems.[20] Yet there were always genuine adepts of masonic lore who felt that there was still some secret key to knowledge which they had not attained or who were dissatisfied with the rituals of the lodges they belonged to, or with their trifling social activities. One such was the publisher Nikolai Novikov, who moved to Moscow in 1779 to take over the University Press and who, together with Prince N. Trubetskoi and others, founded their own 'scientific' lodge, Harmonia, in Moscow in 1781. This was going to lead to a further great split in the Russian masonic movement. One of the recruits to the new lodge was I.G. Schwartz, a German from Transylvania who had found employment in Russia first as a teacher, then as a professor of philosophy at Moscow University. Schwartz, on behalf of the lodge Harmonia, attended the Masonic Convention of Wilhelmsbad of 1782, which had been summoned to bring some order into the chaos of the various masonic systems. It elected Duke Ferdinand of Brunswick Grand Master; it discarded the theory that freemasonry was descended from the medieval Order of the Temple, and re-named its members *chevaliers de la bienfaisance*; and it set up an VIIIth province, namely Russia. Prince N. Trubetskoi was appointed acting head of the Russian province, but the top post was left vacant in the hope that the Grand Duke Paul, who had set out on a long tour of Europe in 1781–82, would occupy it. Sweden refused to acknowledge the rejection of the connection with the Order of the Temple, and withdrew from the central control of Duke Ferdinand.

There were now three systems operating in Russia: the Yelagin/Reichel system; the Swedish system; and the VIIIth province of strict observance masonry under Prince N.P. Trubetskoi, dependent on Duke Ferdinand of

19. *Ibid.*, p. 431.
20. There was in addition a masonic system, affiliated to that of Yelagin, run by General P.I. Melissino, the founder of the lodge Mars in Jassy in 1774, who later set up his own lodge in St Petersburg, with his own system of seven degrees. In the seventh degree 'il s'agit de faire de l'or' wrote the Chevalier de Corberon, who hoped to be received into it. See *Un diplomate français à la cour de Catherine II, 1775–1780, Journal Intime du Chevalier de Corberon*, ed. L.-H. Labande, Paris, 1901, II, p. 3.

Brunswick. But a struggle developed when the officials of the VIIIth province established in Moscow attempted to extend their control or 'prefecture' over the Yelagin/Reichel system in St Petersburg.[21] It is not known, however, how many of the Petersburg lodges defected to the VIIIth province.

Yet within the new strict observance VIIIth province set up by I.G. Schwartz there was also a secret esoteric group of masons who pursued a different system, the Rosicrucians. Novikov and Schwartz were already aware of the existence of a secret Rosicrucian 'theoretical degree' before the Wilhelmsbad Convention, and Schwartz made contact in Berlin in 1782 with two of its Prussian leaders, Johann Christoph von Wöllner and Johann Christian Theden, and brought back their charters and degrees to Moscow. In fact the connection between the Russian VIIIth province and Duke Ferdinand of Brunswick was almost non-existent, and the masons of the VIIIth province, all unbeknown to them, thanks to Schwartz's skilful secret organization, were entirely under the direction of the Prussian leaders. After Schwartz died in 1784, a new representative was sent from Prussia, Baron G.A. von Schröder.[22]

Some Russian masons also joined lodges or systems which had been founded abroad. V.N. Zinov'yev in 1784 became a close friend of the French mason, J.B. Willermoz, in Lyon. He also met Louis Claude de Saint Martin and accompanied him on a trip to Paris. Subsequently, Saint Martin went to London to meet Zinov'yev and the Russian ambassador to England, long a mason, Simon Vorontsov. Admiral S.I. Pleshcheyev, an aide de camp of the Grand Duke Paul, made an extensive tour of Europe in 1788. He met Willermoz in Lyons, Saint Martin in Strasbourg, and joined the sect of New Israel in Avignon, to which Prince N.V. Repnin also belonged.[23]

Students of Russian freemasonry have drawn up extensive lists of known Russian masons, but there were evidently many more masons whose names were never recorded. One of the major experts in the field, G. Vernadsky, has worked out that among approximately 2,500 known masons in the 1770s and 1780s, there were, in 1777, four out of the eleven-member Council of State; eleven out of 31 gentlemen of the bedchamber; two out of five senators in the first department of the Senate; and one in each of the remaining departments. Two out of the five members of the board of the College of Foreign Affairs were masons in 1777; there were none in the College of War; in the Admiralty College, the vice-president, I.G. Chernyshev, was a mason.[24] In the Legislative Commission of 1767 a large number of the noble deputies were masons. Undoubtedly the best known masons belonged to the highest aristocracy:

21. Yeshevsky, *op. cit.*, p. 249.
22. A useful summary of these events can be found in In-Ho L. Ryu, 'Moscow Freemasons and the Rosicrucian Order', in *The Eighteenth Century in Russia*, ed. J.G. Garrard, Oxford, 1973, pp. 198–232.
23. Corberon eventually joined this sect and lived in Avignon at the end of his life. He was a fervent mason, and it is certain that his very successful social life in St Peterburg was forwarded by his masonic contacts. See his *Journal Intime, passim.*
24. Vernadsky, *op. cit.*, pp. 86ff.; see also T. Bakounine, *Répertoire biographique des francmaçons russes*, Paris, 1967.

families of ancient pedigree like the Repnins or the Trubetskoys, or of great wealth like the Stroganovs, or high position like the Vorontsovs and the Panins, and there were many of them. Many army officers were masons, as for instance in the appropriately named lodge Mars, founded in Jassy in 1774, or in the lodge Bellona in St Petersburg. The navy had a long masonic tradition and the lodge Neptune, founded in 1781 in Kronstadt by Admiral Greig, brought together many naval officers, often British.[25] Among governors of provinces a large number of the most senior and distinguished, such as Prince N.V. Repnin, J.E. Sievers, A.P. Mel'gunov and R.L. Vorontsov, were masons, as well as a very large number of officials of various ranks. There was thus a network of masons, almost a *nomenklatura*, within the bureaucracy and the intelligentsia, able to act in a concealed manner to support and promote each other.[26]

Officers were all *ipso facto* nobles, but it is difficult to assess to what extent non-noble Russians were admitted to masonic lodges on an equal footing with nobles, and to what extent masonic egalitarianism was dropped at the threshold of the lodge. In the Russian Academy, of 60 members, thirteen were masons in 1787. In the University of Moscow very many Russian and foreign professors, and in the 1780s two out of three curators, were masons. In the Yelagin lodge of the Nine Muses set up before Yelagin's merger with Reichel's system, the membership reflects the fact that he was director of spectacles at court. At least five members were actors, three were court musicians, two were architects, one a composer and one a writer. Some of these were foreigners, but among the Russians one cannot tell, without examining their *curricula vitae*, what their official, and therefore social, rank was. It can fairly be said that in the second half of the eighteenth century almost all poets, playwrights, authors and intellectuals were masons, and there was not a periodical which did not contain poems, odes, or other pieces in which masonic symbolism was not reflected.[27]

There were also 'brother servants', who prepared and served meals at the frequent banquets, and cleaned, heated and cared for the premises in which the lodges met. These were sometimes serfs or freed serfs (there were two serfs in Urania in 1773, and five in Neptune in 1781).[28] In theory, in accordance with the original constitutions of English masonry, only free people could be brothers. Some masons acquired the reputation of being inclined to free their serfs, or of arranging for their education, like V.N. Zinov'yev, who

25. Cross, *op. cit.*, pp. 58, 66.
26. Vernadsky, *op. cit.*, pp. 198–9. Using T. Bakounine's figures (which are not complete), In-Ho L. Ryu has worked out that 80 per cent of the nobles in state service were masons, as were 33 merchants, 13 professors, 13 doctors, eight musicians, 30 or so writers, three priests and three actors. Unpublished dissertation, p. 121.
27. Cross, *op. cit.*, pp. 63–4; see also S. Baehr, 'The Masonic Component in Eighteenth-Century Russian Literature', in *Russian Literature in the Age of Catherine the Great*, ed. A.G. Cross and Willem A. Meeuws, Oxford, 1976, pp. 121–40. Radishchev was a mason, but not apparently Fonvizin.
28. Bakounine, *Repertoire*, p. XXI.

sent twelve of his child serfs to the Main High School in Novgorod in 1789.[29] On the other hand, some of the most ardent defenders of serfdom like Prince M.M. Shcherbatov or O.A. Pozdneev (a Rosicrucian) were masons. Pozdneev complained bitterly in 1818 that only the Pugachev revolt put a stop to Catherine's intention of emancipating the serfs.[30]

There was also the very occasional priest. One lodge, Urania, admitted two German Jews, possibly for a financial consideration, in 1788.[31] It is noteworthy that 'adoptive masonry', or the setting up of women's lodges, did not apparently exist in Russia. Indeed the Prussian Rosicrucian Wöllner warned Baron Schroeder, the Prussian representative to the Moscow Rosicrucians, against admitting women to masonry: 'Der Bau der Weiber ist nicht zu magischen Arbeiten, der Reinigkeit fällt weg', he exclaimed.[32] As far as is known only one woman was ever admitted to masonic ceremonies as an onlooker, namely A.F. Labzina, wife of the well-known mystic in the reign of Alexander, and herself an adept.[33]

There were also many lodges the members of which were mainly foreigners, and which conducted their business in French or German. Their members were socially officials (some of them noble), particularly in the universities, academies, the professional schools like the Cadet Corps, or the Mining Institute, the medical world, the liberal professions, and also merchants, jewellers, bankers and some whose occupation is not known, as well as a sprinkling of German or other foreign officers. In the lodges set up specifically for the English the majority was non-noble, but a number of Russian nobles and non-nobles sometimes joined.[34]

Why did people become masons? Because there are so few personal memoirs written by masons it is obviously risky to generalize on their motives. They changed over time and place and in accordance with Russian social conditions. Certainly some who joined at the beginning when the lodges were largely run by great magnates in their own houses hoped to rub shoulders with the great and good and attract the eye of a possible patron in their service.[35] But after the manifesto freeing the nobility from compulsory service was issued in 1762 Russian social life became more varied and leisured. The notion of the 'club' as a meeting place made headway, not least because of its early introduction by the English community, when the English merchant Francis Gardner founded the English club in St Petersburg. Musical clubs and dining clubs became very popular in the 1770s. Literary salons developed like the one

29. Ibid., p. 617.
30. Vernadsky, *op. cit.*, p. 224, n. 1.
31. Bakounine, *Repertoire*, p. XXXV; Vernadsky, *op. cit.*, p. 13.
32. Ya. L. Barskov, *Perepiska Moskovskikh masonov XVIII veka, 1780–1792*, Petrograd, 1915, p. 215.
33. *Russkiy Biograficheskiy slovar'*, entry Labzina; see also Cross, *op. cit.*, pp. 57–8.
34. Cross also describes the one and only genuine operative craft lodge in Russia, the 'imperial Scottish Lodge of St Petersburg', set up by the Grand Lodge of Scotland in 1784 for some 60 Scottish craftsmen recruited to work for Catherine's architect, Charles Cameron, in Scotland. Ibid., pp. 61–2 and 71.
35. As for instance Yelagin, see his *Zapiski*, p. 593.

around the poet M.N. Kheraskov (a mason) in Moscow, or N.A. L'vov in St Petersburg. Russians and foreigners took part in private theatricals or in poetry readings.

There were also those who were attracted to freemasonry by a revulsion against the rationalism and the materialism of the culture of the Enlightenment. I.V. Lopukhin (the future Rosicrucian) describes the evolution of his feelings in his memoirs: 'I enjoyed reading Voltaire's digs at religion, Rousseau's refutation, and such works'. But a remarkable event changed his attitude:

> I read with admiration the *Code de la Nature* in which the author of the *Système de la Nature* [Holbach] summarized the whole book, and I translated it. I was pleased with my translation, but it could not be published. I prepared to distribute it in manuscript form, but I had only just made the first copy in my best handwriting when suddenly I felt an indescribable remorse – I could not sleep at night until I had burnt my beautiful notebook and the original. But I was still not at peace until I had written, as a kind of purification, a *Discourse on the misuse of reason by several present-day writers*, which I published if I remember in 1780.[36]

Without necessarily delving deep into occult science, many men sought for a moral or spiritual inspiration in their lives which the Russian Orthodox Church or the current vogue for Stoic morality was unable to provide. A streak of Voltairean anti-clericalism ran through Russian educated society, and though there were distinguished churchmen in the late eighteenth century, notably metropolitan Platon, there were very few priests who were, in the German usage, *salonfähig*. Priests, with their long beards and robes, did not mix in society in the way that French abbés or even English hunting parsons did. A cultured westernized noble, even if deeply devout, might find little common ground with a priest.

In the early days meetings of the lodges often took place in the house of the Grand Master, who was also usually a man of rank and substance. Belonging to a lodge was thus a means of entrance into society for outsiders or foreign visitors.[37] The main business was the admission of new members, or the promotion of members to higher degrees. Some descriptions of the rituals for admission of new members have been published. In Reichel's Apollo lodge a postulant was required to remove all metallic objects, to take off his coat, baring his left breast and right knee, wear a slipper on the left foot, and be blindfolded in a room like a vault, the walls hung in black, the table covered in a black cloth, with a skull holding a burning lamp. There was a Bible open at St John's gospel and an open grave with a skeleton.[38] The symbolism here

36. I.V. Lopukhin, *Zapiski*, Oriental Research Partners, 1976, p. 19, footnote; by a strange paradox, Holbach, at the end of his life, crippled by debt and domestic strife, became a Rosicrucian (Chevallier, *op. cit.*, p. 223).
37. In-Ho L. Ruy, Unpublished dissertation, p. 77.
38. A.M. Pekarsky, 'Dopolneniya k istorii masonstva v Rossii v XVIII stoletiya', *Sbornik statey chitannykh v otdelenii russkogo yazyka i slovesnosti imperatorskoy akademii nauk*, vol. vii, No. 4, St Petersburg, 1889, p. 64.

is clear: death precedes the re-birth of the man as a mason, with his feet on the path to virtue and knowledge, and spiritual redemption.

After the business came the rejoicings, with concerts, performances of specially written masonic oratorios, recitations of poetry, singing of masonic songs, banquets followed by a number of ritual toasts. As the lodges multiplied, special premises were hired, and masons were expected to contribute financially to the costs of meetings, banquets and wine. In the English lodge Parfaite Union there was a scale of fees for reception according to the degree. A special masonic feast for St John's day was organized in 1771 by the English lodge in 'the English playhouse' which was an old barn transformed into 'the likeness of a theatre' in which an English company had been performing plays in the course of that winter.[39]

Masonic contributions were also used for funeral expenses of the brothers, as for instance the magnificent funeral arranged for Admiral Greig by the lodge Neptune in 1788.[40] Masonic treasuries could be filled up from fines, entrance fees, payments for admission of guests etc., or from fees for playing billiards or cards. Collections were also made for alms giving, or for the maintenance of charitable institutions. (The Moscow Rosicrucians made substantial payments to their masters in Berlin, for charitable Rosicrucian activities in Prussia.[41]) One should not, however, exaggerate the extent of the philanthropic activity of the masons. Vernadsky rather sarcastically points out that the money collected for alms was much less than that collected for the banquets, and the well-known distribution of corn in 1787 by Novikov in the area of his estate, Avdot'ino Tikhvin, for which he borrowed 50,000 rubles from a fellow mason, was to be paid back by the recipients in cash or in labour services.[42]

The masonic movement also developed in the provinces, often because an individual government servant who was a mason was appointed to a prominent position. The governor of Yaroslavl' in 1777–88, A.P. Mel'gunov, was both a fervent mason and a broad-minded, humane and enlightened governor. He founded a lodge in Yaroslavl' which lasted as long as he lived, and he was responsible for the development of schools and other welfare institutions. He was also known for his fairness in judicial matters. Count Jacob Sievers, governor of Novgorod and Tver', was also a mason and in every way a high-minded and public-spirited man.[43] Another method by which the provinces were drawn in was by means of the periodicals published in St Petersburg

39. Cross, *op. cit.*, p. 53.

40. Cross, *op. cit.*, p. 51; the lodge Neptune practised the Swedish rite, but it joined Yelagin's system in 1786, well before the outbreak of war with Sweden in 1788. See also Pypin, *op. cit.*, p. 162.

41. In-Ho L. Ryu, Unpublished dissertation, pp. 224ff.

42. Vernadsky, *op. cit.*, pp. 200–1; M.T. Belyavsky, 'Novikovskoye Avdot'ino v 1792 g', *Problemy istorii obshchestvennogo dvizheniya i istoriografii. K 70-letiyu akademika M.V. Nechkinoy*, Moscow, 1971, pp. 49–61.

43. L. Trefoleyev, 'Aleksey Petrovich Mel'gunov, general gubernator Yekaterinskikh vremen', *Russkiy Arkhiv*, 1885, pp. 931–78; Robert E. Jones, *Provincial Development in Russia. Catherine II and Jakob Sievers*, Rutgers University Press, 1984. Mel'gunov and Sievers were friends.

and later in Moscow. Novikov's periodical *Morning Light*, which was strongly masonic in content, had subscribers in Archangel, Kazan', Vologda, Kolomna, Ryazan', Astrakhan and Poltava, who served as a nucleus around which sympathizers congregated, and from which masonic teachings and manuscripts emanated.[44]

As the search for mystical enlightenment played an increasing role, so some of the masons devoted themselves at meetings to the study of masonic texts, which entailed much translating and copying, since many circulated in manuscript only; and to the reading aloud of extracts, or the delivery of lectures on specific aspects of masonic or hermetic knowledge. This kind of activity was by no means universal, and it seems to have developed along two lines, one in St Petersburg, the other, and better known, in Moscow. Some attention must now be given to this.

When I.G. Schwartz returned from Germany in 1782 and introduced the Moscow masons to the secret or theoretical degree, leading up to the even more secret seven degrees of knights of the Rosy Cross, he launched them on a path of open educational activity and secret exploration of esoteric lore. The foundation by Novikov and his friends in 1779 of the Pedagogical Seminary in Moscow at which young people were to be trained as future teachers in the moral principles of higher degree masonry; of the Union of University Alumni which would care for the physical and moral welfare of students; of the Translators Seminar in 1782 to provide texts for the University Press; and finally of an officially constituted society, the Friendly Learned Society, opened with much pomp and with the apparent approval of the commander in chief in Moscow, General Z.G. Chernyshev (a mason), and archbishop Platon, were all steps in a well-thought-out and ambitious programme which was intended to take over the education of teachers, and through them of the educated class in general. The purpose of the Friendly Learned Society was explained as the bringing together of people of different ages, styles of life, profession, and fortune to use their leisure hours for profit, learning and private well-being. According to one source, Schwartz's ultimate object was the destruction of the Russian Orthodox religion.[45]

Nothing could better serve the aim of spreading masonic moral principles and hermetic science than the control of a printing press, indeed of several printing presses, after Catherine's decree of 1783 which allowed anyone to set up a press provided it was registered with the police. In order to provide the reading matter for the members of the Moscow lodges, both for the students at the lower level, and for the members of the secret theoretical degree at the higher level, the members of the translation seminary were kept busy translating works which were either published in Novikov's periodicals or circulated in manuscript, or printed on a secret press without the permission of the

44. Vernadsky, p. 85. There were lodges in Archangel, Vladimir, Vologda, Kazan', Kiev, Kremeuchyg, Kronshtadt, Mogilev, Nizhniy Novgorod, Orel, Penza, Perm, Ryazan, Simbirsk, Khar'kov, Yaroslavl'.

45. In-Ho L. Ryu, 'Moscow Freemasons and the Rosicrucian Order', pp. 222–3.

police, as required by law. It is impossible to give here a detailed outline of the enormous quantity of English, French and German mystic or masonic literature which passed through the hands of Novikov, and I.V. Lopukhin, who ran the secret press. Novikov's private library, confiscated in 1792, contained 3,500 books, within which there was a separate masonic library, comprising original printed or manuscript versions of the literature of the first Rosicrucian enlightenment of 1609–27, and of its revival in the backlash against eighteenth-century materialism. The works of J. Boehme, J. Arndt, Mme Guyon and Saint Martin figured largely. There were manuscripts of A.I. Kirchberger's *Annulus Platonis*, the *Chemische Hochzeit Christiani Rosenkreuz*, *L'Etoile flamboyante* of Baron Tschoudy, several works by Swedenborg, and of course works by or attributed to Paracelsus, Henricus Cornelius Agrippa, 'Hermes Trismegistus' and various works on Egyptian rites. There was also *The New Chyropaedia or The Travels of Cyrus* by A.F. Ramsay,[46] and the strange allegorical tale of the alchemical transmutation of matter, *Chrysomander*, published anonymously in German in 1773.[47]

There were seven Rosicrucian degrees: the lowest was the 'iunorat', the highest the magus, of whom there were apparently none in Russia. The reading matter expounded in the course of meetings of the lodges was carefully graded to the degree reached by the masons. Teaching in the lower degree concentrated on natural history, the action of the stars, on God and nature, coupled with extracts from Jacob Boehme; in the higher degrees, the Cabbala, magic, and alchemy were taught. A frequently used text was the *Paracelsi Handbibel*, a handbook of texts from the Bible drawn up by Johann Thölde, which was published in a Russian translation by Novikov, while another much-used text was the 'Pastorskoye Poslaniye' or *Hirtenbrief* by the German mason, Count Christian von Haugwitz, later a minister of Frederick William II.[48]

Schwartz seems to have been a charismatic figure who left a deep impression on students who attended his course of sixteen public lectures on 'the three different kinds of knowledge', namely rational, of the heart, and by revelation, during 1782, and his attacks on materialism obviously met with a very great response. According to A.F. Labzin, who attended the lectures, he refuted Helvetius, La Mettrie, Rousseau, Spinoza. Though the lectures have

46. See Kenneth Craven, 'The First Chamber of Novikov's Masonic Library', in *Russia and the World of the Eighteenth Century*, pp. 401–10; and cf. my 'Alcune nuove publicazioni su Nikolaj Ivanovic Novikov' in *Rivista Storica Italiana*, Anno XCVII, Fascicolo III, 1985, pp. 872–83 for the list of 716 manuscripts and printed works in *Chteniya v imperatorskom obshchestve istorii i drevnostey rossiskikh*, 1871, part 3, sect. 5, pp. 17–46, with the sometimes very funny comments by the censors.

47. One may speculate whether this work, published in Quedlinburg in 1774, was not in fact written by the prolific author of Hermetic works, H. Fictuld (pseudonym of I.G. Schmidt), in view of its final paragraph: 'Grüsse mir aber den allen Natur Priester Herrmann Fictuld . . . und sage er soll mich besuchen. Es wird ihm aber schwer werden mich zu finden: denn ich bin der Mann der keinen Namen und beständige Hütte hat.' *Chrysomander* was translated into Russian in 1785 by A.A. Petrov, a Rosicrucian.

48. See Vernadsky, *op. cit.*, p. 128. Christian Graf von Haugwitz was a disciple of Lavater, Mesmer, St Germain and Cagliostro, and very close to Frederick William II. He published the *Hirtenbrief an die wahren und ächten Freymäurer alten Systems* in 1785.

not been published, they were taken down by one of his students and exist in manuscript. Man has a dual nature, spirit and matter, argued Schwartz. Below him are animals and minerals, and chaos; above him are the archangels and the cherubim and the supreme force, God. Man is where spirit and matter meet. Man carries within him the secret of creation, but how will he discover it? Reason is not enough. Schwartz went on to propound his solution based on the teaching of Jacob Boehme to which he added Paracelsian alchemy.[49]

Meetings of the higher degrees of the Rosicrucians were austere and took place in rooms hung with black cloth. Members took a simple oath to worship the eternal all powerful Jehovah, to reject the vanities of the world, to love their brothers and to keep silent on the affairs of the order. There were no banquets, only simple ceremonial meals at which bread and wine were served, and after the reception of a new brother, the leader distributed bread and wine in a form of communion service. However, a lighthearted note could occasionally be introduced. Midsummer's day, the principal masonic feast, was celebrated at Novikov's modest estate in 1788 with specially written verses, flower-decked bowers, wreaths, fireworks, hymns, including 'Kol slaven' written by the masonic poet Kheraskov to music by the Ukrainian composer Bortnyansky specially for masonic festivals, a church festival dinner and the distribution of 10 kopeks to each of the poor.[50]

The Rosicrucians were organized in a strictly hierarchical order; only a small number belonged to the highest degree, and only they knew all the members. Only they too knew the sources from which extracts of hermetic wisdom were used in their teaching. It seems to have been this authoritarianism, rather than the hermetic content of the masonic teachings, which alienated Prince Gagarin, the head of the Swedish masons in Moscow, and Yelagin in St Petersburg from the Moscow Rosicrucians. 'Is not this the teaching of the destroyed Jesuit order?', exclaimed Yelagin, comparing the leadership of the Rosicrucian masons with that of the General of the Jesuits in Rome.[51] The exclusiveness of the Rosicrucians only increased when a *silanum* or suspension of activities was proclaimed by their Prussian masters in 1787, probably as a result of the accession of Frederick William II to the throne of Prussia on the death of Frederick II in 1786. Rosicrucian activity certainly continued, but in a more private form.

Yelagin, and other masons in the capital, had also evolved away from the simple club-like activities of the early St Petersburg lodges. Largely under the guidance of Reichel, Yelagin, who does not appear to have had the temperament

49. R. Labry, 'L'enseignement de I.G. Schwartz, Rose-Croix, professeur à l'université de Moscou et son influence', *Mélanges en l'Honneur de Jules Legras*, Travaux de l'Institut D'Etudes Slaves, vol. XIX, Paris, 1939, pp. 189–200.

50. W. Gareth Jones, *Nikolay Novikov, Enlightener of Russia*, Cambridge University Press, 1984, pp. 200–3.

51. Yelagin's *Zapiski*, quoted in Pekarsky, pp. 99–103; see *ibid.*, pp. 126ff. for Prince Gagarin's extremely hostile account of the Rosicrucians in 1785 to Prince A.A. Prozorovsky, the future commander-in-chief in Moscow. Gagarin was the source of the rumours that Novikov had set up schools and a hospital in Moscow, which was not the case.

of a mystic but to have felt the need of something more than he was deriving from existing freemasonry, began to read. The work which above all affected him was Louis-Claude de Saint Martin's *Des erreurs et de la vérité*.[52] This work, he explains, had been mocked by some as crackbrained; others thought it was not a real masonic work, but a concealed Jesuit system; some thought it emanated from the Illuminati, and deserved to be destroyed. As Yelagin further explains in his memoirs, his masonic teacher had told him that true wisdom 'had remained concealed in the temples of the Chaldeans, the Egyptians, the Persians, the Phoenicians, the Jews, the Greeks and the Romans and in the Hellenistic mysteries; and in the schools of Solomon . . . Sinai, John, and in the Desert, and in Jerusalem . . . ; and wisdom was also to be found in the lodges or schools of . . . Pythagoras, Plato, and among Indian, Chinese, Arab, Druid, and other peoples famous for knowledge'. Yelagin therefore concentrated on reading the Old and New Testaments, the church fathers, such as Origen, Eusebius, Justin, Cyril of Alexandria, Gregory Nazanianzen, Basil the Great, John Chrysostom, John Damascene etc., as well as Pythagoras, Anaxagoras, Socrates, Epictetus, Plato, 'Hermes Trismegistus', Orpheus and Homer, Zoroaster and many more. With Dr Ely, a converted Jew and a mason, Yelagin studied Hebrew and Cabbala, theosophy, physics and chemistry, Egyptian traditions, and thanks to Ely he was able to understand Saint Martin's *Des erreurs et de la vérité* (which is indeed a very obscure work) and the writings of Robert Fludd. One of Yelagin's closest friends, 'whose soul doubtless now inhabits the dwellings of eternal bliss', asked for his help in understanding Saint Martin. Whereupon Yelagin began to prepare written explanations of the most difficult passages of a work which 'opened up real knowledge, following the style of the wise men of old, particularly Pythagoras'. The man to whom Yelagin acted as tutor in the mysteries of Saint Martin was none other than the foreign minister of Russia, Count Nikita Panin.[53]

Evidently foundering in this sea of learning, Yelagin attempted to draw up a compendium of masonic teaching, which he did not finish. The first part was to deal with masonry from Adam to the establishment of the Order of the Temple; the second would examine the Talmud, the Cabbala, the teaching of the Sephiroth and the names of God, and then move on to more specifically masonic studies. Judging by his reading, Yelagin seems to have been far more attracted to gnosticism than to the alchemy which fascinated the Moscow Rosicrucians.[54]

Catherine had tolerated the masonic movement, but she had two reasons for disliking it. The first was that it represented an essentially masculine movement, which excluded her and other women, and though she was no

52. Published anonymously in 1775 by 'le philosophe inconnu' in Salomopolis. Translated into Russian in 1785, it had a profound influence, though Saint Martin himself moved away from the external rites of masonry. Masons were generally, if erroneously, known as 'martinists' after him.
53. Yelagin, *Zapiski*, pp. 586ff.
54. Pekarsky, *op. cit.*, pp. 96ff. For his information on the Christian fathers, Yelagin turned to a French source, C. Fleury, *Histoire ecclésiastique*, 36 vols, Paris, 1691–1737.

feminist, it was only too easy to believe that the lodges could provide the pretext and the venue for conspiracies against her. Secondly she remained to her death wedded to the commonsensical rationalism and to the intellectual approach of the Enlightenment as expressed in Diderot (who was not a mason),[55] the Encyclopaedists, and Voltaire, who became a mason only in the last year of his life in rather special circumstances. Catherine had also little sympathy for the sentimentalism of Rousseau, whose political and educational ideas she distrusted, a sentimentalism which was very influential as one of the sources of the cult of sensibility among many masons, for instance I.V. Lopukhin.

The visit to Russia in 1779–80 of Count Cagliostro, who founded lodges in Mittau and Riga, and was expelled in 1780, convinced Catherine of the charlatanry inherent in freemasonry.[56] The Empress did not really distinguish between alchemy, freemasonry, mesmerism, mysticism and theosophy. She started her anti-masonic campaign with the publication of a pamphlet she wrote anonymously in 1780, *Le secret de la société anti-absurde devoilé par quelqu'un qui n'en est pas'*,[57] in which the ritual of reception of new members was faithfully described (Catherine's many masonic friends could doubtless keep her informed) and the masonic cathechism and corresponding emblems were caricatured. She carried on her campaign to put an end to the 'engouement avec les sciences occultes' which was beginning to affect Russia[58] in three plays, which to her great satisfaction were successfully staged not only in Russia but in Germany. In 1785 she launched her attack on the publication of books full of what she called 'nonsensical lucubrations' (*kolobrodstvo*). Novikov was the main sufferer, because he was the main producer of such books, and in 1786, 461 of his titles were impounded; of these 22 were condemned by the Church as likely to induce error. Catherine eventually only banned six, including Saint Martin's *Des Erreurs et de la vérité*, Ramsay's *The New Chiropaedia* (she had not read it)[59] and *Chrysomander.* In 1789 Catherine did not renew Novikov's lease of Moscow University Press, but not until 1792, against the background of the French Revolution, did she proceed against the Moscow masons, and then because of the discovery in Novikov's house of stocks of the books banned in 1786 and of the evidence that the Moscow masons had been trying to win over the Grand Duke Paul to join them, and had maintained secret, direct relations with Wöllner, who was now one of the ministers of the King, Frederick William II of Prussia.

55. Chevallier, *op. cit.*, p. 270.
56. Cagliostro took refuge from his creditors in Yelagin's cellar where, according to Catherine, he got drunk, and was finally persuaded by Yelagin to leave in a kibitka, not by flying through the air. Catherine to Melchior von Grimm, 9 July 1781, in *Sbornik Imperatorskogo russkogo istoricheskago obshchestva* (*SIRIO*), 23, pp. 212ff.
57. Ostensibly published in 1759, in fact in 1780; translated from the French into Russian by A.V. Khrapovitsky, the Empress's secretary, also a mason, translator also of Ramsay's *New Chiropaedia* from the English into Russian.
58. Catherine to Grimm, 11 March 1785, *SIRIO*, 23, p. 375. For her plays, Catherine drew on the article 'théosophe' of the *Encyclopédie*, *ibid.*, 17 February 1786, p. 374.
59. Catherine asked her secretary why *The New Chiropaedia* had been banned; see *Dnevnik Khrapovitskogo*, 7 August 1793, pp. 437–8.

There is no doubt that Catherine was suspicious of the educational work carried out by the Moscow masons, which did not fit in with the secular programme laid down for her schools in the Statute of Education of 1786, and which was intended to create a nucleus of younger adepts of the occult and hermetic sciences, 'sciences' which she regarded with the same distaste as nineteenth-century Russian historians of the Moscow masons, such as A.F. Pypin. She certainly asked the governor of Moscow to investigate the whereabouts of the young seminarists who had been educated in Novikov's pedagogical seminary, and subsequently planted in parish churches in the provinces. Two years later, in 1794, Catherine ordered the closure of all the lodges.

This takes me to some final remarks on the political aspects of freemasonry. The system preached by Reichel had always warned adepts against any masonry which had political aims, which he regarded as false. This attitude may explain the reluctance of the St Petersburg masons, who were close to the court and the government, to join the Swedish lodges, so closely under the control of a member of the Swedish royal family. It does not seem that the St Petersburg lodges were distinguished by any kind of political orientation. Yet there were many individual masons in the capital, and even more in Moscow, who constituted a latent opposition to Catherine as a person and to her policies. In the first place the immorality of the Empress's private life scandalized the more straitlaced and puritanical of the masons, like Prince M.M. Shcherbatov in St Petersburg[60] and the Rosicrucians in Moscow. Secondly some of Catherine's policies, notably the annexation of the Crimea and the second Turkish war, were frowned upon by many, including the Grand Duke Paul, who thought Russia was large enough.[61] In a society in which there was no legitimate outlet for political dissent, criticism of the government or its policies could only be manifested in small groups, such as the lodges, and by means of attachment to a rival centre for power, namely the heir to the throne.

From Catherine's earliest years, the Panin brothers had constituted a nucleus around the Grand Duke in opposition to her, and many courtiers oriented themselves towards the masons, though the evidence that Paul actually joined a lodge is not conclusive. But he entertained almost treasonable relations with the Prussian envoys in Russia and with the Prussian government through the Russian envoy in Berlin, M. Alopeus, a mason, at the time of the Ochakov crisis in 1791, when Prussia was attempting to force Russia by threats of war to give up her conquests at the expense of the Porte. Catherine read the intercepts of dispatches, and it is likely that she was well aware of the atmosphere of intense disapproval emanating from Paul's friends. The Rosicrucian lodges in Moscow certainly sang hymns in praise of the Grand Duke, welcoming his eventual accession. That it was the attempt to recruit the Grand

60. See Prince M.M. Shcherbatov, *On the Corruption of Morals in Russia*, ed. and tr. by A. Lentin, Cambridge University Press, 1969, *passim*. Shcherbatov's idea of the ideal masonic state is expounded in his 'Utopia', the *Journey to the Land of Ophir* a blueprint for a totalitarian state.
61. See R.E. Jones, 'Opposition to War and Expansion in Late Eighteenth Century Russia', *Jahrbücher für Osteuropäische Geschichte*, 32, 1984, pp. 34–51.

Duke into an association conducting clandestine contacts with Prussian ministers which destroyed the Moscow masons, rather than the specifically occult content of their teaching, is to a great extent proved by the contrasting treatment meted out to the St Petersburg lodges. There is not much difference between the freemasonry practised in the St Petersburg lodges (those of the Yelagin/Reichel system and the Melissino lodge) and that of the Moscow lodges. But the St Petersburg masons did steer clear of politics.

The hostility of the Moscow masons was also concentrated against one person, namely Prince G.A. Potemkin, who was not a mason.[62] It will have been observed that there were no masons in the College of War of which he was vice-president and later president, though of course many senior and junior officers were masons. But joining a lodge was not a means of winning the good opinion of the most important of Catherine's ministers. Moreover Potemkin had opposed the pro-Prussian policy of Nikita Panin, and of the Grand Duke Paul, whom he took no pains to conciliate. It is worth speculating why Potemkin was not a mason. He was a deeply religious and very devout son of the Russian Orthodox Church, and it is possible that precisely because he was more in tune with traditional Russian religious feeling, he did not need to seek for a refuge against materialism in occultism or hermetic sciences. He is known to have written a deeply felt Kanon shortly before his death, and his portable press, which he had with him in Moldavia during the second Turkish war, printed translations of Pope's *Essay on Man* and of J. Arndt's *On True Christianity*, both dedicated to him.[63] But Potemkin was tolerant, and it is possible that if he had still been alive in April 1792, Catherine would not have been so heavy-handed in her treatment of the Moscow masons and Novikov in particular.[64] At any rate the combination of the publication of literature frowned on by the Church, seemingly seditious contacts with persons in high places in a country with which Russian relations were extremely tense, attempts to lure the Grand Duke into these seditious contacts, Catherine's increasing fear of the rising tide of revolution in France and Poland, and the loss, by death, in 1791–92 of the support and advice of the two men who had served her in the army and in domestic affairs for years, Potemkin and Prince A.A. Vyazemsky, the Procurator General, who was also not a mason, may have contributed to the darkening of the horizons in Russia in the last years of her reign.

62. The author of the extremely hostile account of Potemkin's career, published under the title *Pansalvin Fürst der Finsternis* in 1794, J.F.E. Albrecht, was a mason, and probably a Rosicrucian (Vernadsky, *op. cit.*, p. 236).

63. *Svodniy Katalog Russkoy pechati XVIII veka, 1725–1800*, vol. V, entry under Potemkin' portable press in Yassy. Because he was devout, some masons feared him as a wolf in sheep's clothing.

64. Catherine's attitude to religious dissent is reflected in a note she wrote, probably to Platon Zubov, on 17 September 1792; she stressed that it was important that there should be no harassment of Old Believers or Old Ritualists as a result of the banning of masonic lodges 'and similar secret and absurd assemblies'. It was important not to place any obstacle in the way of the meetings of the Old Believers, who in any case did not admit people who did not share their views. *Russkiy arkhiv*, 1864, col. 116.

CHAPTER EIGHT

Catherine II and the foundation of the Russian educational system

Throughout her reign, Catherine was passionately interested in education, which she firmly believed could remodel and improve human nature and, with the passage of time she came to regard herself as a great expert in the field. On her accession, she found Russian education in total disarray. As so much in the country, it had been transformed by Peter I, but it had subsequently diverged from the paths he had laid out. Primary schools in the countryside were few and far between. Where they existed they were mainly private schools run by the local priests, and they existed more often in the Ukraine. On court estates there were some primary schools for the training of peasants in literacy and in the skills necessary for the exploitation and administration of the estates. Landowners, like Peter Orlov of Klin, occasionally set up schools on their estates – though in the mid-eighteenth century this was very rare. The priest in the village and minor clerics in the towns took private pupils or ran schools, day or boarding, on a very *ad hoc* basis. So occasionally did the wives of *kuptsy* or of non-commissioned officers.

Secondary education was just as patchy. The groundwork had again been laid by Peter with the modernization of the Moscow Academy, which became a classical gymnasium modelled on the Kiev Academy; in turn the Kiev Academy had been modelled on the classical Jesuit grammar schools common all over Europe.[1] By 1764, there were 26 diocesan grammar schools, academies or seminaries of this kind with some 6,000 students all told. The majority of the pupils were drawn from the clerical estate (though they were not necessarily destined for the church and its dependencies) but a few children from other walks of life received a classical education in these seminaries and went on to careers in the armed forces, or to form the nucleus of the 'professional classes' in the third estate.[2]

1. See M. Okenfuss, 'The Jesuit Origin of Petrine Education', in J.G. Garrard, ed., *The Eighteenth Century in Russia*, Oxford, 1973, pp. 106–30.
2. These schools, because they were church foundations, are frequently called seminaries in Russian and English works on education. This gives the impression that they all trained exclusively for the priesthood, which was not the case.

The so-called 'cypher schools' which Peter I had ordered monasteries and dioceses to set up in 1716 for boys from the age of ten to fourteen, under the direction of the Admiralty College, had never been popular with teachers[3] or pupils,[4] and by 1744 there were only eight left. They were designed to train youngsters in disciplines necessary for naval service, their teachers were drawn from the Naval Academy, they were under the direction of the Admiralty College on the one hand, yet attached to a diocese on the other. Since the dioceses already ran diocesan classical grammar schools, they had no interest in promoting the rival cypher schools which died a natural death.

Parallel to the cypher schools, but longer lasting and more effective, were the army garrison schools (which eventually absorbed the remains of the cypher schools). Their existence was formalized in the 1730s, and they provided an elementary education for the children of poor nobles and officers, of church nobles, private soldiers and non-commissioned officers, and for vagrant and orphaned children.[5] The teachers were drawn from the officers, and were paid out of regimental funds. These schools did in fact serve a useful purpose and the literate ex-soldier became a not uncommon feature of Russian urban and village life.

There were in addition in Russia at mid-century a number of vocational training schools, mainly concerned with the Armed Forces, such as the Naval Cadet Corps, the Army Cadet Corps, and the Engineer and Artillery School. These professional schools had moved away from the narrowly utilitarian curriculum originally devised for them. The Noble Army Cadet Corps, in particular, founded in 1731 for 200 pupils, acted as a forcing house for the first generation of Russian intellectuals[6] and by 1762 it had 600 pupils. Nevertheless, though these armed forces training schools now provided an education in the more polite arts of society, they were still designed to turn out professional officers.

The Academy of Science gymnasium in St Petersburg and the gymnasia attached to Moscow University were civilian in character. From the first, Peter I had intended that the Academy of Sciences should carry out educational

3. The salary of a teacher was 36 roubles p.a., but only too often it was unpaid for several years. See M. Vladimirsky-Budanov, *Gosudarstvo i narodnoye obrazovaniye v Rossii XVIII veka*, Yaroslavl', 1874, p. 39.

4. Children had frequently to be sent from a long distance to attend these schools, and in order to prevent them from running away they were lodged in prisons or kept under guard. See in general the survey by D.A. Tolstoy (the Minister of Education under Alexander II), *Vzglyad na uchebnuyu chast' v Rossii v XVIII stoletii do 1872* in *Sbornik Otdeleniya russkogo yazyka i slovesnosti Imperatorskoy Akademii nauk*, vol. 38, No. 4, St Petersburg, 1886, pp. 1–100, at p. 3.

5. The rector of the higher and secondary educational establishments of the Academy of Sciences in 1750 was S.P. Krasheninnikov, who was a 'soldier's son'. In May 1763, there were 8,775 soldiers' children in garrison schools and 752 waiting to enter, according to an *ukaz* of 14 May 1763: *Polnoye sobraniye zakonov Rossiyskoy Imperii* (hereafter *PSZ*), xv, No. 11816. In 1765, of six students taken as copyists into the Senate from the Academy of Sciences gymnasium, five were soldiers' sons, one was the son of a state peasant: M. Shtrange, *Demokraticheskaya intelligentsiya Rossii v XVIII veke*, Moscow, 1965, p. 120.

6. Among its graduates in the mid-eighteenth century were the poets Sumarokov and Kheraskov, I.P. Yelagin and A. Olsuf'yev (both to become secretaries of Catherine II). The Naval Cadet Corps was established in 1752, for 360 cadets; it brought together the Petrine Naval Academy and Navigation School.

as well as scholarly tasks (the draft of its statutes dates from 1724). But as was common at that time, it proved very difficult to recruit pupils, particularly after the court moved to Moscow in the reign of Peter II. The Academy gymnasium was thus filled with 'the children of the sort of parents who did not at all require this type of education for them . . . soldiers, carpenters, joiners, blacksmiths, peasants of Prince Menshikov'.[7] Moreover it never recovered from the foundation of the Noble Army Cadet Corps which made it less attractive than ever for noble children, since graduation from the Cadet Corps granted them officer's rank. In 1747, new statutes laid down that the Academy should provide 20 scholarships for the gymnasium, open to all classes of society except those who paid the poll tax (i.e. excluding almost everyone except nobles, *raznochintsy* such as soldiers' children, and children of non-commissioned officers, priests and some church servants). Nobles and *raznochintsy* could also attend on a fee-paying basis. The gymnasium continued to be filled mainly by people of humble extraction including the children of the household serfs of the President of the Academy, Kirill Razumovsky.[8]

The gymnasium was supposed to prepare children for the 'university' attached to the Academy. It failed dismally in this task; though here too the Academy provided scholarships, which by 1760 were worth 100 roubles per annum, there were practically no students.[9] The same need to set up secondary and university teaching simultaneously was felt when Moscow University was founded in 1755. Two gymnasia were established at the same time, one for nobles, one for non-nobles, but graduates from both these establishments were taught together in the university. The conditions of entry to the non-noble gymnasium were much more flexible than in St Petersburg, reflecting no doubt the views of the prime mover in the whole scheme, the polymath Lomonosov. The non-noble gymnasium was open to pupils of all classes including children of serfs freed by their owners in order to enable them to be educated. These children were to bring their letters of emancipation with them, which would be returned to them on completion of their studies, 'so that no one could reduce them to bondage again'.[10] At first the gymnasia were supposed to provide 50 studentships each for nobles and non-nobles and a different education. By the early 1760s the numbers were raised to 120 for nobles and 60 for non-nobles, and the difference in teaching programme gradually vanished, particularly as most of the nobles with studentships were poor or landless. There were of course also fee-paying noble students.

7. D.A. Tolstoy, *Akademicheskaya gimnaziya v XVIII stoletii*, in *Sbornik Otdeleniya russkogo yazyka i slovesnosti Imperatorskoy Akademii nauk*, vol. 38, No. 1, St Petersburg, 1886, pp. 1–114.

8. In the fifteen years 1751–65, of 590 pupils who passed through the gymnasium, 80 were poor, mainly landless nobles; 22 were *kuptsy*; 13 came from the clerical estate; 80 were children of clerks. The largest group, 132, was composed of soldiers' sons; 50 were sons of craftsmen in the Academy or the Admiralty; 16 were children of household serfs; 2 were children of peasants; 93 were foreigners; and 23 miscellaneous: Shtrange, *op. cit.*, p. 33.

9. D.A. Tolstoy, *Akademicheskiy universitet v XVIII stoletii*, in *Sbornik Otdeleniya russkogo yazyka i slovesnosti Imperatorskoy Akademii nauk*, vol. 38, No. 6, St Petersburg, 1886, pp. 1–67.

10. M.T. Belyavsky, *M. V. Lomonosov i osnovaniye Moskovskogo universiteta*, Moscow, 1955, p. 293.

As in St Petersburg, the first year's intake of students into Moscow University itself had to be drawn from the classical grammar schools but subsequently the gymnasia provided recruits for the university, though the numbers continued small.[11] Most of the students came from poor families. The teaching until 1767 was mainly in French or Latin. The dramatist D.I. Fonvizin has left a brief and very unflattering picture of the way his teacher helped the students to cheat their way through examinations; but he remembered with gratitude the fact that he had at least learned Latin in the gymnasium and thus laid the foundations for his own future self-education.[12]

In 1758, the Academy of Arts was founded in St Petersburg, and provided one further avenue for advancement to the non-nobles, the *raznochintsy* and even serfs given their letters of emancipation as in the case of Moscow University. The first intake of students was drawn from the same varied background as in the St Petersburg Academy of Sciences and the students were taught painting, architecture, sculpture, engineering, music etc.

State schools and private establishments were not the only means by which the benefits of education were disseminated in Russian society. The practice of engaging foreign tutors was widespread among the nobility, though unfortunately they more often than not proved both morally unsuitable and intellectually unqualified. A brief glance at the memoir literature of the time suggests that as between a school and a private tutor there was little to choose in terms of brutality to children, and not much in terms of pedagogical skills. Alarmed by the influx of French adventurers, the government issued a decree in 1758 insisting that potential tutors should first be examined by the Academy of Sciences in St Petersburg and the University of Moscow to pronounce on their fitness to teach.[13]

In general, from the eighteenth century onwards education was one of the avenues of promotion into the hereditary nobility. Graduates from Moscow University were awarded ranks twelve to fourteen in the Table of Ranks; those who achieved distinction were granted the tenth rank. Non-noble graduates who volunteered for the armed forces were given the fourteenth rank (equivalent to commissioned officer) after six months, and thus became hereditary nobles. Professors were awarded the ninth rank (non-hereditary nobility for those in civil employment). Graduates of the Academies were given similar privileges.[14]

11. In 1759, 18 pupils entered the University; in 1760, 20; 1763, 25; 1764, 23; 1769, 18; a total of 318 in the period 1756–75.

12. D.I. Fonvizin, *Sobraniye sochineniy*, Moscow–Leningrad, 1959, vol. II, pp. 87–8. Remarkable among the teachers at the time was J.M. Schaden, rector of the gymnasium attached to the University, professor of ethics and philosophy, who also took in boarders, and who taught Fonvizin and later the historian Karamzin. A gymnasium was also founded in Kazan' in 1758, among the first pupils of which was the poet G.R. Derzhavin (*Zapiski Derzhavina*, in *Sochineniya Derzhavina*, ed. Ya. Grot, vol. VI, St Petersburg, 1874, pp. 407ff.).

13. There are examples of such examinations in the protocols of the University of Moscow, e.g. the certificate of proficiency to teach French awarded to Jean Louis Bouquet on 26 June 1767. See *Dokumenty i materialy po istorii Moskovskogo universiteta vtoroy poloviny XVIII veka*, ed. N.A. Penchko, 3 vols, Moscow, 1963, vol. III, p. 49.

14. See V.V. Poznansky, *Ocherk formirovaniya russkoy natsional'noy kul'tury*, Moscow, 1975, p. 24.

From the moment she seized power, Catherine had manifested an interest in education. 'La manie de cette année [1762] est d'écrire sur l'éducation' she wrote; and the object was 'la fabrication de l'homme idéal et du citoyen parfait'.[15] The dominant intellectual influences in these early years of her reign were Locke, whose *On Education* had been translated in 1759; Fénélon, whose *Télémaque* and *Éducation des Filles* had been translated several times by mid-century, and the *Encyclopédie*. Rousseau's influence was ambiguous. The banning of *Émile* in 1763 had in all likelihood nothing to do with his educational theories. But Catherine did not care for them: 'Je n'aime point surtout cette éducation d'Émile';[16] moreover, insofar as Rousseau denied the power of formal education to 'educate' his ideas were rejected. It was regarded as axiomatic that education would be a powerful force for the creation of the 'ideal man and perfect citizen', since there were no 'innate ideas'.

In 1763, Catherine appointed as her principal adviser in the field of education I.I. Betskoy, Director of the Cadet Corps, President of the Academy of Arts and charged with the supervision of palaces and public buildings. Betskoy (1703–99) was the illegitimate son of Prince Ivan Yur'yevich Trubetskoy, allegedly by a Countess Wrede who fell in love with him when he was a prisoner of war in Sweden. Recognized by his father (according to Russian custom his name is a truncated version of his father's) Betskoy moved in the highest circles at home and abroad.[17] On his foreign travels he visited educational establishments and hospitals. He was recalled to Russia by Peter III, but though he was present with him at Oranienbaum on the fateful June day, he was, like others on that occasion, an adherent of Catherine's.

Betskoy, though a man of considerable culture, humanity and good intentions, seems also to have been fussy, vain and impractical. Nevertheless, he was to remain for years one of Catherine's most tolerated collaborators.[18] Through him Catherine collected information from Russia and from other countries on educational principles and establishments.[19]

15. S.V. Rozhdestvensky, *Ocherki po istorii sistem narodnogo prosveshcheniya v Rossii v XVIII–XIX vekakh*, vol. I, St Petersburg, 1912, p. 314.
16. Catherine to Madame Bielke, 13 September 1770, *Sbornik Imperatorskogo Russkogo istoricheskogo obshchestva* (hereafter *SIRIO*), 13, pp. 36–7.
17. Trubetskoy's daughter Anastasiya married Dmitry Kantemir and thus became the stepmother of the poet Antiokh. Anastasiya's daughter by Kantemir married Prince Dmitry Mikhaylovich Golitsyn, an extremely wealthy and cultured *grand seigneur* who became Russian ambassador in Vienna in 1760 and stayed there until 1792. Anastasiya herself, after Dmitry Kantemir's death, married the Prince of Hesse Homburg, and was close to the Empress Elizabeth. She was able to advance the career of her illegitimate brother. See P.M. Maykov, *Ivan Ivanovich Betskoy, Opyt yego biografii*, St Petersburg, 1904.
18. He was reputed to have been the lover of Catherine's mother, the Princess of Anhalt Zerbst, both on her visit to Russia in 1744 and after the death of her husband; it was also rumoured that he was Catherine's father, which was most improbable.
19. The Rector of Moscow University was, for instance, ordered to supply Catherine regularly with the results of university and gymnasia examinations, and a survey was ordered in 1764 of the number of students, from which estate, cost to the state if any, food, clothing, academic regulations etc.: Rozhdestvensky, *op. cit.*, p. 250.

It was typical of Catherine that her first step in the field of education was to set up a Commission, composed of G.N. Teplov, T. von Klingstedt, F.G. Dilthey (professor at Moscow University) and the historian G. Müller. In addition the Rev. Daniel Dumaresq, who had been chaplain of the English factory until 1762, was recalled to Russia by Catherine in 1764 and appointed to the Commission. The Commission studied the reform projects which had already been put forward by I.I. Shuvalov under Elizabeth, and under Peter III, and submitted its own recommendations for the establishment of a general system of education for all Russian Orthodox subjects from the age of five–six to eighteen, except serfs.[20] Nothing was done, however, to implement the many plans put forward by the Commission, in all probability because its deliberations were overtaken by the calling of the Legislative Commission.

Education was touched on in Catherine's *Bol'shoy Nakaz* (*Great Instruction*) very briefly, merely to proclaim that it was necessary and to put forward a few general principles of what it should contain, but not how it should be organized. Catherine admitted that it was impossible for the state to provide universal education for 'a numerous people . . . in houses regulated for that purpose'.[21] But one of the sub-commissions set up by the Assembly was charged with the preparation of plans for national education. The Sub-Commission received the references to education in the instructions submitted by the deputies of the various estates and institutions and collated them. It must be said that the demand for education played a relatively small part in the instructions of the deputies to the Commission.[22] But where education was mentioned, the instructions painted a gloomy picture of existing facilities in the provinces and complained that the nobility could not serve the state unless the state saw to their education. In Vereya, the nobles complained that the illiterate children of poor nobles, unable to afford school in the capitals, had to enlist in the army as private soldiers. The townspeople too complained of the shortage of schools, but seemed less convinced of the need for the state to provide them. Least of all was said about the education of the peasantry, though a few local government offices, a few nobles (including the favourite, G.G. Orlov), a bishop and some of the peasant deputies urged the necessity to set up parish schools for peasant children from the age of five to twelve in winter.[23]

20. *Ibid.*, pp. 272ff. Dilthey produced a separate plan for schools of four different levels, the lowest of which was for serf *dyad'ki*, i.e. serf servants of noble children. See also N. Hans, 'Dumaresq, Brown and Some Early Educational Projects of Catherine II' (*Slavonic and East European Review*, hereafter *SEER*, vol. XL, No. 94, December 1961, pp. 229–35).

21. W. Reddaway, ed., *Documents of Catherine the Great*, Cambridge, 1931, pp. 271–2, Chapter XIV, articles 347–56.

22. According to M.D. Kurmacheva in 'Problemy obrazovaniya v ulozhennoy kommissii 1767g.', *Dvoryanstvo i krepostnoy stroy Rossii XVI–XVIII vv.*, Moscow, 1975, pp. 240–64, problems of education were mentioned only in 83 *nakazy* or less than 10 per cent of the total; 24 per cent of the noble *nakazy* discussed the problem, only 5 per cent of the urban *nakazy* and 0.65 per cent of rural *nakazy* (a doubtful figure, since so many of these remain unpublished and unstudied).

23. For an analysis of the demands in the noble *nakazy* see P. Dukes, *Catherine the Great and the Russian Nobility*, Cambridge, 1967, pp. 189ff. The instruction of the Academy of Sciences also

The Sub-Commission on Education also received a special instruction from Catherine herself, pointing out that education in the home had been referred to another sub-commission, and that the present one was to concern itself not with the subtleties of sciences, but with primary, secondary and higher education, the purpose of which was to teach children the duties required of those who have to live in society. According to Catherine this meant the setting up of schools in towns and villages, in which the catechism and the laws should serve as text books.[24]

The Sub-Commission started its labours in May 1768 and extended its search for models to English universities, the Prussian system of national education and 'Irish schools'. It also studied the various projects of Catherine's first Commission on Education, but again by the time the Sub-Commission's activities ground to a halt in 1771, though a variety of projects existed on paper, nothing had been put into a form which could be presented to the Empress as a finalized plan. But if the search for a model system of education had produced no results in ten years, Catherine had achieved some progress on the definition of educational principles and the establishment of individual institutions or the reform of others, in which they could be applied.

On 12 March 1764, Betskoy's *General Plan for the Education of Young People of Both Sexes*, approved by Catherine and possibly dictated in part by her, was published.[25] It set out the principles which were, in theory, to be applied in all Russian educational institutions. The emphasis was on the creation of a 'new kind of person', a new generation, which could only be achieved by isolating the child completely from the age of five to twenty-one from the harmful influences of parents and an illiterate, brutal and corrupt society. Schools were to stress not professional or vocational training but the creation of good citizens and accomplished human beings. Education was to be by precept and moral persuasion. Two years later Betskoy produced a continuation of the general plan dealing with the physical aspect of the education of children from birth to youth. These instructions, 'selected from the best authors', are extremely modern in conception, with the emphasis on hygiene, simplicity, fresh air, loose clothing, well-fitting and low-heeled shoes etc. The regulations rejected Locke's views on corporal punishment and are worth quoting:

> Children must almost never be beaten, and the example of cruel punishments by mindless and savage schoolmasters must not be followed, since by such punishments children are humiliated and lowered: a slavish cast of mind and baseness is bred in them, they learn to lie and sometimes acquire serious vices.

---

demanded more schools. Both the instruction of the Academy and that of Moscow University demanded noble status, the right to wear swords, and the right to own serfs for professors. See *SIRIO*, 43, pp. 371–2.

24. See Catherine's Instruction, Reddaway, *Documents*, Chapter x, article 158: 'Children should be taught to read alternately out of the Church books and out of those which contain the Laws.'

25. *PSZ*, xvii, No. 12103, 22 March 1764: General'noye Uchrezhdeniye o vospitanii yunoshestva oboyego pola.

> All forms of beating, apart from the pain, are, in accordance with all knowledge of all physical principles, harmful to health.[26]

The purpose of these regulations was didactic. They were to be printed and distributed to all the relevant government offices throughout the country, and to the Holy Synod.

Practice followed hard on the heels of theory. The decree (*ukaz*) setting up a Foundling Hospital in Moscow, to which a women's lying-in hospital was attached, had been signed in June 1763 and the Hospital opened its doors in April 1764. The Foundling Hospital was to be a private foundation, not a state body, that is it was placed directly under the Empress and was not accountable to any government institution. It received no public money and was to rely on subscriptions from society, and the operation of an insurance fund for widows with which it was also charged. In its first years the Hospital was very well supported. Catherine and Paul gave lavishly; so did the Metropolitan Dmitry (40,000 roubles) and Prince D.M. Golitsyn (22,000 roubles); a merchant gave the interest on 180,000 roubles for eight years. When gifts began to drop off, the Hospital lived off the various 'privileges' it had been granted such as the proceeds of taxes on playing cards,[27] and the widows' insurance fund.

The Foundling Hospital not only represented an opportunity for new educational theories to be tried out. It also fitted into Catherine's general concern with population policy, and in particular into the fashionable effort to create a third estate in Russia. All abandoned children, whether illegitimate or legitimate, would be received in the Hospital, and precautions were taken to ensure that on leaving they were free and remained free. They were to be trained in a craft or a skill, while the brighter children would go on to Moscow University or the Academy of Arts. Girls were given a dowry of 25 roubles on marriage, and all were provided with 1 rouble on leaving to tide them over.[28]

The Hospital had difficulty in providing the kind of education in the kind of conditions which Betskoy's *General Plan* had laid down. Moreover it suffered from the same initial tragedies which plagued foundling hospitals in other countries, namely the very high mortality rate.[29] But Archdeacon Coxe visited it in 1778, and was favourably impressed. The dormitories were large

26. *PSZ*, XVII, No. 12785, 16 November 1766, article 88. However not all recommendations would be so acceptable today: all musical wind instruments were regarded as harmful to health but a moderate medicinal use of tobacco was advised for those of phlegmatic temperament, or those given to head colds (article 118).

27. *PSZ*, XVI, No. 11908, 10 June 1763. The hospital may have been modelled on the Foundling Hospital set up by Thomas Coram in London: see J. Brownlow, *The History and Design of the Foundling Hospital*, London, 1858. Betskoy had also visited the Foundling Hospital in Lyon. See also *SIRIO*, 27, p. 235, Catherine to Panin (n.d.) refusing to grant G.N. Teplov a monopoly for the manufacture of playing cards.

28. 'On ne vit pas un mois avec un rouble' wrote Diderot but it could and did provide sustenance for a month at a low level. See D. Diderot, *Mémoires pour Catherine*, Paris, 1966, p. 188.

29. 14.03 per cent in 1777; 7.45 per cent in 1778; 8.65 per cent in 1786. Mortality was even higher in the nineteenth century. See Maykov, *op. cit.*, pp. 162–3.

and airy; each child had its own bed, clean linen was frequently provided, and there were no unwholesome smells. Cradles were not allowed and rocking was particularly forbidden. Infants were not tightly swaddled according to the custom of the country but loosely dressed.[30] Coxe was impressed by the spontaneity with which the children crowded around the Director, taking hold of his arm, pulling at his coat, kissing his hand. He could not, he said, judge if they were well instructed, but he could see that they were healthy and happy. He was less satisfied with a performance of Rousseau's *Le Devin du village* which they put on for him, since all this singing and dancing 'must unavoidably take off their attention from the manufactures'. In this respect Coxe echoed the views of the Encyclopedists. D'Alembert had criticized drama as a means of tuition, as for instance used by the Jesuits, in 'useless plays in which Grand Prince Solecism and Grand Prince Barbarism defeat the Marquis of Conjugation', while Diderot exclaimed: 'point de gymnastique, point de musique, point de comédies, point de tragédies dans vos écoles publiques . . .'. They were to be replaced by public exercises in which lazy children and bad schoolmasters could be made to feel ashamed.[31]

The general principles governing the setting up of foundling hospitals in Russia were duly drafted and published by Betskoy in 1767,[32] and were followed by the setting up of such hospitals in St Petersburg and in a number of other towns. Some were founded by nobles, others by priests or peasants, one by a serf, all at their own expense.[33] After the local government reform of 1775, they came under the general supervision of the local governors and the Boards of Social Welfare as and when these boards were set up.[34]

30. This was one of Catherine's particular fads. Tight swaddling in her view should only be used to correct deformed limbs. Her medical adviser in these matters, it should be noted, was the Sefardi, Doctor Sanchez, who had been expelled from Russia in the anti-semitic phase of Elizabeth's reign. One of Catherine's first acts was to restore his pension. See *SIRIO*, 7, p. 119.
31. W. Coxe, *Travels into Poland, Russia, Sweden and Denmark*, 2 vols, London, 1794, vol. I, p. 350; W. Coxe, *Account of the Prisons and Hospitals in Russia, Sweden and Denmark*, London, 1781, p. 18. Coxe's remark draws attention to what was the weakest point in the education provided by the Foundling Hospital, namely the training in craft and skills. The hospital had no facilities and had to rely on local merchants and manufacturers who tended to regard their pupils as cheap labour. See also *Encyclopédie*, entry 'Collège', and Diderot, *Mémoires pour Catherine*, pp. 134–5.
32. These were Parts II and III of the General Plan for the Education of Young People. Part I had been published in 1763 with the plan for the Foundling Hospital. (See n. 27.) *PSZ*, XVIII, No. 12957, 11 August 1767. The plans of 1764, 1766 and 1767 were translated into French by M. Clerc, and published in 1774 in the United Provinces, under the supervision of Diderot, with the title *Plans et Statuts des différents établissements ordonnés par sa Majesté Impériale Catherine II pour l'Education de la jeunesse et l'utilité générale de son Empire.* (There are two simultaneous editions, one in 4° (The Hague), one in 8° (Amsterdam). The French 4° edition contains on p. 113 a biting indictment of serfdom as it affected the education and tuition given to children which is not to be found in the versions printed in *PSZ*. It does not appear that this was added by Diderot (according to the experts in Diderot studies); it may have been added by M. Clerc, or even by Betskoy. It must certainly have been known to Catherine; it provides an example of the difference between the image of Russia presented to Russians and that presented to the West.
33. Maykov, *op. cit.*, p. 148, n. 1.
34. For Maykov, it is axiomatic that such a supervision implied less social participation and hence the eventual decline of the hospitals. His conclusion cannot be accepted without further research.

Soon after the setting up of the Moscow Foundling Hospital came the establishment of the famous St Petersburg Smol'nyy Institute for Noble Girls, in May 1764, followed by the parallel Novodevich'ye school for girls of the third estate.[35] The former was the first school for girls set up in Russia and was broadly modelled on the original Saint Cyr of Madame de Maintenon. The curriculum included scripture and the catechism, but also good manners and morals, foreign languages, music and dancing. The 'bourgeois' girls were given the same education, though in their case architecture and genealogy were omitted.

This first instalment of Catherine's educational reforms of the 1760s was continued with the remodelling of the Cadet Corps for which new regulations were issued in 1766.[36] It too was now to take children from a very young age, and educate them until the age of 21. The curriculum was broadened still further to include natural sciences, philosophy, ethics, history, international law, etc. Though the Cadet Corps remained primarily a professional military school, it now also became to some extent a 'political and civil school',[37] modelled on the Ritterakademie such as the Berlin Académie des Nobles, or even more the École Militaire Royale in Paris.[38] The new spirit in the Cadet Corps influenced also the teaching in the Naval Cadet Corps, and in the Engineering and Artillery Schools.

During the war of 1768–74, though no progress was made with setting up a national school system, Catherine herself continued to follow educational theory and practice in other countries, notably the work of Johann Basedow in Germany. Basedow had devised a full-scale system of education which could be adapted as required, and in 1774 he set up his 'Philanthropin' in Dessau, which attracted immediate attention. Simplicity, the open air life, teaching about *Realien* or real things, learning by play, co-education and non-denominational religious instruction give an astonishingly contemporary sound to Basedow's ideas. Catherine encouraged one of his disciples, C.H. Wolcke, to open a Philanthropin in St Petersburg, ordered large numbers of copies of his works which were distributed in Russia and sent him a substantial monetary gift, as did the Grand Duke Paul.[39] It was, however, Diderot who

35. *PSZ*, XVI, No. 12154, 5 May 1764, sets out here too the principles to be followed. Children were to enter at 6 years of age, and their parents were to agree on no account to remove them until they reached 18. The education was designed to produce virtuous young ladies, with all the graces and a good knowledge of domestic economy. The regulations covered health and hygiene in great detail.

36. *PSZ*, XVII, No. 12741, 11 September 1766; new regulations for the school attached to the Academy of Arts were also drafted.

37. *PSZ*, XVII, No. 12338, 7 March 1765, quoted in Shtrange, *op. cit.*, p. 78.

38. See the article in the *Encyclopédie* which describes it as 'le plus bel établissement du monde . . .'. The article was written by the then director.

39. Basedow's main works, published in Leipzig, were *Vorstellung an Menschenfreunde* (1768); *Methodenbuch für Väter und Mütter der Familien und Völker* (1770) and *Das Elementarbuch für die Jugend und für Ihre Lehrer* (1774); see Rozhdestvensky, *op. cit.*, p. 317. The *Methodenbuch* was translated into Russian in 1771. Wolcke ran one of the most reputable boarding schools in the capital from 1784 to 1801. See M. Woltner, *Das Wolgadeutsche Bildungswesen und die russische Schulpolitik*, Leipzig, 1937, p. 7, n. 3.

pointed most clearly to the fact that what Russia needed was not theorizing about education but theorizing about educational systems, which was done better in Germany than in France and by Protestants than by Catholics. At any rate in his *Essai sur les Études en Russie*, sent to Catherine in 1773, Protestant Germany is put forward as a model.[40]

After the war and the defeat of Pugachev, when Catherine turned again to domestic policy, she took up the question of education still in a somewhat piecemeal manner within the context of the Statute on Local Government (*Uchrezhdeniye o guberniyakh*) of 1775. The obligation to establish schools at *guberniya* and *uyezd* level was laid on the Boards of Social Welfare (*Prikazy obshchestvennogo prizreniya*) which were to be set up with the participation of elected representatives of the three free estates (article 388 of the statute). The boards were given an initial sum of 15,000 roubles, partly for capital expenditure and partly for recurrent expenditure out of interest. In addition many of the fines inflicted by the law courts were to be paid over to the boards for the use of the schools.

As the new local government institutions were progressively introduced in the *guberni*, existing schools were taken over, or new ones were established by the boards. How successful the various boards were depended a great deal on the local governors, and the co-operation, personal and financial, of the local nobility. A tour of inspection, carried out by Catherine herself in north-western Russia in 1780, gives some idea of what had been achieved in five years, and of what still had to be done. In Pskov, for instance, her officials told her that the nobles had produced a very decent sum for a school but that there was as yet no school for the townspeople. Catherine gave 1,000 roubles for the town school, 500 roubles for a seminary, 300 roubles for the orphanage, and 400 roubles for the almshouse.

The town of Polotsk, which became Russian at the first partition of Poland in 1772, was a town in name only, with almost no townspeople apart from Jews. But in 1780 there were six schools in the guberniya with 300 noble pupils and 130 townspeople's children. Mogilyov already had 34 schools with 858 pupils in the guberniya, Smolensk had twelve urban schools (apart from the classical grammar school) for 359 townspeople's children. In Novgorod guberniya which had 350,816 inhabitants, there were ten urban schools with a

40. 'Essai sur les Études en Russie', in D. Diderot, *Œuvres Complètes*, ed. by J. Assézat and M. Tourneux, 20 vols, Paris, 1875–77, vol. III, pp. 415–28. Diderot's Essai seems to have impressed Catherine more than his 'Plan d'une université en Russie', which he forwarded to her in 1776 (*ibid.*, pp. 429ff.). The 'Plan' shows Diderot's anti-clericalism at its most cynical: 'L'athéisme peut être la doctrine d'une petite école, mais jamais celle d'un grand nombre de citoyens . . . Je ne conserverai donc pas les prêtres comme des dépositaires des vérités, mais comme des obstacles à des erreurs possible et plus monstrueuses encore; non comme des précepteurs des gens sensés mais comme les gardiens des fous; et leurs églises, je les laisserai subsister comme l'asile ou les petites maisons d'une espèce d'imbéciles qui pourraient devenir fous furieux si on les négligeait entièrement . . . , *ibid.*, pp. 517, 519. It has now been suggested that the 'Essai' is by Grimm (S. Karp, verbal communication).

total of 1,173 pupils. The capital of the Board of Social Welfare had risen to 27,000 roubles.[41] The nobles of Kursk and Oryol had contributed 10,000 roubles for educational purposes by 1783. The *Magistrat* of Kaluga contributed 1,200 roubles; the merchants of Yaroslavl' gave twelve stone houses, those of Tver' 2,000 roubles. A prosperous peasant of Yaroslavl' contributed 300 roubles for the upkeep of a good local midwife.[42] The Moscow Noble Boarding School (*Blagorodnyy pansion*) set up by H. Schaden was the model which many provincial noble assemblies copied.

In St Petersburg, both state and private initiative was reflected in educational development. In 1777, a 'commercial' school for the *kuptsy* was set up on state initiative. In the same year, the publicist N. Novikov announced that the profits from his new venture, the publication of a monthly periodical entitled *Utrenniy svet* (Morning Light) printed on the press of the Cadet Corps, of a strongly masonic cast, would be devoted to the setting up and maintenance of two schools in the capital. In November 1777, a school called St Catherine's for day pupils and boarders of both sexes and all free classes, both fee-paying and with free places, was founded, attached to the church of the Madonna of Vladimir; a second school, St Alexander's, was founded in August 1778, on the same lines. Both schools were solemnly inaugurated by the Archbiship Gabriel in full canonicals, supported by the ecclesiastical hierarchy; and they were maintained by donations from charitably inclined lay and clerical patrons, including one of Catherine's secretaries, and even the head of the Secret Investigation Section of the Senate, S.I. Sheshkovsky, and Pushkin's grandfather, I.A. Gannibal. So successful were the schools in collecting donations, that in the end it was they who subsidized the periodical *Morning Light*, and not the other way round as Novikov had originally intended.[43]

Catherine herself founded at her own expense a school in the capital attached to St Isaac's Cathedral.[44] Six more schools were founded in the same year, attached to churches, and under the supervision of the Board of Social Welfare. Pupils were mainly drawn from the children of merchants, officers, clerks, soldiers, court officials and servants of nobles. By 1781 there were 486 pupils (of which one-twelfth were girls) and the Board of Social Welfare in St

41. *SIRIO*, I, pp. 384ff. 'Dnevnaya zapiska puteshestviya E.I.V. chrez Pskov i Polotsk v Mogilyov . . .'. At every stop, Catherine gave generous sums to support schools and almshouses, and to assist in putting up stone buildings.

42. Rozhdestvensky, *op. cit.*, p. 450; H. von Storch, *Annalen der Regierung Katharina der Zweyten, Kaiserin von Russland*, Leipzig, 1798, pp. 104ff. Storch gives many other examples drawn from current newspaper reports.

43. See W. Gareth Jones, 'The *Morning Light*, Charity Schools, 1777–80' (*SEER*, vol. 56, No. 1, January 1978, pp. 47–67). In all likelihood support for this venture was strongly masonic. We do not know any details of the setting up of the schools, the teachers, nor whether they came under the Board of Social Welfare in the capital or under the archbishopric.

44. *PSZ*, XXI, No. 15121, 16 February 1781, in which the hope was expressed that citizens in other quarters of the town would set up their schools. See also A. Voronov, *Istoriko statisticheskoye obozreniye uchebnykh zavedeniy Sankt Petersburgskogo uchebnogo okruga s 1715 po 1828 god vklyuchitel'no*, St Petersburg, 1849, p. 10.

Petersburg had raised the capital sum at its disposal to 31,663 roubles from private benefactions and official sources.[45] Novikov's two schools had 95 pupils in 1781.[46]

It was not only theorists like Basedow, Bielfeld and Justi[47] who directed Catherine's attention to German models, by which the state created its useful and loyal citizens; in both Prussia (1769) and Austria (1774) national educational systems had been founded.[48] Melchior von Grimm, as usual, had kept Catherine in touch, and had even been approached by her to take charge of a Russian educational system – a proposal which he wisely refused on the grounds that he did not know Russian.[49] The visit of Joseph II to Russia in May 1780 provided Catherine with a first-hand opportunity of hearing about the successful re-organization of Austrian education which had been rendered necessary by the abolition of the Jesuit Order, and which in turn was an adaptation to a Catholic country of teaching methods devised in Prussian Silesia by the Augustinian abbot Johann Ignaz von Felbiger. These new teaching methods involved the provision of uniform textbooks, and the organization of the teaching of the same subject to a number of children at the same time. Children were taught by reading aloud together, by memorizing, based on the use of tables and blackboards, using the initial letters of words as mnemonics. The system of question and answer was also used. The advantages of this method were that all children were involved simultaneously in the process of learning.[50]

An advisory commission was set up by Catherine in 1782 to study the various models of educational systems. The leading spirit was the mathematician F. Aepinus, a distinguished scientist, who had been a tutor of Paul's at

45. Catherine gave 1,000 roubles to 'her' school and 600 roubles to the other six schools. Paul gave 2,000 roubles: Voronov, *op. cit.*, p. 12.

46. Gareth Jones, *op. cit.*; Novikov's schools cost 1,937 roubles 40 kopecks. In 1780 St Catherine's cost 499 roubles 90 kopecks (of which 200 roubles was spent on the building) and St Alexander's 1,398 roubles of which 237 roubles $9\frac{1}{4}$ kopecks was spent on teaching staff. In the other schools the salary of a teacher averaged 60–90 r.p.a.: Voronov, *op. cit.*, p. 12.

47. J.F. von Bielfeld on education in *Institutions politiques*, 4 vols, Paris, 1762, vol. I, Chapter IV. J.G. Justi in *Die Grundsätze zu der Macht und Glückseeligkeit der Staaten*, 2 vols, Königsberg and Leipzig, 1760–61, had stressed the fact that the state must not merely foster education, if it wanted good and loyal citizens, it must create and direct a system of education. The very fact that education was conceived of as a system was new, and clearly only the state could be charged with such a duty. See Rozhdestvensky, *op. cit.*, pp. 387ff.

48. For the Prussian and Austrian educational systems, see A. Beer and F. Hochegger, *Die Fortschritte des Unterrichtswesens in Culturstaaten Europas*, Vienna, 1867. The Russian programme may also have been influenced by the Polish Commission of National Education, set up in 1773 to take over Jesuit property. See A. Jobert, *La Commission Nationale d'Education en Pologne, 1773–1794*, Paris, 1941 and S. Truchim, *Współpraca polsko-rosyjska nad organizacją szkolnictwa rosyjskiego w początkach XIX wieku*, Łódź, 1960, Łódzkie Towarzy stwo naukowe, No. 30, pp. 1–140. (I owe this reference to the kindness of Dr J. Tomiak.)

49. D.A. Tolstoy, *Gorodskiye uchilishcha v tsarstvovaniye Yekateriny II, prilozheniye k LIV tomu zapisok Imperatorskoy Akademii nauk*, vol. 41, St Petersburg, 1886, pp. 1–213, at pp. 4–5.

50. I. Matl', 'F. Ya. Yankovich i avstro-serbsko-russkiye svyazi v istorii narodnogo obrazovaniya v Rossii', *XVIII vek*, 10, Moscow, 1975, pp. 76–81.

one time, and later became head of Catherine's code-breaking section in the College of Foreign Affairs.[51] Aepinus came out strongly in favour of the adoption by Russia of the Austrian three-tier model of *trivial*, *real* and *normal* schools at village, town and provincial capital level. He approved of the question and answer method of teaching adopted in the Austrian schools, but he warned that in Russia progress would be slower than in Austria where there were plenty of teachers who knew *what* to teach, and who only needed to be shown *how* to teach. In Russia it was necessary to start by teaching the man before training the teacher, and moreover the priesthood could only be drawn upon if its own educational level was improved.

Aepinus's most significant piece of advice to Catherine was to ask Joseph II to send her an adviser, Orthodox in religion and with a knowledge of a Slavonic language. Joseph, on the advice of Felbiger, proposed F.I. Jankovich de Mirjevo, who had taken a leading part in introducing the Austrian reformed system in the Serbian-speaking provinces of Austria. He arrived on 4 September 1782, was received by Catherine on 6 September, and on 7 September an *ukaz* was issued setting up a Commission of National Schools, under P.I. Zavadovsky.[52]

The Commission was charged with organizing a national school network, training the teachers and providing the textbooks. The first step was to arrange for training teachers, and a High School was opened in the capital in 1783 with a teachers' training school attached to it. Meanwhile Jankovich saw to the translation and adaptation from the German or the Serbian of a whole range of textbooks by or approved by Felbiger, on such subjects as history, geography, the three R's, Latin, Greek, grammar, etc.[53] Jankovich also produced a catechism which was highly approved of by Aepinus, and presumably by Catherine. He had 'tellement écarté tous les points de controverse en s'attachant à la morale la plus pure qu'il n'y avoit aucune des religions chrétiennes qui ne puissent faire usage de ce catechisme'.[54]

Meanwhile the Commission extended its control over all existing private schools in Russia in order to ensure that they should conform to the emerging national pattern. In the course of 1782 the new teaching methods were

51. Other members were Field-Marshal A.M. Golitsyn, I.I. Melissino, then director of the Noble Cadet Corps, and the geographer and explorer S. Pallas. On Aepinus, see R.W. Home, 'Science as a Career in Eighteenth-Century Russia: The Case of F.U.T. Aepinus' (*SEER*, vol. 51, No. 122, January 1973, pp. 75–94).

52. The other members of the Commission were Aepinus, P.I. Pastukhov (a secretary of Catherine's) and Jankovich who was co-opted as the expert adviser. See *PSZ*, XXI, No. 16507, 7 September 1782.

53. Jankovich left the Commission in 1785 to concentrate on directing the Teacher Training School and was replaced by O.P. Kozodavlev; he returned later to the Commission. See also Voronov, *op. cit.*, pp. 10–11. Twenty-seven textbooks were ready by 1786: *ibid.*, p. 38 and n. 2.

54. A. Beer and J. Fiedler, *Joseph II und Graf Ludwig Cobenzl: Ihr Briefwechsel*, Vienna, 1901, p. 399: Cobenzl to Joseph II, 15 March 1783. The catechism prepared by Metropolitan Platon went a long way in the same direction, Aepinus had added, but Jankovich's was even better.

introduced into the schools in the capital. In 1784 the Commission was ordered to inspect all private schools and boarding schools (of which there were by then 26 in St Petersburg alone, mainly for foreigners) and examine their teachers. As a result of this inspection one foreign school was closed and the rest were placed under the Commission; all the Russian schools were closed and their pupils advised or compelled to transfer to the new national schools. In October 1785, a similar order was issued for the inspection of schools in Moscow, which was also to ensure that only authorized books were used in teaching.[55] In the two capitals state schools were opened from 1783 onwards. The two schools opened by N. Novikov and his circle in St Petersburg disappeared now as independent entities.

It is a commonplace of Russian and Soviet historiography that Catherine deliberately sought to stifle Novikov's work of 'enlightenment' and to keep control of all education, allowing no independent social initiative. A note of hers has survived, in which she asked for an inquiry to be made into the schools maintained by *Morning Light*, 'their needs and deficiencies'.[56] This has been interpreted as singling out Novikov's schools for particular condemnation. But in view of the fact that *all* private schools were at the time being inspected and remodelled on uniform principles, it would be much more surprising if the *Morning Light* schools had been excluded from this process.[57]

On 5 August 1786 the Russian Statute of National Education was promulgated. It provided for the setting up of a two-tier network of high schools and primary schools in guberniya capitals and primary schools in uyezd towns, free, open to all the free classes in the country and co-educational. No provision was made for rural schools, though these had figured in Catherine's early drafts. The Commission for National Schools supplied the funds for the initial capital expenditure, but thereafter the local Boards of Social Welfare were supposed to provide funds for the maintenance of the schools from the interest on their capital and from donations from the public.

The Statute regulated in great detail the subjects to be taught at every age and the method of teaching. The primary schools, comprising two classes, each of one year, concentrated on reading, writing and arithmetic, with religion and moral education. The high schools comprised four classes (the last of two years) and taught in addition geometry, architecture, mechanics, physics, history, geography, drawing and languages useful for Russians such as Latin, Greek

55. *PSZ*, XXII, No. 16058, 5 September 1784; No. 16275, 7 October 1785. From 1 January 1785 no boarding schools were to be opened without permission from the Boards of Social Welfare, and all schools were to teach in accordance with the rules laid down by the Commission.

56. G. Vernadsky, *Russkoye masonstvo v tsarstvovaniye Yekateriny II*, Petrograd, 1917, p. 206, n. 3.

57. The German school attached to St Peter's Lutheran church was also ordered to conform to the national pattern in an *ukaz* of 7 September 1783. See Gareth Jones, *op. cit.*, and Rozhdestvensky, *op. cit.*, pp. 14–16. If Catherine disapproved of Novikov's schools, which is an unproven assumption, it may have been because the teaching was imbued with a *bondieuserie* which was quite alien to her. On one occasion the pupils did without breakfast and supper for a month to collect 50 roubles for the poor which they hoped would be received 'as Jesus Christ received the widow's mite': Gareth Jones, *op. cit.*, p. 63. Catherine was not likely to approve of fasting by children.

in the southern provinces of Russia, Tatar and Arabic in the south-east, and Chinese in Irkutsk and Kolyvan′. French was relegated to private tuition.[58]

In addition to the textbooks diligently translated by the Commission, teachers were provided with guidance on the moral duties of a teacher. The *Guide to Teachers* issued in Russian in 1783 was based on a Serbian translation of a work by Abbot Felbiger which had been prepared for non-uniate Orthodox schools in Austria.[59] The work was divided into four parts dealing with teaching methods, the subjects taught, the behaviour of the teacher, and the running of a school.

It set out in all the detail beloved of Catherine the qualities of the ideal teacher: he was to be Christian, honourable, loving (in a dignified way), bold, patient, zealous, unprejudiced and condescending; he was to remember that his role was not merely to impart knowledge, but to 'educate' or bring up. His every step and his every gesture must therefore be carefully calculated to fulfil that aim.[60]

Pupils too were provided with guidance over and above the catechism, namely the little book entitled *The Duties of a Man and Citizen* published in 1783, designed to inculcate respect for the law and government. It was divided into four parts: chapter one dealt with duties to God and man; chapter two with health and hygiene; chapter three with duties to society; and chapter four with domestic economy. The child is enjoined to love God (but not specifically the Christian God), and to be dutiful. Most interesting is chapter three, which explains the formation of society: people come together because they need each other's help. Some groups place themselves under one leader. In other groups 'several people concern themselves with the general welfare, and have that power which in a realm belongs to the ruler. These societies are called republics.' But whether one or many rule, all must obey. Rulers would not be where they are if God had not willed it. As well as this justification for government authority the book preaches acceptance of the division of society into masters and servants, and indeed, basing itself on the First Epistle to the Corinthians, into masters and slaves.[61]

58. Latin was still taught in the church grammar schools. See *PSZ*, XXII, No. 16421. The Statute included an 'Instruction on the Teaching of Foreign Languages', with a detailed timetable. Matl′ suggests that French was excluded as the language of subversive thought (*op. cit.*, p. 80). It is more likely that Catherine thought that those who wanted it could afford to pay for it.

59. Matl′, *op. cit.*, p. 80. The Serbian version had been published in Vienna in 1776–77.

60. I have used the third edition: *Rukovodstvo uchitelyam pervago i vtorago rozryada narodnykh uchilishch Rossiyskiya imperii, izdannoye po vysochayshemu poveleniyu tsarstvuyushchiya Imperatritsy*, St Petersburg, 1794, 145 pp. Tables, unbound, 20 kopecks.

61. I have been unable to see a copy of this work, which was based on *Rukovodstvo k chestnosti i pravosti* (in Serbian) by Athanasius Sekeret, Vienna, 1777, who had in turn used a text by Felbiger which I have also been unable to track down. The German original is entitled *Anleitung zur Rechtschaffenheit oder das für die in den Trivialschulen Lernende Slavonisch-serbische nicht unirte Jugend bestimmte Lesebuch*. Part 5 of this text, addressed to the peasants, was apparently not published in Russian. See *Svodnyy katalog russkoy grazhdanskoy pechati XVIII veka*, vol. III, p. 488, n. to Nos 4736–44. Extracts of the Russian version can be found in German in *Russische Bibliothek*, ed. H.L.C. Bacmeister, vol. 9, St Petersburg, Riga and Leipzig, 1784, pp. 19ff.; in Russian in M.I. Demkov, *Istoriya russkoy pedagogiki*, II: *Novaya russkaya pedagogika*, (*XVIII vek*), Moscow, 1919, and in N.I. Zhelvakov, *Khrestomatiya po istorii pedagogiki*, vol. IV, pt. I, Moscow, 1938, pp. 172ff.

Nineteenth-century Russian historians of education, notably D.A. Tolstoy, have commented adversely on the *Duties of Man and Citizen* as totally unsuitable as a reader for children. It mentioned various 'infectious diseases' about which children should know nothing, and it spoke of republics in objective terms.[62] It was rumoured in the winter of 1794 that the book had been withdrawn as subversive. This does not seem to have been the case since it was reprinted eleven times until 1817, when it was finally banned at the instigation of Metropolitan Filaret who held that consciousness of one's duties should be based on religion and not on secular morality. The Minister of Education ordered the book to be withdrawn from circulation and sold for pulping at 50 kopecks a *pud*.[63]

It was the secular tone of the Statute of 1786, and of all the material it published, which shocked the nineteenth-century Minister of Education Dmitry Tolstoy: 'In all the 113 articles of the Statute the church is not mentioned, as though the Christian and moral enlightenment of the people were none of its concern.'[64] Religion was taught in the new schools, but it was not taught by priests, and it was taught with textbooks provided by the Commission, not by the church. Tolstoy thought that this did not reflect anti-clericalism on the part of the Commission so much as contempt for the low educational level of the priesthood, and hence a refusal to let them take part in teaching. Such an opinion suggests Tolstoy's own failure to appreciate the extent to which Catherine herself was personally committed to a secular education. The tone of her own pedagogical work, *An Elementary Civil Primer*, prepared for her grandchildren, Alexander and Constantine, is completely secular.

In this primer, consisting of two separate series of some 210 moral maxims graded in Catherine's view to a child's understanding, God is mentioned only twice: in the first series, in No. 35, 'God alone is perfect', and in the second series, in No. 111, 'Honour God first, then your parents', where the maxim is attributed to Xenocrates; Jesus Christ is not mentioned at all, while Socrates, Plato, Demosthenes, Alexander the Great, Julius Caesar etc. are all drawn upon. The question 'what is a hero?' is asked, but never 'what is a saint?'[65]

62. Tolstoy, *Gorodskiye uchilishcha*, pp. 57–8.

63. According to J. Parkinson, *A Tour of Russia, Siberia and the Crimea, 1792–1794*, London, 1971, p. 223: 'Orders have certainly been given to neglect the schools all over the Empire, with a view to continuing the people in their ignorance, it being feared if they become enlightened, that it may not be possible to govern them.' The book was printed in editions of 10,000 copies in 1786, 1788, 1791 and 1796; the 1817 edition was the eleventh. See N.I. Zhelvakov, *Khrestomatiya*, pp. 172ff., and particularly p. 197, n. 10.

64. Tolstoy, *Gorodskiye uchilishcha*, p. 102.

65. See Catherine to Grimm, 14 May 1780: *SIRIO*, 23, p. 176. Catherine's 'abc' for her grandchildren was published in Russian in two parts, composed of 1–107 and 108–209 maxims, under the title *Grazhdanskoye nachal'noye ucheniye*, in 1781 and 1783. The ensemble of Catherine's stories and her maxims were published in a German translation as *Bibliothek der Grossfürsten Alexander und Constantin*, by I. K. M. d.K.a.R. (Ihre Kaiserliche Maiestät die Kaiserin aller Russen), 4 vols, Berlin, 1784. The *nachal'noye ucheniye* is translated as *Grundlehren des Bürgerlichen Unterrichts* and is published in vol. 2, pp. 1–38 and pp. 133–76. For a study of the models (mainly German) on which Catherine drew, see N. Lavrovsky, *O pedagogicheskom znachenii sochineniy Yekateriny Velikoy*, Khar'kov, 1856.

In the 1760s Catherine had had the opportunity to use the Church as the instrument with which to develop Russian education. Proposals had been put before her by the Commission on Church Estates in the 1760s for the reform of the church grammar schools and the establishment of a Clerical Academy in Moscow. These reports were forwarded to the Sub-Commission on Education of the Legislative Commission and ended there. Again in 1771 a detailed project for national education run at all levels by the Church, after receiving the approval of the College of Economy in 1772, was forwarded to Catherine and went no further.[66] The Orthodox Church traditionally taught only those who were or might become priests or nuns, and there were no great teaching orders. But under the enlightened guidance of Metropolitan Platon, the standards in the church grammar schools and seminaries improved, both from the academic and the disciplinary point of view, and numbers rose from 6,000 at Catherine's accession to 11,329 in 1783.[67] Judging, however, by the experiences of the young Speransky, life in a church school was still incredibly harsh.[68] The educational level of the village priesthood continued so low, that even had she wished to, Catherine would have been unable to utilize priests as primary school teachers.

In one respect Catherine's pedagogical principles, as expressed in the Statute of 1786, were in advance of her times, and ran counter to contemporary tradition and practice. Not for her the German schoolmaster who in the course of 51 years and 7 months of teaching had administered '22,763 notabenes mit Bibel, Katechismus, Gesangbuch und Grammatik' among other – and far more painful – punishments.[69] Corporal punishment of any kind – even pulling the children's hair – was completely banned from her schools.[70]

The Statute of 1786 required the governors in 25 guberniyi to proceed at once with setting up the new schools, and in 1788 a second *ukaz* ordered the opening of schools in a further 16 guberniyi,[71] including the Livonian provinces and the three Little Russian guberniyi, as well as Tobolsk and Irkutsk. In 1786, there were already 165 schools with 394 teachers, 10,230 boys and 858 girls; by 1792 the numbers had almost doubled to 302 schools, 718 teachers, 16,322 boys and 1,178 girls. The numbers dropped after Catherine's death but rose again in 1800, and by the end of the century there were 315 schools, 790 teachers, 18,128 boys and 1,787 girls. All ten uyezds in Moscow guberniya had schools by 1800, in Ryazan′ all twelve.[72]

The National Commission of Schools continued to operate as a kind of Ministry of National Education though its functions seem to have been mainly supervisory and judicial; it was charged with co-ordination of curricula, qualifications of teachers, salaries, textbooks etc. It provided the initial capital

66. Rozhdestvensky, *op. cit.*, pp. 309ff.
67. Demkov, *op. cit.*, pp. 395ff.
68. M. Raeff, *Speransky*, The Hague, 1963, pp. 5ff.
69. Quoted in Lavrovsky, *op. cit.*, p. 46, n. 2.
70. *Rukovodstvo*, p. 106. So also were dunces caps, asses ears etc.
71. *PSZ*, XXII, No. 16726, 3 November 1788 (cf. 16147).
72. Rozhdestvensky, *op. cit.*, p. 606.

expenditure for the schools, but afterwards the Boards of Public Welfare were supposed to use the interest on their own capital (15,000 roubles) as well as donations from the public and the receipt of fines from the courts. The governors in the guberniyi retained overall supervision of the schools, which were to be supervised locally by a director who was a member of the Board of Social Welfare and in the uyezds by an appointed inspector; it was the duty of the Police Office (*uprava blagochiniya*) to see that no schools were opened without the permission of the Board – and the Board was to ensure that only the textbooks and teaching methods prescribed by it were used.[73] At a lower level, not only was it necessary to lay down the salary structure, it was also necessary to decide upon the placing in the Table of Ranks of members of the newly created profession of school teacher. The teachers in the top two classes of *guberniya* high schools (who gave 27 lessons a week) were paid 400 roubles p.a., with lodging, heating and light, and proportionately less for the lower classes and the primary schools. The high school teacher, according to an *ukaz* of 1790, started in the twelfth rank in the Table of Ranks (*titulyarnyy sovetnik*); other teachers would start in the fourteenth or lowest rank. With the automatic system of promotion in force in Russia, a high school teacher could acquire hereditary noble rank (*kollezhskiy assessor*, eighth rank) after 22 years' teaching, a junior school teacher after 36 years.[74]

As usual in Russia, government employees were bound to government service, and came under the jurisdiction of the corresponding service. Hence, to prevent the flight of school teachers from the service after they had reached personal noble rank, those educated at the cost of the state were forbidden to leave. Teachers committing misdemeanours were punished – sometimes very severely – by order of the Commission of National Schools.[75] Apart from the armed forces, the school teaching profession was the first professional, functional corps to be set up in Russia, and the first civil functional corps. Though the procuracy had achieved some unity, it could not be regarded as a functional corps within the bureaucracy since there was no specific training for it, and procurators could exchange posts within the bureaucracy and the armed forces. The school teachers were bound to their profession and promotion could only be achieved within it.

The 1780s thus saw a rapid multiplication of schools throughout Russia, accompanied by the extension of state supervision over the type and quality of education given in all schools, and by the extension of Russian control over

73. The firm of Breitkopf was licensed to publish these textbooks in St Petersburg. Novikov got into trouble for reprinting two of the Commission's textbooks in breach of copyright as a result of which an order was issued prohibiting the publication of these textbooks anywhere in the country except in St Petersburg, by Breitkopf, under the immediate supervision of the Commission. *PSZ*, XXII, No. 16086, 1 November 1784. The Lutheran St Peter's Church in St Petersburg was given overall supervision of all German language schools in Russia, and published German translations of the textbooks: Woltner, *op. cit.*, pp. 36–7.

74. Statute of 1786, and *Polnoye sobraniye zakonov, Kniga shtatov*, vol. 44, p. 200. See also *PSZ*, XXII, No. 16930, 16 December 1790, and Rozhdestvensky, *op. cit.*, pp. 581ff.

75. *Ibid.*, pp. 584ff.; Tolstoy, *Gorodskiye uchilishcha*, pp. 112–13.

the non-Russian schools, including those of the Baltic provinces.[76] Russian language high schools were now set up.[77]

At the same time as the national network was being founded, Catherine turned a coldly critical eye on the institutions which had been established in the 1760s under Betskoy's inspiration, and which had signally failed to produce a new race of men. The Commission of National Schools was ordered in April 1783 to inspect the Smol'nyy Institute for girls. It reported that the teaching was mainly in French, there was no proper timetable, and the teachers were poorly qualified. The Commission set about reforming this situation by introducing teaching in Russian, a fixed timetable, and its own teaching methods as laid down by Jankovich de Mirjevo, who also supplied a special Instruction to teachers.[78] The Cadet Corps were also reformed at the same time, and some of the less military subjects, such as sculpture, were cut out of the curriculum; the number of lessons per week, which had risen to 45, was also reduced.[79]

The most important questions now arise: how successful was this educational programme? How effective were these educational principles, and how effectively were they applied? The judgement of the nineteenth century was highly critical. Catherine was always accused of failing to make enough money available to support her educational programme. It would require a more detailed study than has as yet been made of the financing of education in Russia to elucidate this question. Much larger sums were made available for the special and professional schools in the capital than for the national schools, ranging from the interest on 2½ million roubles p.a. for the schools for noble and non-noble girls (which at the usual rate of 6 per cent would give them an income of 150,000 roubles p.a. together) to the 46,000 roubles p.a. allotted to the Naval Cadet Corps in 1783, which rose to 187,000 roubles p.a. in 1792.[80] It is probable that the government had little experience of the actual financial needs of primary schools.[81]

76. Primary schooling had already – in law – been introduced in Livonia by a decree of the Landtag in 1765, which provided that its members must introduce schools for peasant children to attend from Martinmas to Easter. Each parish was to have a school from which the school teacher was to be drawn. Estonia followed suit. Catherine confirmed the decree in *ukazy* of 1765 and 1785, and by 1787 there were 35 parish schools and 223 communal schools in Estonia. See Board of Education, *Special Reports on Educational Subjects*, vol. 23, Education in Russia, Cmd. 4812, 1909, cited hereafter as *Darlington Report*.

77. Tolstoy, *Gorodskiye uchilishcha*, p. 107.

78. Here again the changing ideas of the eighteenth, nineteenth and twentieth centuries are worth noting. D.A. Tolstoy, commenting on the Instruction to teachers given to the Smol'nyy Institute in 1783, approved of the fact that the girls should be taught to bring up children, but strongly disapproved of the fact that they should be taught how to deal with pregnancy and breast-feeding which he regarded as quite unsuitable to their age: Tolstoy, *Vzglyad*, pp. 54–5.

79. Tolstoy, *Vzglyad*, pp. 22ff. The other state educational establishments, such as the Naval Cadet Corps, the Artillery and Engineering Schools, the Corps of Pages, the School of Mines and the Medical Schools (which were attached at first to hospitals) were all reformed in the course of the 1780s and brought into line with the relevant elements in the new plan.

80. Tolstoy, *Vzglyad*, *passim*.

81. In the 1760s, Professor Dilthey thought that 3 universities, 9 gymnasia, 21 minor schools, 2 peasant schools and a central government educational administration could be run on 104,721

As regards the contribution of society the response was doubtless uneven, and much depended on the local governor. A.P. Mel'gunov, the governor of Yaroslavl' (a mason), inspired the inhabitants of his guberniya to put up 30,000 roubles, and a stone house worth 20,000; in addition he founded a school for all poor children of both sexes (excluding serfs), joined to an almshouse for orphans, widows with small children, and the old and crippled, for which local nobles and merchants raised a further 30,000 roubles which provided the keep for 40 children.[82] By the end of the century the nobility of Tver' had advanced 77,000 roubles for education; Penza levied a tax on the nobles of 5 kopecks per male soul, which produced 9,000 roubles. In Ryazan', a stone house was built by the governor, of which the upper floor was reserved for assemblies of the nobility, balls and masquerades, and the ground floor provided rooms for a *pansion* for well-born children.[83] This was better for the children no doubt than the school lodged under the same roof as an eating house, a cookshop and an alehouse![84] If serfs belonging to private owners were – in theory – excluded, girls were specifically included. John Parkinson, present at one of the twice yearly public examinations of the pupils in Astrakhan' in 1791, was 'suprised to see four girls in the first class'.[85] But numbers were not everything. Many nobles were reluctant to send their children to the national – and classless – schools; private education too, therefore, received a fillip, and an increasing number of private boarding schools was founded. The poet Derzhavin, when governor of Tambov, pandered to this class exclusiveness by arranging that teachers from the national school should, for a moderate sum, teach grammar, arithmetic and geometry in his own home to girls and boys whose parents found it improper for them to attend public schools.[86]

Two years after the inauguration of the educational programme a member of the National Commission was sent on a tour of inspection and brought back a somewhat depressing picture. Society's response to the state programme had been very patchy. While the nobility and the more enlightened urban

---

roubles p.a. with 150,000 roubles for the initial buildings. The budget for a high school was given as 2,500 roubles p.a. (Rozhdestvensky, *op. cit.*, p. 597). A schoolmaster received 400 roubles p.a. for the two senior classes in high schools, 200 roubles p.a. for the second year and 150 roubles p.a. for the first year. In the junior schools, teachers were paid 100 roubles for the first year and 150 roubles p.a. for the second. Teachers of languages received 300 roubles p.a. and teachers of dancing 60 roubles p.a.: Tolstoy, *Gorodskiye uchilishcha*, p. 113, n. 1. For comparison it may be noted that primary school teachers received on average 200–50 roubles p.a. in 1898; at an urban school, a highly qualified teacher received 600 roubles p.a., others 480 roubles p.a. in 1892 (see *Darlington Report*, pp. 261ff.).

82. *PSZ*, XXII, No. 16344, 10 March 1786, and G. Vernadsky, *Russkoye masonstvo v tsarstvovaniye Yekateriny II*, pp. 203–4.

83. Rozhdestvensky, *op. cit.*, pp. 602ff.; *Istoricheskaya zapiska Ryazanskoy muzhskoy gimnazii*, Ryazan', 1904, p. 6.

84. *PSZ*, XXII, No. 16443, 22 October 1786, *ukaz* ordering this to stop at once, and *Istoricheskaya zapiska Ryazanskoy muzhskoy gimnazii*, p. 6; see also Rozhdestvensky, *op. cit.*, p. 602.

85. Parkinson, *op. cit.*, p. 177. However, according to Dubasov, *Ocherki iz istorii Tambovskogo kraya*, from 1788 to 1804 in Oryol, of 3,008 pupils, 1,041 or 34 per cent were serfs. See also V.I. Semevsky, *Krest'yane v tsarstvovaniye Yekateriny II*, 2 vols, St Petersburg, 1903, vol. I, p. 286, on the presence of serf children in schools.

86. G.R. Derzhavin, *Sochineniya*, vol. V, p. 557.

dwellers had put up quite generous sums of money for the schools, most of the merchants and townspeople regarded the education in the humanities provided by the third and fourth classes of the high schools as utterly useless. 'It was well known that to secure a job in the civil service, good penmanship was all that was required' was the common view. The townspeople also turned against the junior schools with their newfangled pedagogical methods, and their conglomeration of poor nobles', peasants', soldiers' children etc. The wealthy nobles too preferred to send their children to the various Cadet Corps or to good private boarding schools. It also proved difficult to recruit qualified people to the Boards of Social Welfare designed to supervise the schools. Moreover, as directors of schools were appointed by governors, they tended to be changed as each new governor chose his own man.

To what extent did this lukewarm social response arise from lack of consultation and the repression of social initiative – as some nineteenth-century historians have argued? There is no doubt that Catherine's policy, as carried out by the Commission, aimed at complete control of education and the establishment of uniformity throughout the country. Underlying this monopolistic attitude was the firm conviction that the government was more enlightened than society, a view which many of Catherine's foreign advisers, from Diderot to 'Estimate Brown', ceaselessly dinned into her ears, and in which she was only too prone to believe.[87] Precisely because the government knew best, it was essential to ensure that its model was followed universally and that individuals should not be allowed to teach according to their fancy: they must avoid all 'widely nonsensical ideas thought up by deceit and ignorance' or 'strange subtle philosophizing'.[88] The first of these warnings was directed against ecclesiastical obscurantism, the second against masonic obscurantism. Both reflect Catherine's determination to put Russia's children on a strictly rationalist diet, incorporating a useful dose of utilitarian religion. Nevertheless, it would be hard to defend the view that more would have been achieved had 'society' been left free to act according to its own lights. It had not achieved very much before 1786 and the initial response was in fact surprisingly good. Society reacted adversely not so much to the schools, as to the kind of education provided.

How effective was Catherine's enlightenment in the surrounding gloom? What happened to the prohibition against the use of corporal punishment? In 1784, some pupils of the Foundling Hospital were birched for having allegedly complained of ill-treatment. I.I. Betskoy, still in theory connected with it, was extremely angry, not so much at the punishment as at the injustice,

87. See for instance D. Diderot, 'Plan d'une Université pour le gouvernement de Russie': 'elle [Sa Majesté Impériale] a devant elle un champ vaste, un espace libre de tout obstacle sur lequel elle peut édifier à son gré . . .' (*Œuvres Complètes*, vol. III, p. 441). And see also N. Hans, 'Dumaresq, Brown and Some Early Educational Projects of Catherine II' (*SEER*, vol. XL, No. 94, December 1961, pp. 229–35) for the expression of very similar ideas.
88. *PSZ*, XXII, No. 16344, 10 March 1786, warning A.P. Mel'gunov; No. 16362, 27 March 1786 to governor Bruce of Moscow warning N.I. Novikov.

since the boys had not in fact complained of ill-treatment. By then some of his own earlier idealism had worn off, but he could still insist that if the foundlings were *not* to receive a 'refined education, it should not however be so coarse and severe as that of the basest kind of people, so that the feelings inculcated in these pupils should render them worthy of the status of free citizens . . .'.[89] Baron Shteyngel′, the future Decembrist, described with feeling the physical ill-treatment he was subjected to in the Naval Cadet Corps in the 1780s.[90] There is not much evidence to go upon (Russians were not so addicted as the English have proved to be to the composition of their autobiographies at the age of 21) but human nature is much the same everywhere, and brutality to children is still with us today. Given the principal defect of Russian school teachers – drunkenness – it is likely that brutality also flourished. The life of a school teacher could indeed be hard. He might look forward to noble status – in 22–36 years time. But in the meantime if he got drunk, he could be sentenced by the National Commission to detention on bread and water, and even, as happened occasionally, to serve as a common soldier.[91]

The pupils in the newly founded national schools by no means exhausted the number of those actually receiving primary or secondary education outside the home in Russia. To these figures must be added those attending the professional schools of the armed forces (some 1,980 pupils) and the garrison schools (some 12,000 pupils), and those attending the School of Mines and other technical schools. All told it is estimated that some 62,000 pupils were being educated in some 549 state institutions at the end of Catherine's reign – a drop in the ocean, compared to the size of the population.[92] There are no figures at all for educational facilities in the countryside, but some undoubtedly existed, if only in the form of the village priest or the retired soldier. Indeed one of the greatest defects of Catherine's educational policy was the failure to concentrate on the training, intellectual and moral, of the school teacher. The special Teachers' Training School in the capital was allowed to lapse into a high school, on the assumption that new teachers would be drawn from the graduates of the high schools, seminaries etc. The standards of the teachers fell rapidly as a result.

Nineteenth-century historians have frequently expressed themselves somewhat scathingly regarding Catherine's efforts to construct an educational system. The twentieth century, with greater experience of the immensity of the task of eradicating illiteracy in a backward society, may show more understanding of the problems implicit in setting up a nationwide system of education, and of the limitations necessarily encountered.

89. Maykov, *op. cit.*, p. 181.
90. See 'Zapiski Barona V.I. Shteyngelya' in V.I. Semevsky *et al.*, *Obshchestvennyye dvizheniya v Rossii v pervuyu polovinu XIX veka*, vol. I, St Petersburg, 1905, pp. 283ff. Fagging also existed in the Kronstadt Naval Cadet Corps, possibly reflecting the strong British influence in the Russian navy.
91. Tolstoy, *Gorodskiye uchilishcha*, pp. 112–13.
92. According to another calculation, between 1782 and 1800, 176,730 scholars passed through the national schools, of which 7 per cent (12,595) were girls (*Darlington Report*, p. 281).

In particular, Catherine has been criticized because she did not make education compulsory. This was clearly impossible until enough schools existed to accommodate the children. But there are other problems. The first country to exact compulsory attendance at school was Prussia in 1763, and the example was followed by Austria in 1774. But in neither country was compulsory education free. The next country to set up a nationwide school system was Russia in 1786. Education was free, but not compulsory. There is a paradox here. Compulsory education, if it is not free, becomes a burden for the poorer classes. On the other hand free education, if it is not compulsory, tends to be monopolized by the better off. The ideal is to introduce both principles together, though generally compulsory education has preceded free education. Russia is the one exception: free education came before compulsory education. This may reflect a greater regard for the interests of the better off; it may also reflect the very low level of education of even the lower nobility and the *kuptsy*, who had not yet learnt to value education enough to pay for it.[93] Some of Catherine's critics have also failed to allow for the fact that the education of society takes more than one generation. The crop of Catherine's sowing was to be gathered by Alexander.

93. Secondary and higher education remained free until 1829, when fees were introduced for secondary schools and universities. Elementary schools remained free until the Soviet government introduced fees for non-proletarian groups in 1923. For comparison it may be noted that compulsory education was introduced in England in 1870, and free education in 1891. In France free elementary education came in 1881 followed by compulsory education in 1882. In Poland free elementary education was introduced in 1775, and compulsory education in 1919.

PART THREE

Catherine II, Russian Society, and the World of Ideas

CHAPTER NINE

Catherine II and enlightened absolutism

Believers in the theory of enlightened despotism thought that Russia was the ideal country in which to apply their ideas. Since it had no ancient institutions which would need to be rooted up, it was a blank page on which the *philosophe* might inscribe what he wished.[1] Nothing could be less true. When Catherine seized the throne in 1762, Russia was an absolute monarchy, placed at the despotic end of the spectrum which extended through the Prussia of Frederick II to the France of Louis XV.[2] There were no institutional limitations on the power of the ruler, who was even entitled to name his, or more often her, successor. There were no constituted bodies or 'estates', no 'intermediate powers' of the kind that existed elsewhere in Europe. As head of the executive the sovereign exercised authority through a series of functional colleges headed by boards under presidents, whose work was co-ordinated by an appointed administrative Senate of some twenty or thirty people. This misleadingly named body had no legislative powers, which were lodged entirely in the ruler. Local administration had been allowed to collapse into an under-financed chaos when Peter I's top-heavy organisation was dismantled in 1727. Vast *guberniyi*, divided into provinces, then into districts, were placed under governors and *voyevodas*, almost the only officials who received a salary. The rest were supposed to live off the people whose lives they administered, and whose lawsuits they adjudicated.

If the organs of government were too few and too slack, society itself was very tightly regimented. Russia had remained much as Peter I (Peter the Great) had left it, with a very small nobility of some 50,000 males, some 200,000 registered townspeople out of approximately 1.1 million towndwellers, and about 10 million male peasants. It had a population second only to that of France, and the lowest population density in Europe.

1. N. Hans, 'Dumaresq, Brown and some early educational projects of Catherine II', *Slavonic and East European Review*, 40 (1961), 481–91.
2. For a discussion of the use of the terms autocracy and absolutism, see Isabel de Madariaga, 'Autocracy and sovereignty', *Canadian-American Slavic Studies*, 16 (1982), 369–87.

Bondage of one sort or another pervaded Russian society. Until 1762, the noble was bound to serve the state in a military or civil capacity, as long as he was called upon, usually some twenty-five years or more. His service life and social status were regulated by the Table of Ranks, instituted by Peter I, a code of precedence in military, civil and court life, modelled on codes in use in Western countries such as Prussia, Denmark, and even England, but applied with far more rigidity. All commissioned officers in the fourteenth rank became hereditary nobles (unless they were already nobles by birth), while civil employees acquired hereditary nobility, as distinct from personal nobility, with the eighth rank. Since the ownership of estates with serfs was limited to hereditary nobles, there was tremendous pressure for promotion among non-nobles, while noble officers tried to climb the ladder leading to rank and wealth. However, the self-image of the noble had undergone a remarkable change for the better in the brief reign of Catherine's deposed husband, Peter III, when, in the manifesto of February 1762, the nobility was freed from compulsory service.

The townsman was registered in his town; he was responsible, together with his fellow townsmen, for the collection of the poll-tax and for the performance of a number of unpaid duties on behalf of the state. The peasantry was, in 1762, divided into three broad groups: private serfs, church peasants and state peasants. The private serfs formed about 56 per cent of the peasantry. They were bound to their villages for tax purposes and for military conscription, but landowners were entitled to remove them and re-register them in other estates, to sell them individually or as families, with or without land, and to take them into domestic service. By the middle of the eighteenth century their position had been assimilated to that of earlier Muscovite slavery, indeed almost to slavery in the Western sense. Their masters were legally bound to provide for them in times of famine, and in old age, and were responsible for the payment of the poll-tax on their behalf. They exercised jurisdiction over them for all petty offences, but major crimes such as rioting, brigandage, or murder went before the state courts. The situation of the church peasants was slightly better since they could not be sold. State peasants paid the poll-tax and an additional sum in quitrent to the state, intended to counterbalance what the serfs paid to their masters. They could be conscripted to work on state building or engineering projects, in foundries, mines or other industries. An enterprising state peasant could however move to a town, make enough money, and eventually change his status from peasant to towndweller, even to registered townsman. All these social groups, except the nobles, were liable to conscription in the armed forces. These were the deep-rooted social institutions that any reforming ruler would have to confront. But in this society, so strictly divided into different orders, there were no established corporate structures, no noble assemblies, no urban corporations, which could be entrusted with a share in internal administration. The country was at that stage, already superseded elsewhere, when the government needed to draw upon the co-operation of members of the various estates in the tasks of administration, and in order to recruit them effectively, had first to organise and give legal form and rights to the necessary corporate institutions.

In the years before she seized the throne, Catherine had occupied herself with systematic reading of political literature, ranging from Plato to Bayle's *Dictionary*, from *Henri IV* by Hardouin de Péréfixe (a ruler whom she greatly admired) to the *Encyclopédie*. Throughout her life she continued in a completely pragmatic and empirical way to borrow ideas from authors who struck her as modern, sensible and rational. She worked systematically and very hard, with a small number of chosen advisers, and in the case of major administrative reforms, she tried them out on a small scale before introducing them throughout the empire. Most of her senior servants remained with her for decades, strengthening the impression of stability of her government, in spite of occasional changes of direction. She was also very attentive to manifestations of public opinion.

Catherine set out her political theory in the famous *Nakaz* or *Instruction*, which she wrote for the Legislative Commission, summoned in 1767 to draft a Code of Laws for Russia. Both have been widely misunderstood, at the time and later. The *Instruction* has been viewed as a Code of Laws, or even as a 'constitution'[3] which was never promulgated, the Commission as a Parliament which failed. As with many of Catherine's policies, there were precedents in previous reigns. But previous legislative commissions had been small *ad hoc* separate consultations with deputies from the nobility and the towns alone. What was novel about Catherine's experiment is that, only five years after her *coup d'état*, she felt sufficiently confident to embark upon the kind of large-scale consultation advocated by Diderot in the *Encyclopédie* (article *représentants*), by calling together representatives of all the free estates of the realm, government bodies, and non-Russian peoples, to examine the chaotic state of Russian law, and to draft a new code. Over 500 deputies were elected, each bringing with him an 'instruction' from his electors setting out local grievances, and the whole enterprise was managed with considerable pomp and publicity. Such a public consultation had not been held for more than a hundred years in Russia, and was not to be made again until the meeting of the first Duma in 1906.

It has been pointed out by Catherine's critics that the serfs were not represented. This is of course correct, but it has to be seen in the context of contemporary theories of representation. In *ancien régime* institutions it was not individual opinion but corporate interests which were represented, and in no country at that time were peasants represented in diets or estates except in Sweden. And in Sweden it was only the peasants living on crown land, the equivalent of the Russian state peasants, who elected deputies since the interests

3. D. Griffiths in 'Catherine II, the republican empress', *Jahrbücher für Geschichte Osteuropas*, NF, 21 (1973) 323–4, is guilty of an anachronistic judgment in an otherwise very balanced article. So also are V.S. Nersesiants and S.I. Shtamm, 'La politica e il diritto penali nella Russia della seconda metà del XVIII secolo', in *La "Leopoldina": Criminalità e giustizia criminale nelle riforme del settecento europeo*, Siena, 1986, preprint, II, pp. 1731–44, at p. 1740.

of peasants living on noble land were held to be represented by the noble landowners. Thus, in Russia, serfs were held to be represented by their landowners, while state peasants sent deputies to the Commission. The Commission thus did not reflect individual opinion, let alone party opinion. Any deputy who attempted to set himself up as the advocate of the private interests of his electors, to run a 'surgery', was promptly called to order.

The clearest evidence of the influence of both Enlightenment and cameralist thought on Catherine is provided by the *Instruction* she wrote in 1765–68 to guide the Commission in its labours. In it she analysed the government and society of Russia as she thought it ought to be, and expounded the general direction she wished to follow. Her principal source was Montesquieu's *L'Esprit des lois*, from which some 294 out of 526 articles were almost literally copied. She has been accused not only of plagiarism (to which she freely admitted), but of distorting Montesquieu's views, in that she applied to Russia (which he regarded as a despotism) the maxims which he applied to a 'moderate' monarchy; that she located the limitations on absolutism, the *pouvoirs intermédiaires*, in the bureaucracy and not in social groups such as the nobility; and that she rejected the doctrine of the 'separation of powers'. This judgment is partly true. Considering the low regard in which despotism was held, Catherine naturally rejected its application to Russia, and preferred to argue that the ruler of Russia must be absolute in view of the size of the country. She justified her argument by postulating the existence in Russia of fundamental laws and the acceptance of a degree of self-limitation in the ruler's use of absolute power. Catherine does not, it is true, locate the *pouvoirs intermédiaires* in social forces such as the nobility or the town corporations, and in this she can be said to deviate from her mentor – but we must remember that neither the nobility nor the towns had as yet any corporate structure in Russia. However, in considering the lawcourts as intermediate bodies she does follow Montesquieu's principles. The courts were part of the bureaucracy in Russia, but then they were part of the state apparatus in France – a fact not appreciated by many commentators[4] – where the Parlements were not independent elected bodies, but emanations of the king in his capacity of supreme judge. Finally, though Catherine does not even discuss the separation of powers in her *Instruction*, one must remember that Montesquieu does not discuss this concept except in relation to one specific form of monarchy, which has political liberty as the main object of its constitution, namely the English monarchy. But she did endorse the separation of functions, i.e. the principle that the sovereign should not act as a judge, and that the judiciary should be separate from the executive.

4. See e.g. I. Fedossov, 'Europe Centrale et Orientale et la Russie' in *L'absolutisme éclairé*, ed. B. Köpecki, A. Soboul, E.H. Balàzs and D. Kosàry (Budapest and Paris, 1985), pp. 233–54, at p. 244; see also D. Ransel, *The Politics of Catherinian Russia: The Panin Party* (New Haven, Conn., 1973), p. 179 and n. These distortions all go back to the misreading of Montesquieu not only by these authors, but by their common source, F.V. Taranovsky, in 'Politicheskaya doktrina Nakaza', in *Sbornik statey po istorii prava posvyashchennyy M.F. Vladimirskomu Budanovu* (Kiev, 1904), pp. 44–86.

Though Catherine had no sympathy for the theory of the social contract on which Beccaria's analysis of society was based, she was influenced by his utilitarianism, and by his humanitarianism, which coincided with her own personal inclinations. His ideas are reproduced throughout the chapters of the *Instruction* dealing with the judicial process, torture, the nature of evidence and the nature and object of punishments, and Catherine put before the Russian public a condemnation of cruelty which had never been heard in Russia before, let alone from the throne. While the influence of Montesquieu predominated in the chapters dealing with social organisation, cameralist ideas were echoed in the sections of the *Instruction* dealing with public order and the economy.

The *Instruction* was not a code of law, nor did it have any legal validity. But it exercised a considerable influence on the intellectual climate of Russia in the eighteenth century and even in the nineteenth, since it opened the way to public discussion of many issues which had never previously been openly debated. Though its circulation seems originally to have been limited to officials, the Instruction was nevertheless freely available to the public from the beginning, since it was advertised as for sale in the Senate bookshop for 50 kopeks as early as 1768. Though its natural law principles, which paid scant regard to Russian positive law, led to its having but slight influence on subsequent Russian legislation, the *Instruction* had a beneficient influence on Russian practice, particularly in the field of penal law, when it was frequently quoted in favour of moderation and the reduction of penalties.

As a codifying body, the Legislative Commission proved both unsuitable and unsuccessful, though the at times acrimonious debates, and the materials collected by it and through it, were to prove invaluable in subsequent legislation. It was prorogued, not dissolved, on the outbreak of war with the Ottoman Porte in autumn 1768, since it was impossible for Catherine, with the resources in manpower and money available to her, to embark on reforming programmes while Russia was at war. It is very probable that the Pugachev revolt which raged from September 1773 to August 1774 explains the failure to recall it, though we have at present no direct evidence of Catherine's thoughts upon the subject. But the need to restructure Russian local administration had revealed itself to be so great that Catherine could not wait for the leisurely process of codification, and adopted a different method, namely the preparation and promulgation of laws by means of consultation with chosen advisers.

In 1764 Catherine had already put through a small-scale reorganisation of the civil administration, introducing salaries for all officials, and pensions after twenty-five years of service, inaugurating an intensive anti-corruption drive, and strengthening the network of procurators whose function it was to supervise the legality of the decisions of the executive, and who were responsible directly to the Procurator General, in turn responsible directly to her. At the same time the collection of the poll-tax was removed from the military and handed over to civilian officials.

The Statute of Local Administration of 1775, many of whose provisions lasted until 1864, some until 1917, was not simply the continuation of policies adumbrated in previous reigns. It represents a quite novel amalgamation of earlier Russian attempts to solve the problem with the doctrines of Catherine's *Instruction*, particularly those derived from Montesquieu, and a substantial dose of cameralism introduced by her Baltic German advisers. One of them, Count Jacob Sievers, also reinforced the English influence on Catherine. He had lived in England, greatly admired the British political system, and no doubt helped the Empress to thread her way through its mysteries as expounded by Blackstone, whose *Commentaries on the Laws of England* she was reading at the time in a French translation.[5]

The reform of 1775 was based on a number of specific principles, namely the multiplication of administrative centres in the provinces, and the corresponding transfer of functions from the centre to the localities; the separation of functions previously combined in one instance; the establishment of specific institutions for the free estates of the empire; and some degree of corporate organisation of these free estates to enable them to participate in the election of representatives forming part of local administrative institutions.

By the division of the vast *guberniyi* of Russia into smaller units, subdivided into districts of some 30,000 inhabitants, the various judicial instances were multiplied and brought much closer to the people, and a number of settlements of varying size, some extremely small, were raised to the status of towns. The separation of functions took quite elaborate forms: general administration, including what would today be regarded as welfare and was then grouped under the general heading of police, was entrusted to the governor, assisted by a board of appointed councillors, and a Board of Social Welfare, on which sat elected representatives of the various free estates. Financial administration including the collection of taxes and the administration of the state peasants became the responsibility of the deputy governor.

The judiciary was completely reorganised, and it is here that the 'estate' principle and the participation of elected assessors are particularly striking. At the apex of the system in each *guberniya* there were a civil and a criminal court, from which appeal lay to the Senate (the governor was specifically forbidden to act as a judge). Three separate sets of courts were established below, in three tiers, for the nobles, the townspeople and the state peasants respectively, to which these social groups elected a number of assessors. The only court of first instance for all classes was the so-called Conscience Court. Here again we have an institution which has no roots at all in the Russian past, and was taken over entirely from foreign models seen through a Catherinian prism.[6] For the Conscience Court was to act as an equity court, a concept hitherto unknown in Russia, and which, it must be said, remained unclear both to the founder of the whole system and to the judges who operated it. The court was supposed to temper the harshness of the law, but it was given additional functions, namely

5. Catherine commissioned a Russian translation of Blackstone prepared by the Russian jurist who studied at Glasgow University, S.I. Desnitsky, which was published in 1780–82.

6. The origins of the Conscience Court are much debated and have been sought in the *Encyclopédie* and also in the Ukrainian court of arbitration.

dealing with cases concerning minors, sexual offenders and witchcraft, etc. But it was also to this court that an entirely new function was entrusted: anyone detained for more than three days without charge could appeal to the Conscience Court to be released on bail, except in case of serious crimes such as *lèse majesté*, or murder. This was a complete departure from Russian practice, clearly borrowed from the English example of habeas corpus, though not from any specific English court. The extent to which this right was actually made use of in Russia remains shrouded in mystery.[7]

At the lowest level, the policing of the countryside was entrusted to a 'lower land court', presided over by a land commissar, with two noble assessors elected by the local nobles, or where there were few nobles, appointed by the crown, and with elected peasant assessors. The Russian Statute clearly describes this institution as a court, but states that the land commissar is not empowered to act as a judge on his own. Nevertheless historians have often remarked that this police organ was wrongly called a court. The confusion may arise because of failure to appreciate that here again there are traces of English influence, notably that of the procedure of indictment by justices of the peace. The English J.P. was not an agent of the executive; he operated by judicial means, i.e. by prosecuting offenders for failing to carry out specific duties (e.g. repairing bridges or clearing manure off roads), and since the land commissar was charged with many of the duties carried out by Justices of the Peace, it is possible that Catherine endeavoured to establish an institution with in-built guarantees against arbitrary misuse of powers such as the English system might seem to provide in her eyes through her reading of Blackstone.[8]

The participation of representatives of social groups in local government institutions, except in the administration of finance which remained firmly in government hands, was provided for by election at the lower levels, by appointment at the higher levels. A rudimentary corporate structure of the nobles and the towns was laid down in the Statute, to organise the elections: the nobles of a district met to elect a marshal, who became the lynchpin of the subsequent establishment of local noble assemblies. The towns elected a town chief, who in turn became the centre for the future development of urban corporate organisation. In these institutions we have pale shadows of Montesquieu's '*pouvoirs intermédiaires*'.

The Statute of 1775 was introduced only gradually throughout the Empire. Even so there were serious difficulties in implementing a policy which was in so many ways designed for a more advanced society than Russia. It did not take account of the enormous variation in type of population (serf or state peasant); of the presence of resident noble landowners; of the size of towns and the presence of enough educated merchants and townsmen to fill elective

7. See J.M. Hartley, 'Catherine's Conscience Court – an English equity court?' in *Russia and the West in the Eighteenth Century*, ed. A.G. Cross (Newtonville, Mass., 1983), pp. 306–18. The Conscience Courts continued to function until the 1840s.

8. See R.E. Jones, *The Emancipation of the Russian Nobility* (Princeton, 1973), p. 230; J.P. LeDonne, *Ruling Russia: Politics and Administration in the Age of Absolutism* (Princeton, 1984), p. 93.

posts; of economic potential, communications, racial homogeneity, and the need for a considerable infrastructure of surveyors, doctors, teachers, clerks, etc. Nevertheless the new institutions did bring life to provincial towns, where energetic governors proceeded to erect new stone buildings, set up schools, hospitals, inoculation centres, to open libraries, patronise the theatre, give balls and enliven social and intellectual life, and encourage manifestations of local initiative in the field of social welfare.

But in spite of the increased services available to the local inhabitants, both urban and rural, and the presence of some conscientious and honourable officials, there is little doubt that Russian local administration continued to be inefficient, corrupt, and often brutal. In spite of new attitudes of mind inculcated into the elite,[9] the mental outlook of centuries could not be changed overnight. The habits of servility to superiors and bullying of inferiors were deeply ingrained, the notion of public service as a vocation and not a burden or a means of enriching oneself still limited to the most enlightened. Even more difficult, because so alien to the Russian tradition, was the attempt to introduce the concept of legality in the judicial process. The total absence of legal training (the first professor of Russian law was appointed only in 1768) helps to account for the failure to grasp the first principles of the rule of law among even governors, whose experience was often entirely military. The efforts of the government to provide better trained officials only began to have results in the nineteenth century.

Judging by contemporary accounts, the brigandage and disorder endemic in some outlying areas was now brought under some degree of control. It is almost invariably assumed by historians that the land commissar, the lowest rural official elected by nobles to police the countryside, always acted in the interests of the nobility. Some were undoubtedly local despots, but what is known of their behaviour is almost entirely based on memoir literature, not on archival sources. Strange as it may seem, there has been scarcely any modern study, based on administrative or judicial records, of the actual functioning of any of the institutions set up in 1775. Some work has been done on a few of the Conscience Courts, but nothing is known about the work of the local government boards; there is no study of the work of any single Board of Social Welfare.[10] Thus the historian can analyse the policy but must suspend judgment on its implementation.

If the Statute of 1775 reflected the ideas of Montesquieu in the elaboration of separate institutions for the different estates, the Police Ordinance of 1782 was closely modelled on cameralist legislation. It incorporated all the aspects of paternalistic social engineering associated with the seventeenth-century concept of 'police', and included detailed rules on how the police was to perform its function of moral guidance, borrowed probably from the *Traité de la Police* of Nicolas de la Mare, which in turn resumed the experience of Louis XIV's

9. M. Raeff, *The Origins of the Russian Intelligentsia* (New York, 1966), p. 125.
10. But see J.M. Hartley, 'The Boards of Social Welfare and the financing of Catherine II's state schools', *Slavonic and East European Review* 67 (1989), 211–27.

great lieutenant of police, La Reynie.[11] Police jurisdiction was limited to trivial offences for which they were authorised to inflict minor summary punishments. All other offences had to go before the courts. In accordance with the practice of *Polizeiwissenschaft* elsewhere, the police was charged with the regulation of fire fighting, public hygiene, street lighting, weights and measures, public decency, the control of public assemblies, and the arrival and departure of strangers.

If the new system of local administration was to work at all, it had to draw on the voluntary participation of elected representatives of the free estates. Catherine therefore considered it necessary in the two Charters of 1785, to the Nobility and to the Towns, to enumerate and enact the basic civic, property, status and corporate rights of these estates, and to define their membership. From now on, nobles could not be deprived of rank, honour, property or life without trial by their peers. The noble's immunity from corporal punishment and personal taxation was confirmed.[12] Noble land was freed from any state restrictions on its exploitation, and the noble's right to buy land with serfs was expressly stated, as was his right to set up manufacturing enterprises, to leave Russian service, to travel and to serve abroad. The Charter extended the corporate rights granted in 1775, authorising the nobles in each *guberniya* to meet every three years to elect their marshal, who acted as the head of the local corporate nobility. A register of the nobles was introduced on a *guberniya* basis: the nobles were divided into six groups according to their origin, though all equal in rights, and the register was to be kept in the office of the local noble assembly. To some extent the decision as to who was a noble was thus placed in the hands of the nobles themselves. The corporate nobility was also allowed to 'make representations' to the Senate or directly to the Empress on local needs. It was this right which was used by the noble assemblies, for example in Tver, in the period leading up to the emancipation of the serfs in 1861.

The Charter to the Towns granted the same kind of personal property and civil rights to the townspeople, though corporal punishment was banned only for the wealthiest groups, namely rich merchants and entrepreneurs, and for a new category of 'distinguished citizens', mainly professional people. The Charter of 1785 also provided the towns with an elaborate system of local administration, in which elected officials took part, an extension to the towns of the provisions of the Statute of 1775.

Catherine's doctrinaire approach is illustrated by the unpromulgated Charter to the State Peasants which dated roughly from the same time. The Charter divides the peasants into six groups according to their origin in almost exactly the same terms as those used for the other social classes. It sets out their

11. Marcel Le Clère, *Histoire de la Police* (Paris, 1964), pp. 32–4.
12. The fact that nobles did not pay the poll-tax should not surprise one since it was designed for the maintenance of the armed forces, and most of the nobles served in the armed forces; even if all males had paid it, however, the total raised would not have been more than 50,000 roubles – a drop in the bucket of Russian military expense.

personal, property and civil rights, and the upper stratum of the peasantry is also granted immunity from corporal punishment. A number of provisions were made for the election of elders and the organisation of communal self-government. The sheer absurdity of the attempt to force the Russian peasantry into the same kind of social mould as the nobles and the townsmen may explain why the Charter was never promulgated. It is also possible that Catherine was persuaded to abandon a scheme that might easily lead to unrest among the serf population. Or the outbreak of the second Turkish war in August 1787 may have led her to shelve this, as so many other plans.

The decentralisation of administrative functions by transferring them to provincial centres led to the phasing out of a number of central government colleges, particularly of a commercial or economic type, such as the Colleges of Mining or Manufactures, or the College of Estates. We know that in the 1780s Catherine was thinking of a fundamental reconstruction of the central government of Russia, for which the Charters to the free estates were in some sort a preliminary. She was working on the reform of the Senate, and she even drafted a plan for an imperial council, and a high court of justice with some legislative functions, to which assessors from the nobility, the townspeople and the free peasants would be elected. These drafts were to a great extent anticipations of the projects which emerged among the advisers of Alexander II in the late 1870s. In this case we know also that Catherine laid these projects aside on the outbreak of war in 1787.[13] There was not enough qualified manpower, nor did the ageing Empress have enough energy to proceed with elaborate plans for reform in the middle of a war, and from 1787 to Catherine's death Russia was almost never at peace. The French Revolution also probably made her abandon ideas of thoroughgoing reform. Yet, if we take the Statute of 1775 and the two Charters of 1785, as well as the Police Ordinance of 1782, it is clear that many of the demands put forward in the Legislative Commission were met. The laws represented that codification which the Commission itself had failed to produce, and introduced major social and administrative changes into the structure of Russian government and society.

What remains paradoxical is that Catherine II was attempting to create and give legal form to a society of orders (*Ständegesellschaft*) at a time when this type of society was being increasingly undermined by other, more radical, centralising reformers, such as Joseph II. This was not just a question of more or less conservative opinion, but a reflection of the state of the social and economic development of Russia. The country was simply not in a position to entrust internal administration to a class of literate officials with a tradition of public service, such as had been produced by the universities of Germany for their princes. Hence administrative tasks had to be delegated to the only social group qualified by years of military experience to undertake them. By

13. M. Raeff, 'The Empress and the Vinerian Professor: Catherine II's projects of government reforms and Blackstone's *Commentaries*', *Oxford Slavonic Papers*, New Series, 7 (1974), pp. 18–41.

attaching rank and salary to the various posts, Catherine was hoping to attract the poorer nobles, who had left service, to continue to serve in the provinces. It is a matter of controversy among historians whether in delegating service in this way the state – if it existed[14] – was abdicating its rights into the hands of a power-hungry and greedy class of nobles, or whether an autonomous state maintained its ultimate control over the resources of the country, allocating the largest portion to that class, the nobles, to which it had entrusted administrative and military duties.

One of several reasons why Russia had not been able to evolve a class of competent non-noble government servants was the educational backwardness of the whole country. Peter I's attempt to introduce secular education had met with but limited success; Moscow University was only founded in 1755, and senior Russian public servants were totally untrained in law or public administration except for those (and the number was increasing) who pursued mainly government-subsidised studies in German, French, Dutch, English and Scottish universities.

Concern with education was central to Enlightenment thought, whether in absolutist Prussia and Austria, or in the Polish gentry republic. Catherine, however, was no admirer of Rousseau's educational theories; on the whole she preferred Locke, though she disagreed with him over the issue of corporal punishment, which she totally rejected. Her early experiments centred around the somewhat fanciful notions of her adviser, I.I. Betskoy, to create 'a new race of men' (and women) by sedulously shielding children from all contamination by the coarseness and brutality of the surrounding world. It was a programme suitable for an elite, but not for a national school system, which Catherine had adumbrated in the Statute of 1775. The moving spirit behind her subsequent educational reform was Joseph II, who in the course of his visit to Russia in 1780, informed her of the policy pursued in the Habsburg lands after the expulsion of the Jesuits. Joseph sent her an Austrian adviser, F. Jankovich de Mirievo, an Orthodox Serbian, expert in the methods devised by the educational reformer, Abbot Felbiger, who had applied them first in Prussian Silesia and then in the Habsburg Monarchy. Catherine's Statute of National Education of 1786 set up a comprehensive system of high schools and junior schools, free, secular, co-educational, open to all classes including serfs if they had the permission of their masters. A centrally devised curriculum was imposed, teaching aids and textbooks were produced including elaborate regulations on the duties of teachers and a textbook setting out the moral and political principles to be inculcated into the pupils, designed to produce dutiful and obedient citizens.

There was inevitably a considerable discrepancy between an ambitious plan and a more modest achievement. The Boards of Social Welfare, charged with setting up and running the schools, had neither the funds nor the staff. There

14. LeDonne argues (*op. cit.*, p. 16) that since 'the state is synonymous with the ruling class . . . it has no separate existence'.

was an enormous shortage of qualified teachers, and though they were not ill-paid compared to other public servants, and though they were given positions in the Table of Ranks, with the possibility of rising to hereditary nobility after twenty-two years service (the ladder by means of which Lenin's father rose to noble rank) the teachers were too uncouth, and the members of the Boards of Social Welfare too inexperienced to be widely successful. Moreover the education provided was still too sophisticated to respond to the basic needs of Russian townspeople, who did not demand more than the three Rs and the ability to read devotional works.

Nowhere was Catherine more truly a daughter of the Enlightenment than in her patronage of arts and letters. St Petersburg became one of the most beautiful European cities, once the banks of the Neva were clothed in granite and the canals spanned by elegant bridges. Less visible to the general public was Catherine's private sponsorship of a wide programme of translations into Russian which she subsidised to the tune of 5,000 roubles a year. In fifteen years the Translation Society formed by her was responsible for the publication of 112 translations, thus giving employment to many noble and non-noble intellectuals.[15] The works selected included the best that France could offer, selections from the *Encyclopédie*, Montesquieu's *L'Esprit des Lois*, works by Corneille, Racine, Voltaire, Mably (translated by Alexander Radishchev), and many of Rousseau's writings, though not the *Social Contract*.

The numbers and the titles published far outpaced the capacity of the reading public to absorb them, and the problem of marketing translations became crucial. It must be remembered that most cultured nobles and non-nobles could read the classics of the French and German Enlightenment in the original languages. German had not yet been ousted by French in St Petersburg – if it ever was – and there may have been a larger market for German books than for French. Indeed the works of J.G. Herder, and those of Immanuel Kant, were published in German in Riga, where Herder became head of the gymnasium before he left for Weimar, and the complete political works of Rousseau were published in Riga in German translation in 1779–82.

Catherine's critics have found it difficult to explain why in 1783 she authorised the establishment of printing presses, hitherto a state monopoly, by anyone, subject to registration with the police. The most recent scholar in the field suggests that Catherine believed that the independent presses 'posed no serious political or ideological threat to the government' and that it was the desire to let private enterprise rather than the state bear the losses on publishing which proved the most significant consideration.[16] Until 1783 the government presses were all self-censoring; after 1783 there was still no central censorship, though works had to be submitted to the local chiefs of police to ensure that they contained nothing offensive to order, religion or public decency. Until the French Revolution the Russian censorship was laxer than

15. G. Marker, *Publishing, Printing and the Origins of Intellectual Life in Russia, 1700–1800* (Princeton, 1985), p. 91.
16. *Op. cit.*, p. 108.

ever before or since, with the exception of a few years at the beginning of the reign of Alexander I. How lax it was is illustrated by the police chief's approval of Radishchev's *Journey from St Petersburg to Moscow* in 1790.

Only recently has the hitherto widely accepted account of Catherine's relationship with the publisher N.I. Novikov been revised by Soviet and non-Soviet scholars. The traditional view presupposes a duel between the elderly (she was 39 years old!) and reactionary Catherine and the 24-year-old radical Novikov, conducted in 1768 in the pages of *All Sorts of Things*, edited by Catherine's secretary, and *The Drone*, edited by Novikov. Yet it was not known at the time that the Empress took a personal part in *All Sorts of Things*. All the journals which appeared in the 1760s indulged in backbiting and satire against each other, as well as with *All Sorts of Things*.[17] It used to be stated that Catherine closed down Novikov's *The Drone* because of his attacks on her. There is no evidence to support this, whereas there is evidence that she supplied him with 200 roubles to assist him with publishing his next periodical *The Painter*, in which he published even more biting satires on uncouth nobles and impoverished serf villages. The subsequent rift between the Empress and Novikov, culminating in the latter's arrest and incarceration in Schlüsselburg in 1792, arose as a result of Novikov's participation in the Rosicrucian masonic movement, directed from Prussia, which was alleged to have attempted to recruit the Grand Duke Paul, at a time of great tension between Russia and Prussia. There is also no evidence that Catherine resented the attempt of Novikov and other Moscow masons to undertake social welfare independently of the state, though she was perturbed at the huge sums of money they seemed to dispose of.

By 1790 Catherine woke up to the dangers implicit in unrestricted publication, not only of masonic obscurantism but of revolutionary ideas. Until 1789, and well into 1790, Russians had been surprisingly well-informed about events in the United States and France. Novikov had published, in a supplement to the *Moscow Gazette*, a series of articles praising George Washington as the 'founder of a republic which will probably be the refuge of freedom, exiled from Europe by luxury and depravity'. The French 'Declaration of the Rights of Man' of 1789 was published in No. 74 of the *St Petersburg Gazette* in that same year. There were graphic descriptions of peasants burning chateaux in France, of the invasion of the French royal family's apartments in Versailles, reports of the debates in the National Assembly. French Revolutionary pamphlets, leaflets and periodicals were on sale in Russian bookshops.

The first indication of Catherine's dismay at what was being published came with Radishchev's *Journey from St Petersburg to Moscow*. It is very probable that until then she had felt able to allow tirades against foreign, or irrelevant classical, tyrants, but she drew the line at attacks on herself or her government. This explains the eventual exile of Radishchev to Siberia (in conditions

17. For a modern account of the satirical journals, see W. Gareth Jones, 'The polemics of the 1769 Journals: a reappraisal', *Canadian-American Slavic Studies*, 16 (1982), 432–3.

infinitely more comfortable than the modern gulag, since he lived with his sister-in-law and his servants, and was allowed to receive both books and money).

By 1790 even the advertisements of books for sale had to be submitted to the police,[18] and in 1791 the Academy of Science was given directives on what foreign news to publish in order to eliminate items about Russia, and to present news from France in a hostile light. Finally, in September 1796 Catherine withdrew the freedom she had once granted, and set up formal censorship of imported and locally printed books. One cannot help wondering what political events dictated this extremely severe reaction in 1796. It may not have been events in France, but the situation in Poland, where the second and third partitions had led to a veritable war against Russia which had undertones of revolutionary fervour about it.

Catherine II has on the whole been harshly treated by historians, particularly in the late nineteenth and twentieth centuries. Even non-Marxist historians have been conditioned by Marxist interpretations. Many have totally rejected her claim to be counted among the enlightened despots.[19] The somewhat disparaging portrayal of her personality and her reign now current is based on a number of issues which have been differently viewed at different times. These include the murder of her husband, her numerous lovers, the charge that she did nothing to put the 'liberal' maxims of her *Instruction* into effect, and that they were designed by a consummate hypocrite to throw dust in the eyes of the *philosophes* in Paris; that in her reign serfdom was both intensified and extended; that she brought unnecessary wars on Russia and that she partitioned Poland. Let us take them in turn.

At no time can one overlook the murder of Peter III, which casts a shadow on Catherine's reign. She did not order it, but she must have been aware that it was inevitable. She benefited from it, and was therefore an accessory after the event. The murder of a husband has always been perceived by society as a more heinous crime[20] than the murder of a son (Peter I) or of a father (Alexander I), or of the lover of one's wife (George I's Hanoverian father had it done for him). Coupled with Catherine's licentious private life, which offended Victorian susceptibilities far more than those of her own time – as Alexander Herzen put it in 1859, 'the history of Catherine cannot be read to ladies'[21] – it led historians to conclude that she was incapable of any virtuous

18. *Svodnyy katalog russkoy knigi grazhdanskoy pechati XVIII veka 1725–1800*, IV, entry 110, pp. 104–5.

19. See for instance Gabriel Ardant, 'I have not mentioned Catherine II on purpose because she cannot qualify as a reformer. She duped a certain number of great European writers . . . but she cannot fool history', in 'Financial policy and economic infrastructure of modern states and nations', in C. Tilly (ed.), *The Formation of National States in Western Europe* (Princeton, 1975) at p. 204, n. 34.

20. It counted as 'little treason' in England and the penalty was still burning alive in the eighteenth century.

21. See his introduction to the Memoirs of Princess Dashkova, repr. in Yekaterina Dashkova, *Zapiski 1743–1810*, ed. G.N. Moiseyeva (Leningrad, 1985) at p. 214.

action, let alone enlightened reform. The judgment is still repeated, even though its moral basis has been totally eroded. The permissive twentieth century may perhaps take a more charitable view of Catherine's private life. She was not in fact promiscuous, and the procession of her lovers was very orderly.

The charge that Catherine tried systematically to deceive the *philosophes* can be easily dismissed. Probably the most cultured person ever to sit on the Russian throne, and a genuine blue-stocking, she belonged by right to the cosmopolitan circle of intellectuals who subscribed to the *Correspondance Littéraire et Politique*, edited by her friend Melchior von Grimm. Her own temperament shines out in her letters to Grimm and to Voltaire – gay, witty, pragmatic, totally secular in tone. We do not know what she said to Diderot, but the notes he prepared for his discussions with her show how free and wide-ranging they were. If Diderot was disappointed in Russia, though not, it seems with Catherine herself, it was because he saw it before she had undertaken any of her great reforms, and because his visit burst the bubble of 'le mirage russe', the illusion that Russia was a blank sheet on which a *philosophe* could trace new institutions with the stroke of a pen. Diderot never commented on the Statute of 1775, and he died before the promulgation of the Charters of 1785 or the Statute on National Schools of 1786. He was in fact very ill-informed about Russia.

Similarly the charge that Catherine failed to put the maxims of her *Instruction* into effect belongs to a period when her major internal reforms were viewed from the perspective of liberal, populist or socialist historians, who never expected any good to come from the tsar. It also derives from the assumption that the *Instruction* represents a 'liberal' period in Catherine's reign. Yet there is nothing liberal in the political sense in the *Instruction*, though many of its provisions were in fact implemented in a variety of ways and little by little. The attempt to introduce the rule of law in the courts, organised on estate principles; the abolition of torture in law and to a great extent in fact; the distinction introduced between detention pending trial and imprisonment as a punishment; the introduction of release on bail, these are but a few of the specific recommendations of the *Instruction* which were put into effect. The Charters of 1785 also represent the translation into law of some of the basic ideas expressed in the *Instruction*. What Russian liberal historians missed was any attempt to establish a permanent representative institution, or to limit absolute power by means of a constitution. Catherine never for one moment contemplated any dilution of her political power, and never deceived anyone in this respect. The first attempt to force her, as a woman with but a tenuous claim to the throne, to govern in consultation with a council of high officials, appointed by her but with the right to countersign laws, was brushed aside by December 1762. But to nineteenth-century liberal historians, the Enlightenment was identified with constitutionalism. This is a highly anachronistic approach, particularly if we bear in mind that the Legislative Commission met twenty years before the American constitutional convention.

It is necessary to refine the precise meaning of the concept of Enlightenment in the context of Catherinian reform. Like her contemporaries, she believed that it was desirable to maximise and hold on to state power in order to achieve reforms necessary for the welfare of the people. Many of the policies she considered useful had their origins in German cameralism. But by the middle of the eighteenth century, they were expressed in the 'rhetoric' of the eighteenth-century Enlightenment.[22] The style of government, the language in which policies were explained, reflected the values of the Enlightenment. The classical paternalism of the 'police' state was disguised in the language of 'progress'. This is particularly noticeable in the series of edicts of the years 1775–86 which laid down the basic parameters of a uniform administration and uniform rights throughout the empire, with scant regard to historical tradition. The language of the Enlightenment is also used to support the domination of the state over the church coupled with religious toleration in practice, if not in law. Catherine asserted her right to regulate Catholic, Protestant and Moslem religious organisation, including the appointment of Catholic bishops, while the Jews were not only granted religious toleration but more extensive civil rights than anywhere in Europe at the time. The educational programme was totally secular, and priests were not allowed to teach in state schools. The regulation of health and hygiene and the provision of inoculation centres and hospitals belongs more to the world of cameralism, as does the whole undercurrent of the control of national resources, improvement of communications, the land survey, efforts to improve agriculture (including the introduction of the potato with instructions on how to cook it), the freeing of manufacture from state shackles, but the language is still that of the Enlightenment.

The most damning indictment of Catherine is that she did nothing to improve the lot of the serfs. This has increasingly become the sole criterion for judging her claim to be an enlightened despot. Again, it is a criticism which only began to be made in the second half of the nineteenth century, when the peasant question dominated Russian political thought. It was given substance and weight by the massive and scholarly study of V.I. Semevsky published in 1903.[23] It was one sentence used by Semevsky which set the general tone: under Catherine, serfdom had become more intensive, 'in depth and in extent', not his overall judgment of her policies.

Nowhere was state initiative in fact likely to be more dangerous for the government than in matters concerning the peasantry. Serfdom was fundamental to the stability of the state, and the most important tax, the poll-tax, depended for its assessment and collection on the registration of the taxpayers where they lived. But at the beginning of her reign Catherine was able to implement a policy, already adumbrated by her predecessors, namely the

22. This point is very effectively made in M. Raeff, *The Well-Ordered Police State. Social and Institutional Change Through Law in the Germanies and Russia, 1600–1800* (New Haven, Conn., 1983), p. 233.
23. *Krest'yane v tsarstvovaniye Yekateriny II* (2 vols, St Petersburg, 1901).

secularisation of the church and monastic lands, thus winning the praises of Voltaire, and turning about one million serfs into state peasants.

Serf riots tended to mark the beginning of a new reign, since there was always the hope that the new ruler would take over private estates and turn them into state lands. There had indeed been a larger number than usual of riots on serf estates in the years 1765–68. It is difficult to pinpoint the causes, but in all probability serf awareness of the manifesto freeing the nobles from compulsory service deprived serfdom of legitimacy in the eyes of the serfs since it should logically have been followed by their own emancipation. Serfs were also well aware of the calling of the Legislative Commission to which the state peasants, many of whom lived in the same districts as the serfs, were sending deputies. It was also in these years that Catherine sponsored some experimental projects on court estates, with a view to trying out new methods of land tenure, and an essay competition which launched public discussion of the peasant question.

Unrest declined in the first two years of the Turkish War, but the cumulative impact of increased conscription, higher taxation, rising prices, sporadic food shortages, the plague which raged in Moscow and South Russia in 1771–72, the resentment bred in some of the borderland Cossack hosts by 'militarisation' and the heavy-handed repression of a local but quite serious Cossack mutiny led to the great rising which goes by the name of its leader as the Pugachev Revolt. Described as a peasant war, above all in Soviet historiography, it was in fact Cossack inspired, organised and led. It drew for support on the workers and peasants attached to industrial enterprises, on disgruntled Cossacks and state peasants, on Old Believers and on non-Russian tribes such as the Bashkirs. When the revolt moved into areas in which serf estates existed or predominated, the serfs of course joined in. It was typical of the 'monarchist illusions' of the leadership that Pugachev bound his followers to him by asserting that he was the legitimate tsar, Peter III, who had survived his wife's attempt on his life, and set up a court and a government modelled on that he intended to overthrow, down to the very titles of Catherine's courtiers.

In spite of the large area over which it eventually moved, the revolt of Pugachev never acquired enough consistency to threaten the heart of Russia, and its undisciplined hordes could not stand up to professional soldiers. It was over by August 1774, and was followed by a brief but savage period of repression. In more ways than one it was a tragedy for the peasantry. Their somewhat inchoate hopes for a Cossack Utopia were defeated. And the government saw to it that no such rising should ever occur again by disbanding the wild Zaporozhian Cossack host of the Dnieper, and binding the Don Cossacks, who had not taken part, even more closely to its service. But the revolt also put paid to any attempt by the government to regulate relations between serfs and their masters on a nationwide basis. Fear of an outbreak of the same kind led Catherine to prefer to consolidate the administration of the countryside in the hands of the class both qualified and desirous of performing such duties.

More than eighty years after he made it, the time has surely come to re-examine Semevsky's verdict quoted above. For instance, the law enabling landowners to exile serfs to Siberia for settlement antedated Catherine, and it extended the same power to state peasants, church serfs and townspeople. The peasants were the only social group to preserve this power until the twentieth century. Landowners, it is true, were empowered to send serfs to hard labour in the Admiralty (not in Siberia as frequently stated) without any form of state trial, but Russian legislation was so confused that Alexander I thought this power had been withdrawn with the Statute of 1775. The most severe law, of August 1767, which prohibited complaints against landowners, except in cases of treason, on penalty of the *knut* and hard labour in the mines of Nerchinsk, repeated a provision of the Code of 1649 still in use, and seems to have been a temporary measure which was never repealed. The 'extension of serfdom' to the Ukraine is a misnomer. In the interests of uniformity, as advocated by Catherine, the poll-tax was extended both to the Baltic Provinces and to the Ukraine in 1783. This involved no change in the status of the peasants in Livonia, who were already fully enserfed. But in the Ukraine it implied the loss of the right to move from one estate to another, subject to the landowners' permission, which the peasant on privately owned land still enjoyed in theory. Whether this involved the extension to the Ukrainian landowners of the full rights of Russian landowners (sale of serfs without land, removal from one estate to another, etc.) has not been adequately explored.

Catherine has also been criticised for making grants of settled estates, i.e. land with peasants, totalling some 800,000 people of both sexes, as rewards to servitors and favourites, thus turning 'free' state peasants into serfs. Semevsky himself, however, pointed out over eighty years ago that more than three-quarters of Catherine's land grants were in fact made from estates in territories annexed from Poland in the three partitions. It was thus Polish crown peasants and church and private serfs who were granted away, in accordance with the method, traditional in a country poor in specie like Russia, of rewarding faithful service. Catherine made very few grants from Russian state peasants, and she had a further reason for distributing Polish lands, namely the desirability of introducing Russian landowners and hence officials into non-Russian lands.

The assertion frequently made that Catherine's land grants were made in order to win the support of the nobility does not hold water if one examines the dates on which the bulk of the land grants were made. Until 1772, that is to say during the early period of Catherine's reign, when she was most in need of support, some 132,000 peasants of both sexes were granted. The remaining grants all date from after 1773, when Polish lands first became available, 260,000 being granted in what was to prove the *last* year of her reign. Finally one should note that Catherine limited the number of people allowed to own serfs, and stopped all previously existing means of enserfing free men and women (including self-enserfment) which had in the past led to many abuses.

Though Catherine certainly pursued traditional Russian aims in foreign policy, attempting to complete the work Peter had left unfinished, namely the acquisition of a foothold on the Black Sea, her extremely high-handed manner of conducting foreign policy provoked both the first and the second Turkish wars at a high cost in blood and treasure. War was taken for granted in eighteenth-century Europe as a means of acquiring territory and hence power, and in this respect Catherine does not compare unfavourably with her fellow monarchs. But her role in the destruction of Poland is particularly unsavoury. It is not so much that she took the initiative in the first partition of Poland, for the first hint came from Frederick II, as well as the ultimate pressure. It is rather that the whole of her policy towards Poland, from the election of Stanislas Poniatowski onwards, created a situation which rendered partition possible and the extinction of Poland inevitable after the Polish revolution and the constitution of 3 May 1791. Though Catherine shares the guilt for the partitions with the rulers of Prussia and Austria, yet she adopted bullying tactics almost unequalled at the time.

If one is to sum up, it is time that Catherine as a ruler should be re-evaluated. She was a rational human being; she worked hard, with well-chosen advisers, whom she trusted and who stayed in their posts for decades, not one of whom was ever sent into exile even when he was dismissed. She did not go about in snuff-stained coats like Frederick the Great, or shabby uniforms like Joseph II, and her court outdid theirs in brilliance and extravagance. In private life she preferred simplicity; she lit her own fire and made her own coffee in the morning, because she disliked being waited on, and her private parties at the Hermitage were remarkable for the ease and informality which prevailed. But in public and on state occasions she still believed in using the magic of monarchy, regarding the court as a necessary mechanism of government, a means of holding the allegiance of those who hoped to win power, fortune and favour, and of impressing the illiterate multitudes. She travelled extensively in her wide domains, attempting to acquaint herself with conditions.

Perhaps her main service to Russia was that she created a framework for government and society, more civilised, more tolerant, more free than ever before or after. But she did not find it possible to improve the lot of the private serfs, and it is this contrast between the freer and more orderly life of the upper classes, and even to some extent of the state peasants, and the unreformed state of private serfdom, which produces the impression that the situation of the serfs worsened during her reign. Yet they evidently benefited too from the increase in agricultural production, the growing domestic market, the development of craft industries, and even sometimes from facilities for education and promotion.

The difficulty about making a final assessment, or embarking on a political or sociological interpretation of Catherine's reign, is that though we know a great deal about the laws she enacted, we know so little about how they actually worked in practice. Was torture really no longer used? Was corporal punishment never inflicted in state schools? What sort of justice did the new courts dispense? Were the guarantees of property, life and honour observed?

Were the rich and the powerful able to bend the law in their favour? Was Catherine merely the willing tool of a rapacious nobility, or did she, as she believed, preside over an autonomous state? In view of the present state of research we must suspend judgment for the time being. Experience suggests that practice lagged far behind theory, and many of Catherine's reforms were distorted in her reign already, and certainly in that of her son Paul, so that their ultimate import is hard to grasp. Nevertheless, in what she attempted to do, and in her style of government, she belongs clearly in the tradition of those who governed in what they believed to be the interests of the people and who go by the name of enlightened despots.

CHAPTER TEN

Catherine II and the philosophes

Historians, it seems to me, have always adopted very different attitudes towards two of the 'philosopher kings' of the eighteenth century, Frederick II and Catherine II. It is a commonplace of the historiography of Russia, whether native or foreign, that Catherine's relationships with Voltaire, Diderot, d'Alembert and others were intended to throw dust in the eyes of enlightened Europe. To my knowledge, however, Frederick II is never accused of hypocrisy, of attempting to buy himself a good press. Yet he subsidised newspapers, paid pensions to *philosophes* and entertained them in Berlin. One may well wonder indeed whether the much younger Catherine was not merely following his example.

In criticising Catherine, historians have argued that she failed to implement the policies put forward by the *philosophes.* The trouble is that those who make this criticism never trouble to point out *which* particular policy, put forward by *which philosophe*, Catherine failed to adopt. She is condemned in sweeping terms for having failed to take seriously the views of Montesquieu (the separation of powers), Rousseau (the social contract perhaps?), Diderot (who opposed the separation of powers and advocated some form of national representation), Voltaire (who approved of enlightened despotism – the so-called *Thèse royale* – in underdeveloped societies), and many others.

It is unfortunately also often the case that Western historians of ideas, experts in the work of the various *philosophes*, and who are only marginally concerned with Catherine, get their basic facts about Russia wrong. One need only turn to the chapter on Voltaire and Catherine in Peter Gay's *Voltaire's Politics*, which bases itself on G. Sacke's out-of-date and distorted interpretation of Catherine's policies and thus gives a totally false picture of her reign.[1] The same spirit can be detected in the otherwise very balanced work by

1. P. Gay, *Voltaire's Politics: The Poet as a Realist* (Princeton, 1959), pp. 171ff.: Catherine is described as 'an ambitious and energetic woman who skilfully disguised her ruthless procedures behind humanitarian rhetoric'. Gay's account, and his polemics with other historians in the footnotes, are seriously misleading.

Carolyn Wilberger on 'Voltaire's Russia'.[2] There are so many inaccuracies in the chapter dealing with Catherine and Voltaire, that it is seriously misleading. The annotator of the latest edition of Diderot's letters and writings is just as misleading and misled. Indeed one wonders sometimes why it is considered permissible for historians of the Enlightenment to take such liberties with Russian history, to take so few steps to check their facts.[3]

To return to my main subject: which of the various policies advocated by which *philosophe* should Catherine have followed? To what extent did the *philosophes* agree with each other? I propose to explore here some of these tangled relationships in the context of particular issues, starting with the triangle Voltaire–Rousseau–Catherine in their relationship with Poland, and moving on later to the more complex triangle of Catherine–Montesquieu–Diderot.

I

It is well known to all that Rousseau quarrelled with everybody, indeed, to all intents and purposes he abandoned the camp of the *philosophes*.[4] He quarrelled of course violently with Voltaire. And Voltaire, who did not in any case share Rousseau's philosophical or political views, added an extra edge of virulence to the campaign he waged against 'ce fou de Jean Jacques'. It was with real dismay that, in 1765, Melchior Grimm noted in the *Correspondance littéraire* the rumour that an anonymous work entitled *Sentiment des citoyens de Genève*, which revealed the secret that Rousseau had sent his five children by Thérèse Levasseur to the Foundling Hospital, had been written by Voltaire. He could not believe that Voltaire could sink so low. Yet Voltaire was indeed the author of this pamphlet, and was avenging himself for the fact that Rousseau had betrayed Voltaire's authorship of a violently anti-Christian work entitled *Le Sermon des cinquante*, which Voltaire had so far been able to pass off successfully as by La Mettrie.[5]

The gulf between Voltaire and Rousseau was intellectual, moral and temperamental. Voltaire was irritated by the vagueness and imprecision of Rousseau's language, by his belief in the virtues of primitive man before he

2. Carolyn H. Wilberger, 'Voltaire's Russia: Window on the East', in T. Besterman (ed.), *Studies on Voltaire and the Eighteenth Century*, CLXIV (Oxford, 1976), pp. 145ff., particularly pp. 151, 154–5.

3. Denis Diderot, *Oeuvres complètes*, 15 vols, ed. and annotated by R. Lewinter (Paris, 1971). See for instance XII, pp. 806–9 and notes, on the role of I.I. Shuvalov in the preservation of the Jesuit order in Russian-annexed Poland, and contrast with Catherine to Grimm, 16–27 May 1780 in *Sbornik Imperatorskogo russkogo istoricheskogo obshchestva (SIRIO)*, XXIII (St Petersburg, 1878), pp. 177ff. and particularly p. 182.

4. See e.g. Diderot, *Oeuvres*, XIII, p. 627, 'Note sur la désunion de Diderot et de J.-J. Rousseau': 'le citoyen Rousseau a fait sept sceleratesses à la fois, qui ont eloigné de lui tous ses amis . . . en verité cet homme est un monstre . . .'.

5. *Correspondance littéraire philosophique et critique de Grimm et de Diderot, depuis 1753 jusqu'à 1790* (Paris, 1831), IV, p. 176. J.-O. de la Mettrie (b. 1709) was a doctor two of whose works were condemned in 1745, as a result of which he went into exile in Holland and subsequently settled in Berlin under the patronage of Frederick II. He was the author of *L'Homme Machine*, one of the most systematic materialist treatises, and was by then safely dead.

had been corrupted by civilisation, and by the element of enthusiasm which infused Rousseau's deism as opposed to Voltaire's profoundly rational attitude of open-minded scepticism. Nowhere does this undercurrent of irritation, mounting to overt hostility, emerge more clearly than in the marginal notes Voltaire made on a number of works by Rousseau, notably the *Discours sur l'origine et les fondements de l'inégalité*, the *Contrat social*, and *Emile*. Rousseau's description of the original social contract, 'le pacte social', aroused Voltaire's particular scorn.

His view of *Emile* can be briefly stated: 'C'est un fatras d'une sotte nourrice en quatre tomes avec une quarantaine de pages contre le christianisme des plus hardies qu'on ait jamais écrites'. Voltaire could not sympathise with the rhapsodic tone of the vicaire savoyard, nor with Rousseau's meanderings on the beauties of religious ritual. But the crux of their disagreement on *Emile* goes back to Voltaire's criticism of the *Discours sur l'inegalité*, to Rousseau's belief in nature as against civilisation. Rousseau exclaims: 'trouvez vous qu'un enfant ainsi parvenu à sa quinzième année ait perdu les précédentes?'. Voltaire replies: 'Oui, car c'est une brute qui ne connais pas une seulle vertu socialle'.[6]

Thus the two *philosophes* disagreed on any number of subjects, including the formation of society, religion, education, and women, but more strictly relevant to the present topic are their diverging opinions on history in general and Russia in particular. These have been excellently analysed by Carolyn Wilberger in her 'Voltaire's Russia', and there is no need to go into great detail here. But one should, I think, stress that Voltaire was a historian (of sorts), which Rousseau was not. For Voltaire history was a school which taught contemporary mankind what to learn from the past, and what to condemn and discard. The standards of the most enlightened men of his own day were the only valid ones, and they were universally valid at all times and in all places. History was made by men and particularly by great men. It was the triumph of the rational man of action over the passive resistance of the dumb hordes of 'canaille'.

Voltaire's interest in Peter I and Russia began early. Peter was for him the outstanding example of the ruler who by his own almost unaided efforts – however ruthless – had moved his country forward along the continuum from primitive barbarism to civilisation. The first volume of his *Histoire de l'Empire de Russie* was published in 1762, a matter of months if not weeks before the *Contrat social* and *Emile*. It is thus quite possible that the critical remarks on Russia made by Rousseau in the *Contrat social*, which do not figure in the original draft, were added to the version since it was published after he had read Voltaire's *History*.[7]

The debate between Rousseau and Voltaire to some extent anticipates the debate between Slavophiles and Westerners. Rousseau accused Peter of having

6. For particular examples, see George R. Havens, *Voltaire's Marginalia on the Pages of Rousseau* (Columbus, Ohio, 1933), pp. 13, 15, 26, 44, 45, 68, 72, 77.
7. Wilberger, p. 203.

Westernised Russia indiscriminately, of distorting Russian national character as a result, and, by attempting to civilise her too soon, of losing the chance of civilising her for ever. Liberty once lost cannot be regained, wrote Rousseau. 'Il est pour les Nations, comme pour les hommes un tems de maturité qu'il faut attendre avant de les soumettre à des loix. . . . Les russes ne seront jamais vraiement policés parce qu'ils l'ont été trop tôt.' Peter was an imitator, not a creator. He made Germans and Englishmen when he should have made Russians. 'L'empire de Russie voudra subjuguer l'Europe et sera subjugué lui-même. Les Tartares, ses sujets ou ses voisins, deviendront ses maitres et les notres', concluded Rousseau.[8] When he read these remarks in 1762, some time before the beginning of his correspondence with Catherine, Voltaire noted in the margin: 'polisson, il te sied bien de faire de telles predictions'.[9]

If one were to sum up the controversy, both Voltaire and Rousseau started from the assumption that pre-Petrine Russia was a lawless wilderness. But for Voltaire, Peter had been a genius capable of dragging Russia screaming into the eighteenth century, while for Rousseau Russia was still too barbarous to become civilised, and in any case Western civilisation, as distinct from the development of her native culture, could only corrupt her.

Until the 1760s the attitude of both these writers to Russia had nothing to do with Catherine personally. But from her accession Catherine began to cultivate Voltaire, whose works she had long admired. It was from him that she had imbibed the cult of Henri IV (the author of the famous quip about the 'poule au pot' for which Catherine has so frequently been reviled), a cult which she also shared with Diderot. There is, however, some ambiguity from the beginning in Catherine's attitude to Rousseau. She presumably read his contributions to the *Encyclopédie*. It is probable that she read the *Contrat social* not long after its publication (and condemnation), judging by a remark of hers in a letter to Voltaire of 15 October 1763. Referring to Rousseau's prophecy in the *Contrat social* that Russia would one day be subjugated by her Tartar subjects, Catherine replied 'Je répondrai à la prophétie de Jean Jacques Rousseau en lui donnant, je l'espère, aussi longtemps que je vivrai, un démenti fort impoli'.[10] It is true that in 1763 the French edition of *Emile* was banned in Russia, together with a life of Peter III and a work with the unusual title *Lettres juives* . . .[11] But the ban against *Emile* was directed in Russia, as in France, Geneva and Berne, against the *profession de foi* of the savoyard vicar, with its total rejection of revealed religion, and it seems to have been very soon forgotten, since a translation of the *profession de foi* appeared on its own, in 1770.

8. Rousseau, *Contrat social*, in *Oeuvres complètes*, IV (Paris, 1964), p. 386.
9. Havens, p. 55.
10. Rousseau, *loc. cit.*; Catherine to Voltaire, in W. Reddaway, *Documents of Catherine the Great. The Correspondence with Voltaire and the Instruction of 1767 in the English Translation of 1768* (Cambridge, 1931), p. 1.
11. *SIRIO*, VII, p. 317, Catherine to Glebov. The last work was probably the Marquis d'Argens's *Lettres Juives ou correspondance philosophique, historique et critique, entre un juif voiageur en differents Etats de l'Europe et ses Correspondans en divers Endroits*, 6 vols (The Hague, 1783). (I owe this reference to Professor L. Lewitter.)

Most of Rousseau's other works, including the *Discours sur l'origine de l'inégalité*, were published in Russian translation – in full or abridged – during Catherine's reign.[12] And though the *Contrat social* did not appear (it did after all contain very unflattering reflections on Russia), there is no record of any prohibition of its translation. A few years later, moreover, in 1765, after Rousseau's quarrel with David Hume, Grigorii Orlov issued a pressing invitation to Rousseau to make his home in Russia – an invitation which cannot have been made without Catherine's approval. Rousseau declined it and resisted all further pressure to visit Russia.[13]

It was Catherine herself who first indirectly approached the patriarch of Ferney, and it was natural for Voltaire to transfer to Catherine the admiration he had felt for Peter I, once he was sure that her seat on the throne was secure. But what particularly brought the old man and his young disciple together was an aspect of Catherine's mentality and political programme which was after Voltaire's own heart.

It is difficult today to recreate the atmosphere of deep hatred and loathing of Christianity in general, organised religion in particular, and especially Catholicism, which prevailed within some groups among the *philosophes* and was to culminate in the proscription of the Catholic Church in France in 1793. We must remember that censorship was largely religious. It was not for their political doctrines, but because they undermined the foundations of the faith, that the *Encyclopédie, De l'Esprit* of Helvétius, or *Emile* were banned. It was in France that the Huguenot Calas was broken on the wheel in March 1762 for allegedly murdering his son when the latter expressed a wish to be converted to Catholicism. It was in France in 1766 that the nineteen-year-old Chevalier de la Barre was convicted, together with a seventeen-year-old friend, of blasphemy, namely mutilating a wooden cross. The two youths were typical eighteenth-century hooligans, out to challenge the establishment. But their offence was not explained away by social factors, such as unemployment or relative deprivation. De la Barre was sentenced to be burnt at the stake after various barbarous mutilations, a sentence which was carried out in full on 1 July 1766 – a copy of Voltaire's *Dictionnaire philosophique*, said by the young man to have led him astray, was burnt together with his body.[14]

Such incidents roused Voltaire to paroxysms of fury difficult to measure, and rendered more acute by the ever-present fear for himself – hence his refusal to acknowledge the authorship of many of his works (and his rage against Rousseau for betraying his authorship of one of them); hence his campaign, throughout his life, for religious tolerance, for the separation of the church

12. See *Svodnyi katalog russkoi knigi grazhdanskoi pechati XVIII veka*, 5 vols (Moscow, 1962–68), *passim*.
13. See A. Lortholary, *Le mirage russe en France au XVIIIe siècle* (Paris, 1951), pp. 245–6. See also Iu.M. Lotman, 'Russo i russkaia kul'tura XVIII veka', in *Epokha Prosveshcheniia* (Leningrad, 1967), pp. 208–81, and, above all, pp. 215–16, n. 24, where Lotman states that discussion of the doctrines of popular sovereignty and of the social contract were not at this period banned by the censorship.
14. Gay, pp. 278–80.

from the state, for state control of the church, of all churches; hence his more generic campaign against the Catholic Church, summed up in his slogan, 'écrasez l'infame'.

The policy of religious toleration appealed also to Catherine, who was temperamentally opposed to persecution for the sake of persecution in any field, who regarded torture as counter-productive as well as uncivilised and hated cruelty. She could not, however, embark immediately on her accession on a policy of religious toleration. Her position in her early days was too insecure, she needed the support of the Church, she had put herself forward as the guardian of Orthodoxy. In practice, however, throughout her reign her influence was thrown into the scales in favour of toleration whenever practicable (though she may have concealed from Voltaire the fact that prosecutions for blasphemy or sacrilege still actually took place in Russia).[15] The Soviet scholar Iu. Ia. Kogan mentions a number of cases of prosecutions for blasphemy in the second half of the eighteenth century – cases which reached the capital by appeal or by reference to the Tainaia ekspeditsiia. In none of the cases he quotes was corporal punishment inflicted unless the accused was also charged with *lèse majesté* – the two frequently went together since unseemly references to the queen of heaven were easily followed by similar outbursts against the queen of the earth. One case in particular illustrates the process: a *kantseliarist*, Petr Borshchevskii, of Glukhov, son of a Cossack *sotnik*, allowed himself to revile the Empress and her various works and also declared that God had no mother. Arrested and charged, Borshchevskii put up the usual defence that he was drunk. The lower *rasprava* court condemned him to death; the higher *rasprava* court upheld the conviction but altered the punishment to 200 strokes of the whip, nostril clipping, and hard labour on the Dnieper line. The criminal court of the *guberniya* upheld both conviction and sentence, but the local people were reluctant to carry it out on a nineteen-year-old and sent the case to the Procurator General in 1783. His sentence confirmed by Catherine was eight days on bread and water and six months in a monastery to confirm him in the faith.[16] Clearly the closer to the throne, the lighter the penalty.

Voltaire was impressed by the speed with which Catherine revived and put through a policy dear to his heart, namely the secularisation of the estates of the Church. He had greatly admired the subordination of church to state enacted by Peter I. Catherine was now completing the task – already once begun by Peter III – by freeing one million serfs and turning priests into paid servants of the state. And it was Voltaire's hatred of Rome which led him to support Catherine's policy of securing political rights for the dissidents in Poland. The

15. Catherine certainly seems to have indulged in prevarication in connection with the activities of the church courts. She assured Voltaire that there were no 'billets de confession' in Russia. This was in fact not true, since a certificate of annual communion in a parish church was required as a means of searching out Old Believers. See Reddaway, *Documents*, p. 112, Catherine to Voltaire, 24 May/4 June 1771.

16. Iu.Ia. Kogan, *Ocherki po istorii russkoi ateisticheskoi mysli* (Moscow, 1962), pp. 93–5.

tale of his descent into the Polish imbroglio has been told by A. Lortholary, but he was not alone in supporting Catherine. Helvétius for instance wrote: 'qui dans ce moment même ebranle le trone de Constantinople et ravage la Pologne? Le fanatisme. C'est lui qui, défendant au catholique polonais d'admettre le dissident au partage de ses privilèges, ordonne de préférer la guerre à la tolerance . . . Le papisme est l'auteur caché des malheurs de la Pologne.'[17]

Soyez donc triomphante
Et du saint père et du mufti,

wrote Voltaire to Catherine, underlining thus his equal hatred of the oppressors of classical Greece and of classical Rome.[18] Pamphlet after pamphlet, impromptu or commissioned, was churned out by his facile pen. Yet Voltaire was not primarily defending Russia. He was attacking the Catholic Church. His weakness was seized on by Frederick II who knew him well. Writing to him on 12 January 1772, Frederick slyly recalled the terrible enemies of Henri IV during the sixteenth-century wars of religion: 'Vous savez donc que mes confédérés, moins braves que vos ligueurs, mais aussi fanatiques, n'ont pas voulu leur céder en forfaits . . . Montesquieu aurait perdu son temps à trouver chez eux les principes des republiques ou des gouvernements souverains . . . Au lieu de philosophes vous y trouvez des esprits abrutis par la plus stupide superstition, et des hommes capables de tous les crimes que des lâches peuvent commettre.'[19] Frederick enclosed in this letter a few cantos from a poem, a *Pologniade*, which he was writing, which for lack of taste is hard to beat.

In Voltaire's honour be it said, however, that he had not expected his championship of Catherine to culminate in a partition of Poland. Partition had so often been talked of in the past, as far back as the days of Peter I, that perhaps he was slow to recognise the signs that it was actually happening. His first reference is in a letter to Catherine of 29 May 1772. He speaks of Catherine taking the noble role of destroying the anarchy in Poland – 'en rendant à chacun ce que chacun croit lui appartenir, et en commençant par elle même' – and expresses the hope that one day she will advance to liberate Byzantium. Frederick II, who attributed the partition entirely to the moderation of Catherine, invited Voltaire to commemorate her achievements: 'C'est à votre muse à la celebrer dignement. Je ne fais que balbutier en ébauchant son éloge.'[20]

The partition of Poland divided the camp of the *philosophes*. The great names, d'Alembert, Grimm, vociferously approved. D'Alembert went about reciting Frederick II's *Pologniade* in the French salons; Grimm rejoiced that

17. Helvétius, quoted in Lortholary, p. 110.
18. Reddaway, *Documents*, p. 25, Voltaire to Catherine, 26 February 1769.
19. Frederick to Voltaire, 12 January 1772, in Voltaire, *Oeuvres*, ed. L.E.D. Moland (Paris, 1877–85), XLVIII, p. 4. See also Frederick II, *Oeuvres*, XIV (Berlin, 1850), pp. 183–236, 'La guerre des confédérés, Poème', dedicated to the Pope, in six cantos.
20. Reddaway, *Documents*, pp. 161–2; Voltaire, *Oeuvres*, XLVIII, p. 173, 16 September 1772.

'tout s'arrangera au grès des prelats prussiens, autrichiens et russes inspirés par le Saint Esprit'.[21] But there were those like Mably, Mercier and Mme du Deffand who were loud in their condemnation of this breach of international law.

Thus far Catherine had shown herself a faithful disciple of Voltaire. And the old man of Ferney had remained wedded to his belief in the '*thèse royale*', the theory that, in relatively large and undeveloped countries, an enlightened absolute monarchy was the only means of achieving good government. Against this background it is instructive to compare Voltaire with Rousseau. For whereas the Jesuit-educated Voltaire became an ardent champion of the partitioning powers, the ex-Calvinist Rousseau became the adviser of the Confederate Poles. His *Considérations sur le gouvernment de Pologne et sur sa réformation projetée* was probably written in 1771, at a time when Voltaire and Grimm were conducting their propaganda campaign against the Confederate government in France. He was approached by Claude Carloman de Rulhière (he who had written the suppressed *Anecdotes* on Catherine's seizure of power), who was not only an old acquaintance of Rousseau's but also a protégé of the deeply anti-Russian Choiseul. Rulhière had been engaged in writing his *Histoire de l'anarchie de Pologne* for the edification of the Dauphin, and was in touch with M. Wielhorski, one of the Confederate leaders. It was he who put Wielhorski in touch with Rousseau, and the latter could not fail to respond to the appeal of the Poles, fighting for their nation, as he had responded earlier to the Corsicans. Wielhorski provided Rousseau with material on the history of Poland in general, and on the Confederate programme, including their manifesto of November 1769 which had aroused Voltaire's ire, an essay by Mably who had spent a year in Volhynia and was reasonably well informed on Poland, and other materials. But Rousseau's *Considérations* were overtaken by events. The fall of Choiseul in December 1770 led to the dismissal of Rulhière, and was followed in early 1772 by the first partition. By April 1772, Rousseau's text, which he had been promised would remain secret, was already circulating in manuscript, and it was reviewed by Grimm in the *Correspondance littéraire* of January–February 1773.[22] It was finally published for the first time in 1782, after Rousseau's death.

The *Considérations* were intended for Poland, but some of Rousseau's proposals are of a more general application. He was after all trying to apply the principles of the *Contrat social* to a concrete case, yet the concrete case, the Polish Commonwealth, in its confederate version, bore little resemblance to the ideal Republic of Sparta. This is not the time or the place to analyse this work in detail, but some of Rousseau's recommendations should be quoted. Always a defender of national identity, Rousseau urged the Poles to keep alive

21. Lortholary, p. 114. D'Alembert greatly admired Frederick's poem. 'Je connais quelques philosophes qui ont pris en pitié ces pauvres confédérés' . . . he wrote to Frederick on 2 January 1772. Frederick replied on 26 January: 'je plains les philosophes qui s'interessent à ce peuple méprisable à tous les egards'. Cf. *Oeuvres*, XXIV, pp. 553 and 556.

22. *Correspondance littéraire*, VI, pp. 335ff. For the *Considérations*, see Rousseau, *Oeuvres*, III, pp. 951–1041.

their devotion to the Republic and to their nationhood by means even of the maintenance of their national costume. No Pole should appear at court dressed in French style, he recommended, and he criticised Peter the Great for his reckless abandonment of Russian national customs and dress. The spirit of the Confederation of Bar must permeate the whole of Poland, wrote Rousseau, if Poland is to be free. 'If you cannot stop them [your neighbours] from swallowing you, become at least difficult to digest.'[23]

Rousseau did not advocate total social equality. There should be distinctions of rank, but all the people should join in public festivals, and great differences of wealth should be avoided (though Rousseau realised this might be difficult). Education too should be national, designed to create Poles, and should be the same for all. In the political sphere Rousseau admitted some degree of representation because of the existence of the binding mandate in Poland. 'L'Angleterre qui jouit du premier de ces avantages a perdu sa liberté pour avoir negligé l'autre', he wrote.[24] 'Si les Confédérations ont sauvé la patrie [Poland] ce sont les diétines qui l'ont conservée et c'est là qu'est le vrai palladium de leurs libertés'[25] (i.e. the reverse of democratic centralism). His warnings against a hereditary monarchy, his preference for open as against secret voting (since the representative is bound by his electors) and his interpretation of the *liberum veto* go back to the *Contrat social*. In Book IV, Ch. II he had written: 'Il n'y a qu'une seule loi qui par sa nature exige un consentement unanime. C'est le pacte social.' Thus, in the Polish context, unanimity was necessary for the constitutive laws which formed the body politic, and could continue to be used for constitutional matters. But the *liberum veto* was oppressive in other fields.[26]

There is one remarkable chapter in the *Considérations*, entitled 'Vice Radical'. Here he warns against chimerical enterprises. Is it possible, he asks, to 'reformer le gouvernement de Pologne, c'est à dire donner à la constitution d'un grand royaume la consistance et la vigueur de celle d'une petite republique?'. The size of nations and states, he exclaimed, were the source of all evils which undermined 'les peuples policés'. Small states, whether republics or monarchies, prospered *because* they were small. In large countries delegation was essential, which leads to oppression. It was surprising, went on Rousseau, that a large country like Poland had remained in a state of anarchy rather than foundering in despotism: 'Commencez par reserrer vos limites si vous voulez réformer votre gouvernement. Peut-être vos voisins songent à vous rendre ce service [the first hint at the partition]. Ce seroit sans doute un grand mal pour les parties demembrées; mais ce seroit un grand bien pour le corps de la nation.' Thus Rousseau advised the Poles to reduce the size of the country, and to base their government on the dietines, and he further proposed that they should adopt a federative system.

23. Rousseau, *Oeuvres*, III, p. 962.
24. *Ibid.*, p. 975.
25. *Ibid.*, p. 979.
26. *Ibid.*, IV, p. 440.

It will have been noted that Rousseau's effort to adapt the *Contrat social* to the Confederation of Bar does not offer much in the way of practical advice to enlightened despots or indeed to unenlightened ones, or even to confederated Poles. But there is one remarkable paragraph which Catherine seized on at once when she read this work. It occurs in the section discussing the 'orders' of which Poland was composed. Traditionally they were the King, the nobility and the Senate. Rousseau, however, expressed his preference for a division into 'les nobles qui sont tout, les bourgeois qui ne sont rien, et les paysans qui sont moins que rien'. Turning to the problem of serfdom he showed his awareness of the difficulties implicit in emancipation. He feared not only the self-interest of the masters, but also 'les vices et la lâcheté des serfs'. The whole page is worth quoting:

> La liberté est un aliment de bon suc mais de forte digestion; il faut des estomacs bien sains pour le supporter. Je ris de ces peuples avilis qui, se laissant ameuter par des ligueurs, osent parler de liberté sans même en avoir l'idée, et, le coeur plein de tous les vices des esclaves, s'imaginent que pour être libres il suffit d'être des mutins. Fière et sainte liberté! Si ces pauvres gens pouvoient te connaître, s'ils savoient à quel prix on t'acquiert et te conserve, s'ils sentoient combien tes loix sont plus austères que n'est dur le joug des tyrans; leurs foibles âmes, esclaves des passions qu'il faudroit étouffer, te craindroient plus cent fois que la servitude; ils te fuiroient avec effroi comme un fardeau prêt à les écraser.
>
> Affranchir les peuples de Pologne est une grande et belle opération, mais hardie, périlleuse et qu'il ne faut pas tenter inconsidérément. Parmi les precautions à prendre, il en est une indispensable et qui demande du tems. C'est avant toute chose, de rendre dignes de la liberté et capables de la supporter les serfs qu'on veut affranchir. . . . songez que vos serfs sont des hommes comme vous . . . n'affranchissez leur corps qu'après avoir affranchi leurs âmes.[27]

'La liberté n'etant pas un fruit de tout les climats n'est pas a la portée de tous les peuples. Plus on médite ce principe etabli par Montesquieu, plus on en sent la vérité', Rousseau had written in the *Contrat social* (Book III, Ch. VIII). Is it surprising that Catherine should take him at his word?

In a letter to Grimm, of 12 May 1791, i.e. just after the Polish Revolution of 3 May, Catherine underlined the connection of these Polish events with Rousseau's *Considérations*, stressing particularly the warning about liberty which Rousseau had given in the paragraphs quoted above. Events in Poland were 'bien propre à discrediter pour longtemps la liberté et à la rendre odieuse à tous les peuples . . . Rousseau a dit: je ne sais ou, si vous voulez être libres, preparez vous a supporter non seulement les épouvantables malheurs qui vous y mèneront, mais encore ceux qui accompagnent et sont la suite de la liberté.' In a note attached to this letter, she copied out the sentence beginning: 'fière

27. *Ibid.*, III, p. 974.

et sainte liberté' and then added: 'NB: il est bon de lire ce qui précéde cette exclamation; cela n'est pas moins juste. Frottez les nez camus de ça.'[28]

But it is with regard to the more acute problem of serfdom that Rousseau's words are particularly relevant. For in this quotation, he takes the side of those who believed that emancipation could only come after the serfs had been raised to the status of men, and not the side of those who believed that in order to raise serfs to the level of men, they should *first* be freed; he took the side of Princess Dashkova (in her conversation with Diderot)[29] rather than that of G. Korob'in, whoever he may have been the spokesman of in the Legislative Commission.[30]

II

I would like now to turn to the second of my two examples, namely the triangle Catherine–Montesquieu–Diderot. The link between Catherine and Montesquieu needs no elaboration. However, the link between Montesquieu and Diderot is perhaps less well known and deserves close scrutiny. First of all, I would like to place the relationship between Catherine and Diderot in its proper setting, something which to my mind none of the authors who have dealt with the matter has done.[31] There are three relevant periods: up to 1773; Diderot's actual visit to St Petersburg in 1773–74; and the years after 1774 to his death in 1783.

Until his visit to Russia Diderot's attitude to Catherine expressed admiration conditioned by gratitude. Her religious policy and the summoning of the Legislative Commission were in themselves enough to win the admiration of *philosophes* living in the France of Louis XV. For in France there was severe ecclesiastical censorship, and Diderot was deeply depressed at the course political events had taken when Chancellor Maupeou dissolved the Parlements in 1770 and replaced them by a network of royal courts. It is extremely significant of the political gulf between Diderot and Voltaire, that whereas Diderot saw the destruction of the Parlements as the victory of royal despotism over popular institutions which protected Frenchmen from the exercise of arbitrary power (and which also of course comprised valuable pieces of property),

28. *SIRIO*, XXIII, pp. 537 and 538, note 2. Rousseau's responsibility for revolutionary literature was clear to Catherine. 'Rousseau les a mis à quatre pattes', she wrote to Grimm, commenting on the literary and political disorder in Paris. *Ibid.*, pp. 517ff. at p. 520, 29 April 1791.
29. See K. Fitzlyon (ed.), *The Memoirs of Princess Dashkov* (London, 1958), p. 122: '. . . when the lower classes of my fellow citizens become more enlightened they will deserve to be free . . .'. It is noteworthy that in his extremely scholarly study of Rousseau's influence in Russia (see above, note 13) Lotman does not mention the *Considérations sur le gouvernement de Pologne* at all. It is as though Rousseau had never written this work.
30. There is still considerable controversy among Soviet scholars as to whether Korob'in was the mouthpiece of Catherine in the Commission. See I. de Madariaga, *Russia in the Age of Catherine the Great* (London, 1981), pp. 175ff.
31. E.g. V.A. Bil'basov, *Didro v Peterburge* (St Petersburg, 1884, reprint Newtonville, Mass., 1972, with an introduction by A. Lentin); D. Diderot, *Mémoires pour Catherine*, ed. and introduced by P. Vernière (Paris, 1966); M. Tourneux, *Diderot et Catherine II* (Paris, 1899).

Voltaire welcomed the abolition of the Parlements as bastions of unrepresentative privilege arrogating powers to themselves which they did not possess, meting out the sort of justice which had led to the death sentences on Calas and de la Barre.

In his personal relations with Catherine, Diderot could not but be grateful for the purchase of his library (he needed money for a good dowry for his daughter). Catherine moreover had offered to help the publication of the *Encyclopédie*. Diderot gave her artistic and literary advice, and tried to help her by suppressing the *Anecdotes* of Rulhière.

Some authors have suggested that Diderot's views on Russia can already be gleaned from the references to Russia in Raynal's *Histoire des deux Indes* in the 1770 edition. This seems unlikely for Diderot only began to contribute in 1772. In the 1770 edition, however, Raynal makes himself the echo of Rousseau. Russia for him is a vast unpeopled desert, without laws, liberty, wealth or industry; in the last century Russia had gone back rather than forward; the great lawgiver (Peter) had exhausted it in forming an army, a navy and a port, and his heirs had completed the ruin in order to keep up these vain and unnecessary establishments.[32]

We come to the second phase, to Diderot in Russia: whom did he meet there? Where did he get his information from? This extremely important aspect of his attitude to things Russian has not been sufficiently explored. We know that he saw Catherine, that he addressed a number of questions to her – very detailed questions on population, industry, agriculture, social structure. Many of these Catherine answered herself and some of her answers are very revealing: Diderot for instance was quite wrong about Russian social structure, which he saw as divided into ecclesiastics, nobles, '*adnodworzi*' (free men) and peasants. Catherine put him right, pointing out that the Russian 'estates' were the Church, the nobility, with exclusive right to ownership of land, townspeople, with exclusive right to trade, and peasants of two kinds, i.e. those who owned and cultivated land, and the subjects of the nobility, 'apart from crown peasants and one-homesteaders'. (It is of these wealthy *odnodvortsy* incidentally, not of serfs, that Catherine repeated to Diderot Henri IV's quip which she had once quoted to Voltaire, saying that they could eat turkey every day since chicken was too common.) Questions dealing primarily with foreign trade and tariffs Catherine referred to Count Munich.[33]

Who else do we know that Diderot actually met? Obviously Falconet, not a reliable friend, not a very reliable source;[34] young A. Naryshkin, kind, but not

32. Abbé G.T.F. de Raynal, *Histoire des deux Indes* (Amsterdam, 1770), II, pp. 204–5. Raynal's unfavourable view of Russia may also be derived from Le Mercier de la Rivière – see the latter's letter to Raynal from St Petersburg, 19/30 October 1767: 'tout est à faire dans ce pays. Pour parler mieux encore il faudrait dire tout est à défaire et à refaire': Bil'basov, pp. 149ff. Wilberger, p. 247, points out that this passage is omitted in the 1774 and 1780 editions of Raynal, when Diderot's 'expert' knowledge could be drawn upon.

33. Diderot, *Oeuvres*, X, pp. 811ff.; Tourneux, pp. 532ff.

34. See the *Correspondance de Falconet avec Catherine II 1767–1778*, ed. by L. Réau (Paris, 1921), *passim*.

a luminary; the Vice-Chancellor, Prince A.M. Golitsyn, cousin of Diderot's friend D.A. Golitsyn at The Hague; Dr. N.-G. Le Clerc, professor at the Academy of Fine Arts. His circle of acquaintance was in fact extremely limited. The Grand Duke, for instance, would have nothing to do with such a libertine.[35] His most frequent Russian companions seem to have been I.I. Betskoy and his daughter, Anastasia Sokolova, one of the Empress's favourite maids of honour. What could he learn from them? Much about Betskoy's educational establishments (he visited the Smol'nyi Institute with Catherine). But also something about the temper of the great figures at the Russian court. It is not amiss to quote here from a report by the French envoy, Durand de Distroff, to his principal in Paris, of 24 September 1773, i.e. not long before Diderot's arrival in St Petersburg. Durand reports on the discussion of an episode in which the police chief N.I. Chicherin was alleged to have been responsible for the beating up of some servants belonging to a magnate in the course of carrying out an arrest of one of them. What can they do, exclaimed the three magnates, whose words Durand reports, to prevent this sort of thing? And they gave the reply themselves: 'C'est nous réunir en corps et faire voire à l'impératrice l'indécence, l'injustice, et les suites funestes d'une violence semblable'. But when one of these magnates complained to Catherine, she merely replied: 'Je ne mets aucune difference entre mes sujets, pourquoi voulez vous que Cziczerin y en mette. Il n'a pas tort. Il faut que justice se fasse.' The disgruntled trio then continued to bewail the fact that the only privilege granted to the nobility by the manifesto of 1762 was that of hanging about in waiting rooms.

> L'oukase de la liberté . . . nous a rendus amphibes . . . nous a fait indistinctement rats de terre et rats d'eau . . . nous n'avons point d'existence, nous ne sommes rien de solide, on nous confonds avec les derniers maroufles, on nous hausse, on nous baisse selon le caprice ou le moment de faveur. Il n'y a pas plus de vraie noblesse en Russie actuellement qu'il n'y a de justice, d'honneur, de droit des gens. . . . Comment est-il possible qu'on se pique des beaux sentiments, de philosophie . . . et qu'on se conduise ainsi. Comment peut-on se laisser mener par les discours des Orlows, des Weszemki, des Cziczerin, gens ignorans, grossiers et à mauvais conseil?

Durand's own opinion was that between ruler and people there were only 'des oppresseurs et tyrans subalternes. La liberté donnée à la noblesse, les privilèges qu'on accorde à des entreprises, les Loix projettées a grands frais ne sont que les scènes du théatre despotique ou jouent toujours les ministres. On en murmure et le chagrin doit être grand pour que des gens en place se fassent des confidences mutuelles.'[36]

35. D. Kobeko, *Tsesarevich Pavel Petrovich* (St Petersburg, 1883), p. 107. See also Sir Robert Gunning's despatches of 22 November 1773 and 7 April 1774 in *SIRIO*, XIX, pp. 339, 397–8.
36. Archives des Affaires Etrangères, Quai d'Orsay, Correspondance Politique, Russie, vol. 93, Durand de Distroff to d'Aiguillon, 20 November 1773.

In a much later dispatch Durand revealed the names of the three who took part in the conversation he quoted at such length. They were the Vice-Chancellor A.M. Golitsyn, Betskoy and Anastasia Sokolova. These were therefore the sort of sentiments and opinions which Diderot was likely to hear from those he saw most of at the Russian court. Thus he would have been led to believe that there was a strong undercurrent of frustrated demand for aristocratic participation in decision-making, and resentment against the levelling absolutism of the Empress. Diderot also probably heard through Grimm or through Durand of the tensions surrounding the majority of the Grand Duke in 1773 and the mysterious plots and counter-plots centring around Saldern at the time.[37] He attended some private and diplomatic receptions, became friendly with the Swedish envoy, met members of the Academy, but in his letters (which are rare) he mentions very few names.

Let us now briefly look at events in Russia and in Europe at the time of Diderot's visit.[38] He arrived in Russia on the eve of the wedding of the Grand Duke, when Catherine edged Nikita Panin out of his post as tutor to the heir to the throne. The Pugachev Revolt was still a distant cloud on the horizon, which grew only too quickly in the autumn and winter of 1773–74. Orenburg was only relieved in March. Secondly, by autumn 1773, Catherine knew that a further campaign against the Turks lay ahead, with all the stresses and strains involved in war. Thirdly, it was just at this period, December 1773–January 1774, that the current favourite Vasil'chikov was dismissed, and Catherine's great love affair with Potemkin began. No wonder that in the winter months Catherine saw less of Diderot. But strangely enough, Potemkin's name is never mentioned by the *philosophe* in his correspondence, then or later, though Diderot showed his usual unexampled tact when he advised Catherine to send the Grand Duke Paul on a tour of the Russian Empire escorted by one of the Orlovs.[39] If we turn to France the picture was very dark: Diderot was bitterly opposed to the dissolution of the Parlements in 1770; he feared for 'la France avilie', and hoped that in Russia he might find a monarch more respectful of the rights of her subjects.

To sum up: Diderot's information about Russia was very limited; he saw nothing of the country, he appears never to have visited an estate. He saw only St Petersburg, and he saw it in winter. He left before the thaw, in March 1774, and it was on his return journey, while he was staying again at The Hague, that he wrote the *Observations sur le Nakaz*. He mentioned that he was

37. See my summary in *Russia in the Age of Catherine the Great*, pp. 260–1. The full story is not yet unravelled.
38. A. Lentin's Introduction to the 1972 reprint of Bil'basov's *Didro v Peterburge* unfortunately contains a number of errors. During Diderot's visit, Pugachev was nowhere near the Volga (p. 20); Catherine could not think of disinheriting Paul in favour of Alexander I before Paul had even married his first wife (p. 21); Lentin fails to distinguish between the *Mémoires pour Catherine*, written for Catherine to see herself, and the *Observations* which Diderot could send to her or not as he chose (pp. 25–6), and erroneously states that Catherine received a copy of the *Observations* in 1776, whereas she saw them only after the death of Diderot. Moreover it is really farcical to speak of Diderot's 'first-hand knowledge of Russia'.
39. Diderot, *Mémoires*, pp. 69ff.

making some note on the *Nakaz* in two letters to Catherine in 1774, but she did not take him up, and the knowledge that he was writing something she might never see probably gave greater freedom to his pen.

It must be remembered that Catherine wrote her *Nakaz* in 1765–66, and Diderot's systematic comments were written in 1774. The time-lag accounts for some of the irrelevance of Diderot's remarks. He criticises Catherine, for instance, for having omitted any mention of her educational establishments in the *Nakaz*. But these had only barely been founded at the time she was writing.

There is, however, one fundamental aspect of Diderot's criticisms which has not been sufficiently highlighted. We know that Catherine borrowed 294 of the articles in the *Nakaz* from Montesquieu, usually copying his formulations quite literally, and she took 108 articles from Cesare Beccaria's *Delle delitte e delle pene.*[40] Diderot commented in the *Observations* on 169 articles in the *Nakaz*. A rough count shows that over 100 articles which he commented on or criticised were lifted bodily from Montesquieu, and over 20 were drawn from Beccaria; a few more come from Bielfeld's *Institutions politiques*. Much therefore of Diderot's criticism goes beyond Catherine's political views to those of her principal mentor, Montesquieu, with whose society of orders Diderot was totally out of sympathy.

It is these *Observations*, addressed in great part to Montesquieu, together with Diderot's contributions to Raynal's *Histoire des deux Indes*, which are usually interpreted as showing Diderot's utter disillusionment with Catherine, Russia and enlightened despotism. The *Mémoires* he wrote for Catherine belong to an entirely different category, though equally interesting as expositions of Diderot's own ideas. They were papers prepared for discussion with the Empress at the time. Even so, Diderot is very outspoken in many of his proposals, even if he is more cautious in his criticisms.

Let us look more closely at some of Diderot's comments on the *Nakaz*. The extent to which he is concerned with the nature of power is very apparent. On the statement in article 19 of the *Nakaz* (quoted literally from *L'Esprit des loix*, II, 4), that 'le souverain est la source de tout pouvoir politique et civil', Diderot comments: 'je n'entends pas cela', and he continues to expound his deeply felt view that power comes from the people, or 'la nation' assembled in some representative form. Similarly the acceptance by Catherine of Montesquieu's formula that sovereign power implies channels through which power *runs down* is rejected by Diderot. 'Je n'aime pas cette façon de voir; elle a une odeur de despotisme qui me deplait.' He believed that fundamental laws could only really be safeguarded against overthrow in a state where these channels transmitted the general will of the people *upwards* from the people to the sovereign, and where they could not be blocked by bribery or destroyed by the ruler. Fundamental laws in any event seemed to him at that time very slender guarantees against arbitrary despotism, in view of the dissolution of

40. The standard work is N.D. Chechulin, *Nakaz Imperatritsy Ekateriny II dannyi kommissii po sochineniiu proekta novogo ulozheniia* (Moscow, 1907).

the Parlements in France. Thus Diderot was more and more convinced of the necessity for a ruler to dispossess himself of part of his power in favour of a representative assembly with fairly limited rights. The sovereign must be a caretaker, a good housekeeper, bound by the laws made by the people. It is an essentially democratic vision which floats before Diderot's eyes. In the *Mémoires pour Catherine*, he had urged the Empress to keep the Legislative Commission in being (and Catherine in 1773–74 had not yet perhaps finally decided not to recall it; it was the Pugachev Revolt which turned her away from political to administrative methods of reform). But when Diderot turns from the theoretical criticisms in the *Mémoires* to practical proposals in the *Observations*, we find echoes of the aristocratic constitutionalism which he has heard of from his Russian friends. 'Qui doit composer ce corps', he asks (the representative body which is to receive part of the sovereign's power) and he replies: 'les grands propriétaires', that is, our friends the great landed magnates.[41] Diderot is aware that the *tiers état*, that is the non-peasant *tiers état*, is negligible in Russia. But he does not know enough about Russia to realise that the bulk of the nobility forms a sort of *tiers état*. His plan to put power into the hands of the great landowners would have created a kind of Polish Commonwealth, or even worse, it called to mind the *Verkhovniki*. Early in her reign Catherine had condemned them: 'Le projet inconsidéré des Dolgorouki à l'avènement de l'impératrice Anne auroit entrainé infailliblement et par consequent la ruine de l'état'.[42]

There was a time perhaps when Diderot had believed in enlightened absolutism, but by 1774 he saw no difference between 'la monarchie pure' and despotism. Among his many visionary statements there is one really moving warning to Catherine in the *Mémoires:*

> tout gouvernement arbitraire est mauvais; je n'en excepte pas le gouvernement d'un maître bon, ferme, juste et éclairé. Ce maître accoutume à respecter et à chérir un maître quel qu'il soit. Il enlève à la nation le droit de déliberer, de vouloir ou de ne pas vouloir, de s'opposer, de s'opposer même au bien. Le droit d'opposition me semble dans une société d'hommes un droit naturel, inaliénable et sacré.

A good despot is like a good shepherd who reduces his subjects to the condition of beasts, making them forget what freedom is like. In a purely Utopian passage, Diderot exclaims: 'si l'on proposait a SMI de voir subitement la constitution de l'empire russe transformée dans la constitution anglaise je doute fort que'elle ne refusât. Libre pour le bien qu'elle veut, liée pour le mal qu'elle ne veut pas, en effect, qu'y perdrait elle?'[43]

This was a political recommendation which Catherine was very unlikely to accept – and Diderot did not really consider the practical means of working

41. 'Observations sur l'Instruction de sa Majesté Impériale', in *Oeuvres*, XI, pp. 207–317. See particularly pp. 207ff., the preamble, and pp. 230–1, comment on Article 39.
42. Catherine II, *Sochineniia*, XII (St Petersburg, 1907), p. 632.
43. Diderot, *Mémoires*, pp. 117–27. The recommendations in these pages in favour of popular representation and limited sovereignty are quite as outspoken as anything in the *Observations*.

it out (let us remember that he is writing *before* the Americans invented the method of popular constitution-making). In other respects the gulf between the practical ruler and the theorist was vast. Diderot kept urging Catherine to enact a law of succession – the one law which she could *not* enact without branding herself a usurper. Some of Diderot's recommendations were also very *sui generis*: for instance he disapproved of the publication of the verdicts of law courts (as recommended by Montesquieu and Catherine).[44] The sentence in a particular case must be consigned to oblivion, and each case must be decided without reference to previous ones. Needless to say, Diderot found a simple solution to the problem of the abuse of serfs: abolish serfdom.[45] He was incidentally often just as critical of articles quoted from Beccaria as he was of Montesquieu.

In an article which appeared some years ago, Sergio Cotta made what seems to me a very perceptive distinction between Montesquieu and Diderot. Montesquieu, he argued, is attempting to construct an empirical science of society as it is, in order to deduce the laws of social development. Voltaire, Rousseau and Diderot are concerned with politics, as the science of what *ought* to be. Hence Montesquieu is a proto-sociologist, while Voltaire, Rousseau and Diderot construct *ideologies*. It is certainly the case that Montesquieu was trying to analyse existing societies: France, England, the Ottoman Porte, the Dutch Republic, Venice. Whereas Diderot's constitutional monarcho-democracy was an ideal construct, it existed nowhere. Both writers are deeply relevant still today, the one as Cotta puts it as an 'empirico-réformiste', the other as 'rationalistico-révolutionnaire'.[46] Diderot's prescriptions are universal, valid for all societies. Montesquieu's are rooted in history. Catherine, influenced by Montesquieu during her formative years, an eclectic empiricist exercising her *métier de roi*, could not be other than a historicist. She for instance echoed Montesquieu's dictum that 'C'est à la legislation de suivre l'esprit de la nation'. Diderot disagreed: 'Je ne crois pas cela: c'est à la legislation de faire l'esprit de la nation'.[47]

At the end of the *Observations* Diderot sums up his view of Catherine: 'Je vois . . . un projet d'un code excellent', but there is not one word in the *Nakaz* about ensuring its stability. 'J'y vois le nom de despote abdiqué, mais la chose conservée; mais le despotisme appelé monarchie . . . Je ne vois aucune disposition projetée pour l'affranchissement du corps de la nation; or sans affranchissement ou sans liberté, point de proprieté; sans proprieté, point d'agriculture'. But the Empress has a noble soul, penetration, enlightenment – to use her own words, the tree she cannot push over, she will undermine by

44. *Observations*, in *Oeuvres*, p. 240, on article 101 of the *Instruction*. See also p. 249, on article 148.
45. *Ibid*., p. 267, on article 254; p. 269, on article 200.
46. S. Cotta, 'L'illuminisme et la science politique, Montesquieu, Diderot et Catherine II', *Revue internationale d'histoire politique et constitutionnelle*, NS, No. 16 (Oct.–Dec. 1954), pp. 273–87. A. Strugnell, in his very perceptive study, *Diderot's Politics* (The Hague, 1973) (more balanced than Yves Benot, *Diderot. De L'Athéisme à l'anticolonialisme* (Paris, 1970)) argues, however, that Cotta goes too far in suggesting that Diderot had rejected the analytic approach of Montesquieu. If Montesquieu had discovered the laws underlying society, he writes, Diderot discovered, if in primitive form, the laws governing the relationship of the individual to society (p. 156).
47. *Observations, Oeuvres*, XI, p. 232, on article 57.

cutting its roots little by little. There is here, therefore, still a note of hope for the future, Catherine will be able to do something, even if the *Nakaz* is not a blueprint for the sort of polity Diderot would approve of.[48]

The tone of the remarks on Russia which Diderot published in the 1780 edition of Raynal, and which have now been identified, is far more pessimistic, and I would like again to make a brief aside. First of all, we must again raise the question about how well informed Diderot was on Russia. The *Observations* were written before the enactment of the Statute of Local Administration of 1775, that is to say when Catherine had not yet embarked on a single one of her major reforms. The question now arises, did Diderot, before contributing to the *Histoire des Deux Indes*, see and study a copy of this statute? We know that Catherine was very proud of it, that she saw it as putting the principles of the *Nakaz* into effect and as greatly superior to it. 'Notre edifice législatif s'élève peu à peu', she wrote to Voltaire, on 29 September–10 October 1777. 'L'instruction pour le Code en est le fondement; je vous l'ai envoyée, il y a dix ans. Vous verrez que ces règlements ne dérogent point aux principes mais qu'ils en découlent.' In an earlier letter Catherine had informed Voltaire that so far the Statute had only been translated into German, but as soon as she had a French translation she would send him one. In the event he received the German edition, but he did not live to comment on it.[49]

Did Diderot ever receive a copy of the French text? He makes no mention of this piece of legislation in any of his commentaries or letters, and he might not have made some of his comments had he known of it. But it appears that none of Catherine's letters to Diderot has survived (if she wrote to him) and that all trace of his letters to her in the period December 1774 to June 1779 has also disappeared.[50] It is certainly strange that a man so interested in Russia should have made no comment at all on such a substantial piece of legislation.

The darker colour of Diderot's writings in 1780 also reflects his increasing despair at events in France, where Turgot had been dismissed in 1776, and his growing fascination with the revolutionary movement in America. Here at last he was seeing his theories put into practice. The revolutionary undertone to his thinking in these years is not so much a reaction to his negative experience of Russia as a welcome to a new dawn over the Atlantic.

It is still difficult to disentangle precisely the exact proportions of Diderot and of Raynal in the paragraphs on Russia incorporated in the 1780 edition of the *Histoire des deux Indes*. Certainly some sentences are fully identifiable paraphrases of portions of the *Mémoires* or the *Observations*. The denunciation of the good despot is even more forcible: 'Le meilleur des princes qui aurait fait

48. *Observations, Oeuvres*, XI, pp. 316–17. It should be added that many of Diderot's remarks in the *Observations* about Russia reflect his total ignorance of the country, e.g. there were no public hospitals in Russia (untrue) (p. 287 on article 346); there were no foundries, no industry for making e.g. nails (Diderot evidently knew nothing about the craft activities of the peasants) (p. 269, article 294).
49. Reddaway, *Documents*, pp. 211, 209.
50. Diderot, *Oeuvres*, XV, p. 1122, n. 4.

le bien contre la volonté générale serait criminel par la seule raison qu'il aurait outrepassé ses droits'.[51]

Strangely enough, however, many of Diderot's responses to Russia are conditioned by Montesquieu's theory of the influence of climate on political systems. 'D'abord', he asks, 'le climat de cette region est il bien favorable à la civilization et à la population?' The long winters, during which but little work could be done, led the people to indulge in gaming, drunkenness and debauch. 'Peut on introduire de bonnes moeurs malgré le climat?', asks Diderot again. Could one uniform code of laws suit such diverse regions, with so many different languages and customs? How can a people, brutalised by slavery, be raised to the point where they might understand liberty? Diderot hoped of course that some day a *tiers état* could be created. But in Russia villages and towns were too far apart, the country was too large, and had much better be broken up into smaller units. Diderot/Raynal is often wrong also on his facts: there was no security for property in Russia (not true); there were no law courts except seigneurial courts (not true); there was religious toleration except for Jews (no longer true). Orthodoxy was of course 'la plus grossière superstition'. Russians' good opinion of themselves was a further obstacle to their improvement and Diderot quotes an alleged 'observateur étranger' who had travelled extensively in Russia as saying: 'le russe était pourri avant d'avoir été mur'. (Diderot always denied that he was the author of this quip – but it was widely attributed to him at the time.[52])

Diderot repeats in the *Histoire* his criticism of Catherine for having failed to change the nature of power in Russia, but his language is somewhat more moderate. In general he comments favourably on some of her policies. There are no statesmen around her, however, he remarks. 'Ce qu'elle a fait seule peut étonner, mais quand elle ne sera plus qui la remplacera?' He feared that the Grand Duke might not carry on the good work she was doing. But if Catherine was successful, then her genius would shine out all the more brightly against the stark background.[53] One phrase which Diderot uses does indeed have a real Russian ring to it: 'Dieu est bien haut, l'empereur est bien loin, et je suis le maître ici'.

Diderot had great faith in education and he approved of Catherine's early attempts to spread it. (He was responsible for the publication of the *Plans et statuts des différents établissements ordonnés par Sa Majesté Impériale Catherine II pour l'éducation de la Jeunesse* at The Hague, on his return from Russia.) But he died in 1783, before Catherine's main educational reform was enacted, the Statute of National Schools of 1786. It would probably have met with his approval since it was entirely secular and started at primary school level. He did not live to see the Charters to the Nobility and the Towns of which he would probably not have approved (too close to Montesquieu). He never

51. *Ibid.*, XV, p. 551.
52. *Ibid.*, pp. 552–3; see also Suard to the Markgraf of Bayreuth, 20 November 1774, *ibid.*, XI, p. 1070.
53. *Ibid.*, XV, p. 556.

commented on the Police Ordinance, or on any of Catherine's other major reforms.[54]

Thus there is no doubt, to my mind, that Diderot's judgments on Russia, as expressed openly in the *Mémoires*, and secretly in the *Observations* and the *Histoire des deux Indes*, were based on inadequate and inaccurate information dating from the early years of Catherine's reign, in fact from the 1760s. Diderot never set foot outside St Petersburg. He knew nothing of the Russian economy, of Russian arts and crafts, of peasant industry, by personal experience. Much of what he heard came from the highly critical – and often ill-informed – foreign colony, and much of what he saw was so strange (and the climate so terrible) as to repel him. Moreover he was a very egotistical man, more concerned to teach than to learn. The information he demanded was designed to enable him to prepare his lessons. He never studied Russian political or economic realities – or he would not have insisted so frequently on the need for a law of succession. The blindness which prevented him from seeing that a usurper like Catherine could not enact a law of succession which was bound to destroy her own legitimacy is quite striking.

Finally, the magnitude of the task of modernising Russia appalled him. Both in her public proclamations (the *Nakaz*) and in her policies, Catherine was not proceeding either far enough or fast enough for him. Repeatedly he reproaches her with merely changing the name of her form of government (autocracy) and not its nature. His bitterness regarding absolute monarchy was also expressed in a short essay written soon after the *Observations*, namely the *Principes de la Politique des Souverains*, directed primarily at Frederick II, but which applied to Catherine too. His visit to Russia had certainly cured him of any remaining illusions about enlightened despots. But he was judging Russia not in terms of what actually existed there but in terms of his ideal polity. The experience of the country, *Russia*, as distinct from the ruler Catherine, shattered the 'mirage russe' which had been nourished in the West by Voltaire's *Histoire de Pierre le Grand*, the optimistic belief that 'philosophic' reform had begun and could continue to come from the East. In the long run neither Voltaire, nor Rousseau, nor Diderot knew Russia as Catherine knew it, and she too did not know it as it really was. But if Diderot was disappointed in Catherine as a ruler, are we not also justified in asking if she was disappointed in Diderot as an adviser?

54. It is permissible to wonder whether Catherine ever realised the extent to which Diderot had contributed to Raynal's *Histoire des deux Indes*, and whether this affected her attitude to Diderot in the 1780s. She was after all the only person to have read the *Mémoires* until that date, and she may well have recognised certain ideas and turns of phrase. However, Catherine, who had sent Diderot 2,000 rubles through Grimm in 1779, paid 1,000 to the *philosophe's* widow in September 1783 which she considered to be five years' pension of 200 livres p.a. in advance (*SIRIO*, XXIII, p. 14, to Grimm, 18 May 1779; p. 318, 9 September 1783). There are three very hostile references to Raynal in Catherine's letters to Grimm in spring and early summer 1782, which suggest that she was then under the immediate impact of reading his *Histoire*. On 2 April 1782, she wrote for instance: 'legislatiren wir ohne viel darauf zu sehen was der abbe Raynal quackt und luğt; unter andren Lügen soll er sagen dass mir nichts geglückt von allem dem, so ich angefangen habe; das ist doch eine sehr grosse Lüge, . . .' (*SIRIO*, XXIII, p. 235; see also p. 231 and p. 247).

CHAPTER ELEVEN

Catherine II and Montesquieu between Prince M.M. Shcherbatov and Denis Diderot

On 14 December 1766, Catherine II of Russia issued a manifesto summoning the various free orders of the Russian empire to send deputies to a Legislative Commission which was to bring order into the chaos of Russian laws by producing a new code. To assist the Commission in its work, the Empress wrote her *Great Instruction* (*Velikiy Nakaz*). The nature of this document has frequently been misunderstood. It is not a series of laws. It is not a constitution for Russia. It is a series of propositions culled from what seemed to Catherine the best and most modern political theorists of her time, integrated into a fairly coherent whole, and setting out the basic principles of a well-ordered government and society.

It is a remarkable fact that this statement of the principles of government, published by a practitioner of the craft actually fulfilling her function at the time, and almost without precedent in the history of Russia, has until recently been the object of relatively little informed analysis. In Catherine's own lifetime, her *Instruction* was widely acclaimed by the *philosophes*. It was banned by the Sorbonne; but in 1770 it was held up as an example to the government of Louis XV, who had exiled his *parlements* only a few years after Catherine had called deputies to collaborate with her in the 'formation d'un corps de loix qui établissent solidement la felicité publique'.[1] A few years later the future leader of the Gironde, Brissot de Warville, reprinted the *Instruction* and the rules for the election of deputies in his *Bibliothèque philosophique du législateur.* 'Le prince que désirera le bien de ses sujets', he wrote, 'imitera donc l'exemple de l'impératrice de Russie, assemblera une commission composée de députés de tous les ordres, de toutes les provinces de ses états, pour travailler à la confection d'un nouveau code de loix.'[2]

In the nineteenth century, historians discussed the *Instruction* in passing, in general histories of Russia and in biographies of Catherine, but devoted little

1. Cfr. André Blonde, *Le parlement justifié par l'impératrice de Russie*, n.d.n.p. (1771?).
2. J.P. Brissot de Warville, *Bibliothèque philosophique du législateur, du politique et du jurisconsulte*, tome III, Berlin, 1783, p. 32.

attention to the analysis of its political content and its relationship to contemporary political thought. To Pushkin, as a young man of 23, writing in 1822, the Legislative Commission was a farce, and the *Instruction*, which served to 'raise Catherine to the level of Titus of Trajan', was a hypocritical document which could only arouse justified indignation.[3]

If one considers the numerous editions in Russian and foreign languages which appeared between 1767 and the end of the century, and the fact that by 1818 1,421 copies were being sold off at 4r.05 kopeks a pood, to be pulped, it is clear that interest in the *Instruction* plummeted downwards after Catherine's death. It is difficult to assess how widely it circulated in the eighteenth century. According to a Senate *ukaz* of April 1768 the *Instruction* was to be distributed to fifty-four government offices in Russia and to the chanceries in each *guberniya*, where once a month it was to be read aloud to the officials above clerical rank. It was not however to fall into the hands of mere clerks. This *ukaz* has been interpreted as limiting the availability of the *Instruction* to the public at large. Since, however, the Russian edition was on sale at the Academy bookshop for 50 kopeks, was frequently reprinted, and was widely advertised by booksellers, it seems to have reached a fairly extensive public. The extent of its influence is difficult to gauge. In the Legislative Commission itself it was common for deputies to quote from the *Instruction* (rather than from Montesquieu or any other writer) because the imperial authorship made the reference safe. There were townspeople, cossacks and peasants in the audience when portions of the *Instruction* were read out every day. It is significant that among Pugachev's followers at least five had been deputies to the Commission, but how far they were influenced by the *Instruction* if at all remains a matter of conjecture.

In the nineteenth century the *Instruction* was not re-published separately in book form until 1893, though all twenty-two chapters were included in Russian and in French in the relevant volume of the *Polnoye Sobraniye Zakonov Rossiyskoy Imperii*, edited by M.M. Speransky, in 1830 and in the 1849 edition of Catherine's *Sochineniya*. Finally in 1907 a scholarly edition was published in Russia, edited and annotated by N.D. Chechulin, who made a thorough analysis of Catherine's sources, and printed the many variants and portions of original drafts which had been left out of the final version.[4] The most penetrating political analysis was published by F.V. Taranovsky in 1904, unfortunately before the appearance of Chechulin's edition.[5] A new translation into English, dating from the eighteenth century, has recently been found in the Library of Congress, and was published in 1977 with an introduction by Paul Dukes, who provides the most thorough analysis of the doctrine of the *Instruction* to appear until now, making full use of Taranovsky, and takes the

3. A.S. Pushkin, *Sochineniya*, ed. B. Tomashevsky, Leningrad, 1936, pp. 661–2.
4. N.D. Chechulin, *Nakaz imperatritsy Yekateriny II*, St Petersburg, 1907.
5. F.V. Taranovsky, *Politicheskaya doktrina v nakaze imperatritsy Yekateriny II*, in *Sbornik statey po istorii prava posvyashchennyy M.F. Vladimirskomu-Budanovu*, ed. by M.N. Yasinsky, Kiev, 1904, pp. 44–86.

matter forward by analysing subsequent Soviet, East and West German and American interpretations.[6]

There were, however, contemporary critics of Catherine's *Instruction.* At almost the same time, in 1774, Denis Diderot, in the house of Prince D.A. Golitsyn, the Russian envoy at The Hague, and Prince M.M. Shcherbatov in St Petersburg, put their criticism on paper. Neither was to see the light of day for a long time. A few pages of Diderot's *Observations sur le Nakaz* were published in 1899 by M. Tourneux,[7] and a full text edited by P. Ledieu was published in 1920 in the *Revue économique et sociale.* A further text appeared in 1960 edited by Yves Benôt, and a version which collates a number of different manuscripts was finally produced by P. Vernière in his edition of Diderot's political writings.[8]

At the time Catherine knew nothing at all about Diderot's *Observations.* Yet according to the latter's friend, Naigeon, Prince Golitsyn had broken open the *philosophe*'s trunk and stolen the original manuscript. If he did so, he did not forward it to the Empress, who only saw a copy when Diderot's papers were sent to St Petersburg after his death. Catherine was furious when she read Diderot's remarks in 1785: 'C'est un vrai babil dans lequel on ne trouve ni connaissance des chose ni prudence ni clairvoyance', she wrote to her *souffre douleur*, Baron Melchior Grimm.[9] Experts in Diderot studies assume that she destroyed the manuscript since it is not to be found in Diderot's papers in Leningrad,[10] though it is possible that she kept it with her own papers and it has simply not been found.

Prince M.M. Shcherbatov's criticisms took even longer to be made public. They did not appear until 1935 when a small collection of his hitherto unpublished works was issued in Moscow, edited by P.G. Lyubomirov.[11] It is with these two contemporary critics that the present essay will be concerned, since they approached Catherine's *Instruction* from such different points of view, the one a radical philosopher, the other an aristocratic constitutionalist.

CATHERINE'S POLITICAL VIEWS

Before embarking on a consideration of Catherine's critics, it is necessary to devote some attention to her own political views in general and as expressed in the *Instruction*; to the extent to which she borrowed or deviated from Montesquieu, her principal mentor; and to the changes which experience of ruling and of Russia brought to her views.

6. P. Dukes, *Russia under Catherine the Great*, vol. II, *Catherine the Great's Instruction to the Legislative Commission of 1767*, Newtonville, Mass., Oriental Research Partners, 1977.
7. M. Tourneux, *Diderot et Catherine II*, Paris, 1899.
8. *Revue économique et sociale*, Paris, 1920, VIII, pp. 273–412; Diderot, *Œuvres Politiques*, Paris, 1963.
9. Diderot, *Œuvres Politiques*, cit., p. 335. All quotations from the *Observations sur le Nakaz* will be taken from this edition. See also *Sbornik imperatorskogo russkogo istoricheskogo obshchestva* (*SIRIO*), 23, p. 372, Catherine to Grimm, 3 November 1785.
10. P. Vernière, in Diderot, *Œuvres Politiques*, cit., pp. 334, 370.
11. M.M. Shcherbatov, *Neizdannyye Sochineniya*, Moscow, 1935.

What do we know of Catherine's opinions on government *before* she seized the throne? A number of her jottings as Grand Duchess and later, as Empress, have been preserved. Most revealing of her own attitude is her condemnation of the attempt by the *Verkhovniki*, or members of the Supreme Privy Council, to limit the power of the crown during the succession crisis of 1730. If successful, this attempt would, in her view, soon have reduced Russia to the level of Poland; the country would have incurred the danger of falling apart and of losing many of its provinces, which might even have been overrun by the Tartars.[12]

Catherine was in the habit of making extracts of works which she had read, and marking passages which impressed her, as well as of making extensive marginal notes. It is unfortunately not always easy to date these extracts precisely. Sometime in 1762, but before she seized the throne, Catherine made some notes on d'Alembert's *Mémoires de Christine, reine de Suède* in his *Mélanges*. 'L'état', she noted, 'dont les loix doivent être sacrées pour les monarques, parce qu'elles subsistent toujours, tandis que les sujets des rois disparoissent, a interêt que tout homme soit jugé suivant les loix.' Further, she noted from d'Alembert's *Analyse de l'Esprit des Loix*: 'La liberté politique, considerée par rapport au citoyen, consiste dans la sureté où il est à l'abri des loix, ou du moins dans l'opinion de cette sureté, qui fait qu'un citoyen n'en craint pas un autre'. Elsewhere, among a number of different jottings, Catherine wrote: 'Il est contre la religion chrétienne et la justice de faire d'hommes, qui apportent tous la liberté en naissant, des esclaves; un concile affranchit tous les paysans serfs autrefois, de l'Allemagne, de la France, Espagne, etc. Faire un coup d'éclat pareil ne seroit pas le moyen de se faire aimer des possesseurs des terres, remplis d'entêtement et de prejugés.' Catherine went on to propose that the solution would be to enact that whenever an estate was sold in Russia the serfs should be freed, and in a hundred years all would be free. In a later jotting, she exclaimed: 'Liberté, âme de toutes choses, sans vous tout est mort. Je veux qu'on obéisse aux lois, mais point d'esclaves. Je veux un but general de rendre heureux, et point de caprice, ni de bizarrerie, ni de tyrannie qui y déroge.'[13]

We do not know when Catherine read Montesquieu's *De L'Esprit des Lois* for the first time, though she was certainly very well acquainted with it by 1760. This is evident from her marginal comments on a work entitled *Lettres Russiennes*, by F.H. Strube de Piermont, which appeared in that year.[14] This

12. *Sochineniya imperatritsy Yekateriny II*, ed. A.N. Pypin, St Petersburg, 1907, XII, p. 632.
13. *Ibid.*, pp. 608, 610; see also D. Ransel, *The Politics of Catherinian Russia*, Yale University Press 1975, pp. 52–3.
14. F.H. Strube de Piermont (or Pyrmont), born plain F.H. Strube, entered Russian service and was for a time secretary to Biron. He was appointed to the Legislative Commission of 1754. The *Lettres Russiennes* were published without indication of date or place. A facsimile edition has been published in 1978, edited by Corrado Rosso, La Goliardica, Pisa, together with Catherine's marginal notes, which were earlier published by A.N. Pypin in *Yekaterina i Montesk'ye*, 'Vestnik Yevropy', 38, No. 5, 1903, pp. 272–300. I am grateful to Miss Pia Pera for drawing my attention to the facsimile edition.

work was an attack on Montesquieu's theory of despotism as a separate form of government, and on his application of despotism to Russia, in *L'Esprit des Lois* and incidentally in the *Lettres Persanes*. Strube argued that there was really no difference of substance between Montesquieu's despotism and his monarchy: the former was merely a monarchy under a bad ruler. This led Strube to attempt his own definition of despotism, which he based on Jean Bodin: 'La monarchie seigneuriale . . . est celle ou le Prince gouverne ses sujets comme le père de famille ses esclaves'. Strube goes on to argue that 'le despotisme, en tant qu'il dénote le gouvernement d'un état composé d'esclaves, au lieu de citoyens proprement dit, n'a pas lui même rien de contraire aux principes de droit naturel et civil'. He thus regarded servitude or slavery as perfectly lawful and indeed even moral, and concluded that both in a despotism and in a monarchy, the ruler was bound by no civil or political laws (whether fundamental or not!). The distinction lay in the fact that in a despotism the ruler ruled over people who 'belonged to him', whereas a monarch ruled over free people and had therefore to concern himself with the public good. There was, pointed out Strube, no difference between the kind of obedience exacted by a despot and by a limited monarch; for those laws which had been legally enacted in a limited monarchy were as absolutely binding on the subjects as were the caprices of a despot. Having posited that the only difference between a monarchy and a despotism lay not in the quality of the power exercised but in the condition of the people over whom power was exercised, that a despotism ruled over unfree people, while a monarchy ruled over free people, Strube went on to argue that 'le gouvernement de Russie n'est pas un gouvernement despotique proprement dit. Pour cet effet je n'ai qu'à faire voire que les peuples soumis à ce puissant empire jouissent d'une veritable liberté civile et ne méritent pas plus le nom d'esclaves que les sujets de tous les autres états de l'Europe où gouvernent les princes absolus.'

It is relatively easy to pick holes in Montesquieu's history; Voltaire, Helvétius, d'Alembert all enjoyed themselves doing so, privately or in public. This aspect of Strube's little opus is not what concerns us here, but rather the nature of Catherine's comments on what he wrote. She did not sympathize at all with the apologia for serfdom. 'L'éloge de la servitude! Et pourquoi l'auteur ne ce [sic] vend il pas pour esclave', she exclaimed. When Strube concluded that the Russian government was not a despotic government 'proprement dit', she noted: 'Monsieur dispute pour le nom, non pour la chose'. When Strube stressed that there was the same difference between the noble and the serf as existed elsewhere in Europe, 'que ce sont les prérogatives et les droits particuliers qu'elle [la noblesse] tient des souverains qui la distinguent des serfs et du Tiers Etat . . . et non le droit d'avoir des esclaves', 'en quoi?' asked Catherine. To his statement: 'que la noblesse russienne n'a jamais été depouillée de ses droits', 'mais quels sont ils?' asked Catherine again.

Dismissing Strube's book as badly argued and dull, Catherine jotted down on a blank page her own view of the government best suited to Russia: 'Un grand empire comme celui de Russie se destruiroit s'il y étoit établi une forme de gouvernment autre que Despotique, parce que c'est le seul qui peut remédier avec promptitude nécessaire aux besoins des provinces éloignées, tout autre forme destruisant par des longueurs cette activité qui donne la vie à tout. Ainsi prions seulement Dieu qu'il nous donne toujours des maitres raisonnables, qui se conforment aux loix et n'en fassent qu'après examen et uniquement en vue du bien de leurs sujets.'[15] Clearly, therefore, while she still was Grand Duchess, Catherine believed that a ruler should be bound by the laws, that Russia was a despotism in Montesquieu's sense of the word, that the Russian nobility – still at that time subjected to compulsory service – had no rights comparable to those of the western nobles, and that the servitude of the serfs was real and contrary to human and divine justice.

THE GREAT INSTRUCTION'S DEBT TO MONTESQUIEU

The *Instruction* combines several different kinds of propositions: definitions of what is: 'en Russie c'est le Sénat qui est le dépositaire des loix' (art. 26); definitions of what ought to be: 'C'est une très mauvaise politique de vouloir changer par les loix ce qui doit être changé par les coutumes' (art. 60); and finally the discussion of alternative methods of achieving the desired aim, often with historical illustrations setting down the advantages and disadvantages of a given course of action: 'D'autres sont de l'avis contraire et soutiennent qu'on peut permettre aux nobles qui ne sont pas au service, de commercer' (art. 331). Catherine summed up her purpose as follows: 'Nous avons cité dans le cours de cet ouvrage tant d'exemples et d'usages de diverses nations que dans la vue de faciliter le choix des moyens qui pourront . . . rendre le peuple russe le plus heureux de la terre' (art. 521). The *Instruction* is thus not the exposition of a coherent political theory; it lays down no blueprint for the future organization of Russian government and society, and shows many signs of the incorporation of last-minute afterthoughts and the acceptance of last-minute excisions.

The way in which Catherine interpreted the ideas of Montesquieu in the compilation of what might be termed the 'constitutional' part of her *Instruction* is a matter of some controversy – using the word constitution in the sense of the 'set of rules' regulating the motion of the state. Did she for instance slavishly copy him, as some critics have argued, simply diverging from his text where his propositions were totally inapplicable to her purposes? Or did she construct her own political doctrine from her borrowings? In order to

15. *Ibid.* It is probable that Strube's book was written some time before it was published, possibly soon after the publication of *De l'Esprit des Lois.* His argument that the difference between nobles and non-nobles in Russia does not lie in the right to own serfs since other estates are also allowed to own serfs suggests that he may have written before the ukaz of 1754 which ordered all non-nobles to sell estates with serfs (except industrialists). See also Ransel, *op. cit.*, pp. 47–54, who however over-estimates the influence of N.I. Panin, and confuses Montesquieu's monarchy with fundamental laws (France) with a constitutional or limited monarchy with the separation of powers (England).

answer this question it is necessary to turn briefly to the great Frenchman's exposition as Catherine might have read it at the time, purged of all amplifications of his thought which scholars, working on his own manuscripts, have later been able to establish.

Two major aspects of Catherine's borrowings must be examined. First, what did Montesquieu say about large states in northern climates, and about Russia specifically? And secondly what did Montesquieu mean by a monarchy?

If we turn to Montesquieu's theory of climate, the character of the Russian people did not quite correspond to Montesquieu's analysis. Though they were indeed energetic and brave, they were not outstandingly self-confident, and they were certainly not lacking in astuteness and cunning. They were, however, characterized by their remarkable resistance to pain and fatigue: 'Il faut écorcher un Moscovite pour lui donner du sentiment', as Montesquieu put it. (Just how wounding sensitive Russians found such remarks is illustrated in a letter from Aleksey Narishkin to Beccaria; he speaks of himself as 'un homme du nord, du pais de ces gens qu'il faut écorcher pour leur tirer du sentiment'.[16]) More to the point is Montesquieu's argument that the changes introduced by Peter I were accepted in Russia all the more easily because the existing habits and customs of the country were not native to it, were alien to the climate and had been brought in from outside by conquest and the mixture of peoples. Russia belonged to Europe and in returning it to Europe Peter I's task was easier than he had thought (Bk. XI, Ch. XIV).

The true monarchy for Montesquieu was the form of government suitable to a state of moderate size, and was distinguished from a despotism by the presence of fundamental laws. Great empires were bound to fall apart or to be divided. 'Un grand empire suppose une autorité despotique dans celui qui gouverne', explained Montesquieu, arguing that it was necessary for speed in decision-making to supplement the slowness of execution consequent on the huge distances over which decisions had to be sent to be implemented. The principle of such a government was 'fear', and law would be arbitrary and lodged in a single head. The separation of powers was not a *sine qua non* of a moderate or true monarchy. It is in the context of a state which has political liberty as its main object that Montesquieu mentions the separation of powers. Different states have different objects: the pleasure of the prince in a despotism; the glory of the ruler and the state in a monarchy; the independence of each individual in Poland, 'et ce qui en resulte – l'oppression de tous'. But *one* nation has political liberty as its main object, namely England, and secures it by means of the separation of powers. If all three powers are united in one hand, then the government is a despotism. But in most of Europe 'le gouvernement est moderé parce que le prince qui a les deux premiers pouvoirs laisse à ses sujets l'exercise du troisième', i.e. the judiciary, which should be in the hands of men appointed from among the people and should not be enshrined in a certain order nor confined to a certain profession.

16. Quoted in C. Beccaria, *Dei delitti e delle pene*, ed. Franco Venturi, Torino, 1965, p. 648.

To sum up, though its climate offered hope of escape, its size condemned Russia to be a despotism. Nevertheless, there are several indications throughout *L'Esprit des Lois* that Montesquieu considered that climate might prevail over size, and that Russia was not irrevocably doomed to have a despotic government. 'Que la noblesse Moscovite ait été réduite en servitude par un de ses princes, on y verra toujours des traits d'impatience que les climats du midi ne donnent point. N'y avons nous pas vu le gouvernement aristocratique établi pendant quelques jours?' is a remark which shows Montesquieu to be informed about and favourable to the efforts of the *Verkhovniki* to introduce limited monarchy in Russia in 1730.[17] Other favourable symptoms were quoted in Bk. V, Ch. XIV: 'Voyez . . . avec quelle industrie le gouvernement moscovite cherche a sortir du despotisme . . . on a cassé les grands corps de troupes, on a diminué les peines des crimes, on a établi des tribunaux; on a commencé à connaitre les loix'.

Yet Russia could not be a true monarchy since it lacked the basic fundamental laws. These comprised the law of succession; the presence of 'des pouvoirs intermediaires subordonnés et dépendans', and 'des canaux par où decoule la puissance'. These 'pouvoirs intermédiaires' were the social orders, namely the nobility, the church, and the burghers. In addition there must be a 'dépôt des loix'. The classic phrase 'point de monarque, point de noblesse, point de noblesse point de monarque' did not imply that monarchy needed the support of the nobility in order to survive, but that if there were no nobility, the 'pouvoir intermédiaire le plus naturel', monarchy would be unlimited and therefore despotic.[18]

If one takes what Montesquieu had to say about despotism, monarchy and limited monarchy, it is clear that he regarded all these forms of government as placed on a continuum ranging from one extreme to another. The following quotations illustrate this point:

> Je ne prétends point par là ravaler les autres gouvernements ni dire que cette liberté politique extrème [of England] doive mortifier ceux qui n'ent ont qu'une moderée. Comment dirai-je cela, moi qui croit que l'excès même de la raison n'est pas toujours désirable, et que les hommes s'accomodent presque toujours mieux des milieux que des extremités?

17. Montesquieu was acquainted with Prince A.D. Kantemir, the Russian envoy to France in the 1740s, who had played an active part in the overthrow of the plans of the *Verkhovniki*. Kantemir was not, however, likely to be in favour of the plans of the Dolgorukiye and above all of Prince D.M. Golitsyn, since he belonged to the circle of Feofan Prokopovich and moreover had a deep personal grudge against D.M. Golitsyn. The latter's daughter had married Kantemir's elder brother Konstantin, who had been declared sole heir to the Kantemir fortune in accordance with Peter I's law of single inheritance. Antiokh Kantemir succeeded in overturning this judgement in a lawsuit as a result of which Golitsyn was sentenced to imprisonment in Schlüsselburg where he died in 1737.

18. R. Shackleton, *Montesquieu: A Critical Biography*, Oxford, 1961, p. 279. Cf. also F. Bacon: 'Toute monarchie ou il n'y a point de noblesse est une pure tyrannie comme celle des Turcs', quoted in Strube de Piermont, *op. cit.*, p. 201.

and

> Les monarchies que nous connaissons n'ont pas comme [England] . . . la liberté pour leur objet direct . . . Les trois pouvoirs n'y sont point distribués et fondus sur le modèle de la constitution dont nous avons parlé. Ils ont chacun une distribution particulière selon laquelle ils approchent plus ou moins de la liberté politique; et s'il n'en approchaient pas, la monarchie dégénèrerait en despotisme.

CATHERINE'S INSTRUCTION

What did Catherine II make of all this? There is of course no reason why she should not have adapted Montesquieu's political analysis to the Russia she knew and hoped to transform. Montesquieu's *Esprit des Lois* is not a sacred text from which it is blasphemy to depart. Catherine was now a ruler, faced with the solution of concrete problems against a specific background of institutions, social groups, religious and cultural conditioning, which she could not ignore. She was not a political theorist but a practitioner of the craft of ruling. Moreover it must be remembered that her *Instruction* is not a description of what Russia actually was, but a mixture of what was and of what ought to be.[19] She thus attempted to formulate the principles which could be relevant to an empire whose political and social structure were still underdeveloped by contemporary standards.

Naturally enough Catherine fully endorsed Montesquieu's conclusions regarding the influence of climate on Russia, and proclaimed Russia to be a European power. The definition of the political structure of the Russian empire presented more problems. In this context it is essential to remember that it is the French text of the *Instruction* which comes closest to Catherine's own thought. She borrowed from authors who wrote in French, and she wrote the *Instruction* herself in French. It was subsequently translated into Russian for her.

As a simple statement of fact, Catherine declared that 'Le monarque de Russie est souverain' (art. 9).[20] But in her very next proposition, Catherine departs significantly from Montesquieu: 'un grand empire suppose une autorité souveraine dans la personne qui le gouverne', she wrote, where Montesquieu had written: 'une autorité despotique'. Her verbal sleight of hand in this context

19. See particularly Catherine's letter to Frederick II accompanying a copy of the *Instruction, SIRIO*, 20, p. 237, 17 October 1767.

20. The Russian version of this article reads: 'Gosudar' est' samoderzhavnyy'. It should be remembered that in the eighteenth century *samoderzhavnyy* was usually translated as 'sovereign' or 'absolute'. See my article 'Autocracy and Sovereignty', *Canadian-American Slavic Studies*, 16, Nos 3–4, Fall–Winter 1982, pp. 369–87. See also Strube de Piermont, *op. cit.*, p. 195, note b: 'On pourrait croire que les empereurs grecs, ayant pris les titres de *Βασιλεὺς* ou de Roi, d'*αυτοκρατορ* ou de souverain . . .'. In his otherwise illuminating article, 'L'illuminisme et la science politique: Montesquieu, Diderot et Catherine II', in *Revue Internationale d'histoire politique et constitutionnelle*, 6, October–December 1954, pp. 273–87, Sergio Cotta wrongly seems to imply that 'autocratique' is closer to despotism than to absolutism.

is quite understandable. Russia was not, after all, the Ottoman Porte, Persia, or Japan, and Catherine was bound to reject the title of 'despot',[21] while insisting that in order to rule such a large state and keep it from disintegrating a single authority was essential.

It remained much more difficult to detect in Russia the presence of any fundamental laws, in Montesquieu's sense of the word. There was no true law of succession. Peter I had enacted such a law, enabling the ruler to choose his heir, but this represented the legalization of the arbitrary will of the ruler rather than the stabilization of the continuity of the state. The absence of any mention of this particular law in Catherine's *Instruction*, however, is not surprising. The Legislative Commission was not empowered to discuss the constitutional structure of Russia, and in view of Catherine's status as an usurper it was a subject on which she could lay down no law.

It is perfectly possible that Catherine, who had a very literal mind, took Montesquieu's rather subtle approach to a fundamental law *au pied de la lettre*, and interpreted a fundamental law as signifying the rules according to which the state operated rather than, as Montesquieu evidently intended, as the presence of social forces (the *pouvoirs intermédiaires*) and institutions (the *parlements*) which functioned as a counter-balance to the power of the state.[22] Thus, it is arguable that in her view the form of government set up by Peter I in the last ten years of his reign represented the constitutional structure (or fundamental laws) of Russia. These could be taken to comprise the Senate, the Procuracy, the Colleges, the General Regulations for the Administration, and the Military and Naval Codes. Orthodoxy as a state religion constituted another fundamental law, enshrined in the Spiritual Regulations.

Much more important from the point of view of the analysis of Catherine's political doctrine in relation to *L'Esprit des Lois* is her attitude to Montesquieu's 'pouvoirs intermédiaires', 'les canaux par où découle la puissance', and the 'dépôt des lois'. Nowhere does Catherine state or imply that the 'pouvoirs intermédiaires' are the social orders, let alone that the nobility in Russia is the most natural 'pouvoir intermédiaire'. In terms of Russian reality she was of course quite right. The privileges of the Russian nobles had not yet acquired the legal status of rights. Catherine's own attitude in the early 1760s to the confirmation of such rights is obscure. She had aroused ill-feeling among some of the nobles by her failure to confirm the law of February 1762 emancipating the nobility from compulsory service (though it was in fact acted upon), and she allowed the report of the Commission she herself had set up to revise the law in February 1763 to lie, taking no further action upon it. Nor did she pursue proposals put to her in the early 1760s to associate elected representatives of the nobility with local administration. Yet in her definition of nobility ('un titre d'honneur qui distingue du commun des hommes ceux qui en sont décorés') she stresses that it is a practice established in antiquity to

21. See the essential discussion of the assonances of the word despotism in F. Venturi, *Despotisme oriental*, in *Europes des Lumières*, Paris and The Hague, 1971, Ch. 6.
22. Shackleton, *op. cit.*, pp. 279–80.

distinguish people who have proved most virtuous or have rendered most service by granting the privilege of nobility. Virtue and merit raise a man to noble status; virtue and honour inspire his conduct. The first duty of a noble is to defend his country but civil virtues can also be rewarded by nobility.[23] The prerogatives, or rights, of nobles are nowhere defined. But then it was the function of the Legislative Commission to codify existing rights and draft new ones, in accordance with the principles of the *Instruction*, not for the *Instruction* to lay down the law in advance. More striking is Catherine's total disregard of the Church as an estate of the realm. It had been deprived of its lands in 1764; it was not invited to send a deputy to the Legislative Commission as a separate order and was simply represented by a deputy elected by the Holy Synod, an official body; religion is not mentioned at all in the *Instruction*, except briefly in Chapter XIV on Education, in which article 351 lays down the duty of parents to bring up their children in the Holy Orthodox faith.

Catherine's discussion of the Third Estate and the burghers is typical of her eclectic approach. For the Third Estate in her view should comprise all those free men who are neither peasants nor nobles. And within the Third Estate is the separate category of those who enjoy the right of citizenship (*le droit de bourgeoisie*). These rights are, however, limited to the town itself in which the burgher is a property owner, and do not, in the *Instruction*, sum up to general rights conferred on a social order.

Yet it was essential, if Catherine was to conform to Montesquieu's pattern of a true monarchy, to have 'pouvoirs intermédiaires' and 'des canaux moyens par où découle la puissance'. Catherine therefore combined the social with the institutional and located them in the law courts, i.e. in the French context, the *parlements*. This has led some commentators[24] to assume that she was placing the 'pouvoirs intermédiaires' in the bureaucracy. Yet judging by the French and English texts of the *Instruction*, which have the words 'tribunaux', 'courts of judicature' or even 'constitutional courts of judicature' for the Russian *pravitel'stva* it is clear that Catherine was thinking of the law courts as such, or of the Senate and the Colleges in terms of their function as a court of appeal and courts of first instance.

The French text of the *Instruction*, as mentioned above, must be taken as the most authoritative, and it is perfectly correct to speak of the French *parlements* in Russian as *pravitel'stva*. The *parlements* were sovereign courts, emanations of the King as supreme judge, which with time had become the bastions of the *noblesse de robe*, who owned their offices as so many pieces of property. This had enabled them to acquire an authority which had at times challenged that

23. See *Instruction de Sa Majesté Impériale Catherine II*, St Petersburg, 1769, articles 360–75. All future references to the *Instruction* are taken from this edition. Dukes, *op. cit.*, p. 16 argues that Catherine 'subordinated the nobility to the bureaucracy. She did not make a noble sense of honour the basis of autocratic government as he [Montesquieu] had made it of the monarchial variety.' I do not find that the French text of the *Instruction* bears this out notably article 364. There is nothing in the whole of the chapter on the nobility to which the authors of the standard French works on 'noblesse' could have taken exception.

24. E.g. Taranovsky, *op. cit.*, and Ransel, *op. cit.*

of the King.[25] But they were not part of the French bureaucracy, in the sense of forming a hierarchy of professionally trained officials, appointed, employed, promoted, and paid by the state.

In Russia, in the 1760s, there was no established system of law courts divorced from the administration. Justice was mainly inquisitorial, governors and *voyevodas* acted as judges at *guberniya*, province and district level; *magistraty* and *ratushi* (composed of elected townspeople from the topmost economic stratum) heard cases affecting members of the urban estate, while at a lower level verbal courts dealt out summary justice. In general, however, judicial functions were simply grafted on to administrative functions, and were carried out by the same people in the same offices.[26] The Russian judicial system was thus quite chaotic between 1727 and the implementation of the Statute of Local Administration of 1775 which introduced the separation of functions between the judiciary and the executive.

Can the Russian courts, such as they were, be called bureaucratic bodies? In fact did Russia in the 1760s have a bureaucracy? Taranovsky, in many ways the most penetrating analyst of the *Instruction*, bases his whole theory on the argument that the 'tribunals' were bureaucratic 'in the wider sense as administration by means of professional *chinovniki*'. For him therefore, the 'samoderzhavnoye pravleniye' (absolute government), as portrayed by Catherine in her *Instruction*, is not a 'soslovnoye pravleniye' or government by 'estates' but a bureaucratic absolutism, or a *Beamtenstaat*, a form of government which he suggests that Montesquieu either did not know of or deliberately passed over in silence.[27] Taranovsky goes on to argue that in adapting Montesquieu's theory of an 'estate' monarchy to her political purposes, Catherine showed considerable originality in formulating her own political doctrine of 'bureaucratic absolutism'.[28] His conclusion does depend, however, both on acceptance that Montesquieu's monarchy ruled by fundamental laws is a 'soslovnoye pravleniye', which it was not, and on the interpretation of the

25. The inherent weakness of the *parlements* was shown up when they were disbanded in 1770–71. It must also be considered whether contemporaries always clearly understood the nature of the *parlements*. Shcherbatov, for instance, thought that the provinces in which the Etats had been abolished in France 'were governed by Parlements, in which peers, judges and clerks (mostly from the third estate) all sat together forming a joint monarchical, aristocratic and popular government'. See his *Razmyshleniye o zakonodatel'stve voobshche*, in *Sochineniya*, e.d. I.P. Khrushchev, 2 vols., St Petersburg, 1896, I, p. 385.

26. The central colleges acted as courts of first instance according to the social estate of the plaintiff or the defendant, and the nature of the dispute.

27. Taranovsky, *op. cit.*, p. 70. He suggests that Montesquieu may be hinting at a bureaucratic monarchy when he speaks of a great European state carrying on a systematic assault on patrimonial and ecclesiastical jurisdictions (Bk. II, Ch. 4). Yet surely in this passage, Montesquieu is referring to England.

28. M. Raeff, in his *The Enlightenment in Russia and Russian Thought in the Enlightenment* (*The Eighteenth Century in Russia*, ed. J.G. Garrard, Oxford, 1973, pp. 25–47) and in *The Well-Ordered Police-State: Social and Institutional Change through Law in the Germanies and Russia, 1600–1800*, Yale University Press, 1983, exaggerates to my mind the 'bureaucratism' of Catherine and her conscious adoption of cameralist principles. They undoubtedly influenced her in detail, but when she wrote her *Instruction* Montesquieu was uppermost in her mind.

word 'bureaucracy'. Here again a semantic problem arises. By the nineteenth century the word *chinovniki* had come to be generally used for officials in the civil and military service and a man could climb in the Table of Ranks by moving from one branch to another.[29] Furthermore, Taranovsky argues that the distinctive characteristics of a bureaucratic system are the replacement of the personal administration of the ruler by a corps of professional *chinovniki*, and the existence of a hierarchical ladder of government institutions. These principles, according to him, were at the basis of the reforms introduced by Peter I, even if its theoretical formulations remained unwritten. Thus, according to Taranovsky, when Catherine II ascended the throne, a bureaucratic order was an established fact in Russia.

It is hard to accept this judgement either about the reign of Peter I or about Russia at the accession of Catherine II. Peter attempted, certainly, to establish a well-organized hierarchical service of paid officials, but they were not professionally prepared, nor were they devoted exclusively to civil service. After 1727 local administration reverted to the Muscovite pattern, only a handful of the higher officials being in receipt of salaries from public funds. This is the system which Catherine inherited. The 'tribunals' she referred to were staffed by nobles who were not professionally trained for civil employment of any kind, and who combined administrative, judicial and even military duties. It is this system which she improved in 1764 and transformed in the Statute of Local Administration of 1775 and the Charters of 1785. Taranovsky is arguing back from the nineteenth century 'chinovnichestvo' and assuming its existence in eighteenth-century Russia. Yet, arguably, in the eighteenth century it was impossible to create a true bureaucracy. So long as civil and military employment and ennoblement remained inextricably linked by the Table of Ranks, every reasonably competent or powerfully protected civil official could hope to become a hereditary noble, entitled to own an estate with serfs, and turn his back on the third estate.

If Catherine did not lay down the theoretical foundations of a bureaucratic absolutism, what were in that case the political principles of the *Instruction*? In a number of chapters of a 'constitutional' content which establish general principles of political structure, Catherine clearly implies that Russia is (or should be when the Code has been drafted) an absolute monarchy ruled according to fundamental laws. The 'laws' are those dispositions 'qui ne sauraient être changées en aucun temps et leur nombre ne saurait être grand' (art. 444). The fundamental laws of Russia are not spelled out in detail, beyond the statement of the existence of a depot of laws, the Senate, and of intermediary bodies, i.e. the subordinate courts, 'par ou découle la puissance'. All these bodies are entitled to make representations to the ruler on current decrees which might be contrary to the Code. At the time the composition of all subordinate courts was appointive, but when she issued the *Instruction*, Catherine

29. See R.D. Givens, *Eighteenth Century Nobiliary Career Patterns and Provincial Government*, in *Russian Officialdom*, ed. W. Pintner and D.K. Rowney, London, 1979, pp. 106–29.

had already reached the conclusion that it was necessary to associate elective representatives of the 'estates' with local administration and justice.[30]

The permanency of the fundamental laws is also stressed in article 508: 'Si les principes sont conservés lorsque la constitution change, le changement se fait en mieux; mais si les principes sont perdu, l'Etat court à sa destruction'. Catherine also openly accepted the self-limitation of the monarch by these fundamental laws, notably in article 512: 'Il est vrai qu'il y a des cas où la Puissance doit et peut agir dans toute sa plénitude, sans aucun danger pour l'Etat; mais il y en a d'autres ou elle doit agir dans les limites qu'elle s'est posée elle-même'.

The social organization of Russia is only briefly sketched in the *Instruction*, since the details of the rights of the various estates were to be supplied by the Legislative Commission itself. The various sub-commissions did indeed produce draft codes for the rights of the nobles, the townsmen, the Cossacks and even some incomplete drafts regarding state peasants and serfs.[31]

To sum up, Catherine saw Russia as being or becoming a true monarchy in Montesquieu's sense of the word. The model of course was not England but France, a kingdom which, *pace* Taranovsky, was not in any sense a 'soslovnoye pravleniye' or 'government by estates', since the 'pouvoirs intermédiaires' played no part in government except to some extent in the *pays d'états*.[32] The rights of the French nobility were fairly fragile and only three years after the publication of the *Instruction* the French *parlements* were swept away by the stroke of a royal pen. If Russia lacked some of the elements which Montesquieu had deemed essential, so did many other acceptable European monarchies, and in any case Catherine was proposing to remedy some of these structural deficiencies. By the time she had finished remodelling the institutions of Russia in the 1780s she had defined the rights of, and granted a degree of corporate organization and a sphere of independent activity to two of the social estates, the nobles and the townsmen, and the judiciary had been established as a functionally separate institution. It was a hybrid structure, part 'estate' based, part bureaucratic. Which way it would develop would depend a great deal on the interplay of central direction and local initiative. Though the activity of the local corporate institutions has scarcely been studied,[33] there is some evidence that the nobles did not make full use of the opportunities offered to them.[34] The emphasis on the 'bureaucratic' nature of Catherine's reforms in much of the historiography of the reign reflects not so much her intentions when she set these institutions up, as their failure to develop in the unfavourable political climate after her death, notably in the reign of Paul. The renewed government stress on the bureaucratic at the expense of the 'estate' element fitted

30. See Isabel de Madariaga, *Russia in the Age of Catherine the Great*, London, 1981, p. 278.
31. These draft projects have been published in *SIRIO*.
32. It is incorrect to translate 'a monarchy ruled according to fundamental laws' as a 'soslovnoye pravleniye' or government by estates, as does Taranovsky. Nowhere does Montesquieu mention the political function of the estates in France, not does he ascribe legislative power to the nobility.
33. Very little attention has been devoted to the study of the activity of the noble assemblies.
34. See Givens, *op. cit.*, and G.S. Vinsky, *Moe vremya*, Oriental Research Partners, 1974, pp. 43–4.

well into the pattern of command/obedience which antedated the reforms of Peter I, was enormously strengthened in his reign, only with difficulty slightly modified under Catherine, and reverted to under her successors.

PRINCE M.M. SHCHERBATOV AND THE INSTRUCTION

The comments of Prince M.M. Shcherbatov on Catherine's *Instruction* are the only detailed, contemporary Russian response to have reached us. They are interesting in themselves, but they acquire added importance in the context of the personality of the man who wrote them. Born in 1733, Shcherbatov came from an old Ryurikid family, with a distinguished record of service.[35] In his youth he employed his leisure hours in the study of political literature, translating works of interest to him, most of which remained unpublished during his lifetime. He does not seem to have travelled abroad, but since he read extensively he was fairly well acquainted with political events in the world outside Russia. Shcherbatov served briefly in the Guards during the Seven Years War, but was one of the first to take advantage of the manifesto on the freedom of the nobility from service and retired with the rank of captain in March 1762. In 1767 he was elected deputy for the nobility of Yaroslavl to the Legislative Commission, where he played a very active part as the spokesman for the political and social rights of the aristocracy, both in the main debates and in the Subcommission on the Third Estate to which he was elected. Yet Shcherbatov never achieved the prominence to which he felt himself entitled. Possibly Catherine disliked his championship of unadulterated serfdom in the Commission at a time when she was seeking means of alleviating its worst features. Perhaps she found his personality uncongenial. The French *chargé d'affaires*, the Chevalier de Corberon, thought him a cultivated man, but very pedantic, and capable of the most unrestrained diatribes against his own country when speaking in private.[36] At any rate, in 1774, at the age of 41, he had only reached the post of Heraldmaster, in charge of the department in the Senate which kept the records of the service appointments of the nobility. Soon after he was also appointed official historiographer and embarked both on the collection of a fine library of manuscripts and on a *History of Russia*.

By 1774, partly out of conviction, partly out of disappointment, Shcherbatov's political ideas had acquired a certain consistency. In his study, between four walls, he advocated as the ideal form of government a monarchy in which the power of the ruler was severely limited by an aristocratic council. In his view, relations between rulers and ruled were founded on a form of contract. Individual men chose to cede some of their freedom to a ruler who would 'fulfill the general will for the happiness of all, and defend

35. The most accessible biographical sketch is in the introduction by A. Lentin to his translation of *On the Corruption of Morals*, Cambridge, 1969.
36. *Un diplomate français à la cour de Catherine II: journal intime du chevalier de Corberon*, ed. L.H. Labande, 2 vols., Paris, 1901, I, pp. 80, 291; II, p. 186.

society against all enemies', but, he argued, quoting Rousseau, it was unnatural to believe that human beings endowed with freedom by nature would cede it without necessity or expectation of advantage to themselves. In all governments monarchy, oligarchy and popular elements were combined, but one form dominated over the others according to the national temperament. Thus France was a monarchy, and England, in spite of appearances, a republic.[37] Despotism, for Shcherbatov, was not a form of government but the perversion of an existing form, namely monarchy.

The most 'beautiful' form of government, wrote Shcherbatov in 1760, was the aristocratic. Laws were decided upon by a majority, and could not be arbitrarily changed. A 'Senate', a permanent institution composed of the wisest men, stood guard against any perversion of the system, and notably against any decline into oligarchy, which was an oppressive form of government.

In his various meditations on different forms of government, written at different times, Shcherbatov analyses, sometimes in considerable detail, the role of the nobility as the first estate, the *pays légal*. He frequently uses the word *narod* but usually only in the sense of those people who should have political rights, not the people as a whole, let alone the common man. He entertained a very high notion of the nature and value to the state of the noble order, and of the concept of *noblesse oblige*. All men might have been born equal, but natural inequality soon manifested itself, and it was hereditary, so that with the passing of generations a noble by birth was made of a totally different clay from the common man. As a result, he argued that in the drafting of laws and the administration of justice learned jurists should be limited to giving advice to nobles 'who from their youth had the needs of the state drummed into them by their parents and relatives, and had acquired the knowledge of the laws from them'. Learned jurists did not have that noble pride which protects them from interestedness, and which is 'innate to the nobility as heat to fire and wetness to water'.[38]

Yet when Shcherbatov defended the right of the nobles to unlimited power over their peasants, a power which he did not trust a ruler to exercise over his nobles, he was championing not only their inbred and hereditary right to rule over others, but their right to the land and those who cultivated it as so much property, paid for by past services but also in hard cash.

What remains obscure is the extent to which Shcherbatov's ideal polity is based on serfdom. As far as Russia was concerned he was at that time totally opposed not only to the emancipation of the serfs but to any regulation of relations between serfs and *pomeshchiki* by the state. Was serfdom in his view an essential consequence of the history and geography of Russia? When, in the late 1780s, Shcherbatov wrote his unfinished version of Utopia, *The Voyage to the Land of Ofir*, a curious blend of social rigidity and political flexibility held together by a strong censorship of behaviour and ideas, the peasants were

37. Shcherbatov, *Neizdannyye Sochineniya*, cit., p. 23 (article 13). See also his *Razmyshleniye o zakonodatel'stve*, p. 386.
38. *Razmyshleniye o dvoryanstve*, in *Sochineniya*, cit., pp. 219–68, at p. 232.

barely mentioned. But clearly they were serfs, since in the 'Moral and Civic Catechism' taught in the schools of Ofir, the pupils are enjoined not to be cruel to their 'slaves' (*raby*), to clothe and feed them and not to overburden them with work.[39] Yet, as will be seen below, he did in principle conceive of the freedom of peasants in general.

The influence of Montesquieu can be detected in nearly all Shcherbatov's political works, particularly as regards his analysis of political structures and institutions. His comments on Catherine's *Instruction* show that he had made a careful comparison with *L'Esprit des Lois*, noting on every article of Catherine's the precise book and chapter from which she had quoted, pointing out any deviations from the original which seemed to him significant.

Shcherbatov's comments on Catherine's *Instruction* developed along two main lines. First he objected to some of Montesquieu's theoretical propositions; secondly he took issue with Catherine over the nature of her own government as it emerged from the *Instruction* or as he interpreted it from his own knowledge. He was thus less concerned with matters of principle than with how a particular ruler ruled in practice.

Let us turn first to Shcherbatov's comments on what might be termed 'constitutional' questions, and the problem of fundamental laws. He objected to Catherine's statement that the ruler of Russia must enjoy absolute power (art. 13), which of course he traced to its source in Montesquieu, though he did not comment on Catherine's deviation from the word 'despotic' used in the original.[40] Shcherbatov argued that if an absolute ruler was hardworking and sacrificed pleasures for the benefit of his subjects, if his orders were wise and just, then such a despotism might be preferable even to the freedom of a republic. But such rulers were rare. Nor did he think that speed in making decisions was to be welcomed when the decisions themselves might be taken by unaccountable rulers who could be swayed by their passions. Where one person ruled, argued Shcherbatov, even if power was limited by law, the ruler could break the law; law would become merely a word, whereas in republics, where the many rulers were accountable, they were forced to rule according to law; it was the law, not they, which ruled.[41]

Coming to article 16, in which Catherine quoted Montesquieu quite literally on the extent to which liberty flourishes in an absolute monarchy, Shcherbatov dismissively remarked that the 'spirit' of liberty was not the same as liberty, that people might for a time be deceived by such a 'mask' of liberty, but would then fall into greater slavery than before.[42]

When in article 18 Catherine stated that 'Les pouvoirs intermédiaires, subordonnés et dépendans du pouvoir suprème constituent la nature du gouvernment', Shcherbatov spotted at once that the words Montesquieu used in continuation ('c'est à dire de celui où un seul gouverne par des loix

39. *Puteshestviye v zemlyu Ofirskuyu*, in *Sochineniya*, cit., I, pp. 749ff., at p. 957.
40. See above, p. 243.
41. Shcherbatov, *Zamechaniya*, in *Neizdannyye Sochineniya*, cit., pp. 22–3.
42. *Op. cit.*, p. 24.

fondamentales') had been omitted. This roused his deepest suspicion. 'The omission of these words', he wrote, 'indicate a desire for unlimited despotic power.' Similarly he attacked Catherine's statement that 'le souverain est la source de tout pouvoir politique et civil'. He pointed out that Montesquieu had said this of a monarchy in which the ruler is bound to rule according to fundamental laws. In such a case, 'issuing or confirming laws with the consent of the tribunals [*pravitel' stva*] he is really the source of all political [*gosudarstvennyy*] or civil power' and is himself bound to obey the law he has established. But this does not happen in states in which the ruler considers himself above the law.[43] Turning to what he regarded as Russian reality, Shcherbatov noted that neither in the *Instruction* nor in the regulations for the election of deputies to the Legislative Commission was there any mention of the drafting of fundamental laws for the state, which should in fact be the first task on which the commission embarked.[44] Hence the *Instruction* tended to the perpetuation of despotic government. This is the only occasion in which Shcherbatov suggests in these observations that the Legislative Commission should have had the function of a constituent assembly, that it should have been empowered to draw up the actual fundamental laws of the state.

As was frequently the case among admirers of Montesquieu, there was some confusion about what he actually meant by fundamental laws. Were they statutorily enacted laws or were they institutions performing functions sanctioned by law and custom? The existence of a 'dépôt des lois' was for instance considered as a fundamental law, and was endorsed by both Catherine and Shcherbatov, though the latter added that Montesquieu had argued that in a despotism there was no dépôt des lois since there were no laws. In Russia, Catherine had declared, the 'dépôt des lois' was the Senate. Shcherbatov considered that this name, chosen by Peter I, gave a misleading impression owing to its association with the Roman Senate. But the Senate in Russia had no legislative power and but little executive power; any difficult decisions were referred to the ruler, who issued orders slavishly obeyed by the senators. Since the Senate had no power to interpret the law, nor to remonstrate against a personal ukaz, it was useless to describe it as a depositary of the laws. It was only a 'mask . . . as in all despotic states where judges are not the guardians of the laws but the instruments of the will of the despot'. The Senate had, it is true, been given the power to make representations about any ukazy to the emperor. But this power had never been used since Peter's time. Why, asked Shcherbatov? Because mistakes were never made? Or because senators were afraid to speak? In all probability, he concluded bitterly, the rulers appointed only inferior and unenlightened persons to the Senate, in order to ensure that their power should not suffer from the opposition of strong-minded men.[45]

43. *Op. cit.*, p. 25, article 18.
44. *Op. cit.*, p. 27, article 23.
45. *Op. cit.*, p. 26, article 21. He was himself made a Senator in 1779.

The various versions of Catherine's *Instruction* render the interpretation of article 28 particularly difficult. The French version again seems the clearest: 'Qu'est ce que le Dépôt des Loix? . . . Le Dépôt des Loix est cette institution en consequence de laquelle les corps établis pour faire observer la volonté du Souverain conformément aux Loix fondamentales . . . sont tenus de se conduire dans l'exercise de leur fonctions.' Shcherbatov, using the Russian text, which has '*nastavleniye*' (instruction) for 'institution',[46] argued that this implied the existence of a law specially designed to protect other laws. He saw a contradiction therefore between this article and article 26, which placed the depositary of the laws in the Senate, i.e. a tribunal, and not in a law. But he did in his argument raise to the category of a fundamental law in Russia the *General'nyy Reglament* or General Regulations issued by Peter I which codified administrative procedures throughout the Russian government. This gives some clue to the kind of legislative acts to which contemporary Russians might have granted the status of fundamental laws of the realm.[47]

Shcherbatov thoroughly endorsed Montesquieu's analysis of the importance of the separation of powers for the preservation of liberty. Indeed he went further than Montesquieu. Liberty did not consist merely in being protected against the misdeeds of other citizens; it consisted in being protected against the unjust power of the ruler (arts 38 and 39). There could be no real freedom where legislative and executive power were united in one person who was not bound by law. In such a society one could not trust in the preservation of one's property or even of one's life. In a work written only a couple of years later than his comments on the *Instruction*, Shcherbatov, discussing the Russian government, remarked that it was completely arbitrary (*samovlastno*) since the legislative and the executive were united in the monarch. In the reigns of Elizabeth and Catherine II, he added, arbitrary power had been used only for mercy. But if virtuous hearts produced good deeds, this did not alter the fact that the basic principle of government was arbitrary.[48] Shcherbatov passes over the fact that Montesquieu considered that a government was 'moderate' as long as the third power, the judiciary, remained separate from the other two. Catherine, who did indeed unite in herself all three powers, was naturally enough silent on this subject in the *Instruction*, except that she did attempt to draw a distinction between the sovereign as legislator and the judiciary (art. 149).

The idea that all men should be equal before the law is accepted by Shcherbatov in the sense that they are all entitled to the same protection for their honour and their property. But there should be no equality of punishment. Arrest and corporal punishment crush a noble, but a commoner remains

46. The Russian word *nastavleniye* renders this article almost unintelligible, and one may wonder whether, when the translation from French into Russian was made, the translator misread Catherine's handwriting and read *instruction* where she had written *institution*.

47. *Op. cit.*, pp. 28–9.

48. *Statistika v razsuzhdenii Rossii*, in *Chteniya v imperatorskom obshchestve istorii i drevnostey rossiyskikh*, 1859, No. 3, pp. 1–96, at p. 65.

unmoved by it. This was a common view at the time and difference of punishment in accordance with social status was a common practice in many countries, so common that Shcherbatov's reaction need cause no surprise.

In his comments on Catherine's chapters dealing with law courts, torture, penal practice and the death penalty, Shcherbatov is on the whole in agreement with the original. He favours the setting up in Russia of a corps of 'pleaders' (*stryapchiye*) to advise litigants for a fixed sum (art. 116); he opposes torture and mutilation, such as branding, though not the death penalty. He defends the right of the accused to object to a number of the judges (or assessors) of the court (182) and his right to be judged by his peers, but he regarded the English habit of locking up a jury without food and drink until a unanimous verdict had been reached as barbarous, and likely to lead to the reaching of a wrong decision as a result of starvation. He suggested that the introduction of a corps of public prosecutors might lead to the elimination of that 'shameful' figure, the informer, and endorsed Catherine's condemnation of the practice of allowing judges to receive presents, however small. Unfortunately the practice of paying salaries to judges had lapsed after the death of Peter, and even their re-introduction by the present empress had not succeeded in eradicating the ingrained habit of taking bribes.[49]

Where Catherine had condemned the confiscation of property as a penalty except in very rare cases, and then admitted the confiscation only of acquired as distinct from inherited property, Shcherbatov condemned the practice outright. The fact that it was possible was bound to induce ill-intentioned people to bring false accusations in order to acquire what they coveted. He also supported Catherine's statement that verdicts should be made public together with the evidence on which they were based. Catherine's views on the death penalty, which she rejected, were set out at length in article 210, based on Beccaria. Here Shcherbatov diverged from her in insisting on the deterrent effect of the death penalty, which should therefore be maintained, though rarely used.[50]

On the question of serfdom, Shcherbatov's comments are ambiguous. There are only thirteen articles in Catherine's chapter XI, the only ones to survive the drastic censorship to which this particular chapter was submitted by her advisers. In her original draft Catherine had put forward various proposals for reducing the number of serfs. She had accepted Montesquieu's proposition that a large number of serfs could not be freed at the same time. But she proposed that the state should guarantee the serf's moveable property so that he could buy his freedom; or that he should become free after serving a given number of years; or that once free he should never be enserfed again (a policy which became law in 1775);[51] or the setting up of peasant tribunals as existed

49. Shcherbatov, *Zamechaniya*, in *Neizdannyye Sochineniya*, cit., articles 124, 130, 139, 140, 141, pp. 41–45. In his *Razmyshleniya o zakonodatel'svte voobshche*, p. 418, Shcherbatov also recommends the introduction of bail, which he confuses with *habeas corpus*.

50. *Zamechaniya*, article 210, p. 47.

51. *Polnoye sobraniye zakonov Rossiyskoy imperii* (*PSZ*), St Petersburg ,1830, XX, No. 14275, Manifesto of 17 March 1775.

in Russian Finland which might 'diminuer la dureté domestique des maitres et des valets', or even a jury system, as in England.[52] In the chapter as published, Catherine did go so far as to state that abuses of, and the danger implicit in, serfdom should be regulated by civil law. Elsewhere, in her chapter on crafts and trade, Catherine stressed that agriculture was bound to suffer where the peasant owned no property, for the obvious reason that he would work harder for himself than for someone else.

It is probably just as well that Shcherbatov did not see the excised portions of Chapter XI, which would have horrified him. He was of course in full agreement with both Catherine and Montesquieu about the dangers of emancipating a large number of serfs at once. The land would be deserted, servants, seeing that more could be earned elsewhere, would abandon their masters. Freedom, he wrote, could only be granted gradually, as a reward for zeal and services, and on condition that the freed serf should be placed in a status in which he would he happy and useful to the state. Yet though here Shcherbatov does appear to conceive of a free peasantry, even in Russia, of a state in which the peasant is not bound to the soil, he seems to have believed that agriculture had suffered, even in western countries, when the peasantry had been emancipated. In his *Zapiska po krest' yanskomu voprosu*, written in 1768, in the midst of the debates in the Legislative Commission, Shcherbatov argued that the rent which peasants might pay the landowner for leased land would never be as much as the income obtained from peasant serfs. Therefore comparison with the freeing of the serfs in western countries was not valid. In France, for instance, thanks to local circumstances, when the serfs had been freed, the seigneurs remained owners of the land; the peasants benefited from their freedom and the owners from their increased revenues from rents. But, added Shcherbatov, considering the decline in agriculture about which there were so many complaints in France, he doubted if the peasants would now be given their freedom on the same terms.[53]

When Catherine tentatively proposed (art. 261) that serfs should be allowed to own property, Shcherbatov rejected it out of hand. 'Slaves cannot have property if it is not linked to freedom; for how can a man defend his property if he has not freedom to defend his body.'[54] Moreover, he argued, though the land in Russia belonged to the landowners and not to the peasants, the former were much too conscious of their own advantage to take their land and property away from the peasant. As a result, he argued, somewhat speciously, peasants do not feel that the land is not theirs – but the introduction of such ideas into their minds had led them to riot, indeed to murder many landowners during the recent Pugachev revolt, which had showed the peasants to be totally unworthy of any kind of freedom.

Shcherbatov is clearly allowing his feelings to run away with him here. Nevertheless his perception that peasant ownership even of moveable property

52. Chechulin, *op. cit.*, pp. xxxIIff.
53. *Zapiska po krest'yanskomu voprosu*, in *Neizdannyye Sochineniya*, cit., pp. 3–15, at p. 12.
54. *Zamechaniya*, p. 51.

would reduce peasant dependence on the landowner and endanger the latter's control of his labour force is for once quite clearly stated. To admit that public order is founded on deceiving the peasant into believing that he is the owner of the land when he is not reveals the extent to which on this particular issue Shcherbatov, even if only subconsciously, put personal advantage above principle and state security. His arguments in this domain do not have the intellectual consistency which characterized his discussion of political and legal issues.[55]

From Chapter XI onwards, Shcherbatov began to run out of steam and confined himself almost entirely to noting the original sources of Catherine's articles in *L'Esprit des Lois*. His interest was only aroused again when he reached the article describing the nobility (360). One should add to Catherine's definition, he wrote, that the nobility 'is the support of the throne and the state'. His argument is a curious one. The peasant owned so little property that it was a matter of indifference to him what changes took place in the state. A conqueror, or a usurper, would defend the peasant just as well as a legitimate ruler. The merchant class were citizens of the whole world (an anticipation of the charge of rootless cosmopolitanism?), unconcerned with the glory and welfare of the state as long as they could enrich themselves. All empires ruled by traders lasted but a short time, as the fate of Carthage and the decline of the United Provinces proved. But the nobility, deriving their advantage and honour from the advantage and honour of the state, identify their personal destiny with that of the state. Hence, because the noble had better opportunities to serve the state, he should use his privileges to perform such services, and in turn the state was obliged to provide him with both opportunity and privileges. Catherine's *Instruction* did not come up to Shcherbatov's expectations in one important respect: there was no reference to the need to maintain the prosperity of the noble estate, 'for nothing so degrades the heart of man as poverty'. The nobility in Russia used their private fortune to educate their children and make them fit for service, to supplement the small salary they received for state service, and to increase the splendour of the court. Hence their very debts were useful to the state since they encouraged the circulation of money and the development of arts and crafts. Shcherbatov was consistent in rejecting all kinds of sumptuary laws (useless in any case in view of the extravagance of the court). But though in principle he approved of partible inheritance, he thought some great families should receive state assistance in the form of larger salaries and allowances for their younger sons, in order to enable them to keep their fortunes intact.[56]

Shcherbatov did not comment on any of the remaining articles of the first 20 chapters of the *Instruction*, beyond again noting the corresponding sources in Montesquieu. It is a pity, because Catherine reverts to general political issues in articles 501–17. His views on the social and political structure of Russia are not systematically expounded in his comments on the *Instruction* for

55. *Op. cit.*, articles 370–77, pp. 52–3.
56. *Op. cit.*, articles 360, 374, 375, pp. 58–60.

he is simply following Catherine's text. He is therefore more concerned to express his doubts about the validity of Montesquieu's analyses, in the light of his own experience of what seemed to him to be a despotism, both in theory and in practice. For a systematic exposition of his ideas one must turn to his later works, his critique of the Statute of 1775, of the Charter to the Nobles of 1785, and above all to his *Journey to the Land of Ofir.*[57] If one leaves aside Shcherbatov's defence of serfdom, in which his own self-interest is so clearly involved, he remains the first consistent theorist in Russia of a new trend of thought, which could only have been formulated after the reign of Peter I. For he combined acceptance of the mobilizing role of the state with the diffusion of state power among the elite. In his view, the protection of personal property and security could be secured only in what he defined as 'a republican form of government', i.e. a polity less anarchic than Poland, less commercial than England.[58]

DIDEROT'S *OBSERVATIONS SUR L'INSTRUCTION DE L'IMPÉRATRICE DE RUSSIE*

Diderot arrived in Russia in October 1773 and left in March 1774. He never left the capital and his brief sojourn did not turn him into an expert on Russia. Though he was – rightly – pleased with his reception by the Empress, he was clearly immensely disappointed with the country, the people, the political structure and the possibilities for change, and above all the climate.

As in the case of Shcherbatov, the *Observations* do not constitute a systematic exposition of Diderot's ideas, because he is following Catherine's *Instruction* article by article. He approached it, however, from a diametrically opposed political pole – though strangely enough, his recommendations to Catherine sometimes coincided with those of Shcherbatov. More than Shcherbatov he aimed his shafts at the analysis of government and societies by Montesquieu which lay concealed behind Catherine's *Instruction*. Diderot commented on over 169 articles from the *Instruction*, and of these, over 100 were borrowed from Montesquieu, and some 20 from Becaria.[59]

Did Diderot really intend to send his *Observations* to Catherine? The original manuscript might or might not have been stolen by Prince D.A. Golitsyn, but Diderot had copies, and he could have copied one out and submitted it to the Empress had he wished. He did not. And in a way this is not surprising.

57. Apart from the introduction to A. Lentin's translation of *On the Corruption of Morals in Russia* relatively little has been published on Shcherbatov in recent years. The dissertation by J. Afferica, 'The Political and Social Thought of Prince M.M. Shcherbatov' (Harvard) remains unpublished. An article by M. Raeff dates back to 1960, while the short volume by I.A. Fedosov was published in 1967. Since then E. Donnert has published an article in *Zeitschrift fur Slawistik* (XVIII, 3, 1973) and André Monnier has published a brief note on the *Journey to the Land of Ofir* in *Cahiers du Monde russe et soviétique*, XXIII, 2, pp. 187–96,

58. *Razmyshleniye o dvoryanstve*, p. 256.

59. See my article 'Catherine and the Philosophes' in A.G. Cross ed., *Russia and the West in the Eighteenth Century*, Newtonville, Mass., Oriental Research Partners, 1983, pp. 30–52.

The tone of his remarks in sometimes so violent, the underlying trend of his ideas so critical, that it is highly unlikely that he would have addressed his comments, in the form in which they have come down to us, to a ruler who remained throughout his lifetime his principal benefactress.

In the short space available here, only comments Diderot made on the political theory of the *Instruction* will be considered. Already in the *Encyclopédie* Diderot had expounded his belief in the secular and popular origin of all government. He rejected the divine right of kings and placed sovereignty squarely in the people. The *Instruction* should have begun, he wrote, with the proclamation that the only true sovereign is the nation, the only legislator the people. A well-made code must start by binding the ruler in writing, and the use by the sovereign of the power granted to him must be publicly verified by a national representative body at regular intervals. Such a body should also be the source of all civil and political power.[60]

There was not, in Diderot's eyes, any difference between a despotism and 'la monarchie pure'. The despot did what he wanted; the monarch 'est assujetti à des formes qu'il néglige quand il lui plait et qui ne font que suspendre ses volontés sans les changer quand il les respecte . . . C'est l'esprit de la monarchie pure qui a dicté l'instruction de Catherine seconde. C'est donc une mauvaise forme de gouvernement.'[61] Even a *monarchie temperée* provided no guarantee against a return to 'pure' monarchy.

Turning to the intermediary powers, Diderot argued that their rights should be defined and laid down in such a way that neither the ruler nor his heirs could alter them. Again, he goes beyond Catherine to Montesquieu. If intermediary powers are dependent on the supreme power (Bk. II, Ch. IV)[62] they are nothing. 'Un peuple libre ne diffère d'un peuple esclave que par l'inamovibilité de certains privilèges appartenant à l'homme comme homme; à chaque ordre de citoyens, comme membre de cette ordre, et a chaque citoyen comme membre de la société.' Here again there is the contrast between Diderot's concept of universally valid, rational laws, and Montesquieu's sense of the constant changes brought about by time in the delicate balance between the ruler and the 'pouvoirs intermédiaires'.

Diderot agreed that a 'dépôt des lois' was essential, but far more important in his view was to ensure that the 'depot' should not be violated, 'par le souverain ou par le magistrat'. The right to make representations (art. 21) was useless. 'Faire des representations!', exclaimed Diderot. 'A quoi servent les representations? Est-ce-que nos magistrats n'en faisaient pas?' And had not the *parlements* been repeatedly overridden, exiled, and finally destroyed? What

60. On Diderot's political thought see *inter alia* Jacques Proust, 'Diderot et l'experience russe; un exemple de pratique theorique au XVIIIe siècle', in *Studies on Voltaire and the Eighteenth Century*, CLIV, 1976, pp. 1777ff.

61. *Observations, Œuvres Politiques*, p. 356.

62. Neither Catherine nor Diderot was to know that Montesquieu had modified his original draft by the insertion of the words 'subordonnés et dependans' in order not to appear to be raising up other authorities against the king. See Shackleton, *op. cit.*, p. 279. See also Diderot, *Observations*, cit., p. 360.

guarantee was there of the survival of this institution? In France 'le parlement n'est plus. En Russie c'est le Senat, mais le Senat n'est rien.'[63]

The main object of any government, wrote Diderot, should be 'le bonheur des citoyens', rather than their glory (art. 15). 'La vie n'est rien si elle n'est pas heureuse', he urged, and explained how happiness could be found and ensured. 'Il faut d'abord que la société soit heureuse; et elle le sera si la liberté et la propriété sont assurées.'[64] Elsewhere he wrote: 'Pourquoi la Russie est-celle moins bien gouvernée que la France? C'est que la liberté naturelle de l'individu y est reduite à rien, et que l'autorité souveraine y est illimitée.' Thus he rejected the definition of liberty in a monarchy put forward in article 16 by Catherine (and Montesquieu). 'La liberté est dans les democraties', he argued. 'L'esprit de liberté peut être dans les monarchies . . . cependant quand on manque de celui-ci, il faut précisément conserver celle-là. Il faut qu'un peuple soit libre, ou qu'il croie l'être.' Let the mask of liberty, the spider's web, conceal 'la tête hideuse du despote'.[65] Liberty was essential to the preservation of property, which in turn was essential to happiness. Only a happy people will multiply, and a people can only be happy where 'la liberté et la propriété sont sacrées'.

Equality meant equality before the law, not social or economic equality. All privileges attached to different estates and orders should be abolished. Even so, natural inequality would inevitably lead to a certain degree of inequality before the law and in society. Inequality was attached to merit. 'Je respecte toutes ces inégalités c'est une portion de la propriété.'[66] On the vexed question of serfdom, Diderot put forward the simple solution of abolishing it.

The virulent anti-clericalism, so typical of Diderot, is manifest from the very beginning of his *Observations*. Both Catherine and Montesquieu were castigated for having placed their work under the protection of the Almighty, which he considered to have been pure expediency on their part. 'Je n'aime point a faire entrer dans les actes de souverainété des gens qui prêchent un être supérieur au souverain', he wrote. 'Le prêtre dont le systeme est un tissu d'absurdités tend seulement à entretenir l'ignorance; la raison est l'ennemie de la foi, et la foi est à la base de l'état, de la fortune, de la considération du prêtre.' The priests' real place in society was 'tout juste au dessus ou au dessous du comédien'. To a ruler ruling over an extremely devout population, such diatribes were bound to reflect the author's total disregard for the sensibilities of the bulk of that same 'people' whose life he wished so much to render happy.

To sum up these brief remarks on Diderot's *Observations* one may note two contradictory conclusions. On the one hand Diderot urges Catherine to adopt a series of measures which would deprive her forever of a portion of sovereign

63. *Op. cit.*, p. 364.
64. *Op. cit.*, pp. 374, 403.
65. *Op. cit.*, pp. 355, 357–8. See above, p. 21 for Shcherbatov's very similar denunciation of the 'spirit of liberty'.
66. *Op. cit.*, pp. 366, 407.

power, in order to prevent the government of Russia from ever reverting to a despotism. To ensure *political* liberty in Russia, Catherine should surrender her authority into the hands of some sort of body representing 'les grands propriétaires', the powers of which would evolve over time.[67] She should have defined the rights of the sovereign in her *Instruction*. 'La liberté politique ne consiste pas a faire tout ce que l'on veut', Catherine had stated in article 36. But, concluded Diderot, 'Cette maxime doit s'étendre également à la souveraineté . . . la souveraineté et la liberté sont limitées l'une et l'autre par la même barrière: le respect de la propriété de la part du souverain, et son usage de la part du sujet.'

On the other hand, in several of his observations, Diderot seems to be urging Catherine to use her despotic power to introduce reforms which would otherwise not be achieved. In article 57, Catherine had written: 'C'est à la legislation à suivre l'esprit de la nation'. Diderot rejected this. Solon had indeed followed the spirit of the nation, but then he was not a despot, ruling over a barbarous and enserfed population. But 'quand on peut tout et il n'y a rien de fait, il ne faut pas s'en tenir aux meilleurs lois qu'un peuple peut recevoir; il faut lui donner les meilleurs lois possibles'.

Diderot's remarks about Russia are often inaccurate, and he wrote his *Observations* before Catherine had embarked on the major programme of reforms which marked the years 1775–86. He should not therefore be taken as a source of information on Russia, nor should his judgements be accepted without reservations. His *Observations* underestimate the difficulties of introducing reforms into any country, let alone Russia. But at times reality pierces through the clouds of *philosophie*. 'Civiliser à la fois une aussi énorme contrée me semble un projet au-dessus des forces humaine', he wrote, commenting on the statement that Russia was a European power. And later on, 'Croyez vous que les paysans d'une contrée qui a huit mois d'hiver puissent ressembler au paysans d'une contrée qui en a à peine deux ou trois'.[68] Diderot's relative lack of interest in Catherine's legislative programme after 1775 suggests that in his heart he turned away from the insoluble problem of civilizing such a vast and backward country, and looked to the more manageable countries whose problems he could focus within the range of his mental camera: the United Provinces, the United States, and of course France.

If Shcherbatov wrote his comments from the point of view of aristocratic constitutionalism, at least they reflect some knowledge of Russian reality, and an awareness that the *Instruction* was not a Code. Diderot, in contrast, frequently criticizes the *Instruction* as though it were a fully fledged Code of laws. Moreover the political solutions he put forward had little relevance to Russia.

67. *Op. cit.*, p. 368. Vernière (p. 369, n. 2) suggests that Diderot proposed this somewhat strange solution because he realized that Russia had no *tiers état*. But see my article 'Catherine and the Philosophes', cit., for the explanation that he was influenced by some of the disgruntled magnates who were his most constant companions in Russia, and who evidently shared Shcherbatov's opinions on the ideal form of government for their country.
68. *Op. cit.*, pp. 370–1.

A government whose main object was public happiness by means of legal guarantees of liberty and property was indeed a far distant ideal – then, and ever since. Sadly, one must also conclude that Diderot's confident claim that 'le philosophe n'a jamais tué de prêtres, et le prêtre a beaucoup tué de philosophes' is no longer true.[69]

69. *Op. cit.*, p. 349.

CHAPTER TWELVE

Russia and the Enlightenment

This is clearly a very broad subject. I shall therefore assume that we agree in general on the use of the word 'Enlightenment' to describe an intellectual movement in which reason was winning the battle over revelation in the field of ideas, the validity of many traditional institutions was being questioned, the authority of the Church was being disputed and, as the eighteenth century wore on, the legitimacy of the dominant form of government on the continent of Europe, namely royal absolutism, was being increasingly undermined.[1] In addition, rulers open to these influences were moved to embark on what was perceived at the time to be programmes of reform, political, social or economic as the case might be, in order to maximize in the most rational way the resources of their respective states. In attempting to analyse the influence of the Enlightenment in Russia, however, one must face the problem of detaching this one particular broad current of ideas from the general cultural life of the country as it was remodelled as a result of Peter I's reforms.

The philosopher Leibniz, who met Peter I several times, and corresponded with his friends Franz Lefort and James Bruce, devised a fundamental programme for the cultural modernization of Russia, which Peter to a great extent adopted and achieved. Leibniz put forward seven measures he thought essential, namely the establishment of an institution in general charge of sciences and art; the recruitment of foreigners; the importation of foreign instruments; granting permission to Russians to travel abroad; the education of Russians within their own country; the assessment of conditions in the country so as to discover its needs and finally supplying them. This programme required a whole range of activities and cultural pursuits new to Russia, such as the setting up of printing presses, libraries, and bookshops, the collection and study of specimens of natural history and of technical instruments, the establishment of schools and academies, and the study of the geography, climate and soil, the

1. This is the revised text of a talk given to a history seminar in St Andrews University in 1984.

people, languages and religions, the agriculture, mineral wealth and communications of the country.[2]

Leibniz's programme, which falls squarely within the German *Frühaufklarung*, is the foundation for, but is not the same as, the Enlightenment. It prepared the way, opened up the channels for the slow penetration of new ideas and concepts, mainly scientific at first, branching out into literature, philosophy and politics as the century wore on. Two at least of Leibniz's recommendations are very relevant here: one was the establishment of a central institution to oversee cultural and scientific life, in the case of Russia the Academy of Sciences, planned while Peter was alive, and founded after his death. The other was the importation from abroad, and the production and distribution within Russia of the printed word. The introduction of the cyrillic civil script in 1707 made both printing and reading easier, though bookshops were still almost non-existent (in Venice there were 67 in the sixteenth century).[3]

The systematic introduction of works published in the West began with Peter I, though in his time it was still a trickle. Fewer than 500 titles were published in Russia in the whole of the seventeenth century, and 95 per cent of these were devotional. With Peter, books of all kinds were imported on a wide scale. Even so, 58 per cent of the works printed in his reign were official documents, 23 per cent were religious in content, and history, geography, technology and science, philosophy and *belles-lettres* all together amounted to 3.3 per cent of the total. The number of titles published continued small in the following 30 years: from 1725 to 1755 a total of 928 titles, of which religious works still came to 41 per cent, were published.[4] These figures are a sufficient commentary on the quantity, if they give no clue to the quality of what was available to the Russian reader. It is instructive to compare them with the flood of books, journals, and ephemera published for instance in England, France and the United Provinces in the same period. It is really only after the middle of the century that the existence of a larger reading public in Russia led to a take-off in publishing: 1,482 titles were brought out in 1755–75, while in the years 1776–1800 the number rose to 7,845.[5] But published books are not everything. They were massively outnumbered by the manuscripts of devotional works, chapbooks, calendars, almanachs which provided the basic reading matter.

It must also be borne in mind that Russians borrowed from the West mainly – though by no means only – the literature which was being published at the time, what was necessary to Russians at the time, what was then contemporary to them. To illustrate what I mean, in the excellent Soviet complete

2. Mechthild Keller, 'Wegbereiter der Aufklarung; Gottfried Wilhelm Leibniz' wirken fur Peter des Grossen und sein Reich', in *Russen und Russland aus deutscher Sicht, 9–17 Jahrhundert*, ed. M. Keller *et al.*, Munich, 2nd ed. 1988, pp. 391–413.
3. Review in the *Times Literary Supplement* by George Steiner.
4. Gary Marker, *Publishing, Printing and the Origins of Intellectual Life in Russia 1700–1800*, New Jersey, 1984, pp. 25, 59.
5. *Ibid.*

catalogue of works published in the period 1725–1800, there is only one reference to Machiavelli in the index. When you look it up, you find that it is the *Anti-Machiavel* of Frederick II of Prussia, not *The Prince* or the *Discourses*.[6] There were no translations in early eighteenth-century Russia of medieval or Renaissance philosophy, politics or theology, though the second book of Aristotle's *Politics* appeared in a monthly magazine in 1757. There were no translations of Descartes, Pascal or Spinoza; Grotius's *De jure belli et pacis* did not appear, but his *De veritate religionis christianae* was published in 1765, 1768 and 1781. Peter himself sponsored the publication of Pufendorf's Introduction to the *History of the Major European Powers* which appeared in 1718 in 600 copies, and again in 1767–77, this time in over 2,000 copies.[7] His *On the Duties of Man and Citizen* appeared in 1726. Quintus Curcius's Life of Alexander the Great and Aesop's fables provided light reading. Most translations from the great Western poets or thinkers were published after the middle of the century, such as Dante, Ariosto, or Erasmus's *In Praise of Folly*. The poet Tredyakovsky translated a life of Francis Bacon from the French in 1760 and included some extracts of his philosophical works. A translation of what may be Hobbes's *De cive* appeared in 1776.[8] A number of Plato's works, including the *Laws*, were published in translation by the Academy of Science in 1780–85.[9] There was no translation of Leibniz.

Of course one cannot judge exclusively by translations. Even in Russia, where to a great extent they reflected the choice of those who commissioned them, and to some extent that of the translators, a great deal of very second-rate literature was translated, such as English romances translated through the French, and other works of dubious value, which nevertheless had a commercial market. If Greek was not part of the cultural baggage of the educated Russian, knowledge of Latin became much more frequent in the eighteenth century (it was taught in the Slavo-Greco-Latin academies and in church seminaries), which opened the way to the reading of much classical literature, and to the philosophical, political and educational literature of the seventeenth century much of which was still written in Latin. In the second half of the century, many translations of classical poets and historians appeared. And the small Russian elite, mainly but not exclusively noble, could also read in French, German, sometimes even English or Italian. But Russia moved into the world of the Enlightenment without that intimate knowledge of the literature of the classical world and of the middle ages which underpins the whole history of thought in the West. The allusiveness which gives grace and lightness and forms so much of the texture of intellectual interchange in the West could not easily be grasped. This seems to have left Russian intellectual life very shallowly rooted in unfertilized soil, and to my mind rather thin. It lacked the essential

6. *Svodnyy katalog russkoy knigi grazhdanskoy pechati XIII veka, 1725–1800*, 5 vols, ANSSR, Moscow, 1964, III, No. 7907.
7. *Ibid.*, II, 5768–70.
8. *Ibid.*, I, 1459.
9. *Ibid.*, III, 5351.

depths provided by previous religious, philosophical and scientific debate. All that went before the enlightened writers of the eighteenth century, all that they had drawn upon, the Russians learnt about later.

It is also easy to forget that the establishment of institutions of higher learning, the increasing numbers of poets, playwrights, scientists of all kinds, the emergence of literary and satirical journals in the first half of the eighteenth century, represented primarily a process of the westernization of cultural forms rather than the influence of specifically enlightened thought as defined above. The institutionalization of Russian culture took place with the foundation of the Academy of Science in 1726, the Cadet Corps in 1731, the University of Moscow in 1755, the Academy of Arts in 1757, and finally, in 1783, the Russian Academy of Letters. These bodies served to bring together the intellectual elite of the country, including the high nobility, the middle nobles, the professional class of teachers, and teachers in the military cadet schools, mainly non-noble and sometimes German, the scientists, also usually German, the grammarians, historians, geographers, of whom Lomonosov became the towering example. It is not surprising that the new culture should have taken some time to establish itself. In spite of the suggestions of some historians that westernization had already begun to make an impact in the late seventeenth century, the whirlwind unleashed by Peter I was a tremendous culture shock. Foreign clothes, foreign ideas, foreign travel, foreign religions, foreign-style architecture, living in stone houses, watching pageants celebrating victories in which Mars and Hercules were praised (and if literate, reading the leaflets expounding their meaning), seeing statues of naked women in the round in Peter's parks and portraits which actually looked like the people they portrayed, all this was bound to lead to some dislocation of the traditional modes of feeling and thinking.

Moreover, a considerable gulf developed in Russia in the eighteenth century between secular and religious thought. Most leading Russian writers in the early part of the century had either been educated in the Slavo-Greco-Russian academies (in Moscow or Kiev) or in theological seminaries. With the foundation of the Cadet Corps, Moscow University (which had no theological faculty) and the schools attached to the Academy of Science and Arts in mid-century, education became much more secular and divorced from the Church. In Catherine's educational reforms of 1786, priests were not admitted to schools even to teach the catechism. Russian writers were familiar with the Psalter, the Church Slavonic Bible and the liturgy and possibly with the Church fathers because primary education in the countryside was often in the hands of the parish priest (when it was not given by a retired soldier!). And there were a few highly educated ecclesiastics, such as Archbishop Feofan Prokopovich in the reign of Peter I, and Metropolitan Platon and Archbishops Evgenii Bolkhovitinov and Evgenii Bulgaris in the reign of Catherine II.[10]

10. The only foreign visitor to my knowledge to have left lengthy descriptions of conversations with Metropolitan Platon and Yevgeniy Bulgaris is Francisco de Miranda, *Viajes-Diarios*, II, Caracas, 1929, pp. 351–2, 359.

But there was not that easy social intercourse between the Russian priesthood and secular society which was so marked in France, and prevailed if perhaps to a lesser degree in England.

Many Western commentators have adopted the practice of Soviet historians of using two concepts in dealing with the Enlightenment in Russia: these are 'enlighteners' and 'enlightening' on the one hand and Enlightenment on the other.[11] In theory these concepts should be kept separate, but they are often confused. An 'enlightener' is by definition 'progressive'. It is in this sense that N.V. Ryasanovsky, in his *The Image of Peter the Great in Russian History and Thought*,[12] speaks of Peter as representing the Enlightenment. But I do not think this view of Peter would be acceptable to most Western historians of Russia and of the history of ideas. The intellectual climate in which Peter operated, the ideas he drew upon, belong more to cameralism, to the German *Frühaufklarung*, to *Polizeiwissenschaft*. He was not concerned with broad philosophical generalizations, but with practical necessities such as how to navigate ships or make guns, organize an army, raise revenue and ensure public order.

The difficulty for Soviet historians is that they are faced by a number of *obiter dicta* by Marx and Lenin which have tended to imprison their scholarship in a straitjacket. Marx identified the Enlightenment with capitalism, the rise of the bourgeoisie and philosophical materialism (and in his analysis the Enlightenment is mainly French). Lenin regarded the Russian Enlightenment as mainly a nineteenth-century phenomenon, characterized by three main traits: firstly hatred of serfdom and the defence of liberty, self-government and the European way of life; secondly a defence of the interests of the popular masses in general; and thirdly the belief that the abolition of serfdom would bring increased prosperity. (This really corresponds rather to an enlightener than to the Enlightenment and is sometimes regarded as a mental portrait of Chernyshevsky.)

The problem in applying these criteria to Russian intellectual history is that eighteenth-century Russia was nowhere near a capitalist society in spite of the efforts of Soviet economic historians to detect the embryonic capitalism in the womb of feudalism. There was only a very small bourgeoisie, and only very few bourgeois were interested in the life of the mind. And very few of the 'enlighteners' were philosophical materialists. That disposes of Marx. As regards the authors, in the eighteenth century, nearly all were noble; a few were *popovichi* or sons of priests, like Tredyakovsky; a few more were *raznochintsy*, that undefinable category of people who did not fit into the estate structure of Russia, who fell between ranks, and to which the budding professional classes belonged; and a very few were peasants or even of serf origin; as the century advanced some were to be found among the merchantry. Nearly all the nobles were interested mainly in noble affairs, and there is very little of that burning concern with the evils of serfdom so typical of the Decembrists and the

11. P. Berkov, *Istoriya russkoy zhurnalistiki XVIII veka*, Moscow–Leningrad, 1952, *passim*.
12. Oxford University Press, 1985.

nineteenth-century intelligentsia until very late in the century. That disposes of Lenin.

In this brief and partial survey I shall confine myself to the traditional use of the concept of 'Enlightenment'. In my view this movement comes into full force in Russia in the second half of the eighteenth century, coinciding broadly with the reign of Catherine II (1762–96). I see it as the circulation among an elite group of secular, rational, scientific approaches to intellectual and cultural life, and to problems of government, administration and the economy. In this latter field it is not so much the adoption and application of specific 'enlightened' policies, but new approaches to the formulation and implementation of new or old policies which strike one. I propose in the first place to analyse the substructure of intellectual life, i.e. the radius in which the Enlightenment operated in terms of the channels for the circulation of ideas, printers, censorship, publishers, booksellers, print runs, and the readership, including private libraries. Secondly I will examine the nature and quality of some of the works published in translation; and thirdly, the nature and quality of a few original works.

The substructure, which Robert Darnton has so brilliantly illuminated for France, has not been so well studied by Soviet historians as might have been expected, though recently an American scholar, Gary Marker, has provided a very useful overview based on intensive research on which I shall draw (as well as on the works of Soviet bibliographers). In seventeenth-century Russia there was one central printing office, forming part of the government apparatus, and the Patriarchate also had its own printing establishment. The only other presses were in the Ukraine, in Nezhin and Chernigov, which had been under Polish overlordship until 1667, and where Polish tradition was strong. Peter I believed in the necessity of explaining his reforms to the people and it is striking how many of his published edicts begin with the word '*ponezhe*', 'because'. As a result most of his major government institutions set up their own printing presses, notably the Senate, the Holy Synod, the Academy of Sciences and eventually the Cadet Corps, the Artillery Corps and other military training schools, and of course the University of Moscow. More by accident than by design maybe, the previous total Muscovite central control of the printed word in Russian was perpetuated under Peter I and his successors. Printing in German in Livonia and Estonia was in the hands of private enterprise.

Any author wishing to have something printed submitted his text to one or other of these official presses and paid for the printing. (Books were usually sold in unbound sheets and the purchaser arranged for the binding.) After the Catherinian reform of local administration in 1775 many of the Boards of Local Welfare[13] set up their own printing presses which not only published local edicts but also locally written prose and poetry, sometimes even written by women, as in Tambov when the poet Derzhavin was governor. This situation continued until 1783, when Catherine introduced freedom to set up

13. Prikazy obshchego prizreniya.

a printing press anywhere, by anyone of whatever social estate. Whereupon a large number of private and commercial presses was set up, by nobles on their private estates and by non-nobles in towns. When Radishchev wanted to print his *Journey from St Petersburg to Moscow* he bought a press and printed it himself.

Very little is known about the policy or the practice of the censorship before 1783. Since until 1783 all printers were attached to government institutions, they were in general self-censoring. Many historians, both pre- and post-Soviet (after all, a lot of nineteenth-century historians were deeply critical of the absolute regime prevailing in Russia), have assumed, judging by tsarist practice in nineteenth-century Russia, that a severe political censorship was practised in Catherine's reign which banned any criticism of the Empress, serfdom, absolute government etc. But there is almost no evidence to support this. There are a few known cases where the Empress intervened in person to forbid a work. Much has been made of the fact that she banned Rousseau's *Emile* in 1763. But this prohibition occurred very early in her reign, probably at the instigation of the ecclesiastical authorities, more concerned with the *Confession de foi d'un vicaire savoyard* than with Rousseau's educational theories. Indeed, Catherine, who did not care for his educational theories either, nevertheless seems to have raised no objection when selections from *Emile* and *Sophie*, including the famous confession of faith of the savoyard priest, were published in the 1770s.[14] Nor did she raise any objection to the publication of a translation of the *Discours sur l'origine et les fondements de l'inégalité* by that great admirer of Rousseau, General P.S. Potemkin, the cousin of her favourite.

The official presses continued to be self-censoring after 1783, but authors using, or owning, private presses were now required by law to submit manuscripts to the chief of police in the nearest district capital, who was supposed to ensure that the criteria adopted by Catherine were enforced, namely that there should be nothing offensive to religion, public morality and the ruler, before authorizing publication.[15] This was a very wide definition which allowed for the publication of very varied original and translated works. No doubt writers and translators developed a sixth sense of what would be acceptable. Tirades against foreign tyrants[16] were not objected to, and I do not know of any proven case of prohibition by the censorship until the French Revolution was well under way, except for the censorship of masonic works (of which more below). Political information about the American Revolution appeared frequently in the Moscow and St Petersburg Gazettes, and the French

14. Translated in 1770 by S. Bashilov, printed on the press of the Artillery and Engineering Cadet Corps (SKRK, III, 6225).

15. K. Papmehl, *Freedom of Expression in Eighteenth-Century Russia*, The Hague, 1971.

16. Radishchev translated G. Bonnot de Mably's *Observations sur l'histoire de la Grèce* (1766) in 1773, and added to Mably's condemnation of despotism his own gloss in a footnote, to the effect that 'Despotism [*samoderzhavstvo*] is the condition most repugnant to human nature . . .' and he asserted the right of the individual to be released from obligation to the ruler if the ruler were unjust. This general condemnation of '*samoderzhavstvo*' met with no difficulty from the censorship.

Declaration of the Rights of Man was published in full in the *St Petersburg Gazette*.[17]

Moscow University Press became in due course a large-scale publishing firm rather than a mere press, particularly after the lease was granted to N.I. Novikov in 1779. He developed an enormous programme of publications, and through his masonic connections established a network of provincial booksellers. But he met with a number of obstacles. The first occurred in 1783, when he published a guide to calligraphy of which the copyright belonged to the Commission on National Education. The question of copyright was a very grey area at the time in Russia, but the Commission complained and Novikov had to surrender the 790 copies remaining out of 1,200 printed and pay for those he had sold. In 1785 he again got into trouble over the printing of masonic works of occult character. Six of these works were eventually banned by Catherine. Again in 1787 fourteen masonic or anti-religious works, published on a secret press run by Novikov and which had not been shown to the chief of police, were banned.[18] But the reasons for these last two prohibitions were not strictly political. There was nothing in the pseudo or semi-mystical literature printed by the Moscow masons which could be regarded as politically seditious, even by an extremely suspicious ruler, which Catherine was not. But she disapproved of wasting the resources of the Moscow University Press on works which she regarded as superstitious lucubrations. In 1789, moved by evidence of the continuation of Novikov's masonic educational activities, she determined not to renew his lease of the university press.

By the early 1790s Catherine was fully alert to the dangers of the French Revolution, and what seemed to her its offshoot, just over her borders, in Poland. Radishchev's publication of his *Journey from St Petersburg to Moscow* in 1790, with its powerful condemnation of serfdom, what seemed to her its implicit approval of Pugachev's rising, and its attack on the commander-in-chief of the Russian armed forces (G.A. Potemkin) in the war with the Ottoman Porte, led to his arrest. For once we have the actual evidence of Catherine's response, for she jotted down her marginal comments in her copy of his book. Sentenced to death by the highest criminal court, the sentence was commuted to ten years exile in the wilds of Siberia.[19] Similarly, V. Knyazhnin's play on *Vadim of Novgorod*, the medieval republican hero who challenges the legitimate sovereign Ryurik, which had passed unnoticed when it was first issued, got into trouble when it was republished in 1793 by an incautious Princess Dashkova. She was bitterly reproached by Catherine and the play

17. M.M. Shtrange, *Russkoye obshchestvo i frantsuzskaya revolyutsiya*, Moscow, 1956, p. 50.
18. See my *Russia in the Age of Catherine the Great*, London, 1981, p. 526.
19. It is frequently stated that Radishchev was sentenced to hard labour in Siberia. He was not. He was allowed to travel to his ultimate destination, Ilimsk, in a leisurely way, stopping off for a while in Tobolsk. He was eventually joined by his sister-in-law (his wife had recently died) and two of his children; he had three more children by the latter but could not marry her, as she was his deceased wife's sister. He had servants to care for them all and his patron, A.R. Vorontsov, sent him money and books.

was banned. (Knyazhnin had died some time before. Dashkova had hoped to benefit his widow and children by reprinting the play.) Several other publishers got into trouble in the 1790s, including Novikov and his masonic friends who had continued to issue banned masonic books, and whose masonic activities were now closed down. Novikov himself was arrested and convicted without a formal trial for treasonable relations with the Prussian Rosicrucian masons, who had now become ministers of the new King Frederick William II of Prussia when Russia and Prussia had recently been on the brink of war.[20] The assassination of Gustavus of Sweden in March 1792 and the execution of Louis XVI in January 1793 in France contributed to Catherine's fears of revolutionary attacks on herself, and in September 1796, rather late in the day it must be admitted, she issued the first formal edict on censorship. All private presses were closed down; all imported books were subjected to censorship at the Russian borders and all manuscripts had to be as before submitted to the chiefs of police. Publishing in Russia never reverted to the freedom it had briefly enjoyed in the period 1762–96.[21]

If publishers were at first non-existent and printers few and far between, booksellers were at first even more rare. One of the few memoirists of eighteenth-century Russia, T. Bolotov, has described his discovery of the existence of bookshops. During the Seven Years War he was with the Russian occupying forces in Königsberg, and was told that such places existed. He went into one, saw unbound copies of books displayed, chose one, arranged to have it bound, and shortly afterwards found himself the proud owner of the first book he had ever bought. Again, in the second half of the century, bookshops as well as other shops became more frequent in the major cities; the printing works at government institutions also sold books, as did the Academy of Science and the University Press in Moscow, and in the countryside books were frequently peddled in market stalls.

The print runs give us an idea of the extent of the readership, and hence of the audience for *all* works published, not merely for the masterpieces of enlightened thought. The Synodal press published a large number of items such as psalters, catechisms, primers and alphabet books, some still in the old orthography, Russian grammars, laws and charters. The textbooks published by the National Education Commission after 1783 were reprinted several times and evidently had a vast captive market. The works by French *philosophes*, including even the great Montesquieu, published by Catherine's Society for the Translation of Foreign Books, found a less ready market, and lead one to wonder whether most of the likely readers read them in French or German.

20. The investigation into Novikov's Prussian connections occurred just before the Russian invasion of Poland preparatory to the Second Partition and only a year after Catherine had been reduced to tears by Prussian threats over the Ochakov crisis. There is still some dispute about the reasons for the condemnation of Novikov, but a careful reading of the documents leads me to the conclusion that though the investigation in all likelihood arose because of an ecclesiastical denunciation for allegedly printing Old Believer books, the condemnation occurred because of his direct contacts with Prussian Rosicrucians who were now ministers of the King of Prussia.
21. *Polnoye sobraniye zakonov Rossiyskoy imperii* (*PSZ*), St Petersburg, 1830, xxiii, No. 17,508.

Some works, like Marmontel's *Bélisaire*, translated by Catherine herself and a group of her courtiers, were reprinted many times, but printers frequently remained with large stocks of unsold copies on their hands, which were eventually disposed of at a discount. A.A. Nartov, the Secretary of the Academy of Sciences, proposed in the 1740s that employees of the Academy should take part of their salary in books in order to shift them off the shelves. The print runs of the satirical journals of the 1760s and 1770s also show surprising variations. In its first year, Novikov's *The Drone* ranged from 800 to 300 copies. The reprint editions in book form seemed to do better (1,200). It was not the censorship which killed off the journals, therefore, but the lack of readers. When Novikov closed down *The Drone*, he prepared to start a new journal, *The Painter*, for which he received a subsidy of 200 rubles from the Empress. One of his later, moralizing and masonic journals, *Morning Light*, which was supposed to make enough money to subsidize two schools, was in the end subsidized by wealthy subscribers to the schools such as Catherine and the baby Grand Duke Alexander. In its first year the print run was 785, in the second year 540, and in the third year 184.[22]

What social class purchased books? Or journals? Or read them? This is a difficult question to answer on present evidence, since not nearly so much work has been done on private libraries in the second half of the eighteenth century as in the first, i.e. on the libraries of those who started collecting books in the reign of Peter I. Some not entirely conclusive figures for subscribers to *The Drone* show that 77 per cent were nobles, 10 per cent clerics, 6 per cent merchants, and 7 per cent miscellaneous. Subscribers to the journals published in the 1770s show an even more overwhelming noble majority, 88 per cent in Moscow, 87 per cent in St Petersburg, and 72 per cent in provincial towns, where subscribers in the priesthood numbered 13 per cent.[23] Readership was of course somewhat wider than these figures suggest since they take no account of multiple readership.[24]

Given the slow spread of education throughout the country, these figures are not surprising. But they were nevertheless a great disappointment to Soviet researchers who had hoped to see in Novikov, for instance, the spokesman for the interests of a middle-class, bourgeois trend, the publisher of bourgeois authors for a large bourgeois readership in a burgeoning capitalist economy. It is clear, however, that throughout the country the bulk of the readership was mainly noble, sometimes clerical, and it was small.

Similarly most of the writers and translators were noble. Shtrange, who has written a good deal on what he calls the 'democratic intelligentsia' (democratic here refers to social origins, i.e. non noble, not to political ideas), lists

22. Gareth Jones, 'The Morning Light' Charity Schools, 1777–80', *Slavonic and East European Review*, 56, No. 1, January 1978, pp. 47–67.
23. G. Marker, 'Novikov's Readers', *Modern Languages Review*, 77, No. 4, October 1982, pp. 894–905.
24. G. Marker, 'Russian Journals and their Readers in the Late Eighteenth Century', *Oxford Slavonic Papers*, 19, 1986, pp. 88–101.

73 non-noble writers and translators, though one would not always agree with his classification.[25] Most of the translators worked for the Society for the Promotion of Foreign Translations set up by Catherine in 1767, with a subsidy of 5,000 rubles per annum, which paid for the translations but not for the printing, and which lasted until its functions were taken over by the newly founded Academy of Letters in 1783, presided over by Princess Dashkova. Many of the translations it commissioned were utilitarian, such as grammars, books on medicine, and other sciences, geography, arithmetic etc. But the selection also reflected Catherine's own taste and choices. It included Robertson's *History of Charles V*, a partial and free translation of the first volume of Blackstone's *Commentaries on the Laws of England*, Bielfeld's *Institutions Politiques*, which Catherine drew upon for her *Great Instruction*, and translations of Homer, Ovid, Tacitus, Suetonius, Terence, Cicero, Julius Caesar. Translations from the classics and from English were important because they were not accessible in general to the ordinary reading public which only rarely knew English. In her later years, Catherine showed a great interest in the English novelists and promoted translations of Fielding and Smollett. *Humphrey Clinker* diverted her when the Swedish gunfire rattled her windows in St Petersburg in the war of 1788–91. One great contribution of Scottish culture to Russian happiness was the translation through the French of William Buchan's *Handbook of Practical Medicine* in 1790–91, which is referred to fondly by the young S.T. Aksakov in his *Years of Childhood*.

As regards private libraries, again information is scanty. The contents of some twenty in the early part of the century is known, sometimes as a result of their confiscation on the disgrace of the original owner. Of those I have studied the content is overwhelmingly political and historical, sometimes there are also manuals of diplomacy and law. These are libraries for use rather than for pleasure, though there are occasional indications of specific tastes, such as gardening or alchemy. James Bruce's library of more than 1,500 books (printed and manuscript) is not typical and is extremely wide-ranging. It was left to the Academy of Sciences on his death in 1737.[26] The architect P.M. Yeropkin, who was caught up in the fate of Artemiy Volynsky and executed in 1740, had a much more modest library of some 319 volumes of which some thirty concerned literature, Russian or foreign.[27] It is likely, however, that as the century advanced the content of private libraries became much more varied and more space was devoted to original and translated literary works and to runs of foreign periodicals. Details of over 3,000 books confiscated from the library of Novikov on his arrest in 1792 show not only the wide selection of masonic, mystical, alchemical and occult works one would expect but also works by Sir Thomas More, Erasmus, Rousseau's *Contrat Social*, Helvetius's

25. Shtrange, *Demokraticheskaya intelligenstiya v Rossii*, p. 276.
26. A.I. Kopanev, ed., E.A. Savel'eva, compiler, *Biblioteka Briusa, Katalog*, Leningrad, 1989.
27. S.P. Luppov, 'Biblioteka P.M. Yeropkina', in *Knigopechataniye I knizhnyye sobraniya v Rossii do serediny XIX v*, Leningrad, 1979, pp. 142–53.

De l'Homme, and all 48 volumes of the *Encyclopédie*.[28] The Library of the University of Moscow was open to the general public on Wednesdays and Saturdays.[29]

To turn now to the nature and quality of the works published in translation, there is again a striking change throughout the century illustrating the shift from *prosvetitel'stvo* to *prosveshcheniye*, from the utilitarian to the cultural. The Svodnyy katalog includes all books and journals printed; many of them were designed purely for entertainment. There were many translated or original stories of adventure, love stories and romances with little or no intellectual or artistic merit. By the second half of the century Russians could read a great deal of Voltaire: his dramas, his satires and occasional pieces – indeed far more than was available to the reading public in Spain for instance. Extracts from the *Encyclopédie* of Diderot and d'Alembert were published, a great deal of Rousseau, including his articles in the *Encyclopédie*, the *Nouvelle Heloise*, and the *Confessions d'un Enfant du Siècle*. *L'Esprit des Lois* of Montesquieu appeared in 1775. Much was translated simply because it was there.

Let me turn for a moment to the question of the comparative influence of French and German enlightened thought. M. Raeff has argued that French literature and social models dominated Russia from the middle of the eighteenth century, but that they did not inform the profounder and more basic aspects of the evolution of Russian culture and thought.[30] It is certainly true that throughout the eighteenth century the current from Germany to Russia flowed very strongly, directly or via the Baltic provinces. Leibniz had recommended individual German scholars to Peter; the ideas of Christian Wolff and the pietism associated with Halle fitted in well with the Petrine conception of service to the state, and the current was maintained through the contacts between the German scholars in the Academy of Sciences (and at this time they were practically all German), and later the many German teachers in the University of Moscow. There was also a very large resident German colony in St Petersburg, so large that the city court of the capital had a special German chamber after 1775 which heard some 20,000 cases a year.[31] German did not need to be translated, there was a fairly substantial readership, and German books were easier to procure than French, because Riga was a centre for book publishing in German. In eighteenth-century Russia, tutors, cooks and hairdressers were French, scholars were German. It is true that, as G. Marker has noted, more works were translated from French than from German (for example in 1756–75, 402 from French, 175 from German) but then the French

28. I. de Madariaga, 'Some New Publications on Nikolay Ivanovich Novikov', in *Studies in History and Politics*, Special Issue in Honour of Ragnhild Hatton, Lennoxville, Quebec, IV, 1985, pp. 171–80, and E. Beshenkovsky and I. Martynov, 'Po sledam biblioteki N.I. Novikova', in *V mire knig*, 76, No. 3, pp. 80–2.
29. *Svodnyy katalog*, IV 16, No. 4.
30. M. Raeff, 'The Enlightenment in Russia and Russian Thought in the Enlightenment', in *The Eighteenth Century in Russia*, ed. J.G. Garrard, Oxford, 1973, pp. 25–47.
31. Miranda, *op. cit.*, p. 466.

wrote more romances, which were popular in Russia.[32] Raeff reminds us that Lomonosov, Derzhavin and Karamzin all knew German before they knew French. So did Denis von Vizin (as he called himself).[33] The Orlov brothers are said to have known only German, and so apparently did the Procurator General, Prince A.A. Vyazemsky. Far more Russians attended German universities than went to France, and if they went to France, then it was to Strasbourg which was German-speaking and Protestant. Raeff is probably right in suggesting that natural law, *Polizeiwissenschaft* and administrative theory came from Germany, while political theory, literature, history and deism came from France, and to some extent England, rather later in the century. German influence was undoubtedly strongest in the first half of the century, under Peter I and until the death of his niece, the Empress Anna, in 1740, while French influence was more noticeable in the second half of the century.

In a different article Raeff has responded to the massive symposium edited by Eduard Winter[34] in East Berlin (*Die Deutsch-Russische Begegnung und Leonhard Euler, 1958*), a book which paints a picture of a growing Russian bourgeoisie pressing for the programme of the 'enlighteners' to be implemented. But as we know, not even the German colony could make up the missing bourgeoisie. Raeff argues that the more original Russian writers among those influenced by French thought in the second half of the century are influenced not by the French generation of the 1750s such as Montesquieu and Voltaire and the Encyclopaedists but by post-1750 French writers such as Rousseau, Mably, Raynal and of course Helvetius.[35] The Russian ambassador to Paris and later The Hague, the enlightened and reformist Prince D.A. Golitsyn, supervised the publication of Helvetius's *De l'Esprit* in 1774 in The Hague, and the latter's influence on Radishchev as well as that of Raynal has been well-established – even Catherine detected it. But one generation did not replace another: the influence of the earlier, pre-1750 writers continued but was overlaid by newer and more radical and exciting authors.

This leads on to the question of the first vehicles for the expression of original Russian thought, namely the literary and scientific journals and above all the satirical journals. Peter I's first newspaper, the *St Petersburg Gazette*, had been intended to inform the public about Russian victories and about European events. But by mid-century the various educational institutions he and his successors had established, military and civilian, ventured into other fields. The middle of the eighteenth century saw the proliferation of the periodical

32. Marker, *op. cit.*, p. 88.

33. A. Strycek, *La Russie des Lumieres – Denis Fonvizine*, Paris, 1976. The von Vizin family (the name is spelt in many different ways) descended from the Knights of the Livonian Order; Pushkin russified the surname in verse to Fonvizin in 'Yevgeniy Onegin' and this spelling finally became current at the end of the nineteenth century. It was not how he spelt his name, nor how he thought of himself. *Op cit.*, p. 17, n. 2.

34. E. Winter *et al.*, *Die Deutsch-russische Begegnung und Leonhard Euler. Beitrage zu den Beziehungen zwischen der deutschen und der russischene Wissenschaft und Kultur im 18 Jahrhundert*, Berlin, 1958.

35. M. Raeff, 'Les Slaves, les allemands et les lumières', *Canadian-American Slavic Studies*, 1, No. 4, 1967, pp. 521–51.

press. Many of these literary or satirical journals were short-lived but they provided an outlet for poetry, drama, odes and prose works, the latter very often translations of Addison and Steele, Swift or Dr Johnson taken from German editions in book form. One of the first literary journals, *Idle Times*, was brought out by the Cadet Corps in 1759, rather as though Sandhurst published poetry and moralistic prose. Catherine herself behind the scenes sponsored a satirical journal, *All Sorts of Things*, in 1769, edited by her private secretary, G. Kozitsky, which indulged in all sorts of backbiting and sarcastic chitchat with other periodicals, notably *The Drone*, edited by the 24-year-old Novikov, *Miscellany*, *This and That*, *Neither This nor That*, and others, and discussed the burning issues of the day, including the exploitation of the serfs, examples of good and bad landowners, francophilia, silly young women. The literary and satirical journals which became more and more numerous from the 1760s onwards reflected both English and French thought adapted to Russian social reality and served also to popularize ideas from the *Encyclopédie* and other French sources. They were usually short-lived, lasting only a year or two. The journals published in the 1760s have attracted most attention from literary critics, partly because this particular crop, following on the appearance of *All Sorts of Things*, led some historians to postulate the existence of a battle between what was regarded as the Empress's journal (though to what extent this was known at the time remains uncertain) and Novikov's *The Drone* on the nature of satire which ended only in the suppression of the latter by an outraged Empress. This interpretation has now been discarded since the discovery that Catherine actually subsidized Novikov's second and even more outspoken satirical journal, *The Painter*, to the tune of 200 rubles.[36] The journals were often reprinted in book form in the following years, and new ones continued to appear.

Probably the most effective introduction to the thought of the French Enlightenment was the *Encyclopédie* of Diderot and d'Alembert, which Catherine offered to publish in Russia when the editors got into difficulties in France. The articles in the *Encyclopédie* provided short, readable summaries of the latest 'enlightened' thought on a vast number of topics, scientific, philosophical, legal, historical, political, artistic and literary. Many selections were translated into Russian,[37] and presumably the wealthy magnates possessed copies in their private libraries. In any case knowledge of French was by the last quarter of the century becoming almost universal in elite court circles.

In the political field, by far the most outstanding and influential original work was Catherine's *Great Instruction* to the Legislative Commission of 1767, if one may be permitted to call a work original which pillages Montesquieu, Beccaria, Justi, Bielfeld, the Abbé Coyer, Nicolas de la Mare and possibly

36. V. Stepanov, 'Novikov i ego sovremmeniki', *XVIII vek*, No. XIV, pp. 211–19.
37. For instance, S. Bashilov translated entries on political and religious topics, Ya. P. Kozels'ky translated entries on such subjects as philosophy, natural law, and politics, and I.G. Tumansky, a translator in the Heraldmaster's Office translated entries on aristocracy, democracy, despotic government, monarchy, sovereignty (*samoderzhaviye*), government, tyrant, in a collection published in 1770. All of these came out under the auspices of Catherine's Society for the Promotion of Translations. See Shtrange, *Demokraticheskaya intelligentsiya*, pp. 276ff., Appendix.

Adam Smith.[38] It was original in its arrangement of these disparate materials. But it was far more original as an intellectual programme put before an untutored assembly of deputies elected from all the free ranks of society, including the state peasants, but excluding of course the serfs. (A number of Western authors such as A. Kahan and J. LeDonne consider the state peasants as serfs of the state and as forming part of the so-called 'spoils' available to be shared out among the nobles. It is interesting to observe that Catherine II at least considered them to form part of the free population of Russia, by granting them the right to elect deputies to the Legislative Commission, modelling herself perhaps on the Swedish constitution, in which peasants on crown lands formed part of the fourth estate, while peasants on noble land did not vote and could not be elected.)

Catherine's *Instruction* reflected the ideas of the Enlightenment in more ways than there is room to deal with here, notably in its totally secular approach to government, in spite of the initial appeal to God which so irritated Diderot; in its political and social analysis, which is largely based on Montesquieu, though not on him alone; in its sociological approach to crime and justice, based on Beccaria; in its advocacy of religious toleration and in articulating for the first time in Russia the principle of freedom of expression.[39] Portions of the *Instruction* were read aloud at the beginning of every session to the 500-odd deputies present. It is very instructive to compare the 'instructions', similar in purpose to the French 'cahiers de doléance' of 1789, which the deputies submitted to the Commission before it met, with the tenor of the debates in the plenary sessions as recorded in the Journals of the Commission. The 'instructions' of the deputies were couched in the traditional language of petitions to the tsar while the debates were often vigorous, and many controversial propositions were slipped in as speakers sheltered behind some article quoted from Catherine's *Instruction*, which they probably had not identified as drawn from a foreign writer such as Montesquieu. The *Instruction* did several things for Russian intellectual life: it put a whole lot of ideas culled from many of the authors of the French Enlightenment into general circulation, and created a climate of thought within which ideas could be measured and tested. Though it never enjoyed the status of law, it was frequently made use of in judicial decisions in order to incline towards the most merciful interpretation of the law. And it made thinking, writing and intellectual pursuits into respectable occupations for the nobility and the non-noble educated elite and helped to create an incipient professional class.[40] The importance of the lead given by the court in this context should not be underestimated.

38. V. Kamendrowsky, *Canadian-American Slavic Studies*, 13, No. 4, Winter 1979, pp. 545–54, suggests that Catherine's source for her ideas on the economy was in fact the *Encyclopédie*, and not as has sometimes been suggested Desnitsky's notes on the lectures of Adam Smith he had heard in Glasgow.

39. See Papmehl, *op. cit.*

40. Catherine's *Instruction* was published at intervals in the last 35 years of the eighteenth century, never in very large print runs. Though a Senate ukaz decreed that it was to be kept from the

One topic which had but very rarely been touched on in previous published and unpublished writings was the vexed question of serfdom, regarded not only in its economic aspect, but as a moral problem. Catherine dealt with it very scantily in Chapter XI of her *Instruction* which had been severely mauled by her advisers. Serfdom was quite simply taken for granted as essential to economic and social order much as was slavery in British, French and Spanish colonies. But the growing emphasis on individual freedom led in all these countries to the questioning of the system in which human beings owned other human beings. Slavery and serfdom formed part of an economic system and they were now to be discussed in Russia in the context of an institution typical of the Enlightenment, namely the Free Economic Society, a body modelled in general on the many societies set up to further agricultural improvement, by the application of physiocratic and enlightened principles, ranging from 1723 in Scotland to 1763 in Leipzig, and to 1767 when the first of the many *sociedades económicas de amigos del pais* was founded in Spain. The Russian Free Economic Society, founded in 1765, was the first private society ever established in Russia (with official blessing) and it was to this society that the Empress proposed that it should announce a competition and award a prize for the best essay on the subject: 'What is the most useful for society – that the peasant should own the land or only moveable property and how far should his rights over the one or the other extend?'. Most of the 160-odd entries submitted were by foreigners (including Voltaire under a pseudonym), and only seven were by Russians, a telling comment on the interest the competition aroused in Russia. The prize was won by a foreigner, but a Russian came second. None advocated the immediate abolition of serfdom, but most of the entries envisaged means of reducing its severity, and of eventually phasing it out. The debate was now launched in Russian educated society. It must be admitted, however, that the overwhelming majority of non-peasant society in Russia was composed of *krepostniki*, upholders of serfdom whether they owned serfs or merely hoped to. A few, including Catherine herself, attempted to introduce modifications of the system on their own estates, but even the peasants themselves did not as yet easily conceive of any other status than that of state peasants.[41] The Free Economic Society also sponsored a vast range of surveys and inquiries on agricultural production and productivity and maintained relations with similar societies abroad (Arthur Young was a member). It lasted until it was closed down in 1917.

Between Catherine's *Instruction* of 1767 and Radishchev's *Journey from St Petersburg to Moscow* of 1790, very little original political writing was actually published in Russia in the form of books. But interesting commentaries

hands of chancery clerks in offices, it was nevertheless widely available since it was on sale at the Senate bookshop and in other bookshops.

41. Prince D.A. Golitsyn, for instance, proposed to Catherine that she should emancipate the court peasants on the assumption that the nobility would follow her lead. She was not convinced. See I. Bak, 'Dmitri Aleksandrovich Golitsyn', *Istoricheskiye Zapiski*, 26, 1948, pp. 258ff.

appeared in translations or in the introductions to translated works. Ya. P. Kozel'sky, Ukrainian, and probably cossack in origin, a captain in the artillery, was one of the critics of serfdom as a (landless) deputy of the nobility in the Legislative Commission. He published his own introduction to his translations from the *Encyclopédie* and a penetrating commentary on his translation of F.K. von Moser's *Der Herr und der Diener geschildert mit patriotischer Freyheit* (Frankfurt, 1761) ('Gosudar i Ministr' 1762).

But at least two important treatises were written and remained unpublished. The first was by the playwright Denis von Vizin, who had made his mark with the satirical play *Brigadir* in 1769, directed at 'gallomania', which was so successful that he read it to the Grand Duke Paul and to the Empress herself. Vizin was employed in the College of Foreign Affairs under Count Nikita Panin, its senior member, and *de facto* foreign minister. Panin had been involved from the beginning in the plot to remove Peter III, but he had hoped to enthrone the young Grand Duke Paul, with his mother as regent, and himself of course as both Governor of the new emperor and senior minister. Catherine and her adherents had frustrated his plans, but he had still made an effort to secure her agreement to a project to limit her powers by forcing her to act within certain specified channels and with the approval of certain specified secretaries of state.[42] Like her predecessor Anna Ioanovna, Catherine had at first signed the draft plan proposed to her, and then torn the paper up. But Panin remained wedded to his idea of limiting the power of the ruler by means of fundamental laws, and it is evident that he discussed these plans, which he hoped to put into effect when the Grand Duke Paul became tsar, with his brother, General Peter Panin, and with Denis von Vizin. But a stroke in 1782 made it impossible for him to write, and the 'Discourse on the Permanent Laws of the State' was eventually written by Vizin, either at Panin's dictation, or more probably as his own work. Written around 1783, when Vizin was no longer the radical satirist of the 1760s, the Discourse is a long argument in favour of the institution of fundamental laws, by which the sovereign is bound, just as 'God instituted principles of everlasting truth, unalterable by himself, whereby he governs the universe, and which he himself cannot transgress without ceasing to be God'. Vizin's definition of political freedom is straight out of Montesquieu, and postulates security of person and an 'indissoluble link between freedom and property', which together with the form of government must be guaranteed by the fundamental laws. If a ruler transgresses these laws, then 'the nation [i.e. the nobility] is now within its rights in restoring its own freedom', for all human societies are based on voluntary mutual obligations. It is not surprising that this document, written with intense feeling, which postulates the existence of a revocable social contract,

42. For details see my *Russia in the Age of Catherine the Great*, pp. 39ff. For the text of Panin's memorandum see M. Raeff, ed., *Plans for Political Reform in Imperial Russia, 1730–1905*, Prentice Hall, N.J., 1966, pp. 56ff.

remained concealed until manuscript copies began to circulate, thanks to Vizin's nephew, General M.P. von Vizin, among the future Decembrists.[43]

Another critic of Catherine's absolutism was Prince M.M. Shcherbatov. He was the spokesman in the Legislative Commission for the interests of the nobility, and defender of serfdom, but this did not prevent him from being deeply imbued with ideas culled from the Enlightenment. He favoured the form of government which can best be described as aristocratic constitutionalism, in which the great nobles enjoyed powers similar to those of the House of Lords in England. Shcherbatov published a multi-volume history of Russia and several works on genealogy. But he did not – could not – in the prevailing intellectual climate publish his most interesting productions, above all the famous *On the Corruption of Morals in Russia*, an indictment of both Peter the Great and Catherine II, and his *Journey in the Land of Ophir*, a terrifying Utopia. More interesting in the present context are his comments on Catherine's *Instruction*, the deviations he traces from Montesquieu, and her failure to maintain the rights and privileges of the nobility. There may well be other undiscovered critics of Catherinian Russia from the 'enlightened' perspective which have remained unpublished, but in original and translated works there was nothing that she could not tolerate until Radishchev attempted to criticize Russian institutions in 1790, denouncing serfdom, and censuring the conduct of the commander-in-chief (Potemkin) of the Russian armed forces in the war against the Porte in the language of the Enlightenment.

Education was also central to the Enlightenment, as reflected in Diderot's *Mémoires pour Catherine*, the documents he prepared as the groundwork for his discussions at his regular meetings with Catherine in St Petersburg in 1773–74.[44] It was also central to Catherine's concerns, not only as a value in itself but as a means to forward her hopes of creating a *tiers état* in Russia. Her adviser in this field was at first I.I. Betskoy, who hoped to use education in order to develop a 'new kind of man' and whose educational plans were published in The Hague in 1774 under the supervision of Diderot. Very influential were Locke, Fénélon, and later German educationalists such as Johann Basedow. But Catherine did not pursue the application of their ideas in Russia. Novikov published his own ideas on the 'Upbringing and Instruction of Children' as a supplement to the *Moscow Gazette* in 1783, ideas to which Catherine could have had no objection since he praised her initiatives, and put forward what one can only call very conservative ideas as to the object of education. He thought that children should be educated in the manner appropriate to their station in life even if his views on the manner in which education

43. For the text of von Vizin's Discourse, see M. Raeff, ed., *Russian Intellectual History – An Anthology*, New York, 1966. Vizin's Discourse contained also a fierce attack on 'unworthy favourites' evidently directed at G.A. Potemkin, who had defeated Panin, Vizin's patron, for control of foreign policy in 1781. Vizin had already published with impunity a disguised attack on Potemkin in his translation of Tsa Hseueh (*Ta Gio*) which appeared in May 1779 anonymously in the *St Petersburg Gazette*. For the English text see Raeff, *op. cit.*, pp. 88ff.

44. D. Diderot, *Memoires pour Catherine*, ed. P. Verniere, Paris, 1966.

was to be imparted were in fact very much in harmony with enlightened theories.[45] The seriousness of Catherine's commitment to education is illustrated by the establishment of a national system in 1786. Its results were patchy and it conformed more strictly to the type of education devised to produce obedient state servants, each according to his station, than to the free and child-centred theories of for instance Basedow. But in one respect it was unique: the use of corporal punishment was banned. It survived of course, though possibly not for girls, except in the boarding house for nobles run by J. Schaden in Moscow which was famous for its humanity.

I come now to the question of the reflection of the 'Enlightenment' in Catherine's policies. It should be stressed that 'Catherine' here is shorthand for 'the Empress and her ministers', advisers and officials in various fields. Catherine worked closely with officials of a like cast of mind. She parted company with her foreign minister Nikita Panin, after nineteen years, in 1781, but he was a formidable champion of 'écrasez l'infame' in his attitude to the Catholic Church in Poland; nor was she ever forgiven for her *coup d'état* by A.R. Vorontsov, the brother of Peter III's mistress, who served her until 1792. But most of the men close to her, including many of those subsequently appointed as governors of the new *guberniyi*, shared her ideas.

The secularization of the lands of the Church was a policy after the heart of Voltaire. It was first thought of under Elizabeth, taken up again by Peter III, dropped at first by Catherine for fear of offending the Church on her accession, and then finally forced through. Contrary to what is frequently stated, the church peasants were not given away to nobles but formed a new category of state peasants or 'economic' peasants. Religious persecution had been condemned by Catherine in her *Instruction*, and while Orthodoxy remained the official state religion, toleration was quietly introduced. After the first partition of Poland Catherine was faced with a large number of Catholics and a large number of Jews, and their religious communities were granted a good deal of autonomy under government supervision.[46] Similarly, from her accession the pressure of the state, though not that of the Church, was taken off the Old Believers and it is possible that the setting up of an Old Believer printing press in Klintsy after 1783 aroused the antagonism of the Synod and launched it on a more aggressive policy in Moscow in the late 1780s which led to the ultimate downfall of Novikov, who was suspected of having printed a book for Old Believers in the characters they used.[47]

The reform of local administration in 1775 was an example of Catherine's combination of 'cameralist' policies with the rhetoric of the 'Enlightenment', and not only the rhetoric since she was profoundly influenced by the *Commentaries*

45. For Novikov's 'On the Upbringing and Education of Children' see Raeff, pp. 668–86.

46. For the arrangements made for Catholics, Uniates and Protestants, see my *Russia in the Age of Catherine the Great*, pp. 503–20; for the Jews see the more recent work of John Klier, *Russia Gathers Her Jews, The Origins of the Jewish Question in Russia, 1772–1825*, Northern Illinois University Press, 1986.

47. For the Old Believers, see Pia Pera, *Vecchi Credenti e l'Anticristo*, Genoa, 1992, pp. 131ff., and her articles cited therein.

on the Laws of England by William Blackstone in devising her new system of law courts, and Blackstone in turn had been influenced by Montesquieu. The real novelty of her policy as far as Russia was concerned was the attempt to separate the courts from the general administration, adding elected assessors to the judicial panels in an effort to achieve trial by one's peers in all the free classes of society, creating the *sovestnyy sud* or court of equity, distantly modelled on the English concept of equity;[48] and setting up the Boards of Social Welfare, also with elected assessors, the first nation-wide system charged under the local governors with establishing and supervising schools, hospitals, workhouses and houses of correction, lunatic asylums and foundling homes etc. It is to the powers granted by the Act to governors to take over the estates of landowners who were exploiting and starving their peasants that Vizin refers with approval in his second famous play, *The Minor*, which appeared in 1781, as an example of the beneficent effect of enlightened absolutism.[49]

Eighteenth-century provincial history is in its infancy in Russia, but in those cases where something is known, it is evident that much depended on the personality of the governor. Where, as in the case of A.P. Melgunov in Yaroslavl, he was wealthy and a freemason, or in that of J. Sievers in Tver, he was wealthy, a mason, and a Protestant, there was genuine devotion to the cause of reform and provincial life was culturally much enriched. Many of the Boards of Social Welfare established their own printing presses, which seemed to have survived the decree of 1796 presumably because they were viewed as government presses. They contributed to the enlivenment of provincial life in a modest way.

A word should be said about the role of freemasonry. Its very existence in Russia is a reflection of the Westernizing process, and the philanthropic activity which masonic ideas encouraged was deeply imbued with the moral idealism of many of the 'enlightened writers'. Many masons were actively concerned with education like Novikov or Kheraskov, others were prominent public officials like Zakhar Chernyshev, at one time governor general of Moscow. Many began to seek in freemasonry an outlet for religious sensibilities which the Orthodox Church no longer satisfied. A second current which developed mainly in Moscow centred on Rosicrucianism, mysticism and alchemy and aroused Catherine's satirical ire. Both broad groups, and the many lodges they formed, provided channels for the transmission of high-minded ideals of personal conduct, moral self-improvement, charitable activity, and the translation of foreign masonic works or the creation of indigenous masonic literature, a lot of it unpublished to this day.[50]

48. On the courts of equity see J.M. Hartley, 'Catherine's Conscience Court – An English Equity Court', in *Russia and the West in the Eighteenth Century*, ed. A.G. Cross, Oriental Research Partners, Newtonville Mass., 1983.

49. Vizin had personal experience of the working of this Act, since the lands of a relative of his mother's, F.I. Dmitriyev Mamonov (also related to Catherine's favourite), had been taken over by the local governor because of his maladministration.

50. See in addition to my own article in this book, Raffaela Faggionato, 'La fine di un'Utopia – Contributo all storia della Massoneria nella Russia de Cateriina II', *Rivista Storicaa Italiana*, cv, I, 1993, pp. 36–179.

Leibniz had urged the preparation of surveys and studies of Russian geography, the soil, agriculture, climate etc. It must be recognised that this part of the Enlightenment programme was extensively carried out. The Academy of Sciences was responsible for a vast number of explorations. Bering's expedition to the straits which bear his name preceded its foundation, but the expeditions of G.F. Müller in Siberia, Gmelin in South-East Russia, Krashenninikov to Kamchatka, cast a new light on Russia's huge colonial empire. The economic surveys carried out in Catherine's reign as a by-product of the general land survey provided the raw material for the formulation of economic policy, and the surveys of individual provinces or *guberniyi*, with their detailed descriptions of towns, buildings, schools, hospitals etc., are equally valuable for the historian today. Russians began to know their country. They also began to know its history. Quite a number of undistinguished historians committed pen to paper, but there were also a number of cultured and critical minds which either approached the task of writing their own history, or attempted the critical analysis of what foreigners wrote about Russia. Among historians one may cite V.N. Tatishchev, Prince M.M. Shcherbatov, who was appointed official historiographer by Catherine, General I.I. Boltin, who attacked the history of Russia by Leclerc, before Karamzin himself came on to the scene at the beginning of the nineteenth century. Catherine herself tried her hand at countering condescending French slander by the Abbé Chappe d'Auteroche in her *Antidote*, and later produced her Historical Notes, genuine attempts at disseminating information about Russia's medieval past.

To conclude this brief and admittedly incomplete and superficial survey, as one might expect, in the reign of Peter I, his daughter Elizabeth and particularly that of Catherine II, intellectual and cultural life originated with the court and radiated downwards from it. Peter was more inclined to the utilitarian knowledge, but there were other sides to his character. Love for his paradise on earth, St Petersburg, led him to architecture, painting, sculpture; he was fascinated by mythology, emblems, orders of chivalry, heraldry and tales of past history. Anna Ioanovna's tastes were coarse, but in one respect she put the Russian court on a path which Russia would make its own by developing opera and ballet and founding a ballet school. Elizabeth presided over the foundation of Moscow University, the development of a more flexible and appropriate use of the Russian language by the playwright Tredyakovsky and above all by Lomonosov, and she fostered the Russian and the French theatre. Under Catherine the court encouraged and fostered literary activity, and by her own writings, by providing an audience and subsidies, by developing a market for books and plays, and by her extensive purchases of paintings and sculpture, Catherine made St Petersburg into a unique cultural capital.

If one were to compare the cultural scene and the prevailing values at the beginning of the century with the panorama spread out before one at the end, the differences would be very striking. In spite of the secularization of Church lands, the Orthodox Church continued to exercise a powerful influence, but was itself by no means immune to Enlightenment ideas. The concept of the individual had emerged – slowly it is true – not only from the clan, but also from subordination to the state, and uncritical acceptance of its values had been to some extent replaced by individual judgement. The possibility of an alternative form of government and a different social structure had been envisaged by at least some more perceptive minds. The increasing emphasis on welfare, however inadequate its practical manifestations, was not much behind the general European standards. The attempt to reduce the role of corporal punishment and of cruelty in general in the judicial field, in schools and the home, and even in the armed forces, reflected a more humane attitude among officials. The civilizing process was acting like a yeast in society, setting higher standards for manners and private behaviour, for relations between men and women, parents and children. Only at the end of the century were the theories of the eighteenth-century Enlightenment overtaken by the new and far more radical ideas of the French Revolution, driving many Russian 'enlighteners' including Catherine herself to view their previous gods with some apprehension.

CHAPTER THIRTEEN

The role of Catherine II in the literary and cultural life of Russia

Pre- and post-revolutionary critics have taken very divergent views of Catherine's literary activity and influence, and it is necessary to turn to the Empress's contemporaries or to nineteenth-century critics to obtain a balanced picture of her role, both as a writer and as a Maecenas. Her own writings occupy twelve substantial volumes of varying quality, and her works must be examined with a clear perception of their different nature, object and impact.[1] Even the purely literary productions usually had a political purpose or content.

The first and most important work Catherine wrote was the *Great Instruction* for the Legislative Commission of 1767, which was translated into many languages and often reprinted in Russian. It was widely known in Russia in spite of initial attempts by the Senate to restrict its circulation. Yet the work is Catherine's only in the sense that she selected and ordered the material which she had compiled from the best political thinkers of the time, Montesquieu, Beccaria, Bielfeld, Justi and even possibly Adam Smith. The *Instruction* was written in French, and translated for Catherine into Russian. It is, however, an underestimated landmark in the history of Russian political thought because, though entirely derivative, it nevertheless outlines a political philosophy of government proclaimed from the throne, and it opened up political debate by legitimizing the use of a number of advanced political and social concepts, which could now be freely bandied about. It was still regarded as a guideline for the principles on which legislation should be based in the early years of Alexander I, and was also called upon to justify moderating judicial verdicts in favour of greater humanity.

Catherine also wrote several versions of her memoirs at different times, for different people. Though probably never intended for publication, they were intended to be read, and to justify Catherine's actions as Grand Duchess and her seizure of power. But they too were written in French, and though manuscript

1. *Sochineniya imperatritsy Yekateriny II na osnovanii podlynnikh rukopisey*, ed. A.N. Pypin, 12 vols, St Petersburg, 1901–7.

copies circulated in the early nineteenth century, they first saw the light of day when Alexander Herzen published Part IV in 1859 in London.

A third essentially political work, written by Catherine in French with the help of A.P. Shuvalov, but published anonymously and not openly attributed to her until the 1840s, was the *Antidote*, a long refutation of the *Voyage en Sibérie* by the Abbé Chappe d'Auteroche. Chappe's book has all the pejorative gloss which French intellectuals applied to countries other than their own, and it was published at a time when Russia was involved in a war with the Ottoman Porte, which had been instigated by France. The *Antidote* refutes every malicious allegation by Chappe with a genuine nationalist fervour and pride in the Russian national character and achievements, including even the merits of Russian literature. But the tone is carping and disagreeable, and the anonymous work met with adverse criticism both from Denis Diderot and Melchior von Grimm. The *Antidote* does not add to Catherine's literary reputation, and in any case her authorship was not known in her lifetime. In the same way, Catherine's correspondence with Voltaire, Grimm, Diderot, the sculptor Falconet or Dr G. Zimmermann was not published in her lifetime and thus had little impact. What was extremely important, however, in the context of Russian literary history, was that the ruler herself gave the example of writing, translating into Russian (she shared with her courtiers in the task of translating Marmontel's *Bélisaire*, reserving for herself the chapter on the enlightened monarch), and corresponding with men and women of letters of very different social classes, expounding a whole range of cultural and philosophical concepts. Catherine made the profession of a 'man of letters' respectable in Russia.

Catherine also wrote extensively in the field of education, in which she grew increasingly interested after the birth of her grandsons, Alexander in 1777, and Constantine in 1779. She read widely in current pedagogical literature and her publications include a *Russian primer to teach young people to read* (1781). It was printed in several editions for use throughout the country, with the addition of various writings specially designed for children, such as a Greek alphabet, a selection of Russian proverbs, a series of completely secular moral maxims entitled *Grazhdanskoye nachal'noye ucheniye* (Elementary civil primer), designed for her grandsons and printed in Russian for the future emperor of Russia, Alexander, and in parallel columns in Greek for the future emperor of Constantinople, Constantine. (They were also published in German.) She also wrote children's tales, 'The Tale of Tsarevich Khlor' (1781) and 'The Tale of Tsarevich Fevey' (1783), probably the first children's tales ever to be written in Russian. We have no means at present of knowing how widespread was the influence of these educational works, but they were intended by Catherine to promote teaching by humane methods, to eliminate the antagonistic relationship between teacher and pupil typical of most schools at the time (though not of educational theory), and to emphasize self-discipline and moral virtues such as honesty, courage, truthfulness and obedience to the call of duty, each in his own station in life.

Catherine's venture into journalism belongs to the field where literature adjoins politics. She was directly instrumental in encouraging a new form of literary activity, namely the satirical weekly, when, in 1769, *Vsyakaya Vsyachina* (*All Sorts of Things*) was launched anonymously. It was assumed by Catherine's contemporaries that the editor was G. Kozitsky, the Empress's literary secretary, and this was enough to suggest that she had a personal interest in the enterprise. The evidence that Catherine may actually have written for the journal is very slight and only emerged in the nineteenth century.[2]

Adopting the *persona* of a grandmother (*babushka*), the editor of *Vsyakaya vsyachina* invited others to follow her example, and within the next few months a whole batch of journals appeared, including N.I. Novikov's *Truten'* (*The Drone*), all indulging in vicious backbiting with each other and with their original progenitor. Only the failure of critics to re-examine the assumptions of nineteenth-century literary historians, such as A. Nezelenov and V. Bogolyubov, which have been echoed in Soviet historiography, can explain the long life of the legend of the challenge allegedly directed by the young Novikov against an elderly and wanton authoritarian ruler (after all Catherine was only 40 in 1769, and had been living in domestic bliss with G.G. Orlov for eight years), and her fierce response. *Vsakaya vsyachina* and *Truten'* undoubtedly diverged on the nature of satire, the former preferring the gentler form of 'satira na porok' (satire aimed at vices), modelled on the English journals, *The Tatler* and *The Spectator*, to the harsher mode of 'satira na litso' (satire directed against an individual), defended, if not always followed, by the editors of the other journals, such as Novikov himself, and the editors of *Smes'* (*Miscellany*), *I to i syo* (*This and That*), and *Adskaya pochta* (*The Devil's Post*). Taken in the context of the time, the polemics between all the journals indicate youthful high spirits rather than a systematic 'oppositionist' frame of mind likely to provoke the Empress to reprisals, and no evidence has ever been produced to prove that any periodical was closed by government action. They continued in being in varying numbers from 1769 to 1775, and the short life of most of them must be attributed to financial failure caused by the small Russian readership, unprepared for such a sudden influx of reading matter. Most of them were reprinted in volume form in later years.

That there was no breach between Catherine and Novikov is confirmed by the fact that she provided 200 rubles to assist him with his third satirical journal, *Zhivopisets* (*The Painter*), *after* it had published its most biting indictment of bad serf-owners (it has also been suggested that she wrote for it), and that she subsidized his later historical publications with more than 1,000 rubles.[3] Catherine, however, soon turned away to other activities which entitle her to a permanent niche in the history of Russian literature.

2. P. Pekarsky, *Materialy dlya zhurnal'noy literaturnoy deyatel'nosti Yekateriny II*, St Petersburg, 1863. See also Pypin, *Sochineniya Yekateriny*, vol. 5, pp. 330ff. Pypin states that Catherine may have been supposed to have contributed to the journal but he does not state it as a fact.
3. The most up-to date discussion of the relationship between Catherine and the periodicals is in W. Gareth Jones, 'The Polemics of the 1769 Journals: A Reappraisal', *Canadian-American*

The theatre formed part of any well-regulated court, and Catherine had from the beginning patronized tragedy, comedy and opera. It is possible that the initial impulse which moved her to write plays herself came from hearing Denis I. Fonvizin read his play *Brigadir* at court in 1769.[4] Satirical comedy could well prove a better way to *castigare mores ridendo* which was one of the aims of Catherine's journalism. From 1772 onwards Catherine wrote a large number of plays which can be broadly divided into groups by period, style and theme. In 1772–73 she wrote five plays in the genre of the bourgeois comedy of manners; in 1785–86 she wrote three comedies satirizing freemasonry and 'obscurantism', while continuing to write comedies of manners. In the same period she began to write plays 'in the manner of Shakespeare', and finally she embarked on a number of comic operas.

Catherine wrote plays 'parce que cela m'amuse'. The plays of 1772 are indeed written with gusto. *O vremya* (*O Time*), the first, is based on *Die Betschwester* by C.F. Gellert, in which the author directs his shafts at the sanctimonious bigot, Frau Richardinn. Catherine at times follows the dialogue quite closely, but she adds further characters, the malicious gossip Vestnikova, and the credulous Chudikhina. She shows considerable talent in turning the original German religious hypocrite into the Russian Orthodox variety, never more closely glued to her prayer book than when her creditors call for their money, berating her servants for interrupting her devotions, turning away the poor and beggaring the beggar.

In *Imianiny Gospozhi Vorchalkinoy* (*Mrs Vorchalkina's Nameday*), which has no model, Catherine indulges in unexpected satirical sallies. She puts in the mouth of Vorchalkina an attack on arrogant nobles such as Spesov (the haughty man – was he perhaps modelled on the spokesman of the aristocracy, Prince M.M. Shcherbatov?): 'Zdes' vse melkiye dvoryanya [sic]; vse rovnyye' ('here we are all minor nobles, we are all equal'). The positive character, Dremov (the somnolent), descendant of a man who was ennobled by a previous ruler while he was asleep, hence his name, endorses this attitude: 'khvalitsya rodom, eto nazyvayetsya khvalitsya chiuzhim' ('to boast of one's lineage is to boast of what does not belong to one'). It is also Vorchalkina who delivers the lines: 'kazna tol'ko chto grabit' ('the treasury does nothing but rob'), which led the nineteenth-century poet and critic Prince P.A. Vyazemsky to comment: 'kak ne uznat' tut tsarskogo pera; postoronnomu ne pozvolili by skazat' eto' ('we cannot fail to recognize here the imperial pen; an outsider would not be allowed to say this').[5]

Slavic Studies, 16, No. 24, 1978, pp. 432–43; see also his *Nikolay Novikov, Enlightener of Russia*, Cambridge University Press, 1984, and A. Monnier, *Un publiciste frondeur sous Catherine II, Nicolas Novikov*, Institut d'Etudes Slaves, Paris, 1981. For Catherine's subsidies to Novikov, see V. Stepanov, 'Novikov i ego sovremmeniki', *XVIII vek*, No. XIV, pp. 211–19.

4. See Ettore Lo Gatto, *Storia del teatro russo*, 2 vols, Florence, 1952.

5. P.A. Vyazemsky, *Zapisnyye knizhki 1813–1848*, ed. V.S. Nechayeva, Moscow, 1963, p. 199. See also Catherine to Melchior von Grimm, 23 April 1785, *Sbornik imperatorskogo russkogo istoricheskogo obshchestva* (*SIRIO*), 23, p. 375.

Catherine's second group of comedies, which are even more didactic in intent, was triggered off by the 'frénésie nouvelle de croire aux sciences occultes dont on est fort engoué à présent en Allemagne, en Suède, et qui commençait à prendre ici', and she found a suitable character to graft them on to in Count Cagliostro, who had made a flying visit to St Petersburg in 1779–80.[6] In 1780 Catherine published anonymously and with a false date – 1759 – a short satire on the rites of admission to masonic lodges, *Le secret de la société anti-absurde dévoilé par quelqu'un qui n'en est pas*, which was translated into Russian by her secretary A.V. Krapovitsky (who was in fact a mason) as *Tayna protivo-nelepago obshchestva otkrytaya neprichastnym onomu*. But Catherine thought comedy was a better way of achieving her object which was 'd'étriller les visionnaires qui commençaient à lever le nez'.[7]

The Empress's distrust of freemasonry and occultism was fed by her correspondent in Germany, Dr J.G. Zimmermann, who dwelt not only on the ideas of the Illuminati of Bavaria, but on the notion of a vast international network of masonic lodges, setting up a state within a state, with their headquarters in Berlin, where Frederick William II who became King in 1786 was himself a Rosicrucian. Drawing on the article 'Théosophes' in the *Encyclopédie*, which began with Paracelsus, Catherine, in the first of her plays, *Obmanshchik* (*The Deceiver*), portrayed Cagliostro in the guise of Kalifalkzherston, affectionately called Kalifalkushka by the character in the play he deceived into parting with his gold and jewels. In the second comedy, *Obol'shchennyy* (*The Deceived*), Catherine spells out one of her reasons for distrusting Russian masons in a revealing bit of dialogue in Act V, Scene 1, which may well refer to the alleged activities of the Moscow masons recently reported to her:

> Bragin: Oni v namerenii imeyut potaenno zavodit' blagotvoritelnyye raznyye zavedenii, kak to: shkoly, bol'nitsy i tomu podobno, i dlya togo starayutsya privlekat' k sebe lyudey bogatykh.
>
> Brityagin: Dela tokogo roda na chto proizvodit' sokrovenno, kogda blagim uzakoneniyam otkryty vsevozmoznyya u nas takim ustanovleniyam udobstvy.
>
> (Bragin: They intend secretly to set up various philanthropic institutions such as schools, hospitals and such like, and for that reason they try to attract wealthy people.
>
> Brityagin: Why undertake such things secretly, when thanks to good laws, every sort of facility is open to us for such establishments.)

Catherine is here protesting not against philanthropic activity but against the alleged secrecy of masonic activity. In this play, too, one character, Radotov, a name surely chosen with the French *radoteur* in mind, is swindled by a couple of charlatans, while the final play, *Shaman Sibirsky* (*The Siberian Shaman*), is a deliberately farcical caricature, with almost no plot.

6. Catherine to Melchior von Grimm, 11 March 1786, *SIRIO*, 23, p. 375.
7. *Op. cit.*, p. 328, Catherine to Grimm, 3 April 1785.

Catherine was very pleased with her anti-masonic plays which she felt would deal a 'coup de massue' to the movement. They were performed in Russia and translated into French and German, and thanks to Zimmerman even staged in Hamburg. 'Le Trompeur et Le Trompé ont eu un prodigieux succés', she wrote to Melchior von Grimm, 'Le public a Moscou . . . ne souffrait point d'autres pièces. . . .'[8]

While still continuing to produce comedies of manners such as *Rastroyennaya sem'ya* (*The Disordered Family*), Catherine now embarked on a novel experiment in Russian literature. She had long been interested in English literature (she sponsored many translations from English) and in the 1780s she was devouring Eschenburg's translations of Shakespeare's plays into German. With her usual enthusiasm she plunged into an adaptation of *The Merry Wives of Windsor* and at the same time embarked on a series of historical chronicles of Russia 'in the manner of Shakespeare'.

Shakespeare was almost unknown in Russia. Sumarokov had written a play, *Hamlet*, which bore very little relation to the original; *Richard III* had been translated from the French in 1783, and Karamzin translated *Julius Caesar* in 1787. But eighteenth-century Russian dramatists were still in general firmly wedded to the classical unities of time, place and action, and the new criticism of Lessing, for instance, was only just beginning to be heard. Catherine gave her own explanation of the attraction of Shakespearean drama in a letter to Grimm: 'ces imitations de Schakespeare [sic] sont très commodes, parce qu'étant ni comédies ni tragédies et n'ayant d'autres règles que celles du tact, du supportable pour le spectateur, je les crois susceptibles de tout; les notres auront exactitude historique autant qu'elle ne sera pas choquante; beaucoup de spectacles, de belles âmes à beaux sentiments . . .'[9] In *Vot kakovo imet' korzinu i bel'e* (*How to have the linen and the basket*), based on *The Merry Wives of Windsor*, Catherine turned Sir John Falstaff into a Frenchified braggart, and followed the broad lines of the comedy faithfully enough. But it was beyond her power to reproduce the dialogue of Nym, Bardolph and Pistol – even Eschenburg had been defeated at times.

Catherine's historical dramas are more interesting as a vehicle for her highly patriotic interest in Russian history, which had already been made public in her *Zapiski kasatel'no rossiyskoy istorii* (*Notes on Russian History*), which appeared first in the *Sobesednik lyubiteley rossiyskogo slova* (*Companion of Lovers of Russian Literature*). This was a periodical published by the Academy of Sciences which came out in 1783–84, and was reprinted in separate editions in 1787–94. Catherine's historical contributions were purely narrative notes on Russian history, written in a simple style, with a conscientious use of historical sources and a not always successful effort to distinguish myth from fact. Her *Notes* were designed for young people, to counter the biased histories of Russia which had been appearing in France, and to provide what was in fact the first

8. *Ibid.*
9. *Op. cit.*, p. 383, Catherine to Grimm, 24 September 1786.

easy-to-read textbooks of Russian history, as distinct from the heavy tomes of historians such as V.N. Tatishchev or M.M. Shcherbatov. Catherine's history is strongly dynastic and emphasizes the virtues of the ruler. Hence, in her first play, *From the life of Ryurik*, an imitation of Shakespeare, which deals with Ryurik, and which has echoes of Shakespeare's play *Henry IV, part I*, Catherine accepts the version of Russian history (later regarded as mythical) in which the Slavonic King of Novgorod, Gostomysl (Henry IV), invites his eldest grandson Ryurik (Henry V), the son of a Varangian or Viking Russ Finnish king, and his two brothers to inherit and rule over his lands. Vadim of Novgorod (Henry Hotspur, Earl of Northumberland), a grandson in a younger line, stands forth as the opponent of this invitation to the Scandinavian outsiders, but is won over by the generosity of Ryurik. The play is totally lacking in dramatic development, and Vadim acts merely from ambition and not out of any principled stand, unlike the hero of Knyazhnin's later play, *Vadim of Novogorod*.

Ryurik was never staged, but Catherine's next venture, written in autumn 1786 and entitled *Nachal'noye upravleniya Olega, podrazhaniye Shakespiru bez sokhraneniya featral'nykh obyknovennykh pravil* (*The first government of Oleg, an imitation of Shakespeare, without observation of the dramatic unities*) was frequently performed and proved very successful.[10] In this play Moscow was founded, Askold expelled from Kiev, Igor married Olga, and most important of all, Oleg conducted a successful campaign against Byzantium. He is welcomed in the Hippodrome, where the Emperor Leo stages a production of three scenes from Europides's *Alcestis* to music composed in the 'Lydian, Phrygian and Doric modes' as resurrected by the Italian composer Sarti. Catherine searched through the *Encyclopédie* for information on Greek dress, and allowed the theatre to draw on the imperial wardrobe for costumes for a cast of some 200 people. She took an active part in the production, attended rehearsals, criticized the acting of the leading actors, and was finally very satisfied with the first performance of this eighteenth-century version of a 'musical' in the Hermitage Theatre, on 22 October 1790. The play was subsequently shown at the Kamennyy Theatre and the spectacle of Oleg hanging up his shield on the column of the Hippodrome must have had the same sort of impact during a war with the Ottoman empire (1787–91) as the resurrection of St Alexander Nevsky by Stalin during the Second World War. An English visitor, the Revd John Parkinson, was present at a performance in December 1792 and wrote that what had pleased him 'most of all in it was the Russian dance, which seemed to be executed with a great deal of grace and animation . . . Many of the tunes are Russian. The ceremony of the Espousal and the marriage is I imagine borrowed from the manners of the country. In the last act the Greek Emperor entertains the Russian General with a theatrical exhibition in imitation of the ancients . . .'[11]

10. On Catherine's adaptation of Shakespeare see A. Lirondelle, 'Catherine II, élève de Shakespeare', *Revue Germanique*, No. 2, March–April 1908.

11. John Parkinson, *A Tour of Russia, Siberia and the Crimea 1792–1794*, ed. W. Collier, London, 1971, pp. 57–8. See also A.G. Cross's account, 'Catherine's *Oleg*: a Bicentennial Visitation',

Catherine's concern with the educative function of the theatre as distinct from the theatre as entertainment is less obtrusive in her comedies of manners than in the anti-masonic plays. It appears again in her historical plays in the Shakespearean manner. These pageants placed events from Russian history, real or mythical, before the public in such a way as to appeal to all the senses and to be easily understood. The plays are written in lofty language, in prose, and the ideas are so simple that the main impact comes from the spectacle, which conveys Catherine's claim that Russia, under both her past and present enlightened rulers, is the equal of other nations.

Nevertheless Catherine was incapable of grasping the inner structure and dramatic depth of Shakespeare, and her own historical dramas are simply the acting out of episodes of Russian history with no development of plot or character. For this reason perhaps, these dramas, unlike the journals and comedies, did not set any precedents in Russia. Possibly only the resources Catherine herself could draw upon made it possible to stage them.

The combination of drama, dance, song, music and extravagant scenery and costumes used in *Oleg* led Catherine to experiment also with comic operas based on her own tales or on Russian tales interspersed with popular songs and dances. Probably the least successful of these was the burlesque, as she herself called it, in which King Gustavus III of Sweden, who had just declared an unprovoked war on Russia in 1788, was caricatured as Gorebogatyr Kosometovich, or Knight of Mischance. The opera was based on a tale by Catherine adapted from a popular story of the beggar Fuflig. It was viewed askance by many of Catherine's collaborators, including Prince G.A. Potemkin, who thought it lacking in taste, and it was not shown to the general public in St Petersburg. Catherine's comic operas had very slender plots and relied largely on additional songs and poems provided by her secretary, A.V. Khrapovitsky, drawn from the published works of Lomonosov, Tredyakovsky, etc.

It is difficult for the present-day writer to assess the literary value of Catherine's plays since it is nearly 200 years since they were last performed. According to the critic Sipovsky, writing in 1914, her influence on Russian comedy was noteworthy in the years 1772–82. Many authors followed her style of depicting the life of different classes. Her dialogue was lively.[12] Rereading *O vremya* in 1830, P.A. Vyazemsky was struck by the number of sharp, witty sallies and epigrams.[13] Catherine introduced a number of themes which others widened and explored. These were among the burning issues of the day, such as the conflict between generations, superstition, bigotry, braggadoccio, cowardice, silly old women and ill-bred young ones, gallomania and French contempt for Russia (the character Oranbar in *Perednyaya znatnogo boyarina* (*The ante-room of the noble boyar*) is undoubtedly meant to portray Mercier de la

Newsletter of the Study Group on Eighteenth-Century Russia, No. 18, 1990, pp. 10–17, and entry on Catherine II by V.P. Stepanov in *Slovar' russkikh pisateley XVIII veka*, Leningrad, 1988.

12. V.V. Sipovsky, 'Imperatritsa Yekaterina i russkaya bytovaya komediya eya epokhi', in V.V. Kallash and N.E. Efron, *Istoriya russkogo teatra*, I, Moscow, 1914, pp. 317–40, at p. 326.

13. Vyazamsky, *op. cit.*, p. 199.

Rivière). Catherine does introduce abstract representations of both virtues and vices, but they are outnumbered by the vivid characters drawn from the lower levels of society, living and thinking 'po meshchanski' (en petit bourgeois). Almost the only positive characters are the servants who defend the rights of serfs against their masters and represent the voice of common-sense.[14]

Not a great deal is known about Catherine's method of work, particularly in the early plays. She left a detailed analysis in French of the character and principles of the Siberian Shaman, to be developed later in the play. Her secretary's diary shows how quickly she wrote, and she rarely revised what she had written. Throughout her life she entertained herself with writing for the theatre, translating a few scenes from Sheridan's *School for Scandal* (from the French) or from a play by Calderón de la Barca (also from the French). There are many half-finished plays in which she obviously lost interest, which were not published until 1907, and though she attempted to procure manuals on the art of play-writing, she remained all her life a dilettante. She herself did not regard her comedies as great works of art. But they were frequently performed and she was very proud of their success, and very vulnerable to the flattery which her position inevitably called forth.[15]

Catherine encouraged controversy within established limits and the *Sobesednik lyubiteley russkogo slova*, founded in 1783, was intended to be an organ of debate. But its official character hampered its role, though it was here that Denis Fonvizin published his famous list of questions – some rather impertinent – to which Catherine supplied the answers. Both questions and answers are trifling, and well below the intellectual capacities of the writers. But their importance has been inflated by critics in an effort to stress the constant struggle of so-called oppositionist writers against an oppressive regime.

The edict of 1783 allowing anyone to set up a printing press provided it was registered with the local police showed Catherine's confidence in the general acceptance of her government by society at large. It led to a great increase in the number of printing presses, but there were still fundamental structural obstacles to the development of publishing and the book trade. In spite of the optimistic statements of Soviet historians such as Berkov or Shtrange, the market for books written in Russian was still extremely small and composed mainly of nobles.[16] Penetration into other layers of society was very slight, which may account for the importance of the visual arts (drama, processions, fireworks etc.).

Censorship of course existed but there was no central censorship operating throughout the nation until Catherine's edict of September 1796, a few weeks

14. Sipovsky, *op. cit.*

15. Radishchev, on his way to exile in Ilimsk, was present at a performance of *O vremya* in Tobol'sk in 1791. See D.M. Lang, *The First Russian Radical – Alexander Radishchev 1749–1802*, London, 1959, p. 208.

16. See in particular G. Marker, 'Novikov's Readers', *Modern Language Review*', 77, No. 4, October 1982, pp. 894–905 and his *Publishing, Printing and the Origins of Intellectual Life in Russia, 1700–1800*, Princeton University Press, 1985.

before her death. Until 1783 presses were almost entirely official and self-censoring. From 1783 the censorship was entrusted to the local police boards (*upravy blagochiniya*) in each province, which could be very casual, as in the case of A.N. Radishchev's *Journey from Petersburg to Moscow*. The general guidelines stated that nothing should be published contrary to the Christian religion, the government or common decency, principles applied in a very haphazard way. Insults to particular persons, or swearing in front of nobles or women, were regarded as violations of decency.[17] Rousseau's *Emile* (in French), it is true, was banned in 1763; but the main cause of the ban, as in all countries, was the *Profession de foi du vicaire savoyard*, which was published in Russian in 1770, while censorship of material opposed to the government did not prevent publication of his *Discours sur l'inégalité* in the same year, or the publication of the *Contrat Social* in German in Riga.

The conflict over N.I. Novikov's publications which began in 1785 was not in fact over politics but over religion, i.e. did books issuing from Novikov's press contain obscurantist alchemical or anti-Christian doctrine? The six books finally banned in 1786 were all masonic in character. Again, in 1787, when not only Novikov's press but the presses of the Academy of Sciences, the Senate, and the Cadet Corps were held to be in breach of the regulations granting the Holy Synod the exclusive and lucrative right to publish religious books, the fourteen titles out of 313 which were seized in Moscow were banned on religious, not political grounds. The tragic end of Novikov had little to do with his defiance of censorship; it was motivated almost entirely by Catherine's fear of an international masonic conspiracy against crowned heads, and of an attempt to lure her son Paul into the secret Rosicrucian circle of which her enemy, the King of Prussia, was the acknowledged leader.

But little is known of theatrical censorship beyond the fact that various playwrights were occasionally asked by local authorities to tone down or omit passages from their plays. Much seems to have depended on local conditions. Catherine, for instance, did not consider that Nikolev's tirades against 'nadmenny vlasteliny tvoryashchie adskiye sud'biny poraboshchennykkh vam lyudey' ('arrogant lords inflicting hellish destinies on those enslaved by you') in his *Sorena i Zamir* applied to her and refused to ban the play in 1784.

As the shadows of the French Revolution spread over rulers and aristocracies, Catherine turned back on the freedom she had tolerated, even encouraged, and on the intellectual heroes of her prime such as Voltaire. Many works which had been published before 1791 were now banned, such as Milton's *Paradise Lost*. To this period belongs Catherine's exaggerated reaction to Radishchev's *Journey*, in which, as Franco Venturi has pointed out, she actually misunderstood what he wrote about the dangers of a peasant uprising.[18]

17. Until Soviet work on eighteenth-century censorship is brought together in a coherent study, the most satisfactory work remains K. Papmehl, *Freedom of Expression in Eighteenth-Century Russia*, The Hague, 1971.
18. See F. Venturi's introduction to Aleksandr N. Radiščev, *Viaggio da Pietroburgo a Mosca*, Bari, 1972, p. 49.

Here too belongs her outburst against Knyazhnin's *Vadim Novgorodsky* (*Vadim of Novgorod*), in which she must have detected a much more acute portrayal of the current European scene than in Nikolev's tirades of 1784 against tsars. The final act came in 1796 with the centralized censorship of locally printed and imported books, and the closing down of private printing presses.

Modern Soviet critics have distorted Catherine's role in eighteenth-century literature because of their commitment to a number of ideological positions. First of all, they assume a degree of politicization of society and culture which did not exist at that time; secondly they assume the existence of a perpetual guerrilla war between enlightened intellectuals and a reactionary Empress, too stupid to see that tirades against tyranny were directed against her; thirdly, they assume that Catherine was a systematic defender of serfdom.[19]

Catherine undoubtedly proclaimed that absolutism was the right form of government for Russia, though she distinguished clearly between absolute monarchy according to fundamental laws, and despotism.[20] But in contrast with her predecessors, she greatly enlarged the sphere of private activity, a sphere in which the government did not interfere. As she stated in article 242 of her *Great Instruction*: 'If we forbid many Actions, which are termed indifferent by the *Moralists*, we shall not prevent the crimes . . . but shall create new ones'. Within the framework of absolutism she tried to inculcate the belief that the government was in fact leading the country, acting systematically to improve its administration, economy, education and welfare. More people agreed with her in general if not in detail than twentieth-century critics have often proved willing to allow. They have seen in her, *because* she was the Empress, a defender of the institution of serfdom, and therefore an opponent of all forms of 'progressive' thought. Yet all the evidence goes to show that she disliked and disapproved of serfdom as such, but saw no way in existing conditions to modify it. This so-called dichotomy between Catherine and 'progressive' writers obscures the fact that until the 1790s the arena of cultural life was sufficiently broad to allow for a rich diversity of ideas, ranging from the aristocratic constitutionalism of people like the foreign minister Nikita Panin, the playwright Fonvizin, or the historian M.M. Shcherbatov, to the more radical ideas associated with Radishchev and writers of the late 1780s.

19. A few of these interpretations must be quoted: G.A. Gukovsky, in 'Yekaterina', *Literatura XVIII veka, Istoriya russkoy literatury*, ed. with V.A. Desnitsky, ANSSR, 1947, IV, 2, pp. 364–80, states that the comic opera *Fevey* (1786) based on a tale written by Catherine for Alexander was a tactical move on Catherine's part in her struggle with her son Paul to prevent his travelling abroad and escaping her domination. This is absurd, since Paul had already travelled abroad in 1781 and had no wish to risk losing his throne by being abroad when his mother died. Similarly, referring to Catherine's comedies of the 1780s, Gukovsky writes that it was obvious that Catherine was trying to defeat Fonvizin with his own weapons. P.N. Berkov, in his *Istoriya russkoy komedii XVIII veka*, Leningrad, 1977, writes: 'the very fact that Catherine was forced to struggle with comedy shows how much importance comedies had at the time' (pp. 371–2). Vsevolodsky Gerngross in his *Russkiy teatr vtoroy poloviny XVIII veka ANSSR*, Moscow, 1960, frequently makes the same kind of observation.

20. See my article 'Autocracy and Sovereignty', in *Canadian-American Slavic Studies*, 16, Nos 3–4, Autumn–Winter 1982, pp. 369–87.

Catherine herself had a basically prosaic and pragmatic mind; she was not at ease with intellectual speculation and philosophical abstractions. But her personal example, her patronage and her enthusiasm made culture fashionable and respectable, and she created a climate in which individual initiatives could thrive. Her influence on Russian literary development went far further than her own writings would suggest. She gave powerful, totally secular direction from the throne. She promoted translations of literary and political works into Russian through the Society for the Translation of Foreign Books which she set up in 1768 and to which she gave an annual subsidy of 5,000 rubles, used to pay an array of well-known or obscure translators. The Society lasted until 1783 when it was taken over by the Russian Academy. By then it had published 112 separate translations, and others were in preparation. It is incidentally a tribute to Catherine's perspicacity and unconventionality that she appointed a woman, Princess Dashkova, already President of the Academy of Sciences, to be President of the Russian Academy. No woman has occupied either post since then, in Russia or anywhere else.

Catherine not only contributed to the diffusion of the classics, both modern and ancient, and of European literature in Russian translation. She also extensively patronized original works in Russian by dramatists, poets and historians. She established a library of Russian works for the use of the servants in the Winter Palace.[21] She subsidized theatrical performances, and encouraged the printing of Russian plays. She spent a great deal of money on theatres in which plays by Russian and foreign authors were produced and recruited outstanding Russian actors and foreign composers like Galuppi, Sarti, Paisiello, Martin y Soler. In 1783 there were seven state theatrical companies, leaving aside the many private companies.

Novikov was not the only author to receive financial help. M.I. Popov's *Dosugi* was published at the expense of Catherine's privy purse; so was M.D. Chulkov's *History of Russian Commerce*. Her 'pocket poet', Vasily Petrov, made a career at court (he knew England and may well have kept Catherine in touch with English literature). But even more striking was the success of G. Derzhavin who, thanks to his brilliant poem *Felitsa*, rose to be secretary to the Empress, governor of a province, and eventually under Alexander I, Minister of Justice.

21. See E. Pavlova, *Imperatorskaya bilioteka Ermitazha, 1762–1917*, Hermitage, 1990, pp. 46–7.

Index